To order or receive additional information on these or any other McGraw-Hill titles, in the United States please call 1-800-822-8158. In other countries, contact your local McGraw-Hill representative.

BC14BCZ

McGraw-Hill
LAN Communications
Handbook

McGraw-Hill LAN Communications Handbook

Fred Simonds

McGraw-Hill, Inc.

New York   San Francisco   Washington, D.C.   Auckland   Bogotá
Caracas   Lisbon   London   Madrid   Mexico City   Milan
Montreal   New Delhi   San Juan   Singapore
Sydney   Tokyo   Toronto

Library of Congress Cataloging-in-Publication Data

Simonds, Fred.
    McGraw-Hill LAN communications handbook / Fred Simonds.
        p.   cm. — (McGraw-Hill series on computer communications)
    Includes bibliographical references and index.
    ISBN 0-07-057442-1
    1. Local area networks (Computer networks)—Handbooks, manuals,
etc. I. Title. II. Title: LAN communications handbook.
III. Series.
TK5105.7.S56   1994
004.6′8—dc20   93-48540
                                                                 CIP

1 2 3 4 5 6 7 8 9 0   DOC/DOC   9 0 9 8 7 6 5 4

ISBN 0-07-057442-1

*The sponsoring editor for this book was Jerry Papke, the editing
supervisor was Kimberly A. Goff, and the production supervisor was
Suzanne W. Babeuf. This book was set in Century Schoolbook. It was
composed by Carol Woolverton, Lexington, Massachusetts, in
cooperation with Warren Publishing Services, Biddeford, Maine.*

Printed and bound by R. R. Donnelley & Sons Company.

For all my family,
and especially for Jim,
whose advice I finally took.

Contents

Preface

This book has only one purpose: to help you understand local area networks and help you use that knowledge to benefit your organization and yourself.

Learning technology is easier than applying it. To that end, Chapter 2 focuses on LANs in the workplace and developing an implementation plan that reflects your organization's real needs. It is based on 20 years of applications experiences—so I know it works.

A LAN is a *system,* not a collection of piece parts. While all the parts interact with each other, the end user sees only the final result. If we are to satisfy end users, our customers, then we must take the same system-oriented perspective.

It is this conviction that led me to write this book. I found many specialized books that addressed one part of a LAN or another—wiring, LAN protocols, servers, and network operating systems galore. The problem of tying them together was left to the reader. It seemed to me that all the necessary information ought to be in one place. That's why this isn't just a book, it's a *handbook*; something to be kept on hand and used in your day-to-day activities.

Each chapter is organized with the most general and conceptual information presented first. More and more detail is then added until you either have learned what you need to know or you need advanced information. The information in this book extends to the intermediate level. For advanced information, you need to consult one of those specialized books.

LAN technology is always being improved, quickly rendering many books about LANs obsolete. Knowing this, I have attempted to summarize long-term trends without becoming caught up in events of the moment. Certain aspects of LAN technology, such as primary IEEE 802 standards, are relative constants so this book is somewhat further insulated from obsolescence.

One example of the inevitable march of time is the retiring of the venerable CCITT label, standing for the International Telegraph and Telephone Consultative Committee. Always a part of the International Telecommunications Union in Geneva, CCITT has been renamed the International Telecommunications Union-Telecommunication Standardization Sector (ITU-TSS). Accordingly, I have applied the latter title throughout this book instead of using CCITT.

If computing is a dynamic marketplace, then computer networking is hyperdynamic. This vibrant technology, offering so much, demands constant awareness and oversight in order to remain current. That fact imposes an obligation on each one of us to keep up with the new trends and technologies as we improve our skills. I hope this book contributes to that effort and stimulates your desire to know more. For one so inclined, there are no limits.

Fred Simonds

Acknowledgments

Thanking people is at once easy and difficult. While many of their names are known to me, it seems inadequate to express my gratitude on a mere sheet of paper. However, I will attempt it.

First and foremost, my thanks to Dr. Sidnie Feit, author of her own TCP/IP and SNMP books and technical reviewer of this work. Her painstaking attention, insistence on rigor, and broad technical knowledge has made this book far better than it would otherwise have been. She caused me to re-examine concepts and explain them precisely and simply. At the very beginning of this project, she put me in touch with the next person on my thank-you list.

Series advisor Jay Ranade scrutinized the original manuscript and suggested the separate chapters on Ethernet, token ring, and FDDI that appear in this volume. He was, and remains, a constant source of encouragement and savvy advice to me as we discussed future works.

Jerry Papke, Senior Editor with McGraw-Hill's Professional Publishing Group, contributed additional encouragement. To his everlasting credit, he gave me the time I needed to thoroughly review the text and exorcise errors to make this book as good as is humanly possible. He was ably assisted by Rachel Hirschfield.

As valuable as they are, motivation and advice don't produce a book. Editing supervisors make it all come together, and Kimberly Goff did just that. She coordinated the preparation of the manuscript and the many reviews through which it passed. Her high standards are emblematic of everyone affiliated with McGraw-Hill with whom I worked.

The manuscript was edited by Louis Poncz, who helped make the copy more readable and flow more easily and eliminated many ambiguities.

The composition of the book, that is, putting it into the form you see, was performed by Ms. Carol Woolverton. In my view, the quality of her work speaks for itself.

I am sure there are many unseen hands who made their unique contribution anonymously. The best I can do is to thank them here.

Last but first, I'm indebted to my family. This one's for you.

McGraw-Hill
LAN Communications
Handbook

What Is a Local Area Network?

Key Terms and Components

A *local area network* (LAN) is a high-speed communications link that connects together computers and peripheral equipment that are within a restricted geographical domain. LANs may be contrasted with *wide area networks* (WANS). WANs cover a large geographic area and use leased telephone lines or other long-haul facilities. LANs cover a much smaller area than WANs and are almost invariably owned by the user. LAN data speeds vastly exceed those of WANs: An Ethernet 10 Mbit/sec LAN is more than six times as fast as a high-speed WAN T-1 facility operating at 1.544 Mbit/sec.

This brings us to the first of three elements, shown in Figure 1.1, that make up a LAN, i.e., the *medium*. The medium in a LAN is usually a twisted pair of wires or a coaxial cable through which data is sent. In a WAN, the medium is a telephone line or perhaps a satellite link.

The second element of a LAN is the *hardware*. Hardware includes:

Network interface cards (NICs) These devices connect data processing equipment to the LAN. There are many types of NICs, varying in capability, price, vendor, and access method.

Servers. These provide services to other data processing (DP) devices connected to the LAN, such as PCs, Macintoshes, and powerful workstations.

Communications devices. These include hubs, baluns, repeaters, bridges, routers, and gateways. We will discuss the functions of these devices.

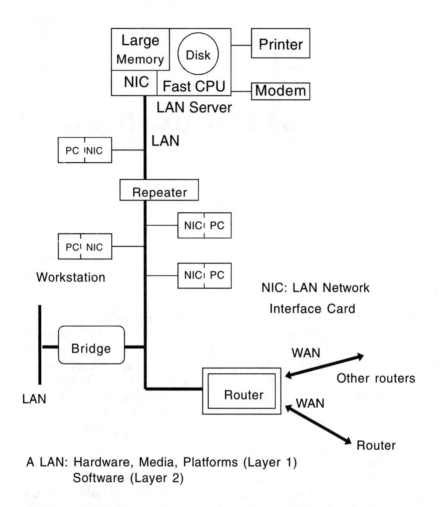

Figure 1.1 Elements of a LAN.

Our third element, perhaps the most important one, is invisible but no less essential. This is the intelligence embodied in the software that drives the LAN.

All LANs require:

A data format.

An orderly way to control access to the medium, called sensibly enough, *media access control* (MAC).

A way to connect higher layer protocols to the LAN. This function is titled *logical link control* (LLC).

Mechanisms to detect faults and errors and recover from them.

A method to manage the LAN. By manage, we include not only monitoring and testing, but providing routine, daily user-related services such as security, resource sharing, and applications services.

A method to route messages reliably and efficiently.

The software in a LAN is organized according to the two lowest layers of the International Standards Organization's (ISO) open systems interconnection (OSI) reference model. As a whole, the model defines all the functions required for communication between any two machines. The ISO/OSI model is divided into seven functional layers to make this possible.

Understanding the model and what each of its layers does is essential for anyone involved in LANs. We will shortly spend some time becoming acquainted with the model and especially how it relates to LANs.

Understanding the OSI model is especially useful when WANs are used to link LANs together, as they often are. The model is also used in diverse areas such as network management and software design. We can expect to see the model pop up in more and more places as the trend toward open systems continues.

LAN Communications Concepts

LAN communication is streamlined and is simpler in some ways than traditional host communications systems.

Traditional host communications tend to be *hierarchical,* with a central computer regulating the flow of information back and forth. Tributary stations cannot communicate between one another directly, only through the central host. The host *polls* tributaries in sequence. Tributaries respond with data traffic or a no-traffic response. One undesirable result of this organization is a significant amount of nondata overhead.

There is no polling in a LAN and no hierarchy. LAN communication is *peer-to-peer,* since all the devices can communicate with each other, and no one machine has greater or less connectivity than any of the others. To borrow from George Orwell, "All animals are equal."

There is a tendency to assign a supervisory role to a server, as if to extend the WAN hierarchy into the LAN paradigm. This should not be done. Servers do not have any supervisory role at all in LAN communications. Technically, you could operate a LAN without any server at all, though it would be of little practical value. There is a virtue here in that a single point of failure, the central host, is eliminated.

In LAN networking, network control is said to be *distributed* among the devices on the network. Specifically, control of the network resides in the NIC firmware in each machine. Therefore, network access and management is not a substantial burden on the workstation itself.

LAN communications may be *connectionless* or *connection-oriented.* Connectionless messages are sent with the expectation that they will be received correctly; there is no acknowledgement of correct receipt. If the message is received incorrectly, a higher layer must ask for re-transmission. Such messages are called *datagrams.*

Connection-oriented communications include the acknowledgement of messages as correct before they are passed on to the recipient. For example, a WAN- or LAN-based Systems Network Architecture/ Synchronous Data Line Control (SNA/SDLC) session is connection-oriented since a logical session is set up between sender and receiver before transmission takes place. The session includes periodic acknowledgement of correct receipt of a message sequence or a request for re-transmission.

LANs have five major communications characteristics:

Medium. This is the means by which data is sent and include shielded or unshielded twisted pair wires, coaxial cable, fiber optics, or, most recently, wireless transmission.

Transmission technique. If the LAN signal is carried directly on the medium, the transmission technique is *baseband.* Techniques which modulate the LAN signal on to an analog carrier signal are called *broadband* systems. These allow several LANS to share the same medium, just as many TV stations share a single CATV cable into people's homes.

Network topology. This is the layout of the cabling. The choices are *star, ring,* or *bus* topologies, or a combination of these.

Access control method. Since a LAN is nothing more than a big party line, there must be some way to control access to the medium. The most common methods used today are *contention* (Ethernet or IEEE 802.3) and *token passing* (token ring or IEEE 802.5).

Data rate. This is simply the raw ability to transfer information in mega*bits* per second. Mixing units here causes confusion, since we gauge information volume in 8-bit bytes rather than bits. Ethernet LANs operate at 10 Mbit/sec or 1.25 Mbytes/second. Token ring systems operate at 4 or 16 Mbit/sec (0.5 or 2 Mbytes/sec, respectively).

The LAN community has developed a convenient shorthand to condense this information with respect to IEEE 802.3 or Ethernet LANs. It consists of the *speed, transmission technique,* and *wire type.* Thus, *10BaseT* refers to a 10 Mbit/sec LAN, using *base*band signaling with unshielded *T*wisted pair wiring. If a number is substituted for the *T,* this refers to the Ethernet coaxial cable segment length in hundreds of meters. So 10Base5 means an Ethernet segment with a maximum length of 500 m. If the cable is not twisted, i.e., no *T*, then it must be coaxial.

Relationship to the OSI Model

The ISO/OSI model is a seven-layer network architecture. A basic working knowledge of the model is useful when working with a LAN, WAN, or any open system. The model's utility in different applications makes it powerful and it will endure.

As shown in Figure 1.2, there are seven layers in the OSI model, one atop the other. Each has a different function, but the common purpose of layers 4–7 is to provide *interoperability,* which means that all the system elements can exchange data regardless of the vendor of the equipment. This is what is meant by an *open system.*

Connectivity is provided in the layers 1–3 of the model. Their combined purpose is to provide a working connection between the sender and receiver, i.e., the ability to move data anywhere in the network, regardless of the transmission technology or medium, and to assure *information integrity* (no errors). Connectivity is a prerequisite to interoperability; if there is no link, there can be no interoperation.

Each OSI layer provides services to the layer above it and maintains a relationship with layers above and below it. Each layer also communicates with its corresponding layer in the other machine. Layers are independent in the sense that changes made within a layer do not affect other layers. *Modularity* is a prime virtue of the model.

A layer communicates with its counterpart in the other machine via a *peer protocol.* Seven OSI layers mean seven peer protocols.

The term "protocol" causes confusion because there are seven protocol layers and multiple protocols within each layer. Thus, to say a LAN is an Ethernet or that it uses TCP/IP is equally descriptive, yet an incomplete characterization. This is because not all the protocols were specified—in this case, just three (Ethernet at layer 2, IP at layer 3, and TCP at layer 4).

It is, therefore, not surprising that there is frequent miscommunication about protocol, since questions are asked and answered incompletely. While protocols have facilitated communication between machines, they have not always made communication easier between people!

In 1983, the ISO released the OSI reference model. This model was the first step in promoting data transfer among multivendor systems. By standardizing the function of each layer, vendors are able to build systems that work together, at least in principle.

In trade papers and journals, the model is referred to as a stack or

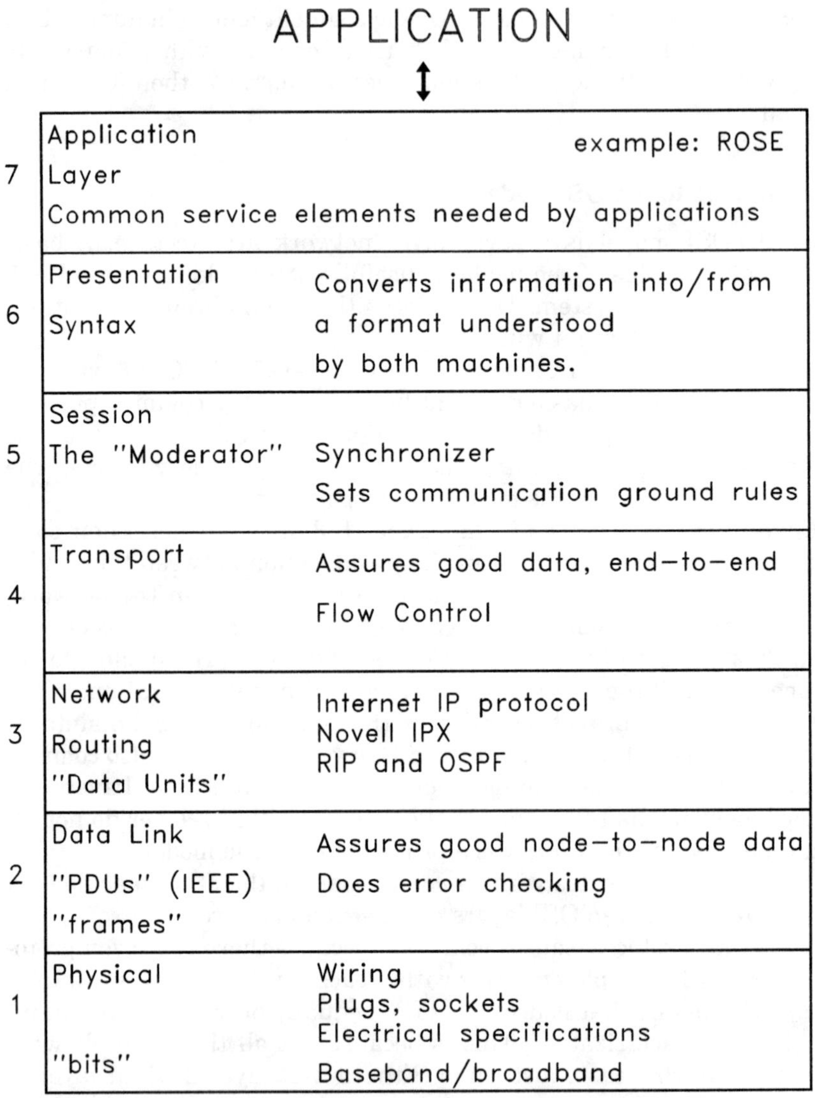

APPLICATION
↕

7	Application Layer Common service elements needed by applications	example: ROSE
6	Presentation Syntax	Converts information into/from a format understood by both machines.
5	Session The "Moderator"	Synchronizer Sets communication ground rules
4	Transport	Assures good data, end−to−end Flow Control
3	Network Routing "Data Units"	Internet IP protocol Novell IPX RIP and OSPF
2	Data Link "PDUs" (IEEE) "frames"	Assures good node−to−node data Does error checking
1	Physical "bits"	Wiring Plugs, sockets Electrical specifications Baseband/broadband

Figure 1.2 The open systems interconnection model.

protocol stack. Systems that use some but not all layers are said to use a *partial* or *short* stack. Other systems may include several implementations of the model, called *parallel stacks*. This is how many vendors implement multiple protocols such as the Common Management Information Protocol (CMIP) and the Simple Network Management Protocol (SNMP)—in separate, parallel stacks. The user needs to just select one (in common, of course) and run with it.

The application layer

Let us begin at the top, as if we were entering data into a system. The application we are interacting with is in turn interacting with the *application layer*, or layer 7. Examples include ITU-TSS* (formerly CCITT) X.400 standards for *message handling systems* (MHSs), better known as electronic mail (e-mail), and *File Transfer and Access Management* (FTAM). The application layer also manages the communication of information between applications entities, such as between sales and inventory programs, using *application layer protocols*.

The presentation layer

The presentation layer, or layer 6, is responsible for the *syntax*. It resolves differences in data formats between dissimilar systems by transferring data in a form common to both of them, i.e., it acts as a "common denominator." Each system then formats the data to suit its needs.

The session layer

The session layer, or layer 5, is the moderator, the "negotiator," between two open systems. The session layer manages the flow of data in both directions and makes sure that it is synchronized.

There can be several session connections that use the same transport connection (at the next layer down), sequenced one after the other, but not at the same time. If a transport connection must be terminated and replaced by another one to maintain service, the session layer insulates the higher layers from noticing the switch.

The transport layer

The transport layer, or layer 4, is a transparent pipe for exchanging data. The transport layer lets processes at each end transmit and receive data reliably, regardless of the system type or their location in the network. Transport layer protocols exchange data in full duplex (both ways at the same time) and ensure correct delivery.

Domestically, *Transmission Control Protocol* (TCP) is the best-known LAN transport protocol. TCP originated in the Department of Defense Advanced Research Projects Agency's Internet, now the world's largest data network.

---

*ITU-TSS stands for International Telecommunications Union-Telecommunication Standardization Sector.

The network layer

Once again, recall that the common characteristic of layers 1–3 is that all three share a role in the process of *connectivity* or creating a communications path.

The one word to describe what the network layer, or layer 3, does, is *routing*. Layer 3 finds the most economical logical and physical paths, routes messages through intermediate nodes, and controls message flow from node to node. A well-known example of a network layer protocol is the *Internet Protocol* (IP). ITU-TSS X.25 packet switching is another well-known network layer protocol. At this layer, we speak of data in terms of *packets*.

Since IP is used as the routing protocol along with TCP at the transport layer, we often hear of TCP/IP because they are inextricably linked. They are two separate protocols, but since they are always used together, they are spoken of as one.

The data link layer

The *data link layer* (DLL), or layer 2, synchronizes transmissions between sender and receiver, including error control over the physical layer below it. This layer ensures error detection and, when implemented, retransmission.

Providing transparency to the physical network elements is also a DLL responsibility. Real-world examples include IBM's SDLC and ISO's HDLC protocols. IEEE 802.3 (Ethernet CSMA/CD), IEEE 802.4 (token bus), and IEEE 802.5 (token ring) are also layer 2 protocols. At this layer we speak in terms of *blocks* for BSC and *frames* for SDLC/HDLC and the IEEE protocols.

The physical layer

The physical layer, or layer 1, handles the electrical and mechanical interface and transmission of signals from one system to another. Plugs, sockets, cables, and connectors all fall within layer 1, as do electrical specifications for signals such as encoding, voltage levels, and grounding. Distances and speeds are part of the specification as well.

LAN cabling and baseband or broadband signaling is part of layer 1. When someone refers to the physical layer, he or she speaks in terms of *bits*.

Protocol rules

Take a look at Figure 1.3. It shows the rules which all layers follow. First, *intralayer entities* have unique addresses and provide services to

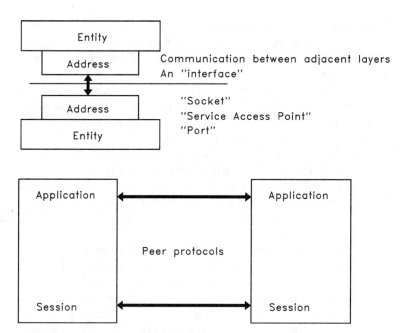

Figure 1.3 Layer rules.

higher layers. Entities can speak upward or downward, but only to their adjacent layers. This layer interface is formally called a *service access point*.

Layers maintain communication with their equivalent layer, or peer, at the other end. They can *never* communicate diagonally with another layer; this would obviously not be peer-to-peer communication. Although layers maintain logical communication with each other, they must go through the layers below them to physically transfer data.

Horizontal communication from one layer to another layer is via a *peer protocol,* whereas up-and-down or hierarchical communication within a stack uses an *interface protocol.* Together, the two constitute an *architecture.*

One definition of an interface is that it provides a junction between dissimilar things. Here they link layers and more specifically, entities. The interface establishes procedures to follow when a layer requests services from or provides services to a layer directly below or above it.

What is a protocol? It is a set of rules needed at both ends to exchange data in an orderly way. For instance, the protocol defines how many bits make a character and the form of a message, i.e., how many characters will be in a message. Once that is set, the data format, where control messages will appear and where data will be sent in a transmission, is determined.

Protocols contain the addressing needed between nodes. Protocols provide orderly message sequencing and a way to detect and correct errors *(error recovery)* without higher layer involvement. Protocols are *nonvolatile* (unerasable) in the sense that the same rules are used again and again for new sessions and communications.

The *addressing* mechanism common to all protocols contains information about who is sending and who will receive a message. Maintaining *synchronization* with the remote end, staying in step, is also a protocol function. Since communication paths are imperfect, *detecting and correcting errors* is a vital protocol task. Regulating the flow of data, called *flow control,* prevents overloading the network or a receiver with data. Flow control prevents data loss into the proverbial bit bucket.

LANs and the ISO model

If the model is really *the* reference for communications systems, then it should be applicable with either a WAN or a LAN. Let us see how the model fits a LAN (Figure 1.4).

The physical layer. LANs have a readily identified physical layer. *Cabling* for local area networks takes four different forms. They include twisted-pair wires, coaxial cable, fiber optic strands, and now wireless systems. Similarly, baseband and broadband signaling and Manchester encoding are characteristics defined at the physical layer. These are discussed later.

LAN protocols. Above the physical layer lies the Data Link Layers. As discussed below, the IEEE LAN protocols divide the DLL into two sublayers, the Media Access Control sublayer and the Logical Link Control sublayer residing above the MAC sublayer.

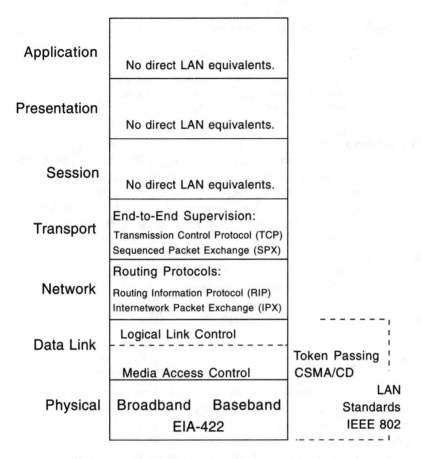

Figure 1.4 The OSI model applied to LANs.

Above Layers 1 and 2, there are no LAN standards.
The model tracks loosely above Layer 2 for LAN protocols.

RIP is an Internet protocol designed to work in routers.
IPX is a proprietary protocol belonging to Novell.
SPX is also Novell-proprietary.

The MAC sublayer is the location of the *access control method*. Some of these, Carrier Sense Multiple Access with Collision Detection (CSMA/CD) and token ring, are well known. Their common purpose is to control and manage the use of the physical layer below.

What does the LLC sublayer do? The LLC services both the MAC sublayer below it and the network layer above. Both of these interfaces are defined by IEEE 802.X as well as the intralayer MAC to LLC communication path. The LLC provides a uniform interface to the network layer regardless of which access method, e.g., IEEE 802.3 or IEEE 820.5, is used.

When one station communicates with another, it is the LLCs in each that exchange data between their *service access points* (SAPs). The SAP is the link to the network layer in each station. Data passed from LLC to LLC is called an *LLC protocol data unit.*

LAN operating systems. Above the LLC layer, things become less standardized. At the network layer, IBM offers its LAN Support Program, implemented as NetBIOS. NetBIOS provides services at the network, transport, and session layers. The object of NetBIOS is to provide a standard interface for linking with applications above it. An alternative to NetBIOS is a peer-to-peer link to SNA/SDLC. This takes the form of an *Advanced Program-to-Program Communication* (APPC/PC) LU 6.2 session.

Vendors have written LAN operating systems working up to and at the application layer to provide the services required in a practical LAN environment. These *network operating systems* are exemplified by Novell's NetWare and Banyan's VINES.

The Need LANs Fulfill

The first *personal computers* (PCs) delivered were stand-alone machines with no communications ability at all. Early efforts to make them communicate with one another used existing WAN techniques, with modems and wires. This quickly proved inadequate, being bulky, too slow for large file transfers, and not allowing sufficient connectivity, i.e., only two PC users could talk at a time.

The origins of local area networking are rooted in the seventies. Dr. Robert Metcalfe was the inventor of what is now called Ethernet, since refined as IEEE 802.3. His invention was developed by a consortium consisting of DEC, Intel, and Xerox, colloquially referred to as "DIX," for the purpose of intraoffice machine communication.

Token-passing was originally conceived as the Newhall ring in 1969 and was developed further by Olof Soderblom of the Netherlands. His firm, Willemijn Holding, holds a token passing patent from 1984, which he licenses to vendors. IBM's research laboratory in Zurich, Switzerland, refined token-passing for practical use. Once introduced by IBM, token ring's acceptance was assured.

LANs fulfill a variety of PC-related needs:

They allow fast file transfers and interactive communication.

They give users the connectivity they need.

Using NICs, processing power is not drained from the PC.

LANs make it possible to share resources, e.g., printers, disks, or files.

LANs are relatively inexpensive to buy, install, and maintain.

LANs diminish duplication in software and reduce PC disk, memory, and sometimes processor requirements.

LANs give users flexibility in connecting dissimilar machines, e.g., Macintoshes, mainframes, midranges, and minicomputers.

LANs make possible new applications such as groupware and multimedia.

LANs are expandable to make possible the on-line corporation.

Client-Server Computing

You may have heard that "the network is [becoming] the computer." In the mainframe era, there was a clear distinction between the computer and the network. The computer furnished the smarts, and the network was little more than a data pipe.

Intelligent networks such as LANs have blurred that distinction. As the network provides more services, it becomes harder to separate the network from the computer. While a LAN can be considered to be a means of linking computers together, we can look at the whole as a distributed, multiuser computing system. In such a system, the resources of workstations linked via the network form a complete computing entity. This is similar in concept to linking memory, disk, a processor, and *input/output* (I/O) on a data bus, where the bus is very fast, but only one bit wide.

In a LAN, we set up what we call a peer-to-peer relationship between machines. There is no master/slave or primary/secondary correlation as is found in hierarchical protocols such as IBM's SNA/SDLC. This homogeneous approach is widely regarded as the wave of the future in computing, and in business social organization as well.

There is, however, a relationship between machines which depends on their respective roles at the moment they interact. Much abused as a buzzword, this is referred to as the *client-server* relationship. Let us discuss exactly what that means.

As shown in Fig. 1.5, servers supply a service of some kind, such as file or communications service. In client-server computing, servers usually do not need to know anything about a client before a client asks for a service; this is necessary only during the service period. Nor does a server usually keep any information about a client after it has provided the service. Servers are therefore often called *stateless* machines.

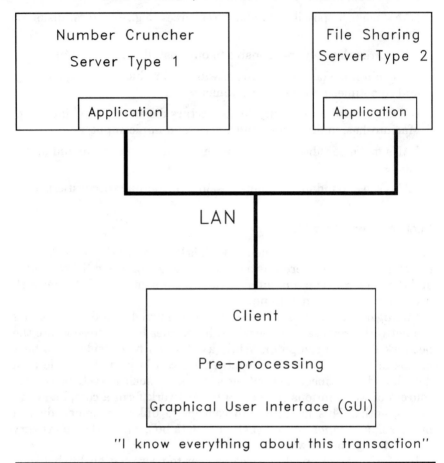

"I don't know who you are, and I don't care"

Number Cruncher
Server Type 1

Application

File Sharing
Server Type 2

Application

LAN

Client

Pre-processing

Graphical User Interface (GUI)

"I know everything about this transaction"

Figure 1.5 Client-server computing.

Clients generally bear all the burden of providing the server everything it needs to perform the service and direct the information back through the network to the client. Further, the client must track the state of the application, i.e., so many records read, number of records processed, and status information. Thus, clients are usually considered *stateful*.

Client-server computing addresses the problem of distributing heavily used applications between two or more platforms. It is a conceptual model of how computers interact with each other. As such, the client-server model is one of many distributed models that have been around for years. By contrast, you may be familiar with the traditional mainframe model. In that *centralized* architecture, most of the intelligence is in the host and little is in the remote devices. However, distributed machines divide the intelligence and are tied together by a network; in client-server-based machines, there is usually a LAN.

Within the distributed model, the client-server relationship is aimed at applications, not data. The application is divided to run in part on the workstation and in part on the server. This model does not insist that the machines be the same, nor even that they use the same operating system. What is required is that the machines be linked by a 1-bit-wide bus: the LAN. Therefore, we have the client-server mantra,

"The network *is* the computer."

Defining client-server

Client-server is one of the most abused catch phrases in the industry. Here are four popular definitions:

1. *A LAN.* We have the incorrect notion that since clients and servers are readily identified, ergo, this must be client-server computing. This definition is inadequate because it looks only at the physical connection rather than the logical relationship between machines. In a conventional LAN, the application runs on either client or server, but not both.

2. *Division of application processing between a workstation and server.* This prevailing definition of client-server computing involves two or more applications processors, each processing their appropriate part of the application. One of those processors is the client workstation, the other is one or more servers.

3. *Networked SQL.* *Structured query language* (SQL) is a syntax for accessing data, not an architecture or an application development language. Client-server relationships deal with applications, not data. Strictly speaking, the client must control every aspect of the transaction to be considered a true client-server relationship. Even so, if preprocessing occurs in the client, networked SQL is generally considered a client-server relationship.

4. *Cooperative processing.* In cooperative processing, several servers work together, often invisibly to the user, to do the job. Each part is done by the server best equipped to service that part of the application. If the client is involved in preprocessing the application and the application is divided by servers, then there is simultaneous use of client-server and cooperative processing. Note that the two can also be mutually exclusive.

What client-server computing is not

Client-server computing is not one operating system controlling more than one central-processing unit (CPU). This is more correctly referred to as multiprocessing or a processor complex. It is also not IBM's *Systems Applications Architecture* (SAA). SAA lets parts of an application run on an intelligent workstation, but SAA does not need a client-server relationship between workstation and server. Unintelligent 3270 and 5250 terminals preclude a client-server relationship as they lack the intelligence to manage a client-server exchange. In a sense, SAA may be the means to push users from 3270s and 5250s toward PC-style intelligent workstations.

Client-server and cooperative processing

Client-server computing should not be confused with *cooperative processing.* In cooperative processing, as the name says, two or more processors share responsibility for servicing a single application. The nature of the interaction between parts of the application is not defined. Today, Sun's *Remote Procedure Calls* (RPCs) and IBM's APPC or LU 6.2 support client-server *and* cooperative processing. The *Open Software Foundation* (OSF) is building the standards framework for cooperative processing through its *Distributed Computing Environment* (DCE) and the DCE's management dimension, the *Distributed Management Environment* (DME).

In cooperative processing, users may not necessarily know where their data resides and where their application is being processed. This task is delegated to the network, which allocates the most appropriate resources to do the job.

Client-server and cooperative processing can work together. There is no reason why RPCs or APPC could not implement a client-server relationship between two machines.

Some people equate a LAN with client-server computing; after all, most LANs have servers and the clients are workstations. While a basic LAN meets this part of the definition, true client-server computing fulfills the larger requirement of sharing heavily used applications among several computing platforms. A basic LAN does not meet this part of the functional definition.

Advantages of client-server computing

The biggest advantage to client-server computing is that it makes full use of the power built into today's workstations. For example, graphical user interfaces such as Windows are best supported on these independent workstations. Supporting them in a central system would place a great burden on the host and any intervening network.

Processing power in the PC or workstation allows for preprocessing, which off-loads the server. Centralized systems require a large portion of their system resources to manage active processes. Distributed processing greatly reduces this requirement.

Client-server computing minimizes differences in network nodes. Network nodes often vary greatly. They may contain different processors or operating systems and may be better suited for one application, e.g., number crunching, than another, e.g., file sharing. While the client and server must agree on a common language, or protocol, other differences are unimportant. How each machine arrives at the protocol is immaterial as long as the protocols match.

Failure recovery is another client-server advantage. Once again, the client is usually responsible for fault recovery. Should a server fail, the client decides how to recover. For example, a client requesting service from a failed print server could make the same request from another one that is working. Conversely, a frozen database server might cause a client to wait until the server has thawed, then it might come back and complete the download.

This is quite a distinction from centralized architectures, where all work in progress is at risk when a fault occurs. In client-server computing, clients assess the potential loss and react accordingly. If the server crashes in the midst of a transaction, the client application, being stateful, will know just where to resume.

Scalability is the ability of client-server computing to grow gracefully. Additions to centralized computing power usually require big incremental investments. Client-server computing calls for only a small machine, perhaps dedicated to an application. Sometimes the application can be loaded on an existing machine. The ability to load each server to capacity makes it possible to balance the applications load and get the most from each server. As an architecture, the client-server's insensitivity to platforms and operating systems makes it possible to mix machines and not be locked into any one vendor's architecture as is typical in minicomputer or mainframe computing.

Finally, when a server is dedicated to a particular service, performance compromises are avoided. The physical machine plus the operating system can be selected and tuned to provide efficient dedicated service. Consequently, performance improves.

Client-server disadvantages

The client-server approach, with the network in the middle, leans on the network heavily. For example, a LAN might have a throughput of

800 kbytes/sec, while a typical transaction might demand 5 kbytes/sec. Thus, 160 transactions per second are possible. This is not very many since thousands of transactions per second are often required. Higher speed LANs, notably 16 Mbit/sec token rings and 100 Mbit/sec *fiber-distributed data interface* (FDDI) are increasingly used in client-server applications. This is particularly true as more servers are added.

Compared to conventional network LAN programs, the load is offset somewhat because client-server computing does not download an entire program as in a conventional LAN. Most of the program runs on the server, i.e., the "back end." Only specified records, not entire files, are downloaded to the client "front end." Nor are concurrency control commands passed through the network to lock files and records.

In the client, tracking the state of the application can take up to 200 kbytes of random access memory (RAM), not including network drivers. This leaves less room for applications. Advanced operating systems, memory managers, and more powerful client processors should reduce the influence of the limiting memory load. For instance, MS-DOS 6.X's MemMaker utility determines automatically the optimum combination of drivers to be loaded into the Upper Memory Block (UMB) space, freeing more of the 640-kbyte base memory for applications.

Security is a major concern, especially regarding viruses and access management. The security problem is clearly more difficult to manage in a distributed system. Tools, e.g., Kerberos, are being developed to manage security and provide management control in distributed environments. The OSF is adapting Kerberos to provide security in its DME.

Access is often granted through a management computer, such as a security server. Once checked in, a user works directly with the desired server. Central security can also provide a list of services. This is a benefit because none of the services can be given a duplicate name. Consistency of passwords and groups is readily attained this way.

Single-purpose LANs may not need a security server if the LAN is departmental. However, several servers on the same LAN can argue with one another and swamp the network with broadcasts. Incorrect disks and wrong network names can cause unstable, even weird, operation. For example, users have accidentally erased passwords on another server. In the absence of a management server, human "liveware" must usually be designated for each server to coordinate usage. This can become time-consuming and expensive.

A variation is to have security information in each server. Sometimes the information comes from a central source, or perhaps the server itself builds its own security. Performance improves because querying the security server is not needed. The problem now becomes one of keeping the security consistent and synchronized between one server and the next. Duplicate information will exist for users with access to more than one server.

The bottom line on client-server

Client-server systems can give great file service performance. The optimum configuration is a combined file and security service in one or two servers that supports 10 to 50 users. It is becoming common to bridge and route such client-server LANs together. Configurations that do not meet the strict definition of a client-server relationship can still provide many of the benefits of a client-server architecture.

Why and When LANs Make Sense

A LAN makes sense when the need for it becomes self-evident. When people start walking diskettes down the hall, or worse, across the complex, time is being wasted. This is called the *sneakernet* phenomenon and is a great way to kill productivity.

When competition for resources starts affecting work flow, a LAN is called for. The best (or worst) example is waiting to use the printer. Printer queues can stop PCs in their tracks and is the end of productive work until the logjam is broken. Bickering and negotiating whose job gets printed next does not help productivity—or morale.

A brute force approach to resources is expensive. The brute force solution means a printer for everyone. This is a poor expenditure of capital. Similarly, providing a modem and a fax or fax board for each user is inefficient. With a LAN, a single communications and/or fax server is much less expensive and provides nearly equal access.

The same holds true for software. Beyond a certain point, operating the multiuser or network version of a program is cheaper than buying one stand-alone copy per user. Further, compatibility is assured in that everyone works from the same program revision. Program software exists in the server and may be downloaded to the user or executed on the server itself. Coresident metering software prevents license violations.

When we refer to a server, we refer to a device that provides service to a user. This is most often a file service. The ability to share a file, and especially to access and/or work on different parts of the same file, is a huge productivity booster. If one worker accesses a file and thereby forces a coworker to wait or do something else, this is a prima facie case for a LAN.

Communicating outside the office can be a legitimate reason to install a LAN. The general thinking today is that the enterprise network of the future will be a LAN in each work area linked to other LANs through a WAN. Such a network will provide uniform access from any area of the company to any other area. FAX and voice traffic, not to mention overnight express and ordinary mail, will all give way to this vision of the on-line enterprise.

This is not science fiction: It is already happening. The viability of groupware, in which workers sharing a common task are linked via LANs, is now established. Geographic separation of groupware members is becoming irrelevant, and there is nothing to say that one person cannot be a member of several different groups. If organizations are assembling workgroups, then groupware is the glue that will bind them together in a common purpose.

New applications are taking hold. The ability to convey a voice and picture as part of an information file is the essence of multimedia. Multimedia's large data content makes a LAN essential. Document imaging, where paper-like looking documents are stored on-line, requires the data-carrying capacity that only a LAN can provide.

Studies show that the number of LAN-to-LAN connections in 1995 will number some 260,000. Message sizes will increase to 150 kbytes in the same time, reflecting the heavy imaging and multimedia traffic. Yet average network transit time will *decrease* from 1.5 to 1.0 sec as LAN speeds increase and advanced switching technologies such as *asynchronous transfer mode* (ATM) begin to appear at user sites.

LAN traffic will grow at the expense of traditional SNA data. Some 61 percent of enterprises rank LAN internetworking as their most important information systems tool with distributed processing second at 42 percent and imaging third at 23 percent.

The trend is established, but what are the common threads here? LANS make possible:

Universal connectivity

Information on demand, in usable form

Optimum utilization of resources

Multiplying, "leveraging," the value of an individual's work

Propelling an individual's work forward, rather than holding it back

Adapting quickly to changing needs

In the next chapter, we will see how these LAN-driven capabilities can and are changing the way we work.

2

LANs in the Workplace

The Establishment of Workgroups

In the last few years, we have seen the establishment of *workgroups,* small numbers of workers who have a common purpose. Workgroups might be likened to the task force concept in microcosm. Workgroups are intended to be cohesive, flexible, and focused, requiring a minimum of overhead and supervision. They are intended to be responsive and adaptable to quickly changing business conditions. Compared to a task force's turning radius of several miles, a workgroup should be able to turn on a dime.

Workgroups are supposed to encourage communication by their peer-to-peer structure. Free of outside interference, creativity is stimulated. By localizing responsibility, management hopes to combine authority with responsibility and so empower employees to do what really makes sense. Ultimately, this amounts to nothing less than the decentralization of management.

Many documented studies show that when employees are given the power to control their work, the resulting creativity, productivity, and morale improvements can be astonishing. Once again, the management pendulum has swung fully from stifling micromanagement to empowerment, from centralized to decentralized control.

Empowering Creativity

The productivity disappointment

Much has been made of the fact that despite huge increases in technology investment per white collar worker, the worker's productivity has not improved very much. According to Morgan Stanley & Co. of New

York, $862 billion has been spent on information technology in the last decade, a 60 percent increase and representing 85 percent of the total information technology that was bought. Believe it or not, the white-collar worker today is surrounded today by no less than an average of *$10,000* in data technology! For all this investment, the corresponding productivity improvement has been disappointing.

Unlocking creativity and productivity

John Brown, chief scientist at Xerox' Palo Alto Research Center believes that *informal collaboration,* e.g., the casual get-together around the coffee machine, is one of the great productivity enhancers. Here ideas are discussed in a totally nonformal, noncommittal, nonthreatening environment. It is not uncommon to find that one worker has been working on something that could help a coworker or vice versa. Maybe a casual conversation creates a new idea, a different view. These chance events are serendipitous, unplanned but fortunate nonetheless, and more of a necessity to the organization than was realized.

Dr. Brown's theory is that office technology to date has been aimed at the individual worker, not at a group, and that those systems set up to support groups have been formal, not casual. The combination has inhibited free exchange of information. This has failed in turn to bring about the atmosphere in which creative ideas can be born.

Another belief he holds is that productivity limits are set by *usability* rather than *technology* and by a person's ability to understand how to use technology in support of group productivity. He said, "Matching technology to the way people are productive will ultimately lead to new ways to be productive. The real value will come from redesigning work practices." Does this sound like "reengineering" to you?

So the object of workgroups is, in part, to build this kind of environment. Designing group software that encourages informality, organizational awareness and a loosely coupled social climate becomes the challenge for groupware vendors.

LANs fit nicely into the workgroup concept. LANs are designed to support groups ranging from a few people to about 250 clients. Since departments are located geographically together, connecting them through a LAN is a natural step.

A LAN itself does not necessarily create a workgroup. More likely it creates several workgroups. If the department is responsible for quality assurance, that is one workgroup. The analytical section is another. The quality assurance staff for each respective product is a third through nth workgroup, and the managers make the nth plus one workgroup. So we can see that each employee is likely to be a member of several workgroups.

Given the physical glue of a LAN, we need some software to make a workgroup really feasible. Such software allows groups of people to share the work on communal projects. This is a good functional definition of what we today call *groupware.*

Bill Gates of Microsoft defines groupware broadly as "any software product that provides for user interaction." Thomas Malone of MIT's Center for Coordination Science defines groupware nearly as broadly as Bill Gates, defining groupware as "information technology used to help people work together more effectively."

And Terry Winograd of Action Technologies, developer of Coordinator, a groupware program, offers the broadest definition of all: "Groupware is a state of mind. I don't think you can point to a particular technology and say, 'that is the technology that makes it groupware.' "

What groupware does

Let us say you need to schedule a meeting with your staff. The first thing you do is check their schedules. (This act can raise a privacy issue if it is not implemented properly.) Then you send each staff member a draft agenda of what is to be discussed. You solicit their input before the meeting and come up with a final agenda, which you then distribute. You also refer each member to several documents that they must read beforehand.

The meeting itself is held in person or through the groupware. In its most basic form, the medium is text messages that are sent back and forth. Some groupware systems are adding audio and video conferencing and video imaging to make groupware meetings more immediate and less cumbersome.

A complete transcript of the meeting is created for later reference. Action items are recorded and draft reports are written and routed automatically for review. Comments are imbedded automatically, and the groupware shows whose comment was added and when. Once edited completely, the final document, which may include integrated audio and video plus text, is routed throughout the organization for review.

More possible groupware applications include:

Work flow management

Making and keeping schedules

Reference services

Conferencing

Knocking down barriers

It does not take much imagination to see how groupware has the power to bind groups together and integrate the functioning of an entire organization. Industry is coming to the realization that an organizational chart is not a communications path chart. To run the activity effectively, members must be free to communicate with whomever is most appropriate, at any level and wherever they are located.

To some extent, groupware blurs if not dissolves barriers created by organizational charts and by geography. As in the computing industry, organizations are moving from a hierarchical to a peer-to-peer structure. It is difficult to say that one caused the other; it seems to be a fortunate confluence of technology and social organization.

A further development will be the continuing evolution of workgroups. They are expected to have less permanence and become more fluid as business needs evolve. The geographical element will all but disappear. More and more decisions will be made at the workgroup level and fewer at the top of the management ladder.

The evolution of workgroups

At the most basic level, a LAN is fundamental to the establishment of workgroups, and it might even be said that the simple act of establishing a LAN creates a de facto workgroup regardless of the software involved. Creating the link creates the group.

A step up from that that point of view is that the most basic software, particularly electronic mail, creates the basic workgroup; Bill Gates would agree with this assertion. In his view, simply adding the send-mail command to the Microsoft Word for Windows and Microsoft Excel file menus in 1989 created a form of groupware.

This was, in fact, a good way to introduce users to the groupware concept, through something familiar. Groupware has not taken off in part because users have been unable to retain their present applications in a groupware environment. Ideally, a groupware package should be invisible to the user. Otherwise, a great deal of training and investment is lost.

Some packages, such as Group Technologies' Aspects, have built-in word processing capability and allow files to be imported. But this is not the same as being able to edit a Lotus spreadsheet in discussion mode among several workgroup members. Ultimately, a standard *applications-programming interface* (API) will be needed so that a standard software interface is presented to applications such as Microsoft Word for Windows or Lotus 1-2-3.

LANs face the same environment-independence problem. Groupware should be independent of the network and the network operating system. This is referred to as *back end independence,* while the side of the software presented to the user is called the *front end.* The object is to decouple the two or to make it possible to mix and match networks and applications in the groupware environment. To see how applications and software interfaces fit together, see Figure 2.1 which illustrates their relationship to groupware.

Mixing and matching is undesirable and causes incompatibility and confusion in buyers' minds. A messaging standard among vendors helps to minimize these problems. Several acronyms have been used for the proposed messaging standard including:

Microsoft's *Messaging Application Programming Interface* (MAPI).

Vendor Independent Messaging (VIM) has been adopted by Microsoft for Excel and Word to make those products compatible with Lotus Notes.

Apple's *Open Collaboration Environment* (OCE).

Novell's *Server Message Format* (SMF).

OSI/ITU-TSS X.400 electronic mail (supported by Novell).

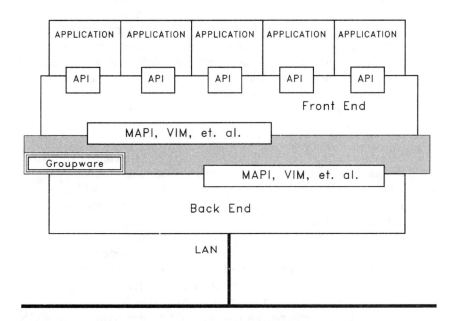

MAPI is Microsoft's Messaging API for Windows.
The MAPI Development Kit contains Dynamic Link Libraries with MAPI calls.

VIM, or Vendor Independent Messaging, is supported by Apple, Novell, Borland, Lotus, et. al.

Figure 2.1 Groupware applications and interfaces.

VIM is gaining momentum not only with Microsoft and WordPerfect, but with the *X.400 Applications Programming Association* (XAPIA). XAPIA will make the final decision on a mail-enabled-*programming interface application* (API) standard. VIM allows users to send messages and files from inside the application without having to exit it first.

These are examples of *middleware,* software that performs protocol translation to permit an interface between an application and a network or between two applications. Middleware provides vital flexibility. If groupware is limited to a few special applications, perhaps only those buried in the groupware itself, then groupware will die of inflexibility.

Knocking down barriers extends to nongroup information as well. Sheldon Laube of Price Waterhouse, a large Lotus Notes user, estimates that a third of the material they receive comes from outside the company. If a customer hands you a document, how do you put it in the groupware data base so that everyone can see it?

To solve this problem, Eastman Kodak is developing software for its Notes' users that will let users enter and retrieve paper documents as stored digitized images. The software will also be marketed by Lotus as Image-Enabling Notes. This will greatly enhance information flow from outside the group into the group. Intel uses a similar system now for applications notes, presentations, and competitive analyses. Kodak is developing a similar capability for NetWare, providing imaging networking groupware to PC-based LANs.

A big learning curve

One of the things that has held groupware back is its complexity. Most packages to date have lacked an intuitive interface that was easy to learn. People simply will not use an unfriendly system, which makes any ensuing productivity and creativity from technology discussion moot. Dr. Brown's comment about usability being a greater productivity influence than technology is right on the mark.

Adds Christine Bullen, assistant director of the Center for Information Systems Research at MIT: "A lot of user interfaces are just not that good. They're not designed for progressive learning, so a user can recall how to use features they learned six months earlier."

A major insurance company's loss prevention department uses ON Technology's Instant Update conferencing product and its Meeting Maker scheduling program. They have on-line meetings, pass claims files plus other documents among one another, and schedule meetings with clients. The company placed so much importance on a friendly interface that they made it a condition of sale.

Even so, software products to date have been so complicated that extensive training has been required even to perform simple tasks. The training expense is squarely opposed to what groupware is supposed to do: Simplify the workgroup operation! A vendor who suggests expensive training should probably be ushered to the nearest egress.

The other side of the training issue is in educating potential users to the point where they can apply what they know about groupware to their own situations. What is called for is the ability to use this knowledge to help solve their real world problems. This is an area where vendors have been weak, and the result has been poor sales. The circumstance is not unlike the Integrated Services Digital Network (ISDN), which is also seen as a technology in search of an application. Once again, Ms. Bullen of MIT said, "Education is the key. You can't expect to give someone a tool they don't know how to use and see benefits. Once users become educated about groupware, you'll see a real change in the way people work."

Hardware concerns

Software so far has lacked platform independence. This is a major problem for LAN users who need to work across a variety of hardware platforms. Some software runs on PCs but not Macintoshes, and vice versa. There is much effort going on to recast PC products into Macintosh versions and the other way around. Lotus Notes runs on the PC but the promised Macintosh version has yet to appear as of this writing. One measure of the importance of hardware is the above-referenced insurance company's decision to standardize on the Macintosh because of its built-in networking capability.

Cross-platform capability is essential if groupware is going to be used across an enterprise network where many different kinds of LANs, WANs, and servers are commonly used. LAN independence is equally important, so that any LAN will be compatible with groupware applications. This is one reason why messaging standards such as MAPI are so important to groupware evaluation.

Market players

The market, expected to be $320 million by 1995, will draw some big players, including Borland, Microsoft (already involved), DEC, IBM, and perhaps Wang. The heavy hitters will legitimize groupware, and they have the deep pockets needed for its development and especially for the presale education process.

Today, Lotus' Notes is generally regarded as the market leader. Other vendors include:

ON Technology's Instant Update and Meeting Maker

Group Technologies' Aspects

Collaborative Technologies' VisionQuest

Groupware summary

Perhaps more than any other factor, education is the key to group-ware's success, both before and after groupware is bought. It is essential that users understand what it can do and how to apply groupware effectively in their own setting before money is spent on it.

After the sale, if people do not, will not, or cannot use it, the dollars will simply have been wasted. Usability supersedes technology!

A major accounting and consulting firm startled the industry by purchasing no less than *10,000 copies* of Lotus Notes. According to their national director of information and technology, the vast majority are still in use. They know because users are charged internally for every Notes ID. Over 85 percent of their people use it more than once per day, and 98 percent use it for electronic mail. Databases are accessed by 80 percent of the users, and 40 percent use Notes to put data into a database. On average, the users look at no less than six databases.

Leveraging the investment in existing software and training is just as important. At the very least, interface software such as middleware APIs and at least one messaging standard such as MAPI, VIM, or OCE should be available. (The great thing about standards is that there are so many of them!)

Ideally, there should be not only seamless software but seamless hardware integration as well. Integration is essential in a multivendor enterprise network. Some vendors are working on porting their software from IBM to Macintoshes and vice versa. On this count, only time will tell.

There is some question about whether groupware should adapt to existing business practices or play a role in reengineering them. Some companies, like Westinghouse, sought a package that fit their way of doing business. Yet others have invested in groupware as a way of reengineering their work processes.

According to Bill Gates, "While I might use a work flow tool to automate the flow of documents in my organization today, I'm more likely to use the introduction of automated tools to reexamine and reengineer the process itself." Would it not make sense to change the process if the automation so dictates it? Even so, this process must take place within the limits of what people know works, company policy, and organizational constraints.

Many believe that yet another generation of groupware will be needed, one that addresses the open applications, training, interface, platform, and usability issues squarely. These are big nuts to crack. The groupware market is still considered to be in its infancy, but a 50 percent growth rate from 1990 to 1995 is expected, resulting in a $320 million market by then, according to International Data Corp.

Where will groupware be then? Bill Gates has said, "I think this whole notion of groupware as a separate category will be meaningless five years from now (in 1997). Today, in the Microsoft Windows environment, every application is enabled for printing and has access to a print monitor or drivers, but it does not know about it because the printing is part of the operating system. This is the same thing that will happen to workgroup applications."

Strategic Business Planning

"When you don't know where you're going, any road will do."—Anonymous

If you do not know the goal, how can you achieve it? So how can you build a LAN that will help your organization meet its objectives if you do not know what they are?

The short answer is that you cannot. More than any other reason, lack of understanding on the part of communications managers and staff is responsible for networks that do not truly serve the purpose for which they were built. The error lay in the sad fact that they were built to match someone's conception, rather than the reality, of what the network should do in support of organizational goals.

In a survey, telecommunications managers reported that only one third of their business' high-level executives do a good job of involving information systems managers in strategic planning.

This is what happens when upper management looks at "computer people" as mere technicians, uninterested in anything other than their intricate and demanding machines. We, however, cannot afford to make ourselves such high priests of *management information systems* (MIS). To get the senior executives' viewpoint, see Robert Townsend's book, *Up the Organization* (Fawcett World Library, New York, NY, p. 19, 1970).

Does the name of the book itself tell you something? For many of us, that priestly mantle once fed our egos and gave us a feeling of indispensability. The 1990s have taught all of us that no one is indispensable.

Your organization has a mission, a role to carry out. For Avis Rent-a-Car it was, in 1970, "to become the fastest-growing company with the highest profit margins in the business of renting and leasing vehicles without drivers." That simple statement of mission was promoted within the organization until everyone working there knew what they were doing there and why. Avis' success speaks for itself.

The next logical question then became, "Is what I'm doing helping us to reach that goal?" The virtue of the question was its power to focus activity, and it could be answered with a simple yes or no. But for you to answer the question, your organization's mission and strategic planning must be clear to you.

Strategic Information Planning

> In the same survey, only 31 percent of senior executives assess the impact of information technology when making strategic plans.

Not only are *consequences* neglected, but how about the *possibilities*?

A *strategic information plan* (SIP) makes sure that information technology is accounted for in the business plan and executed accordingly. *A SIP is the computing implementation of your organization's strategic business plan.* If your organization has set improved customer service as a strategic goal, then a remotely accessible database may be essential to that goal. Both the database plan itself and the steps needed to implement it are a logical part of the SIP. The important thing is that both are traceable back to your organization's strategic business plan.

It is the task of senior MIS management or the *chief information officer* (CIO) task to prepare the SIP. It is helpful if your management allows you to see the actual *strategic business plan* (SBP) and SIP documents; often they are confidential. At a minimum, you should be permitted to see the parts relevant to your LAN project and be able to relate your design to those goals. It is the only way to stay focused, to be sure of accomplishing the objective.

Doing the minimum

Okay, you do not have a SIP, or a CIO for that matter. Now what? *The risk is that your company might build the wrong thing.* At a minimum, you must make your users and management be very specific about what the network is supposed to accomplish. This specifically excludes how to build the network, concentrating instead on what it is supposed to achieve. It should be reduced to paper, so everyone understands and agrees with the objective. For most people, thinking through what they really need is the hardest step.

How to set one up

Accept the fact, as most managers do by now, that information is a resource, no different in principle from financial or personnel resources.

Like these, information exists to meet organizational objectives. Keeping this in mind, technology can be used to put the information in the form and hands of those who can make it pay off. We have changed our thinking from information processing to the outcome of such processing. Most importantly, we're getting closer to our goal of strategic relevance.

The Information Inventory

Take an inventory of the information you have. It may or may not be in electronic form and may exist both within and outside your organization. It should include information kept on paper, in office systems such as word processors, and independent data bases. There may be PCs or file servers containing valuable information that might be useful to other company functions. Find that information and inventory it, with the view that it might be useful to someone else—if they knew it existed.

Think of the information in your organization as a big library, and each information element as a book. A library patron can go to the card catalog and find an organized inventory of the information available and where to find it. Imagine trying to find a book without the card catalog! It would be very time-consuming, and it is most unlikely that the patron would find every possible reference. It is this inefficiency that we as information managers are trying to eliminate.

Continuing the library analogy, we must next *identify and classify* the information we have found. Fiction or nonfiction? Catalogued by author, title or subject?

Information can be subdivided by department or function. Production statistics and sales figures are two examples. Clearly, part of the classification process is the attachment of necessary security restrictions, including the ability to access and change information. Personnel, payroll, and strategic planning information, to name a few items, must obviously be restricted.

While we are discussing access, to whom shall we give a library card? Cardholders might not be restricted to organization members but to outside suppliers, vendors, and customers. If, for instance, we decide to use *electronic data interchange* (EDI), then we might be billing our customers and be paid electronically. If we are working on a project in a joint venture, it is inevitable that our partner will need to access certain files we own.

Now that we know what we have, we are in a position to *devise a plan* to use the information to support our organization's strategic objectives. Do this by asking a question first: What is needed to support this particular objective? Then select the information needed to accomplish that role. As in researching a paper at the library using the card catalog, you will be able to find all the relevant information needed. It is almost certain that you can add information toward attaining the objective that you didn't know you had. *That's using your information resources to full strategic advantage.*

The *information plan* tells us what information resides where and who needs to use it to accomplish a certain objective.

> The information plan should stress related business functions, without regard to the organizational table. If it makes sense for two diverse groups to share information, then so be it.

Do not be afraid to involve users in the planning stage. They have a real contribution to make, and they are the clients who must be satisfied with your efforts. You will defuse much resistance and enlist their support if they participate.

Having determined the end points, we are now in a position to *design a solution* to move data between locations. This is where the hardware, software, and applications come into their own. Modeling tools for the network might be used at this time. At this stage, we conceive the network and its attendant management, in that order, remembering always that function follows need.

Notice that these all fall out of the information plan we have created, and that the information plan is directly traceable to the organizational mission. This is the way it should be, and too often is not.

Too frequently we shortchange the early planning steps in a rush to get to the hardware and wind up with a system that does not meet our needs. Such off-the-cuff planning does not work any more. The stakes are too high and resources too limited. Successful information managers henceforth will have to do it by the numbers.

One of the major goals of the solution is the minimization of barriers. There is no absolute way to know what tomorrow's information map will be. The solution should be as general as possible, and to this end it is necessary to *set standards* that will apply across the board.

Aside from eliminating barriers, standards have their own virtues. We really set standards in two ways. The first is by restricting the range of hardware, software, and applications. Certainly, management of the network is simpler if there are fewer device types and applications to manage. The help-desk staff is able to learn the range of equipment more easily and thoroughly. The organization may be able to take advantage of volume price discounts. Users find they can transport their skills with them if they move from one department to another, and training is simplified.

The second has to do with formal industry standards, such as OSI or TCP/IP. These standards make it possible to manage change, make the most effective use of company resources, and take advantage of opportunities faster and more effectively than competitors. They also offer a way to control costs by reducing the need to make large investments every time the dynamics of the business change.

From a business perspective, standards protect investments against obsolescence and allow owners to derive the full benefit of their potential. The result is very consistent with the business ethic of the 1990s— systems are installed quickly and easily, they are adaptable to changing business conditions, and they are easy to operate.

One warning about standards. They are not deities. If a standard conflicts with job performance, relax the standard. Do not be inflexible. Users will be less resistant to a SIP approach if they do not feel their job performance and autonomy is at risk.

The SIP must contain a *budget* for the necessary resources to implement the plan. Establishment of the budget is the result of the *design solution* we developed earlier. Accordingly, the budget includes money for the network and its management.

In a SIP environment, budget support comes more readily because it is directly based on the organization's strategic plan. Upper management knows that the budget, right from the first premise, is designed to facilitate the organizational mission. This aspect alone makes the budget easier to justify and so obtain management approval.

To round out the SIP, it should have two additional sections. Although usually based on shorter-term needs (a year or two; consistent with the strategic plan), a segment on long-term plans is desirable to add perspective and show a migration path. The last section should be a cost-benefit metric to assess the productivity increases, improved decision-making, and enhanced service for customers that results from a SIP implementation. This is an area where the network management system's fault, performance, and accounting functions, if implemented, can make a contribution.

The ability to handle diverse and changing tasks without major dollar infusions, minimization of staff expense, and discovery of new markets using the unified information base are all tangible examples of the value of information processing within the organization. The input of users, as the clients whom we serve, is an outside measurement of the degree of success that we achieve.

In order for a SIP to be created and to succeed, it must have the backing of higher management. A full-blown SIP is a significant effort in staff time.

There lies the key. It need not be an all-encompassing document from the start; a SIP can debut as a bare bones document. As its utility demonstrates itself, it will be expanded. Do not be dissuaded entirely from writing a SIP or be reluctant to start small if you must; *you are on the right track.*

The networking plan

As a subactivity of the *solution* phase of the SIP, the networking plan is first a reflection of the information plan, because the latter has identified who needs to communicate with whom. This establishes the connectivity paths needed and the applications that must be supported. But remember that *users are looking for applications they can use,* not just simple connectivity!

Too often, planners start with the unstated but incorrect assumption that the LAN network should do everything for everyone, the "corporate utility" concept. The implicit idea is that there are economies of scale attained this way, and a single support staff can then be used to manage the whole system. The idea of a single network investment is particularly appealing. But be aware, *the single-solution network is almost never the best solution.*

The reason is that the information carried on any network has declining value over time. For example, stock information's rate of decline is precipitous, meaning the faster it is sent the better. Moreover, the misplacement of a single digit could be disastrous.

So the network serving the stock broker must be fast, accurate, and available. Such a network would lead to a high-speed, low-error rate, bulletproof transmission technology with self-healing backup and comprehensive network management.

Should a facsimile network ride on the same LAN as stock traffic? Facsimile data is much more error-tolerant than stock data, with less time value. How many documents are sent by fax only to sit in someone's inbox for a day or two? Does it make sense to use a LAN server for such an application, or would it be better to set up a simple virtual network with a common carrier to get the best rate?

In the end, the real question becomes the cost to your organization if the information arrives too late to be of value or is received incorrectly. Evaluated in these terms, you can more readily judge the best method of transmission. Initial network designs should carry high priority traffic and haul traffic of lesser importance only if there is no cheaper way to send it.

Remember that every network's traffic builds over time, and it may not make sense to piggyback low priority data if that space will be needed eventually by more important traffic. Also, this approach puts fewer eggs in the new-network basket. This is very desirable since a new network will inevitably have bugs to be worked out.

What the SIP can do for you and your organization

Most importantly, *the SIP makes sure that you build what is really needed.* Not what you think you need or your users think they need or what management thinks it needs, but what you really need. We are differentiating here between *perceptions* and *reality*.

The focus ensures that capital is invested wisely and that staff time is well-expended. Relevance to the SIP helps get budgets approved and inspires continued support from upper management. It also keeps technogurus from going off on pleasant but unproductive tangents.

The SIP is a yardstick for validating a design before it is built and for validating postinstallation additions and upgrades. The SIP forces business planners to take into account the technology infrastructure they will need to accomplish business objectives. Grand plans fail, not necessarily in conception but in execution. "The devil is in the details."

Conversely, business planners can act more aggressively if there is key technology to support them, such as an expert system. Your organization needs every advantage.

A SIP keeps the computer/MIS department *relevant*. It keeps you in touch with your organization. You should never be asked, "What are you doing here?"

The biggest reason that people were laid off in the recent recession was not because of their competence, but because of the relevance of what they did to the organization's goals. If that link was weak or missing—they were history.

Competitive Advantages

Information is a well-known competitive weapon. A firm is at a competitive disadvantage if it cannot utilize the pockets of information found all over the company when it is needed.

A Gallup poll of 100 key Fortune 500 executives revealed 75 who said their competitive advantage was strengthened with technology. But how about the other 25 firms? Was (is) their information technology effort misaligned with their corporate mission as we have discussed?

Not surprisingly, 97 executives said that technology increased efficiency, but technology's importance in providing customer service followed closely at 91 percent. Some 71 percent noted that technology's role in their company is increasing significantly. The primary reason stated was the need for "instant and accurate access to information."

The same applies to expertise. If the skill locked inside an employee cannot be used effectively when and where it is needed, then that firm is at a disadvantage compared to a competitor who can apply the right skill at the right time.

More broadly, information technology (IT), including LANs and groupware, lets unexpected synergies occur, unlocks creativity, and encourages decision-making at the lowest appropriate level. IT improves productivity by helping to get the most and best from each employee.

The morale-building dimension is also not to be ignored. Most employees *want* to do their best and care very deeply about what they do. The idea is to create an environment that frees them to do so, not one that imprisons them.

Properly used, IT systems help you be responsive, timely, correct, and professional. They help your business plans succeed by leveraging technology. The image projected to your customer and prospect base will be unmistakable.

3

LAN Applications

Sharing Resources

Most people think of a LAN as an electronic highway for sharing limited resources within a workgroup. This is a correct assessment but is somewhat narrow in scope. In this chapter we expand our reach to include other facilities that LANs can share.

LANs are also a *common medium* to link dissimilar devices, such as linking Macintoshes into a PC network. Many unlikely devices have LAN interfaces, making possible a degree of connectivity impossible in pre-LAN times. LANs even link other LANs together. Their connectability makes LANs an essential connectivity tool in a company's strategic network plan.

Let us start this chapter with a discussion of what LANs can share and why resource sharing may be desirable. Then we will talk about LANs as a medium of data exchange.

Disk sharing

Shared disk storage was one of the earliest LAN applications. Called *disk service,* several clients could share the same hard disk. LAN buyers thereby avoided placing large drives in each PC in favor of one or more large disks in a server. The problem with disk service was that if two or more users tried to write to the same disk volume, the disk's *file allocation table* (FAT) could become corrupted. Then files would be lost because the allocation table could no longer find them.

In 1982, a small company then called Novell Data Systems segmented disk access to the file level rather than the whole volume. The file server also took control of the FAT. This advance made file sharing and file server security possible. File servers became real *multitasking* devices, handling tasks from several clients at once.

The cost savings were obvious, and there were productivity and administrative pluses, too. Saved files became sharable, within security limits. The administrator no longer needed to hound users to do backups; instead, the backup was done systematically on the server by either the administrator or an automatic program utility.

Disk storage may be classified into two subareas: file service, which retains files owned by an individual, and database servers, which store information used by a group. Let us discuss file service first.

PCs become file servers because software gives it that personality. As implied by the FAT example above, a file server's job is to make sure that shared resources are accessed in an orderly, nonconflicting way. Working with the application programs, servers ensure concurrent file admission when it is needed and prevent it when it is improper.

File servers control access through a variety of *network operating system* (NOS) security mechanisms, and NOSs vary widely in their ability to provide security. For example, NetWare is regarded as having some of the most flexible security in the industry (even though it has been breached on occasion).

There are two kinds of file servers:

Generic servers are based on standard machines. They are not designed specifically to be used as file servers.

Proprietary servers are designed specifically for this task. While providing better performance, they are often tied to a specific vendor's LAN and NOS products.

Either server type can be operated as a *dedicated* server, used for no other purpose, or a *nondedicated server,* which can be used as a workstation, too. The industry trend is away from nondedicated servers doubling as workstations because a processor-intense application will adversely affect server performance.

File servers contain applications software and data files that are downloaded to workstations on request. Because of the heavy demands placed on servers, they are designed for higher performance than an ordinary workstation. Consolidating power, memory, and disk space in the server reduces workstation hardware requirements.

All files have *access attributes*. Files can be set for read only or read and write. Access attributes are usually set by the application and are modifiable by the user.

Network files are different from ordinary files because they may be shared by several users. For example, the *file-sharing attributes* of

DOS become important when a second or succeeding effort is made to access the file. These attributes are:

Exclusive. The file cannot be shared.

Write access denied. The file can only be read by others.

Deny none access. The file can be shared and anyone can read it and write to it.

Usually, an application will assign the access rights, but users can also modify them.

Access control is, therefore, the first step. Step two, *synchronization,* makes sure that file updates do not occur at the same time by different users, causing a scrambled file.

As shown in Figure 3.1, *file locking* is one synchronization technique. Multiple user updates, i.e., writes to the file, are prevented by using the Exclusive or Write Access Denied file sharing attributes. The file can be shared for reading, but only one user can write to the file.

File locking is considered too coarse and inflexible for use in today's networks. Today we use *record locking.* In this scheme, the same limitations apply but to only a portion of the file, called a record, or a series of records.

Record locking is more complex than file locking. Within record locking, two kinds of locks are used: *physical* and *logical.* In DOS, physical locks protect a record or series of records within a file by preventing access to them on the hard disk.

Logical locks are not supported by DOS, but may be used in other systems. A logical lock assigns a *lock name* to the protected record(s). Other applications must check the lock name and its attributes and are barred from the named records.

Since devices besides disks, files, and records are shared on a file server, a way is needed to organize contention for them, too. Some NOSs do this by the use of *semaphores.*

If you automatically think of a sailor waving flags, you are on the right track. A semaphore is an intelligent *bit flag* that can be given a name, set, cleared, and tested. Unlike record or file locks, semaphores can apply more generally to files, records, record groups, or a shared peripheral, perhaps a modem or printer.

With more properties, semaphores are more flexible than a record lock and can be used for more sophisticated control functions. Semaphores can have any assigned meaning, and are more closely related to a logical lock than a physical one. They can be used quite differently by different applications developers and NOS vendors.

File Locking

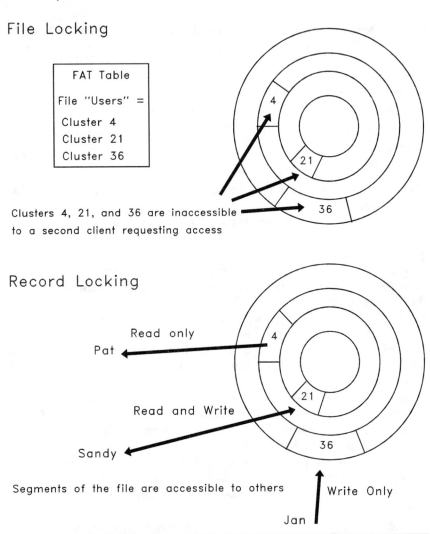

FAT Table

File "Users" =

Cluster 4
Cluster 21
Cluster 36

Clusters 4, 21, and 36 are inaccessible
to a second client requesting access

Record Locking

Read only
Pat

Read and Write

Sandy

Segments of the file are accessible to others

Jan

Write Only

Figure 3.1 File and record locking.

Sharing processing power

A fast LAN server reduces the need for workstation power, RAM memory, and disk capacity. This, of course, has a pronounced effect on direct and indirect costs such as maintenance.

Concentrating processing and storage in the server may permit the use of *diskless workstations*. These are often used in security-conscious, dusty, or otherwise computer-unfriendly environments. Since there is no floppy diskette access, virus infection from a boot or program diskette is not possible. Internal hard disks are often replaced with RAM disks, further reducing the overall failure rate.

The benefits of sharing backup and management

In a server environment, a server can be protected with:

Access management: security and privacy

Periodic backups

Controlled applications availability

Redundancy, e.g., duplicate drives and power supplies

Electrical power management, e.g., an uninterruptible power supply

Clearly defined, professional server responsibility

Many of these disciplines are difficult if not impossible to enforce on individual workstation users. If their workstation crashes, is it likely that they have a backup? You can probably answer this question for yourself!

Management of the PCs and the network should fall on a clearly defined individual or group. A server focuses accountability for every dimension of operating the LAN. Not only are the computing resources shared but so are the valuable people resources.

Small organizations will likely pick the person they perceive as the "power user" or the one most interested in PCs as the LAN manager. We believe this is preferable to "LANarchy" in which everyone, which is to say no one, is responsible for the LAN.

Individual workstation users have their own jobs to perform. LAN administration is not usually in their job descriptions, and productivity is enhanced if a LAN manager and an alternate are delegated specifically. Those individuals will gain experience quickly.

It is remarkable that many of the reasons that justified a mainframe hold true on a smaller scale at the LAN level. Mainframe MIS people are now bringing the same analytical skills, the same disciplines, and the same experience of hard knocks such as the importance of backups and documentation to the LAN server environment. And none too soon!

Specialized servers

In daily use, the term "server" has the adjective "file" implicitly placed before it unless otherwise denoted. Beyond file servers lie an entire family of specialized servers designed for specific applications. These servers are optimized for a particular use, meaning that they have augmented processing power, disk capacity, memory, *input/output* (I/O) ports, and/or card slots to enhance their designated application's performance.

Specialized server applications include:

Database servers

Batch servers

Print servers

Communications servers

Terminal servers

Facsimile, (i.e., fax) servers

Security Servers

These applications are described briefly here and in greater detail in Chapter 5.

Database servers.   Some users reach the point where file service begins to look like a database application. In file service, a database program running in the workstation retrieves blocks of files that are locked until returned. This calls for more workstation storage and processing power, plus database software in each PC. Since *whole files* are downloaded, more files are locked and network traffic is higher.

Database servers divide database processing into a front end application, which runs in the workstation, and back end processing, which takes place in a database server or engine. In this scheme, individual records are downloaded and uploaded, reducing locked data and network traffic. Often, *structured query language* (SQL) running on SQL clients and servers is used in a client-server relationship as we discussed in Chapter 1.

Retention of data in the server makes backup and security as well as providing clean and constant power easier. Management of the database is often required and is easier to do in one place by a designated professional.

Some NOSs include *transaction tracking,* which allows a transaction to be stored in a buffer temporarily until completed. Incomplete transactions cannot, therefore, corrupt the database. This is called *roll-back recovery.* Conversely, some systems use *roll-forward recovery,* which completes the transaction from an audit trail if something goes wrong.

Database servers have extensive disk storage and cache memory to speed disk access. They may also be connected to a *redundant array of inexpensive drives* (RAID) system that provides disk service without interruption even if one drive fails.

Adapting a mainframe technique, database servers may use *hierar-chical storage,* in which often accessed data is kept on-line or to a lesser degree near-line, while off-line storage is used for archived data.

Batch servers. For large processing jobs such as long reports, some LANs employ a batch processing server that handles the job without affecting the interactive file service enjoyed by the other users. These are usually separate LAN-connected PCs.

Printer servers. At some point, the need for print services begins to overwhelm the file server which has been doing double duty. How do you know when a print server makes sense? There is no formula, but there certainly are some clues:

The server runs out of printer ports. Remember that printer ports may be serial as well as parallel!

The server runs out of spooling disk space.

The memory for buffering becomes limited.

The file server performance begins to suffer.

The number of print jobs becomes excessive.

The printers are more conveniently located away from the file server.

Due to the NOS, printers require a separate server.

Print servers take three forms: software-, workstation-, or hardware-based. Software-based servers share the file server's hardware plat-form, but at the expense of server performance and reduced flexibility in locating the printers. Workstation print servers can be anywhere and may be dedicated or nondedicated.

Hardware-based servers offer the greatest flexibility and conven-ience. The best machines install easily on the network and are then forgotten. For example, if the file server goes down, the print server is unaffected. If the power plug falls off the printer, the print server will automatically reload its fonts when the power is restored.

Keep in mind that shared printers on a network do not preclude the use of individual printers on a PC. In fact, these local workstations can be used as printer servers. This requires third-party software, for which some NetWare examples are listed at the end of Chapter 5. All software-based servers require CPU cycles from a workstation or the file server, thereby affecting performance to that extent. Recognize that if the station is turned off, print services disappear until the ma-chine is turned on again!

Communications servers. For many of the same reasons as having a print server, a separate communications server may be desirable. Once again, this form of server allows pooling of resources, only this time it's modems and phone lines rather than printers.

Like printing, communication carries its own set of requirements. Multiple serial ports are usually needed. Communications ports have high interrupt rates, which degrade file server performance. Buffering and management of the communications link is necessary. Communications is inherently less reliable than printer sharing, and some LAN administrators prefer to isolate this possible problem child onto a separate server. Security is usually enhanced: Until the communications server is satisfied, an inbound caller cannot access the LAN.

Terminal servers. As shown in Figure 3.2, it often is convenient or cost-effective to use "dumb" terminals on the LAN instead of more expensive personal computers. Since the terminals are not programmable

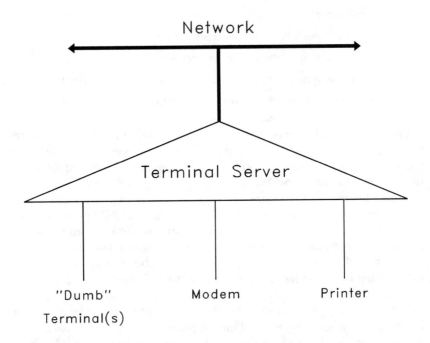

A terminal server can support more than just terminals. It also adds another layer of security to the network.

Figure 3.2 A terminal server.

and are slow-speed EIA-232 devices, a terminal server sits between the terminals and the LAN cable. It is the server that provides the necessary intelligence and buffering to make these two technologies work together.

Usual implementations connect multiple terminals to the server as a way of sharing the machine's expense, which is not generally high. Sometimes terminal ports on the server can be connected to other devices such as modems or printers.

The advantages of using terminal servers include minimum workstation expense, insulation from the possibility of virus entry, and the reuse of existing owned equipment if terminals are already on hand. The disadvantages are that these text-based terminals cannot do graphics, are slow, and may be difficult to get serviced if they are older.

Fax servers. Since everyone in the office sends and receives faxes, fax sharing is a natural LAN application. Consider the number of times people trot down to the fax machine, load it with their document, and then stand there while it goes through, or stand there while one arrives. The opportunity to save them time is an irresistible server application.

In addition, do not forget the added step of converting a disk file to paper so that we can convert it into electronic pulses again as it traverses the fax network. It's estimated that *80 to 90 percent of facsimiles that are sent are available as disk files.* Surely we can streamline this!

One user reduced the time to send a fax from 12 minutes to 2. Multiply that 10 minutes saved times 6 faxes a day, and you have saved a collective hour in staff time. Another estimate showed a total savings, including staff time, fax paper, and toll calls at day rates of over $26,000 annually, given 50,000 pages of fax per year.

Fax servers are ideal for those activities which send high volume faxes; automating the process is essential. Parallel transmission of 20-plus faxes at once is a typical high-volume application. Timed transmission after peak toll hours is essential to keeping the telephone cost under control.

We mentioned in our earlier discussion of groupware that Eastman Kodak is developing imageware to run on NetWare. Fax servers will be able to make use of this software, which takes the form of a *NetWare Loadable Module* (NLM). If some documents to be sent are not on disk, a scanner of some kind will be required to digitize the document and store it as a disk file for transmission.

Incoming faxes from the telephone network are stored in a *peer-to-peer* fax server's hard disk and are forwarded directly to a workstation or are printed. The printer will need at least 1 Mbyte of memory. *Store-*

and-forward fax servers pass the fax to the file server and then on to the workstation.

A received fax can be sent to one or more workstations or kept on the server. In the first case, once the fax is sent, it is no longer retained by the server. A *terminate-and-stay-resident* (TSR) program then advises the recipient that a fax is waiting. The recipient can read and discard it if it does not merit printing.

If the fax is kept on the server, users are given viewing rights, and the fax is archived or automatically deleted after time. It can also be forwarded to as many recipients as desired, now or later.

Security servers.   In some cases, as with the Open Software Foundation's emerging *Distributed Management Environment* (DME) and *Distributed Communications Environment* (DCE), a user must be cleared by a security server before access and privileges may be exercised. Kerboros is one such system, and it is an example of how distributed systems can still have central control.

Sharing applications

There is a break-even point where buying stand-alone copies of application software becomes more expensive than buying a network version. As LAN clients grow, the economic balance shifts from stand-alone to network version. Vigilance is required!

Many licensing arrangements exist for network-available software. There is no current industry standard, although there are moves afoot to standardize license agreements.

It is up to the administrator to prevent use beyond what the license permits. *Metering software* allows the licensed maximum number of active users; subsequent requests for use are placed in a queue.

One problem is that in Windows environments, a user may temporarily iconize an application. All that time, the money meter is running while another user may be waiting on the queue. Sometimes users log into an application and keep it running yet unused.

Automatic log-off software maximizes availability, monitors usage, and provides added security. Matrix Systems' NetOFF[1] is an example. NetOFF automatically logs a user out after a period of inactivity from 1 second (!) to 60 hours. NetOFF monitors all workstation activity such as keyboard and disk usage. It is memory resident, and it requires about 2 kbytes of RAM.

Licensing rules have been followed rather loosely by some users, to

---

[1]Matrix Systems, Houston, TX, (800) 231-0126.

the extent that the *Software Publisher's Association* (SPA)[2] estimates that over \$1 billion is lost per year in the U.S. alone due to illegal copying. SPA has shown a willingness to litigate not only large-scale pirateers, but *bulletin board system* (BBS) operators and corporate violators on behalf of (and at the request of) its 1000 or so members. It is now a felony under federal law to conduct such commercial piracy.

In a more positive vein, SPA conducts a respected antipiracy education program, which includes awareness and self-audit procedures and software tools, all at no charge. Many concerned administrators know or suspect that there is illegal software in their system, but are understandably reluctant to bring themselves to SPA's attention. Nonetheless, SPA claims that litigation is always their last choice.

Thus, we have entered the era of the software police. License *owners* often have the right to inspect the premises of a licensee to make sure that license agreements are not being broken. (Note that SPA is neither an owner nor a fiduciary.) If the infringement is substantial, legal action and a liability judgment could follow.

Differences between single-user, multiuser, and network-aware software

Keep these points in mind as you consider buying applications software. Software fits into three general categories with respect to usage on a LAN:

Single-user. A single copy stored in a file server can be downloaded to one or more workstations via the LAN and run individually on the workstation(s). Utilizing single-user software on a network can be a license violation. This software is often referred to as "networkable."

Multiuser. Multiuser software expands on single-user software by allowing sharing of files created by a single-user program that is properly located in a user's private disk area. File or record locking is used as was described earlier.

Network software. Network software takes advantage of all the shared resources such as modems, printers, or fax servers. It is often called "network aware."

Some stand-alone software packages have configurable options for network use, making it tempting to use it that way, license or no license. Other stand-alone software fits poorly into a network environment. For instance, customized features may not be saved after they

---

[2]The Software Publisher's Association may be reached at (800) 388-7478.

are set up, or they may be modified by others with their own preferences. Files may not be simultaneously sharable as is the norm in a multiuser or network-aware package. The guiding application rule is not so much technical as legal. You do not want to put your organization at risk by using software whether on a network or not when it has not been licensed properly.

Connectivity through LAN Networking

LANs have become the medium to link an unlikely assortment of computers. We have spoken of connecting to IBM-compatible PCs, but they are by no means the only devices which can appear on a LAN.

Of those Macintoshes that are networked, LocalTalk links three-quarters of them and Ethernet links most of the rest. By 1996, Local-Talk, even though it is free, will link only a quarter of networked Macs.

Ethernet is gaining ground in Macintosh networking. This trend toward using Ethernet was thrust forward when Apple officially endorsed Ethernet by shipping it on the motherboard of its high-end Quadra machines beginning in 1991.

Macintoshes can share a LAN with IBM-compatibles. LAN vendor Cabletron offers a *Direct Network Interface* (DNI) Ethernet card for the Macintosh. The card supports 10BaseT and coaxial or twisted pairs. Over 20 other vendors make Ethernet cards for the Macintosh.

As for other LAN technologies, token ring is twice as expensive as Ethernet, but Macintosh token-ring cards are also available. There are even *fiber-distributed data interface* (FDDI) adapters for Macintoshes as well as frame relay interfaces. Arcnet connections are available but have receded in their appeal.

LocalTalk will not disappear. It costs a tenth of an Ethernet connection, but at 230.4 Kbit/sec, it is slow compared to Ethernet's 10 Mbit/sec. LocalTalk will be used mainly in notebook and handheld machines that do not need extensive network capacity.

Apple plans to integrate AppleTalk with IBM and DEC computers and on computers using TCP/IP or OSI. Apple will begin with file and print services, then database access, and finally full integration.

Apple's *Open Collaboration Environment* (OCE) is a software architecture designed to deliver directory, store-and-forward user and application messaging, authentication, and privacy to Macintosh applications. Ideally, user applications can use OCE to provide network services. OCE is architecturally similar to Microsoft's Windows *Open Services Architecture* (OSA). Apple plans to make its software architecture interoperable with Windows OSA.

In the IBM realm, AppleTalk is supposed to be integrated with OS/2, APPN for SNA, AS/400 midrange machines, and network management. Imagine running IBM's NetView network management application on a Macintosh!

Laptops and notebooks

What happens when your sales staff comes in from the road and want to plug their laptop or notebook into your LAN? Can they get there from here?

As shown in Figure 3.3, notebooks that slide into a docking adapter can have a *network interface card* (NIC) card installed in the adapter. But what if you do not have an adapter?

The next best option is to use a *parallel port NIC*. The NIC connects to the notebook's parallel port and may have a pass-through connection

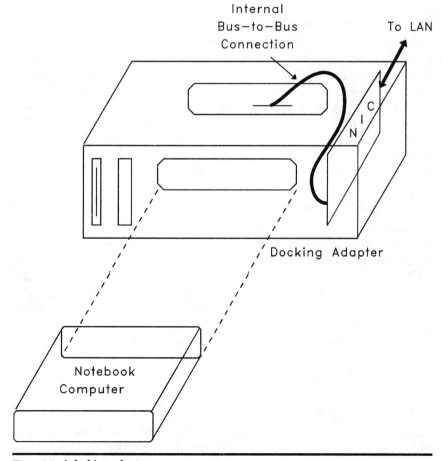

Figure 3.3 A docking adapter.

for a printer. There is, of course, a connection to the LAN cable. It requires a software driver in the computer as well.

The parallel port NIC is also an option when a PC has no available internal slots or if the hardware configuration prevent installing an internal NIC card. The negative side is that the parallel port is only 8 bits wide. This is a bottleneck but a fair trade for having the flexibility to occasionally add a client to the LAN.

Enhanced parallel port (EPP) capability is becoming available to speed up the operation of the parallel port by about a factor of four. Both the computer and the adapter must be so equipped.

A recent development is the PCMCIA 2.0 memory card specification that allows direct access to the computer's internal data bus. For notebooks and laptops, this method yields performance equivalent to an internal NIC.

Minis, mainframes, and front-end processors

Minicomputers, mainframes, and *front-end processors* (FEPs) all have Ethernet and/or token-ring interfaces, making hitherto impossible links possible. A mainframe can be a superserver to a minicomputer or workstation—or even a notebook. *Direct* LAN connections to IBM mainframe bus and tag channels are possible, eliminating the delays caused by a FEP. We will see how these are used in Chapter 11. The point is that the universal LAN has created connectivity among some formerly incompatible machines. This is not the LAN-server model we know, but a new host-to-host LAN model.

LANs connecting LANs

You may have heard the term *backbone LAN*. It refers most often to a LAN which links other LANs together, usually on separate floors. Accordingly, the backbone LAN is often wired vertically, like a backbone, to the horizontal floor LANs (which for some reason are not called ribs). Frequently the backbone LAN will use an FDDI ring at 100 Mbit/sec or a token ring at 4 or 16 Mbit/sec for speed and fault tolerance. The floor-based LANs could be an Ethernet or token ring. Mixing LAN types in this manner is not at all uncommon today. The scheme offers high performance and redundancy in the backbone, lower speed, and less redundancy on each floor.

LANs connecting WANs

Some *wide area networks* (WANs) lack the ability to route traffic at high speed. For this purpose, a LAN may be used as a routing facility to pass messages to their intended destinations. Such LANs are called *network LANs* or *intermediate LANs* because they usually do not connect to workstations directly. Often they connect end-user workgroup LANs together in an *enterprise network*. These distributed client-server networks, with distributed databases and processing power, are regarded as the networks of the future.

LANs between computers

As a method of linking machines together, LANs have much to offer. The interfaces are all standardized, so that otherwise incompatible devices can be connected.

Using a LAN to connect a pair of minicomputers together means that the machines need not be collocated, and their data buses can remain isolated. Even so, the 10-Mbit/sec speed of Ethernet is reasonably close to the bus speeds of the minis, so that Ethernet is not a bottleneck. The point we are making here is that LANs do not just connect clients to servers, they connect networks together as backbone LANs and computers to one another as interhost peripherals.

It is fair to say that the standardization of LANs has created a new connectivity tool. Powerful in its software capabilities and running at high speed, the economics of LAN technology have made it a practical connectivity tool even where very high speed is not needed. The economics have practically disconnected the formerly inelastic relationship between price and performance. That's good news for users!

The All-Important Applications

LAN servers and LAN technology are important but only to the extent that they support user applications. True, we have discussed groupware and database applications. But what capabilities are LANs bringing to our users that they need but do not have today?

Before going any farther, imprint this in your mind:

> Users do not care about connectivity.
> Users care about applications they can use.

They do not care if you use FDDI, TCP/IP, or a wet noodle and a tin can. That is *our* problem. *Their* problem is having the tools before them that let them do their work, be competitive and productive and achieve the organization's goals. Ultimately, their goals are our goals.

Applications in the office

We have already mentioned some basic applications: sharing files, printers and other resources, and fax servers. All of these are valuable tools. In addition, word processing, spreadsheets, modeling programs, and the like are useful and worthwhile LAN-based applications.

Some applications require a LAN environment. For example, LAN technology makes groupware feasible. But suppose you are not ready for groupware. Groupware's core is e-mail. Might e-mail be a viable application for your organization?

Electronic mail

Most often, we think of e-mail as the computer analogue of what comes from the post office every day (derided by the initiated as "snail mail"). For the most part, this analogy holds true in LAN usage. We use electronic mail mainly to exchange messages person-to-person or person-to-group. But e-mail can be used between applications, too. For example, FacSys fax server software recognizes a PC-based e-mail format called *Message-Handling System* (MHS).

MHS. MHS was written by Action Technologies, vendor of a groupware package called Coordinator. MHS has been endorsed by Novell, so NetWare supports MHS. MHS is an open standard, and copies of it are available from either Novell or Action Technologies.

MHS wraps a message in an electronic "envelope," so the message can be in any form. Further, MHS has controls built into it that allow flexible handling of the message from originator to recipient. As a result, MHS can be the framework for message transmission in modes other than e-mail, perhaps in updating distributed databases, in fax server applications, or in multimedia combining text, voice, and video.

MHS uses store-and-forward message switching. It has a central repository that receives messages and stores them until the recipient checks in. Store-and-forward systems are ideal for organizations that cross time zones or for people who are always on the go. For example, MCI Mail is a store-and-forward system, though not based on MHS.

Systems that use MHS as the basis for their e-mail implementations are able to pass messages between them, even though the products come from different vendors. Some e-mail software for LANs provides links to other e-mail implementations, including X.400 gateways.

ITU-TSS X.400. ITU-TSS X.400 (formerly CCIT) is the international standard for e-mail. It has been adopted by DEC, Hewlett-Packard, IBM, and others. X.400 also uses an electronic envelope in which to send data. The content of the envelope need not be just text. It can contain a fax, voice, video, graphics, or a combination thereof called a *compound document*. X.400 does not focus on one type of machine as opposed to another: It is intended for use by any computer, from PC to supercomputer. MHS, by contrast, is intended for PC-based LANs.

Basic X.400 services include many that would be considered intuitive for this kind of service. X.400 includes access controls to provide security and privacy. Along with identifying the sender and receiver, each message is dated and time stamped. Since a message may be in any form, e.g., facsimile or text, the nature of the material in the envelope must be specified so that fax messages will be routed to a fax machine, text file, or whatever is appropriate.

Once sent, the sender will be notified if the message is read by the recipient. Messages can be sent to one destination or to many destinations, and priority levels can be set to indicate the relative importance of a message. X.400 indicates who is the primary recipient as opposed to someone receiving a *for your information* (FYI) or courtesy copy. The sender can tag a reply request to the message if a response is desired.

Since electronic mail raises many issues of privacy, encryption is offered as one way to enhance privacy and security. Some companies have a policy that any message sent on their system is their property and that they have the right to read anybody's mail. More reasonably, other firms believe that an e-mail message is private between the parties involved. If a central store-and-forward repository is used, messages may be archived there in plain text and easily read despite the use of data link encryption.

Most LAN users and prospective users will not have to decide between using an MHS or X.400 package on their LAN. For LAN applications, there are many more MHS packages around. The real decision may be whether to implement e-mail in MHS form on the LAN or X.400 for mail service over a wide area. Perhaps both, linked to one another, will emerge as the ideal enterprise-wide e-mail system.

A checklist of e-mail features include:

Easy to learn and easy to use.

Remote access.

Extra features, e.g., a calendar. Is it worth it?

Hardware requirements, i.e., disk, memory, or modems.

Editing capability, i.e., imports and exports from other programs.

Security and privacy. (Your organization may have a policy regarding e-mail privacy.)

Gateways or links to other e-mail systems.

Managing messages, i.e., directory, priority-setting, and finding.

A repository for sent messages. Is there one?

Flexibility in naming users.

You may already have heard of multimedia, in which text, video and sound all come together on a single machine, in a single file. Both MHS and X.400 are suitable foundations for multimedia applications.

The industry is very divided on multimedia's current state of development. Some observers regard it as a viable business application now, while others cite the need for high bandwidth, expensive video cameras, and codecs, i.e., coders-decoders that digitize voice and then turn it back into sound at the receiver, as obstacles to this informational wonderland. The infrastructure, a way to move these composite files from place to place is as yet underdeveloped. The all-important user interface is yet too difficult for the average office worker to use. We have a long way to go, but tomorrow's vision of the workplace is coming into coarse focus. Without LAN technology, it would not even be conceivable.

E-mail and multimedia represent a taste of the future. These supporting applications will make possible new end-user services organization-wide, allowing immediate access to relevant information wherever it resides. Business success will demand nothing less. LANs are the hardware infrastructure, an "enabling technology" as consultants like to put it, making possible the supporting software applications that in turn will make sophisticated end-user applications feasible.

In Chapter 4, you will gain more insight into the internal workings of a LAN starting with the physical layer, the medium. Picking the right medium for your needs is a key decision, but one that is often made by default. Since this decision has long-term consequences, the medium decision is best made with an understanding of all the factors involved.

4

LAN Topologies and Media

Key Terms

This chapter concentrates on the *physical* portion of a LAN, the part you can see and touch. Based on the ISO/OSI reference model, we must therefore be working at the physical layer, or layer 1.

There are four components to the physical layer of a LAN (Figure 4.1). They are:

The *medium* that carries the LAN signal. Copper wire is the most common medium, but other LAN media include fiber optic cable and wireless radio.

The *electrical* signals themselves, which are either *baseband* or *broadband.*

The *topology,* or the way LAN wiring is laid out on a floor, within a building, or around a campus complex.

The *network interfaces* that connect the media to computers and other devices using the LAN.

Because a LAN is a system, each component interacts with the others. Understanding how they interact is important in making good choices about your network.

Often these decisions are made by default or are implicitly made within other decisions. The result usually works for the short term, but it may not work for the long haul. The broader purpose of this chapter is to ensure that you do not get cornered by short-term thinking.

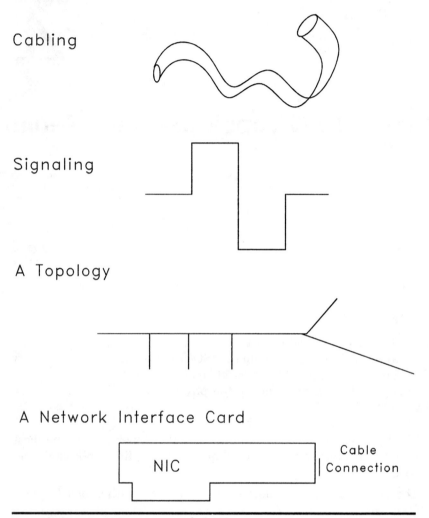

Figure 4.1 The physical components of a LAN.

LAN Media

Cabling for LANs takes three different forms. They include twisted-pair wires, coaxial cable, and fiber optic strands. Each has its own set of characteristics.

Twisted pairs

Twisted pairs have one outstanding virtue: They are everywhere. Any building used for commercial purposes has hundreds of pairs circulating inside it. While most pairs are used for telephones, they have utility as LAN media as well.

These wires consist of 22 or 24 *American Wire Gauge* (AWG) wires, one twisted around the other. The twist tends to cancel out electrical noise from motors and other inductive sources. Often, as in telephone cable, these pairs are *unshielded,* meaning they have no metallic sheath around them to further insulate the pair from noise. This type of medium is *unshielded twisted pair* (UTP). LAN vendors, including IBM, sanction 4- and 16-Mbit/sec token rings on UTP, and 100-Mbit/sec UTP is beginning to appear on the market.

Pairs with shielding are called *shielded twisted pairs* (STPs). (This is not what goes in your crankcase.) Shielding protects very effectively the wires from most sources of interference by grounding the interference before it can get to the wires. STP is high performance media since it can carry high data rates (16 Mbit/sec routinely) for longer distances than UTP.

A few words about UTP. Because STP is more expensive than UTP and because UTP is ubiquitous, there are strong dollar and cents reasons to use UTP wherever possible. Run through walls and ceilings, UTP is cheaper and easier to pull than coaxial cable or STP. UTP is also smaller and lighter, allowing more pairs in limited conduit space. It is flexible too, making it easy to run around corners.

UTP is not suitable for every application. Hub to workstation distances of up to 100 m (328 ft) are suitable UTP applications, but greater distances become problematic for UTP. At this point, STP becomes the cable of choice.

The principal limits to UTP are *near-end crosstalk* (NEXT) and attenuation. NEXT is caused by the strong signal leaving the *network interface card* (NIC) being induced onto the receive wire pair carrying the much weaker received signal. NEXT can drown this received signal.

NEXT is measured in decibels as a ratio of the two. A good NEXT figure is 45 dB and a poor one 21–24 dB. NIC vendors specify their minimum usable NEXT figure.

Attenuation is simply signal loss over distance. The longer the distance, the greater the loss. Attenuation is affected by wire resistance, loose connections, and the like. Signal loss is more rapid over distance as frequency increases, so attenuation is a function of frequency as well.

UTP and STP is graded for quality by Underwriters' Laboratories (UL). Level I is the poorest, while Level V is the best. The UTP in your walls generally meets Level III.

UTP and STP *levels* should not be confused with IBM cable *types.* UL performance Levels I–V and IBM cable Types 1–3, 5, 6, 8, and 9 are *not* the same!

UL performance levels.   The levels are:

Level I   This is for basic communications and power-limited circuit cable, and there are no performance criteria for this level of cable. It is strictly for voice transmission. The cable is marked Level I, LVL I, or LEV I.

Level II   Its performance is similar to Type 3 (multipair) IBM cable. Level II covers cables with 2 to 25 twisted pairs and applies to both shielded and unshielded cable of 22 or 24 AWG. Three parameters are tested: frequency versus impedance, frequency versus attenuation, and maximum DC resistance. It is marked as Verified Level II or Classified Level II.

Level III   It complies with EIA/TIA 568 Commercial Building Telecommunications Wiring Standard for Horizontal UTP. Seven parameters are tested, including NEXT. It applies both to STP and UTP and is marked as above for Level III. Most telco *direct inside wire* (DIW) cable meets Level III.

Level IV   It meets *National Electrical Manufacturers' Association* (NEMA) standard for Low-Loss Premises Telecommunications Cable. It is similar to Category IV of EIA/TIA PN-2841, and it applies to UTP and STP. The same parameters are tested as in Level III but with more test points and tighter tolerances.

Level V   This also meets NEMA's standard but for extended frequencies. It is similar to Category V of EIA/TIA PN-2841 and has the tightest tolerances of all the levels. It is the most suitable for use with 16 Mbit/sec token rings and emerging 100 Mbit/sec networks.

UL publishes a very concise and free brochure titled *UL's LAN Cable Certification Program,* which details their program and performance specifications for each level.[1] The brochure and program also cover IBM Cable Performance Specifications.

Avoiding wiring problems.   Here, as perhaps nowhere else, "the devil is in the details." Problem areas include:

Loosely or untwisted UTP pairs, especially at punch blocks. Replacement of loose twist UTP with tightly twisted pairs may be required.

Incorrect pairs, i.e., a split pair with one wire each from two pairs as revealed by a test set. This situation invalidates the twist benefit. They need to be rewired properly.

---

[1]Call (800) 676-WIRE on the East Coast or (800) 786-WIRE on the West Coast.

Randomly selected pairs may exhibit poor NEXT. Select pair combinations for the best NEXT value, again using a test set.

Using the wrong connector. There are different RJ-45 connectors for stranded and solid wire. They look nearly identical, but using the wrong type will cause intermittent operation.

Placing other digital data traffic in the same cable or wire bundle. This can cause interference with LAN signals.

Excessive cable lengths. Use a repeater if you must.

High temperatures hurt performance. Resistance rises with temperature, causing attenuation. Run the cable through cool areas, not hot ceilings. *Polyvinyl chloride* (PVC) jacketed cable is more susceptible to higher temperatures.

Finally, remember to document everything. Later in this chapter, we will discuss the cabling rules which apply to Ethernet and token rings.

Media filters

UTP token-ring applications require a media filter (Figure 4.2) to reduce noise on the cable and suppress unwanted electromagnetic emissions from the cable which may exceed FCC radiation limits. Media filters connect between the PC's NIC and the cable. Some NICs include them internally. They are needed only with UTP (IBM Type 3 cable).

Media filters are passive; they draw no power. They are *low-pass* filters, which means they pass signals below 4 or 16 Mbit/sec and suppress higher frequencies. These higher emissions are not dangerous, but they may interfere with other electronic devices such as the radio you listen to at work.

Coaxial cable. For high speeds, coaxial cable is often used. As the name implies, "co-ax" has a conducting wire at the center, surrounded by an insulator and then by a concentric shield made of fine wire. This is all bundled inside a protective plastic sheath. Used in Community Antenna Television (CATV) installations, a coaxial cable can carry signals in the range of hundreds of megahertz.

Coaxial cable offers better noise rejection than STP. While it can support data rates of over 100 Mbit/sec, it is usually used at Ethernet speeds of 10 Mbit/sec.

Baluns. Sometimes an Ethernet NIC's interface connector is coaxial, but the available wiring is twisted pair. In this case, an adapting device called a *balun* is used. They get their name, if you have not already guessed it, from what they do: *bal*anced to *un*balanced conversion.

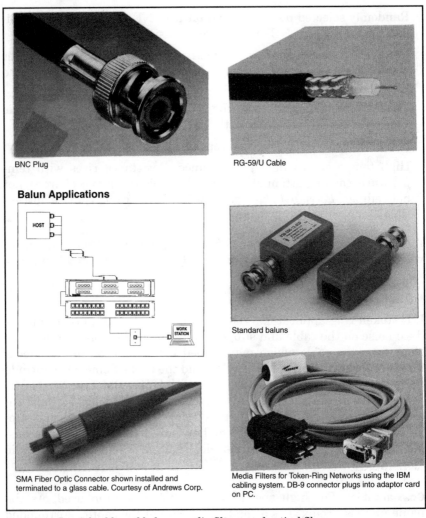

BNC Plug

RG-59/U Cable

Balun Applications

HOST

WORK STATION

Standard baluns

SMA Fiber Optic Connector shown installed and terminated to a glass cable. Courtesy of Andrews Corp.

Media Filters for Token-Ring Networks using the IBM cabling system. DB-9 connector plugs into adaptor card on PC.

Figure 4.2 Coaxial cable and baluns, media filters, and optical fiber.

A balun is nothing more than a transformer. It takes the unbalanced coaxial connection and converts it into a noise-resistant balanced form for transmission down the wire pair. At the other end, another balun reverses the process.

Some Ethernet NICs have an internal balun so that either coaxial or UTP wiring can be used. These are readily identified because they have a coaxial BNC connector *and* an RJ-11 (six wire) or RJ-45 (eight wire) modular connector on the rear.

Baluns are passive. They are very inexpensive, around $30.

Optical fiber. At the highest speed level, optical fibers are used. Using very pure glass, light travels down the center of the fiber through the *core*. The light is kept from dispersing by a surrounding layer called the *cladding*. Because of the difference in the refractive index of the core and cladding, light stays in the core and so can go long distances.

Fiber can routinely carry data rates up to 565 Mbit/sec. Being light waves, fiber is immune to electrical interference, nearly impossible to tap, and runs virtually error free. However, fiber cable is more expensive than wire both to purchase and install, since it has certain installation restrictions such as a maximum bending radius.

The fiber used in LAN applications is *multimode* fiber that works for distances up to a few kilometers. Infrared *light-emitting diodes* (LEDs) provide the light that is invisible to the eye. Fiber is well-suited to token-ring LANs or any point-to-point connection. It can go up to 6500 ft between repeaters, using 100/140 μm fiber cable (IBM Type 5).

What about wireless LANs?

A neat way to circumvent wiring hassles is to use none at all. Wireless LAN vendors promote the notion that their products' cost is offset by the savings in wiring. Would that it were that simple.

First, we need to distinguish between the wireless systems being used as part of a mobile cellular network and the systems that take the place of LAN wiring in a building as shown in Figure 4.3. Interesting as mobile systems are, we are dealing only with the latter here.

Wireless LANs use two media to communicate: infrared and radio. Of the radio systems, some use a single frequency and others use a technique adapted from the military called *spread spectrum*. Spread spectrum techniques were developed to get information through despite the presence of jammers. If you can conceive of your office copier creating interference to a wireless LAN, you can then see the analogy.

Spread spectrum works on the shotgun principle. By spreading the information to be sent across a spectrum of radio frequencies, we increase our chance of success.

Spread spectrum systems use a figure called *chips per bit,* where several frequencies are used to send a single bit of information. In LAN systems, there are 10–32 chips per bit. The penalty is that we must send the information less rapidly since we are using perhaps 32 chips of bandwidth to send a single bit. Thus, wireless systems are slower than wired systems.

It is simpler to use a single frequency, and some systems do. Usually in the 18 GHz range, these signals are fewer in number and dissipate quickly, making "microcells" of 5000- to 50,000-ft radii practical.

Such high frequencies act like light waves. *Line of sight* systems

Infra—Red

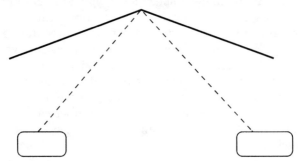

Spread—Spectrum
or Single Frequency Using Microwave Radio

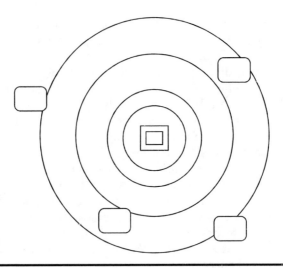

Figure 4.3 Wireless LANs.

must have nothing in between them as any object blocking the path will disrupt the LAN. The system must also build in error-detecting safeguards to maintain data integrity.

Infrared systems use heat waves instead of radio waves. These systems are immune to radio-frequency interference. Infrared waves readily go around corners and are not limited to line-of-sight. They are often used to link wiring hubs in separate buildings.

Lasers or short-distance microwave "shots" offer the benefit of being able to link hubs in nearby buildings at full LAN speed. Disadvantages include the OSHA safety requirements for lasers, weather interference, and potential hassles in licensing the microwave system with the FCC. Vendors will often coordinate this for you.

Where wireless makes sense.   A wireless LAN may make sense under the following conditions:

You need instant hookup, as in a disaster.

A facility is leased; installing permanent wiring does not make sense.

Backup of the wired LAN system is necessary, as in Ethernet.

Temporary connections are needed while awaiting permanent wiring.

Temporary workgroups are formed for a short time.

A wire cannot be run through a building because of its historical value or due to the presence of asbestos.

In local mobile settings, such as warehouses, hospitals, railroad yards, or offices, where people move around a lot.

It makes economic sense to bypass the phone company, as between adjacent buildings or directly across the street.

In electrically noisy environments, as on a factory floor.

Disadvantages of wireless LANs.   These are:

Unlicensed spread-spectrum systems operate on a noninterference basis. If your system interferes with someone else's, you must either stop using your system or take measures to alleviate the problem at your own expense.

The wireless approach is low-speed technology at present relative to wired systems, i.e., roughly a third of the speed of the wired Ethernet.

A wireless LAN must usually work with a wired environment, too. Token ring and Simple Network Management Protocol (SNMP) management are still very new to wireless LANs.

Cost per workstation is 3–5 times that of a wired NIC at about $250. The cost is at best a wash compared to wiring.

A wireless LAN is useless if you are out of town.

Standards are needed. The IEEE 802.11 subcommittee is working on a draft standard, which is due in 1994.

Not all wireless LANs support all network operating systems, multiprotocol support is limited, and some applications incompatibilities are probable.

There may be interference from many sources. Physical barriers, even hanging a coat in the wrong place, can block a wireless LAN signal.

Security can be a real problem. Some wireless LANs offer optional Data Encryption Standard (DES) encryption chips. Do not broadcast your company's secrets out the window.

Wireless LANs are infant technology, largely untested by experience. Their expense and low speed makes them a niche technology for specific applications.

Wireless technology is backed by some of the heaviest hitters in the industry (Table 4.1).

Low speeds do not mean that the system is a poor one. They are often used for peripheral sharing, e.g., of printers, where interactive speed is not necessary.

For the future, the PCMCIA Card 2.2 Interface Standard will make it possible for portable machines' expansion slots to support a wireless transceiver. PCMCIA is the standard for direct bus connections to external devices. The card is approximately the size of a credit card and fits into a notebook's memory slot.

LAN Electrical Signals

Baseband signaling

As shown in Fig. 4.4, there are two types of signals passed through the wiring system. If the signal is *digital,* consisting only of 1s and 0s, then it is referred to as *baseband* signaling. Baseband is also the method used for ordinary coaxial Ethernet and fiber optic transmission, where the light source is simply turned on and off. Baseband is the most common form of LAN signaling.

Baseband signals lose their sharpness with distance. Beyond a certain point, a receiver has trouble telling a one from a zero. For this reason, baseband signals are often regenerated into clean, sharp signals before they deteriorate too much. These devices are called *repeaters* and may be part of a LAN workstation or are inserted in the cable.

Repeaters are active electronic devices that *totally recreate the signal,* losing none of its intelligence and eliminating all distortion and noise. This is the same technique used in T-1 and T-3 communications systems, where the signaling is also baseband.

Baseband systems use the cable's entire bandwidth. Therefore, devices connected to it must share the cable. This is done by means of *time division multiplexing* (TDM). Using TDM, slots of time are allocated to each device for transmission or reception.

TABLE 4.1 Wireless LAN Vendors

Vendor	Product	Remarks
Armatek	EasySpan	2.5 Mbits/sec; no license; supports Arcnet, 802.3, and 802.5
BICC	InfraLAN	4-Mbits/sec token ring; Auburn, MA; used by Shearson-Lehman
AT&T/NCR	WaveLAN	2-Mbits/sec system; spread spectrum; 11 chips per bit
Caliber Tek		Supports Lotus Notes
Cylink	Airlink	64, 128, or 256kbits/sec; 928 MHz spread spectrum; 10-mi radius
IBM (remarket)	Altair Plus	Resells Motorola's Altair; IBM is believed to be working on their own wireless LAN
Infralink	Infralink	40 kbits/sec; infrared scatter system; Arlington, VA
Motorola	Altair Plus	3.3 Mbits/sec; licensed at 18 GHz; 10BaseT; SNMP
O'Neill Comm.	LAWN	Low-speed Ultra-High Frequency (UHF) Ethernet; Princeton, NJ
Photonics	Photolink	200-kbits/sec infrared system; San Jose/Campbell, CA
Proxim	RangeLAN	242-kbits/sec spread spectrum; NetWare support; Mountain View, CA
Symbol Techs.	Spectrum 1	
Spectrix		Infrared LAN
Telesystems SLW	Don Mills	1.3 Mbits/sec; Ethernet; scrambled for security; (Canada)
Ungermann-Bass	Altair Plus	Remarkets Motorola's product
WinData	FreePort	5.7-Mbits/sec system; 32 chips per bit; Ethernet and token-ring. Support; resold by Cabletron.

Data from different devices is interleaved or *multiplexed* together to create a serial bit stream. Controlling access to prevent collisions is the task of the data link layer's *media access control* (MAC) sublayer. MAC is discussed in Chapter 6.

Broadband signaling

Broadband signaling is wave-like (Figure 4.4). The digital signal is modulated onto a carrier signal just as in a modem. The combined waveform creates a broadband, which means using much bandwidth, signal on the medium.

Baseband Signal

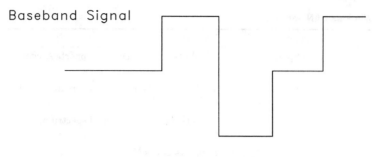

Broadband Signal

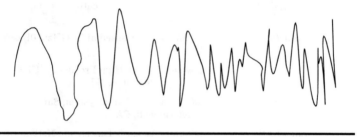

Figure 4.4 Baseband and broadband signaling.

A wave of energy, say electrical or radio, can carry information in three ways—by varying the *amplitude* (strength) of the wave signal; the *frequency* (in cycles per second or Hertz), or the *phase* (place in time).

Baseband signals use only one characteristic: amplitude. This means that only one information path is created. As a minimum, that is all a LAN requires, so most LANs use baseband signals.

Broadband signaling allows greater information-carrying capacity on the cable. By using several frequencies called *carriers,* several different LANs can work on the same cable without interfering with one another. Broadband systems electrically separate channels on a coaxial cable, just the way you tune different stations on your cable television connection or change stations on your radio.

This technique is called *frequency division multiplexing* (FDM). For example, FDM carries some 82 channels of cable TV signals into your home.

It stands to reason that another characteristic, say the carrier's amplitude, must be varied in order to make the carrier frequency actually carry information. This is so, and you hear it on your *amplitude modu-*

lated (AM) radio at home every day. Modulation is the process of changing at least one of the wave's characteristics in time with the information we wish to send. If you prefer the *frequency modulated* (FM) channel, the music you hear is transmitted by varying the frequency of the carrier. It is also common to add the third characteristic, phase, to carry still more information. This is what faster analog modems do: They combine amplitude and phase (called *quadrature*) modulation on a fixed carrier frequency to encode more bits into each wave's transition. Thus, we have the term *quadrature amplitude modulation.*

Baseband and broadband compared

Stations sharing a broadband LAN channel still require an *access control method* to make sure collisions do not disrupt data. As shown in Figure 4.5, single frequency broadband systems allow only *half duplex* (transmission one way at a time). Half duplex is also used in baseband systems. However, two frequencies, being independent, allow *full duplex* (simultaneous transmission and reception) in a broadband system if it is so equipped.

Workstations connected to baseband LANs using bus or tree structures transmit their signals in both directions on the cable. Broadband LANs and baseband rings transmit in one direction only. In the case of *midsplit* broadband, one frequency carries data sent to a head-end frequency converter, which changes it to the receive carrier for transmission back down the cable to the recipient. In *dual-cable* broadband, one cable is used to send and another to receive, but both are unidirectional.

Broadband signals are wave-like in nature. Broadband signals, thus, use amplifiers rather than regenerators. Unfortunately, amplifiers cannot distinguish noise from signal and so amplify everything. This is a negative for broadband systems, but their greater capacity is a positive attribute.

Most LAN systems are baseband. Baseband systems are simpler, but do not offer the speed advantage of full duplex. A broadband system can make very efficient use of the coaxial cable and is one way of adding to or segmenting a LAN without adding more cable.

Unfortunately, the expense of broadband modems and especially the very heavy-duty, expensive, and unwieldy form of coaxial cable all but doomed broadband early in its working life. While some legacy systems survive, new installations are rare. However, the technology is standardized by IEEE 802.3 as 10Broad36.

Ethernet media shorthand

In a continuing effort to obfuscate what we do, the industry has come up with a shorthand to quickly represent a given kind of Ethernet

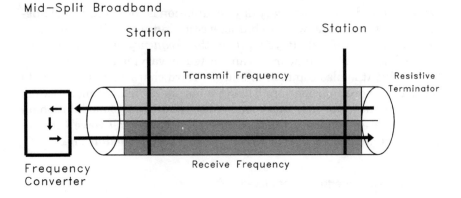

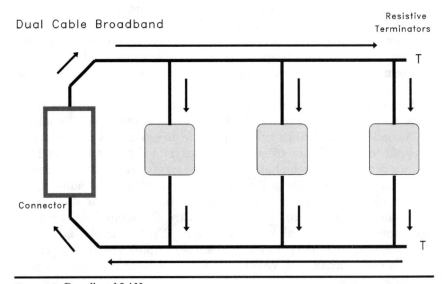

Figure 4.5 Broadband LANs.

LAN. The sequence consists of the LAN's speed, whether it is broadband or baseband, and what kind of cable it uses.

Your have probably heard the term *10BaseT.* In English this means the LAN works at *10* Mbit/sec. Today, only Ethernet runs at this speed. *Base* means it is a baseband LAN. Otherwise it would say *broad* for broadband. *T* means that it uses unshielded twisted pair. We, thus, say 10Base*T.* In contrast, *F* means fiber instead of twisted pair. Therefore, if fiber is used, then 10BaseF is the correct term.

A number instead of a letter means the maximum segment length in hundreds of meters. The cable is always coaxial, though it may be of three types:

2   This indicates 200 m. The cable length is limited by the cable used, RG-58. Since RG-58 is fairly skinny, just under 0.25-in in diameter, it is called *ThinLAN* or *ThinNET*. Because RG-58 is cheaper than its ThickNET or ThickLAN cable cousin, ThinLAN or ThinNET is also called *CheaperNet*.

5   This indicates 500 m. The segment consists of *ThickNET* or *ThickLAN* cable. Heavier than ThinNET, it can go 500 m from one end to the other. The cable is just under 0.5-in in diameter and is often orange or yellow. It resembles RG-8. For the technically inclined, both RG-58 and RG-8 have a 50-Ω impedance if they have a foam dielectric.

36   This means that the cable is heavy, armored coaxial cable used by a broadband system. The maximum segment length is 3600 m.

AT&T's StarLAN is a 1Base5 system. Typical Ethernet systems today are 10Base2, 10Base5, or 10BaseT, with 10BaseT being the most popular and dominating new installations.

Gotchas

Although 2 stands for 200 m, the actual allowed distance is less, 185 m. Call it rounding error.

Even slight impedance changes of a few ohms can cause unwanted signal reflections. For instance, RG-58/A or AU and RG-58 with foam dielectric have impedances of 53 and 50 Ω, respectively (50Ω is the standard). They look the same physically, but their impedances create a signal-reflecting mismatch. Looks can be deceiving!

The same applies to RG-8/A or AU and RG-8 with foam dielectric. Here the impedances are 52 and 50 Ω, respectively. ThickLAN and ThinLAN cables should not be mixed on the same segment.

In twisted pair systems, do not use untwisted modular telephone cables anywhere. Even a few feet of this "silver satin" cable insures a network crash.

Violating these rules can cause the LAN to work poorly or perhaps not at all. The LAN may work acceptably with low traffic and degrade as traffic builds. Symptoms include frame check sequence errors (damaged frames of data), misaligned frames (not terminating on an 8-bit boundary), late collisions (after the first 60 bytes), or total nonoperation.

LAN Topologies (Layouts)

In a LAN, there are only three possible wiring layouts, and they are shown in Figure 4.6. To use the industry term, we call them *topologies* on the principle that one should never use a short, clear, simple word where a complicated and obscure one will do.

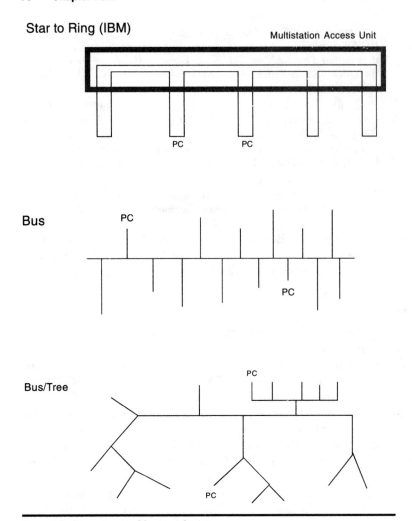

Figure 4.6 Star, ring, and bus topologies.

These topologies are:

The *star,* where wires radiate from a central point outward to clients. Star configurations are becoming the predominant form of LAN wiring.

The *ring,* where the wiring makes a full circle and data circulates around it.

The *bus,* short for data bus, one long party line to which clients are connected. The *tree* is a variation on the bus. Branches can be extended from it to reach clients not situated near the main bus.

Like painters mixing the colors of the rainbow, LAN designers use these topologies to build networks that meet client performance and cost requirements. Like painting, topology selection in complex cases is very much an art.

The star

A star consists of point-to-point links from a central control unit to workstations or PCs. The control unit establishes a connection between two or more units on request. This is typical of voice Private Branch Exchanges (PBXs). A switching hub in a LAN, where cables radiate to workstations in the area, is another example.

A variation of the star is to have subsidiary controllers connected to the main controller with PCs or workstations connected to the subsidiaries, i.e., the "snowflake" configuration.

The star's advantage is its simplicity; all the links are point to point. However, it is wiring intensive and provides no alternate means of communication if the link fails.

The ring

In a ring, the cable forms a large circle or a loop. Stations are connected in series with the ring, receiving everything sent and repeating it down the line. Only messages with a station's unique address are processed.

Thus, the ring is *unidirectional,* circulating messages only one way. A backup ring may carry traffic, control information, or simply be a spare path between hubs as in a token ring. If the ring is cut, the hubs will remain connected via the backup path.

Rings connect together via bridges or routers so that workgroups can communicate with one another. This is called *internetworking* and is discussed in Chapter 11.

Ring topologies are the most difficult to build in terms of cabling, but they offer very good reliability. They may be several kilometers in circumference and are relatively easy to manage using the IBM cabling system or an equivalent. This is the *logical* topology used by IBM, although the *physical* topology is a star.

The bus and tree

The term is short for a data bus (just 1-bit wide) in which a transmission placed on a shared cable is received by all units. Only the one that is addressed accepts the transmission. Sometimes the bus is expanded with tee connectors (for coax media) into a tree configuration. However, it remains essentially a bus where all stations share the line. This is the classic Ethernet arrangement.

Buses and trees are easy to build, but they contain no provision for an alternate path. In addition, coaxial cable is more difficult to work with than simple twisted pair. All the same, there are many Ethernet bus systems in use.

Physical and logical topologies

Discussing topologies requires looking at the wiring scheme from two different vantage points: the way *we* see the wiring versus the way *the system* sees it. We describe this difference in perspective as the *physical* topology and the *logical* topology.

The two may be one and the same, and again they may not. The best example of this dichotomy is the IBM token ring example.

In the IBM token ring, a special message circulates the ring called a token. Client traffic is placed on the ring to its destination, then returned to the originator. The ring may run clockwise or counter clockwise, depending on how it is wired.

IBM knew from the start that ring cuts were inevitable. They also recognized the logistical problems of wiring rings in daisy-chain style from office to office. Most perceptive of all, they anticipated the difficulty of maintaining the ring, finding ring breaks and fixing them.

So IBM rejected the true ring. Instead, IBM uses a *star* wiring configuration. Wires radiate from a central *hub* to a workstation. The sending wires loop through the workstation and return to the hub. The hub connects these wires to the receiving pair of the next workstation on the ring, and so on. The hub shown creates an electrical and *logical ring* (Figure 4.7). Yet looking at the wiring path from above you see a *physical star,* or several stars cabled together.

Selecting a topology

As always, it is important to start with the needs of your organization. Let all the technical decisions be guided by your business needs. This is where many designers go awry. Too quickly, they immerse themselves in an ocean of technology without knowing where they are going. At the beginning, forget about technology. The first and best question to ask is, "What do we want this system to do?"

You may have already concluded that all you really want to do is share the laser printer and a plotter. You do not need e-mail, you occasionally send files down the hall, and the fax machine is pretty quiet. A LAN is too much capability for what you need. Better to buy a nice printer-sharing system and save the difference in costs.

An example of what *not* to do is to start with a preconceived notion that you need a LAN before you really understand the problem. This is a solution being force-fit into a problem. The result in the printer-sharing case would be overkill.

The network looks like this to the system:

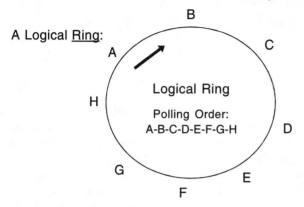

A Logical <u>Ring</u>:

Logical Ring

Polling Order:
A-B-C-D-E-F-G-H

But it looks like <u>this</u> to us:

A Physical <u>Star</u>:

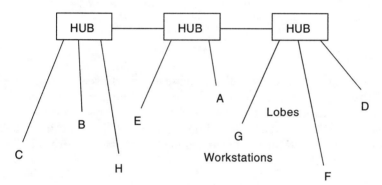

Note that the logical and physical orders do not match.

Figure 4.7 Physical and logical topologies.

Perhaps you have decided that nothing short of a LAN will be adequate. Now you must consider the following:

Who will be the clients? The workgroups?

What will they be doing on the LAN?

How much performance is required?

Where are they, physically?

Is the task mission-critical?

How much client expansion is to be expected?

How big is the budget?

Is there any existing wiring you can use?

What provision is there to detect problems and fix them?

Only the first three questions are not particularly topology-sensitive.

Where are they?

One of the wisest things you can do is to map out where your clients will be located. This can be done from an architectural blueprint of your building or a simple sketch. You will quickly gain an understanding of where your clients are located.

Are they all on the same floor? Where is the telephone company wiring closet? This might make a good wiring hub location.

How far away are they from a possible hub spot? Ethernet and token ring both have strict limits on distances that may be traveled over a certain type of cable. Remember there is a difference between how far they are down the hall and how many feet of cable will be needed to reach them. If you must go up or down at some specified place, the *cable distance* will be greater.

Critical missions

The token ring is inherently self-repairing as we will see later in Chapter 7. Ethernet is not inherently self-repairing. You can justify the generally greater expense of token ring if minutes make a difference in your workgroup's activity. One estimate places LAN availability at 96 percent; much too low without redundancy for mission-critical applications.

Client expansion

The one inviolate rule in networking is that they always grow. Adding Ethernet clients is relatively simple, through a tee connector or a "vampire tap" *medium attachment unit* (MAU) on the cable (Figure 4.8). Token-ring additions require a port on the hub. The hub is called a *multistation access unit* (MSAU).[2] If no port is available, another MSAU must be added.

---

[2]A MAU is an IEEE 802.3 term that carefully defines a device that connects the LAN cable to a workstation. The MAU detects collisions and transmits and receives bits to and from the medium. It inhibits transmission in case of a line collision and interrupts transmission if the maximum frame length is exceeded. The nearest equivalent term and function in Ethernet is a *transceiver*. The industry often says MAU when a MSAU is meant. The choice of the term MAU is unfortunate, because it is easily confused with the token-ring Multistation Access Unit (MSAU). An MSAU is a hub and is functionally very different from a MAU. (*Cont.*)

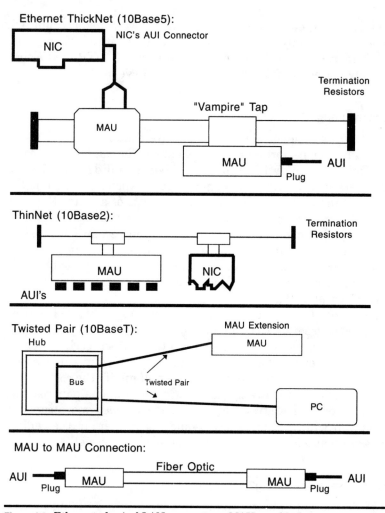

Figure 4.8 Ethernet physical LAN access: taps, MAUs, and hubs.

Ethernet and token ring limit the number of clients per segment: 100 on a Thicknet (the yellow or orange stuff sometimes called "goldenrod") coaxial cable, 30 on ThinNet RG-58 coaxial cable, and 260 on the main ring of a token ring using Type 1 cable (shielded twisted pair).

Failing to consider expansion is an easy way to find yourself in a cor-

---

In industry usage, the "S" often seems to get lost with the result that an IEEE MAU (mainly a transceiver) and a token-ring MSAU (mainly a hub) are both referred to as a MAU. Perhaps this is one reason why IBM is using a newer term, *Controlled Access Unit* (CAU), to refer to its newer hub product. Here we will use the terms as formally defined by IEEE 802.3 and 802.5, respectively.

ner. If you run inexpensive Level 3 UTP cable in your token-ring LAN, it will work fine . . . until you go to upgrade to 16 Mbit/sec. Then what? How much more would it have been to run level 5 UTP in the first place? Surely not as much as reinstalling with Level 5!

How big is the budget?

Token ring wiring is generally more expensive than Ethernet. Its self-healing and higher performance features are valuable, but they come at a cost. Only you can decide if the cost-to-benefit ratio is satisfactory.

Wiring costs are usually the single largest expense in all but the smallest LAN installations. The cable cost is less of a factor than the installation labor costs, which are generally high. Once in place, practically speaking, that cable is there forever. It then becomes our task to make the best use of it under changing conditions.

This is one reason why the decision to install fiber optic cable must be considered carefully. It has strict installation guidelines and needs expensive optics at either end.

Fiber's cost per foot is four to five times that of unshielded twisted pair. It makes sense only if its high bandwidth will be fully utilized or if there is a compelling applications reason to use fiber, perhaps for security or in a high electrical-noise environment. The bottom line is that it is so specialized, you must be sure its use will justify the cost.

A suggestion is to run several pairs since running one pair costs no more than several. If a strand breaks or if you need more capacity eventually, you will be glad to have some "dark fiber" in the ceiling. This suggestion applies to twisted-pair installations as well.

Can we use the existing wiring?

"Yes, but!" is the only answer. Existing wiring in a building is used mainly for voice. The wire gauge may be too thin: modern telephone company cable is usually 24 AWG. Twisted pair installations using Ethernet or token ring require 24 AWG or 22 AWG. (The lower the gauge number, the thicker the wire and the better it is for LAN use).

DIW as the telcos call it may not have enough twist to be usable as LAN cabling. Twist reduces electrical interference. Unfortunately, you cannot simply go, ruler in hand, to the nearest wiring closet to see if your DIW has enough twist. Wire manufacturers have different construction techniques, and the twist per foot can be very different from one vendor's LAN-qualified cable to the next.

Inside wire can go through several junction points at punchdown blocks. These add resistance and noise, so 10BaseT permits only two intermediate punchdown blocks between a MAU and a wiring hub.

Split pairs and other data-killing problems make inside wire a tricky but not necessarily unworkable task.

But let us say you have a lot of direct inside wire and a microscopic budget. Use some of that budget to buy a cable tester and qualify the cable.[3] If it meets specification, use it. Some LAN vendors will not support a LAN whose cable has not been qualified. They know that *60–75 percent of LAN problems originate in the cable.*

The wise move is to hire a competent LAN cable installer. Have them do the mapping and the actual installation. You will be assured that it all meets national and local electrical code specifications, is qualified for your LAN, and is fully documented. They are often listed in the business-to-business yellow pages, or they can be found by asking a local LAN integrator. Some electrical contractors also install LAN wiring. If you are installing UTP, it should comply with EIA/TIA-568 standards, a structured wiring architecture discussed later in this chapter.

Detecting problems and fixing them

The hardest LAN topology to fix is the linear Ethernet segment. There is no way to know where the problem is short of dividing the segment into parts until the problem goes away. This is labor-intensive and is often impractical.

The clear trend in LAN topologies is to do everything through a hub. The hub is where it all comes together. The Ethernet bus and the ring-making connections for token ring are all located inside the hub. Isolating Ethernet problems becomes easy: just disconnect each user from the hub until the problem stops. The hub gives the LAN supervisor an access point from which to manage the network.

Hubs have taken on more popularity as the trend toward using twisted pair in Ethernet has accelerated. Coaxial cable has high noise immunity, low loss, and excellent resistance to damage, but it is relatively expensive and harder to install and work with than twisted pairs.

For that reason, the IEEE 802.3 subcommittee has sanctioned a new wiring option for Ethernet called 10BaseT. Recall that this is IEEE

---

[3]Some LAN cable tester vendors include: (a) Beckman Ind., 3883 Ruffin Rd, San Diego, CA 92123, (619) 495-3200; (b) Microtest, 3519 E Shea Blvd, Phoenix, AZ 85028, (800) 526-9675; (c) Hewlett-Packard Corp, Hewlett-Packard Direct (resells higher-end testers from Microtest), (800) 452-4844; (d) Star-Tek, Inc., 71 Lyman St, Northboro, MA 01532, (800) 225-8528; and (e) The Siemon Co., 76 Westbury Park Rd, Watertown, CT, (203) 274-2523).

shorthand for a LAN that runs at 10 Mbit/sec using baseband signaling over Twisted pair wires. Using 10BaseT requires a hub.

There are over 130 hub models available today from about 60 vendors. With so many products on the market, competition is fierce, and the market has fragmented into low-end hubs with minimum functionality up through high-end hubs that add features such as diagnostics and network management.

Since so many LAN problems originate in the medium, proper documentation is a must. This takes the form of a *cable map* that shows the type of cable used in a segment, how it is routed, and its length. It is not much help if your cable tester says the cable is broken 42 ft away, and you don't know which direction to go or know how the cable is run.

Cable management has become so important that software has been written[4] to help you maintain and manage your cable plant. These systems allow cable performance monitoring, cable break detection, cable pair inventory management, and cable route planning.

Some of the questions above transcend the topology question alone. Network performance depends on much more than the topology, for instance, since the access method, e.g., Ethernet or token ring, server performance, and application software will all exert their own performance influences.

Signaling

Baseband signals may be transmitted by STP, UTP, or coaxial cable. Broadband signals are at radio frequencies, and so they require coaxial cable.

In an effort to simplify decision-making, Table 4.2 illustrates the combinations of topology, media, signaling, and access method.

Media Ground Rules

Ethernet, token ring, and 10BaseT systems all have their own ground rules relating to distances, stations, etc. These rules are summarized and compared for you in this section. The charts include applicable notes for each system. Vendors often improve on these stock figures so do not take these figures as absolutes. While they are standards maxima, they are often not the practical limit.

---

[4]Microtest, among others, offers such a product.

TABLE 4.2   Access Methods and Topologies

	Ethernet (IEEE 802.3)	Token Ring (IEEE 802.5)
Performance	10 Mbits/sec	4 or 16 Mbits/sec
Topology		
Star	Yes	Yes
Ring	No	Yes
Bus and tree	Yes	No
Media		
UTP	Yes	Yes
STP	Yes	Yes
Coaxial cable	Yes	No
Fiber optic cable	No*	Yes
Wireless radio	Yes	Yes
Use existing wiring?	Sometimes	Not often
Signaling	Baseband or broadband	Baseband or broadband
Inherent redundancy	No	Yes

*Not in a bus topology, because tapping fiber cable is difficult. A fiber-based Ethernet is certainly possible in a star-wired hub.

Things the standards do not tell you

A ThickNet LAN segment is basically a 500-m long cable. The cable is usually marked in 2.5-m increments, the minimum distance between taps. Taps should be added at these marks rather than in between. If ThickNet cable is added from different vendors or even different spools, it should be added at 23.5-, 70.1-, or 117-m increments.

Cable consistency is also important in ThinNets. Even a few ohms' difference causes an impedance bump with consequent reflections and signal attenuation. These problems can cause pseudocollisions and failures to detect collisions, respectively.

In Ethernet, terminating resistors are needed at both ends to prevent signal reflections. One terminator should be grounded. All the connectors should be covered with insulating "boots" or covers to prevent accidental grounding. Such grounding can cause circulating currents called *ground loops,* which create electrical noise on the LAN.

10BaseT

10BaseT uses a hub at the center of a physical star wire topology. Segments (also called *lobes*) will run at least 100 m (328 ft). Hubs can be cascaded to form larger networks.

Two devices are allowed per segment. The cable used is 22AWG or 24AWG UTP. Twist is important. Flat ribbon cable used with many phones *will not work.*

Some 10BaseT hubs have an *Attachment Unit Interface* (AUI) port for connections from NICs having only coaxial Ethernet connections. The AUI connection will go to a splitter whose fan-out side has multiple coaxial connectors, one per NIC.

Ethernet media ground rules

Ethernet and token-ring systems each have cabling ground rules which are best considered inviolate. We list the most important ones below:

Ethernet parameter	10Base5 ThickNet	10Base2 ThinNet
Data rate	10 Mbit/sec	10 Mbit/sec
Segment cabling	50-Ω thick coaxial	50Ω, RG-58
Maximum segment length	500 m (1640 ft)	185 m (607 ft)
Segment interface	Coaxial N type	BNC coaxial
Maximum number of segments joined by repeaters	5	5
Transceiver cabling (transceiver to station)	20AWG; 4 shielded pairs	RG-58 or 4 shielded 20AWG pairs
Transceiver interface	D-subminiature 15 pin with slide locks	BNC or D-subminiature 15 pin with slide locks
Maximum number of transceivers per segment	100	30
Maximum transceiver cable length	50 m (164 ft)	12.5 m (41 ft)
Minimum distance between transceivers	2.5 m (8.2 ft)	0.5 m (1.6 ft)
Maximum number of stations per network	1024	1024

No more than four *interrepeater links* (IRLs) are allowed between devices regardless of whether they communicate or not. The maximum number of segments is five. For example, three coaxial plus two 10BaseTs, or 5 coaxial segments, are allowed. The maximum cable length is 4 km (2.4 mi). In addition, transceivers without signal quality error (discussed later) should be used with repeaters, both ends must be terminated in a 50-Ω resistor, and devices are connected to 10Base2 ThinNet by BNC bayonet T-connectors.

Token-ring media ground rules

Token ring.   Maximum ring circumferences vary depending on the cable type, the number of MSAUs, and the number of wiring closets used. We list the important parameters below:

Token-ring parameter	Type 1 or 2 cable (STP)*	Type 3 cable (UTP)†
Data rate	4 or 16 Mbit/sec	4 or 16 Mbit/sec
Maximum net length	Configuration dependent	Configuration dependent
Maximum number of devices per network	260	72
Wire gauge and type	22 AWG STP	24 AWG UTP
Maximum distance from the work area to a wiring closet	300 m (990 ft)	100 m (330 ft)
Maximum distance to more than one closet via punchblocks	100 m (328 ft)	45 m (150 ft)
Maximum distance from wiring closet to wiring closet	200 m (660 ft)	120 m (400 ft) using Type 1 cable
Maximum number of wiring closets per ring	12	2

*An 8-port unpowered MAU counts as 4.9 m (16 ft) of cable on the main ring. One unbridged main ring supports up to 33 eight-port MAUs (4 ports are left unused). At 4 Mbit/sec, a wire repeater extends lobe and ring distances to 770 m (2525 ft). Fiber optic cable (100/140 μm) allows 1980 m (or 6500 ft) between repeaters. Fiber also allows an extension of lobe and ring distances to 2.5 m (4 km). Type 6 or 9 cable counts as 1.33 ft of Type 1 or 2, and Type 8 (under-carpet) cable counts as 2 ft of Type 1 or 2.

†One unbridged main ring supports nine unpowered or eight powered 8-port MAUs. Each network device requires a Type 3 media filter.

Fiber optics. There is no IEEE 802.3 standard for fiber links. Distances to 2000 m are possible with two devices per link. The limiting factor is usually signal loss. Fiber has very low propagation delay. The ThickLAN cable propagation factor should be no less than $0.77c$, and ThinLAN's should exceed $0.65c$, where c is the speed of light, i.e., 3×10^8 m/sec.

Wiring systems. Wiring a floor or building is more than just running a stretch of cable under the floor or above the false ceiling. Moving vertically through risers and then horizontally calls for wiring closets, distribution panels, and planning to ensure that all the system's electrical parameters are met.

National Electrical Code and state and local fire codes apply. For instance, running cable through air plenums usually calls for teflon-coated cable that will not burn. To deal with all these problems, enterprising vendors have come up with *cabling systems* that address all the wiring issues from the logical viewpoint of wiring as a system.

The IBM Cabling System. The earliest system was from IBM, who in 1984 introduced its IBM Cabling System (Figure 4.9). Consisting of standard cable types and connectors, it was among the first to offer an organized approach to cabling. It supports T-1, LAN, or 3270 coaxial

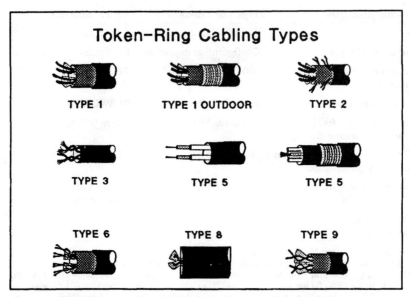

Figure 4.9 IBM cabling system cable types. (*Courtesy of Hewlett-Packard Company.*)

signals. The wiring topology is a chain of stars. User cables at the far end concentrate in a distribution panel at a wiring closet.

STP and UTP can be mixed if the correct distance criteria are observed. You can convert cables lengths and types into equivalent Type 1 ft by dividing the number of feet of cable by the equivalent factor (given below).[5] Use this equivalent to calculate ring and lobe lengths. See the *IBM Token-Ring Network Introduction and Planning Guide* for further data.

Different types of cable are used for different purposes:

Type 1   This cable consists of two individually shielded twisted wire pairs using 22 AWG solid wire. Different sheaths are available for indoor and outdoor use and inside air plenums. Suitable for 4- or 16-Mbit/sec lobes and main rings. The equivalent factor = 1.0 (i.e., it *is* Type 1).

Type 2   This cable is like Type 1 except that it adds four solid 22 AWG wire pairs *outside* the shield for telephone rather than data use. It has the same uses and choice of sheaths as Type 1. The equivalent factor = 1.0.

---

[5]The equivalent factor is the cable's equivalent in terms of Type 1 cable, i.e., if you wish to use 100 ft of cheaper Type 9 cable, then you must allow for the fact that it is equivalent to 152 ft of Type 1 (100 ft/0.66).

Type 3   This cable contains telephone twisted pair. Depending on the version, 2, 3, 4, or 25 twisted pairs are provided. The wire is solid copper, 24 AWG. It is useable at 4 Mbit/sec; it is not recommended in some 16-Mbit/sec cable system networks. The equivalent factor = 0.45.

Type 5   This cable consists of two fiber optic multimode (100/140μm) strands inside a single outer sheath. It is intended for indoor or outdoor use and in dry, waterproof, underground conduits. It is used to extend distances for main ring paths between MSAUs or to connect networks in adjacent buildings. It is recommended to avoid surge and ground loop problems between buildings. The equivalent factor = 3.0.

Type 6   This cable is similar to Type 1 but uses stranded 26 AWG wire so it can bend. It is used for patch panel cables that are inserted and removed often. Wallplate-PC and MAU-patch panel connections use Type 6. It is suitable for 4- or 16-Mbit/sec LANs. Type 6 can be used for runs, but the equivalent factor = 0.75, reducing the distance by one-quarter, i.e., 75 ft of Type 6 is electrically the same as 100 ft of Type 1.

Type 8   This cable is used for under carpets. It is low in profile and high in crush tolerance; it contains two shielded parallel pairs of 26 AWG solid copper wire. It is used for 4- or 16-Mbit/sec networks. The equivalent factor = 0.5.

Type 9   This is low-cost plenum cable like Type 1 but uses thinner 26 AWG wire. It is best used for short MSAU to PC runs where plenum cable is needed. The equivalent factor = 0.66.

The IBM Cabling System includes cables and an array of hardware. It uses a unique rectangular four-conductor *hermaphroditic* (genderless) connector. When unplugged, the transmit pair loops to the receive pair for troubleshooting. This connector has been problematic in supporting speeds above 16 Mbit/sec due to excessive NEXT and is due for redesign.

Some cabling experts consider the IBM system outdated because of its emphasis on STP. The IBM system is sold only through third-party distributors and contractors.

OPEN DECconnect. DECconnect is promoted as being protocol (signaling, really) independent wiring (Figure 4.10). That makes it usable not just for data, but for imaging, sensing, video, and voice traffic. This flexibility is at the cost of having to install many different cables to support these vastly different signal types.

OPEN DECconnect supports IEEE 802.3/Ethernet via 10Base2, 10Base5, and 10BaseT. The system includes *fiber-distributed data interface* (FDDI), Apple LocalTalk, IBM 3270, and AS/400 wiring support.

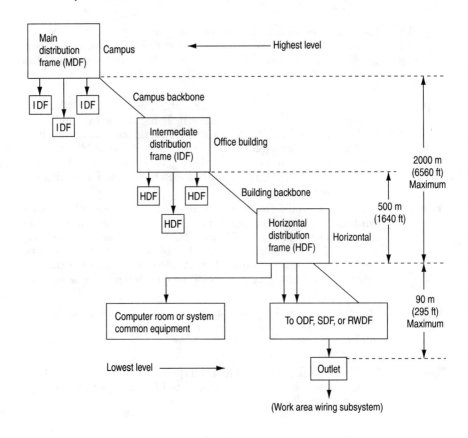

Open DECconnect architecture

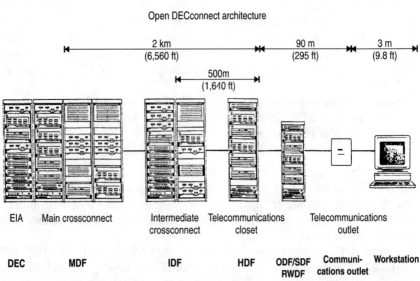

Figure 4.10 DECconnect as an example of EIA/TIA-568. (*Courtesy of Digital Equipment Corporation.*)

OPEN DECconnect supports IEEE 802.5's token ring at 4 or 16 Mbits/sec.

The system is specifically intended to meet LAN wiring needs. FDDI network support for high-traffic applications is supported, with *copper digital data interface* (CDDI) planned; this is ANSI's X3T9.5 TP-PMD. Horizontally, ThinNet and twisted-pair wiring is supported for work area and office connections. Both shielded and unshielded 100-Ω system components are available. DECconnect is a star-structured wiring utility system that ensures physical layer connections between any two network points. It starts at a *main distribution frame* (MDF) where buildings are connected together from *intermediate distribution frames* (IDFs) located in each office building.

The building IDFs connect to *horizontal distribution frames* (HDFs) on each floor. The HDF connects to the work area wiring subsystem, which then goes to the workstations. The administrative subsystem allows cross connects to be changed as needs change.

DECconnect complies with the EIA/TIA-568 Commercial Building Wiring Standard. The standard defines telecommunications wiring for one or more buildings on a campus. It includes wiring topology, distances, media, and connector and pin assignments.

The standard recognizes three kinds of wiring: backbone, horizontal, and work area. MDF to HDF distance cannot exceed 2 km (6560 ft). The IDF-HDF distance limit is 500 m (1640 ft). An HDF cannot extend more than 90 m (295 ft) to a telecommunications wall outlet. The workstation must be within 3 m (10 ft) of the outlet.

DECconnect is sold directly and via distributors such as Anixter and Wesco. DEC offers design, consulting, and installation via its Network Integrated Services Division.[6]

Also refer to the *Building Industry Consulting Service International* (BICSI) Telecommunications Distribution Methods Manual, EIA/TIA-568, and the National Electrical Code (revised every 3 years).

AT&T's Systimax premises distribution system. Relying mainly on UTP and fiber plus modular connectors and cross-connect methods originally created for PBXs, no vendor has more experience with wiring than AT&T. Its product, Systimax, supports Ethernet, STARLAN (AT&T's 1Base5 LAN) and 4- or 16-Mbit/sec token-ring LANs. STP and coaxial cable are also supported. Systimax is updated from the *premises distribution system* (PDS) of 1985.

Unlike IBM, who does not make its cabling system components (al-

---

[6]Those interested in OPEN DECconnect should call DEC at (800) 344-4825 for the OPEN DECconnect Building Wiring Components and Applications Catalog, EC-I1834-29, catalog code: CDB. It is free and exceptionally well written and illustrated.

though they must pass IBM handling and quality-control approval), AT&T manufactures almost every PDS component, assuring that very high quality standards are maintained. PDS consists of three major subsystems:

The *Administrative System,* which provides terminations and cross connects in the satellite closet

The *Horizontal Subsystem* for cable runs from closet to user

The *Work Location Subsystem,* which consists of the workstation attachment adapters, mounting cords, and modular hardware needed to connect almost any device to the PDS

While IBM parts are usually more expensive than AT&T's, the AT&T PDS is generally regarded as more expensive to install.

Like DEC, AT&T sells Systimax directly and through third-party distributors. Their *Architects, Consultants, and Engineers* (ACE) group provides design assistance.[7]

Northern Telecom's Integrated Building Distribution Network.   Northern Telecom is a Canadian telecommunications giant who first marketed *integrated building distributions network* (IBDN) in the U.S. in 1991. Like AT&T, IBDN is aimed at supporting UTP and fiber cable.

IBDN, like DEC's product, follows the EIA/TIA-568 standard. While the standard does not specify non-LAN cabling, IBDN does support both voice and data. More specifically, IBDN handles IBM 3270, IBM System 3X and AS/400, IEEE 802.3 Ethernet, IEEE 802.5 token ring, Arcnet, Wang, and asynchronous EIA-232C.

IBDN offers Level 3 cable for Ethernet and 4-Mbit/sec token ring; Level 4 cable for 16-Mbit/sec token ring; and Level 5 cable for 100-Mbit/sec TP-PMD. These 100-Mbit/sec systems must have patch panels and accessories to support this speed, not just cable. IBDN is sold in the U.S. through distributors.[8]

Additional vendors.   Here are a few additional vendors and systems:

British Telecom's OSCA   MOD-TAP
FASTLAN   Wang's WANGNET

---

[7]For further information call AT&T at (800) 344-0223 in the U.S. or (416) 756-5118 in Canada.

[8]Call (708) 967-2708 in the U.S. or (514) 744-8834 in Canada for further information.

MAUs and MSAUs

These terms cause confusion because they sound so much alike. MAUs are used by *IEEE 802.3* and MSAUs are used for *token rings*. They are incompatible. The terms are often inexactly applied, which adds to the confusion.

As shown in Figure 4.11, a MAU is a Medium Attachment Unit,

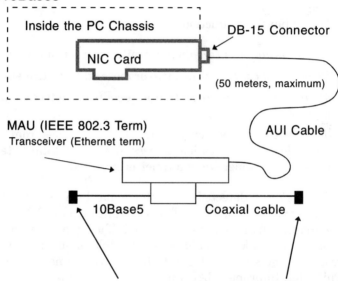

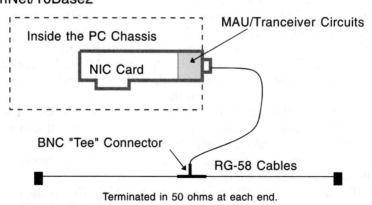

Figure 4.11 An Ethernet MAU and AUI.

which is an IEEE 802.3 term. Its near-equivalent in Ethernet is a *transceiver.* Both devices tap the cable to get the signal off and on. In contrast, a MSAU is a Multistation Access Unit, the most basic hub for token ring. Let us discuss MAUs first, them MSAUs.

MAUs. A MAU is *medium-dependent* because the type of MAU depends on the medium, ThickNet or ThinNet, fiber, or UTP. The MAU may tap into the serial path with connectors or it may tap into Thick-Net LANs using a small pin to puncture the cable. The latter is called a *vampire tap.*

MAUs have five functions:

Transmission and *reception* of traffic to and from the LAN media.

Detection of collisions, i.e., two or more stations transmitting at once.

Monitor mode, i.e., reception and collision detection without transmission.

Jabber detection, which prevents defective nodes from sending excessively long frames called *jabbers* (over 1518 total bytes). The MAU cuts off the jabber when a timer is exceeded.

A *collision* is detected when the signal level on the cable equals or exceeds the combined signal of two transmitters. Collision detection is one reason why repeaters are needed. If a signal from the far end of the cable is too weak, it would not be possible to detect a collision without restoring the signal's strength. Repeaters are needed every 500 m on ThickNet. Improper MAU tap spacing may cause collision detection to fail. Signal reflections can cause false detection of a collision. Taps *must* be spaced in multiples of 2.5 m.

The MAU connects to a PC NIC through an *Attachment Unit Interface* (AUI). A MAU may have several such connections, making it a *multiport MAU,* yet with only one tap needed on the medium.

The AUI cable (also shown in Figure 4.11) may be up to 50 m (164 ft) long and uses STP. It connects to the NIC via a 15-pin D-subminiature connector. The cable carries data both ways and handshaking signals for the NIC to verify contact with the MAU and vice versa.

Chief among these signals is *Signal Quality Error* (SQE). The MAU sends SQE to the NIC whenever the MAU detects a collision or incorrect signal on the cable. The SQE "heartbeat" can be turned on or off in most MAUs, transceivers, and repeaters. Protocol analyzers consider SQE heartbeats to be collisions.

NICs may have the "D" connector for the AUI. This is the most flexible because the NIC can be used with any medium: the MAU insulates the NIC from being medium dependent. A BNC coaxial or RJ-45 modular connector on the NIC allows direct attachment to ThinNet or 10BaseT cable. In the latter case, MAU functionality is within the NIC. NICs have AUI/BNC connectors, others have RJ-45 connectors, and some have both.

MSAUs. A MSAU is the most basic form of hub in a token-ring network, and in fact, creates the ring as shown in Figure 4.12. MSAUs simplify wiring, keep the ring intact, and are a natural control point.

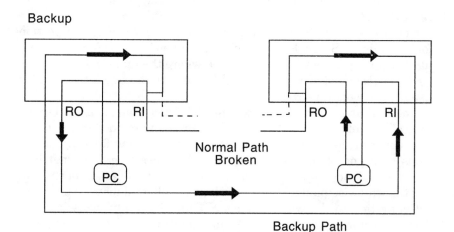

The backup path maintains links between MSAUs *only*

Figure 4.12 How a MSAU creates a ring.

Recall that a token-ring network is physically a star or chain of stars. At the center of each star is a MSAU or a hub incorporating the MSAU's function. Types 1 and 3 MSAUs are used with STP and UTP, respectively. MSAUs connect to workstations through two twisted pair cables called *lobes* and to each other. They are usable at 4 or 16 Mbit/sec unless an internal active component such as a repeater is set for one speed or the other.

A MSAU forms a complete ring unto itself. With no station connected, relays in each port pass signals through the port and loop the workstation on itself through the IBM hermaphroditic connector. Such disconnects can also be ordered by network management, e.g., SNMP, running smart MSAUs.

When a workstation is powered on, its NIC performs a comprehensive self-test. It then tests itself through the lobe. If the lobe test is good, it sends a *phantom voltage* to the MSAU, which opens the port relay and inserts the station into the ring. Token-ring connections are polarity sensitive and must be connected properly.

Phantom voltage remains present as long as the station is on and connected. If it is turned off, the relay drops in. Alternatively, some units such as Thomas-Conrad's automatically initialize whenever a connector is inserted into the port.

MSAUs can be passive (unpowered) or active. Passive MSAU relays take longer to react than their active electronic switching cousins. Unpowered MSAUs come with a relay tool to initialize relay settings. Some MSAUs have a small lithium battery and a master pushbutton to reset the relays.

Notice the *ring in* (RI) and *ring out* (RO) ports, which are connections for cascading MSAUs. Recall that up to 260 nodes or 33 MSAUs can be used in a ring, except for Type 3 cable where the limit is 9. Sometimes a *patch cable* must be inserted in RI/RO to keep the ring intact. MSAUs usually have eight user ports.

Notice that station insertions and deletions change the circumference of the ring. There is usually a backup path provided by an unused pair going in the other direction. If the primary ring fails, the MSAU loops each end of the cable to keep a ring operating. Ethernet lacks such redundancy. However, such a loop doubles the length of the ring. That is why wise planners use only half the allowed distances.

Connection to the workstation's NIC involves only two wire pairs. The connector for STP is a DB-9 subminiature connector. Some NICs also have an RJ-11 for IBM Type 3 UTP.

LAN Hubs

The hub and spoke airline topology has succeeded in the LAN world as well. Hubs (Figure 4.13) are a natural place to concentrate control and

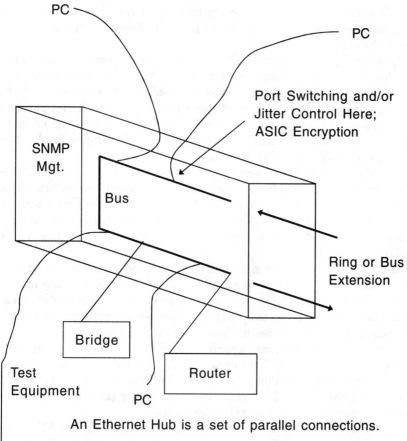

PC

PC

Port Switching and/or
Jitter Control Here;
ASIC Encryption

SNMP
Mgt.

Bus

Ring or Bus
Extension

Bridge

Test
Equipment

Router

PC

An Ethernet Hub is a set of parallel connections.

A token-ring hub creates a ring.

The hub is a natural point for many services: bridging,
routing, security, and management, to name a few.

Figure 4.13 A LAN hub.

give excellent modularity and flexibility in even a small LAN. The
spokes are individual UTP, STP, coaxial, or fiber cables to each user.
These spokes are called lobes, as mentioned earlier.

Low-end hubs can cost as little as $50–80 a port. They are stand-
alone devices or boards which fit into a workstation. The number of
ports is fixed. Often, they are used at the department level to connect a
single workgroup. Sometimes they will funnel traffic into a higher level
intelligent hub. Network management, individual port control, and security are usually not provided for low-end hubs.

Inexpensive hubs are used in a small workgroup setting or to connect remote users. These stand-alone hubs support 8 to 16 users and lack chassis-based slot flexibility. They may have limited intelligence and should be expandable.

Higher-end units typically allow network management down to the port level, have larger port capacity (up to 260 ports), expansion slots and support for different LAN types and cabling. Most token-ring hubs cannot support large numbers of users due to *jitter*, a timing problem that arises when UTP transmits high-speed data. High-capacity hubs often contain *phase-locked loop* (PLL) circuits or ringing tank jitter compensators to reduce jitter to acceptable levels.

The ability to interconnect LANs to one another and to WANs is often found in high-end hubs. The usual configuration is a chassis with plug-in boards to accommodate specific user needs. They offer a natural upgrade path to new LAN users who wish to start at the department level and then add departments gradually until the whole building is on line.

At the upper end of the high-end hubs, individual ports can be activated, taken off line, or even switched. This amounts to being able to walk into the wiring closet and move patch cables from a distance. Remote management is necessary in enterprise-wide networks where local technical talent may be minimal or not exist at all.

Adds, moves, and changes are the second most time-consuming staff support activity, ranking behind help-desk, training, and maintenance. If a port change can be done remotely in 5 min as opposed to 90 min by hand, then the added $125 cost per port quickly pays for itself. Port switching eliminates any travel expense, too.

LAN vendors tend to align themselves with a particular LAN access method. For instance, 3Com Corp. is more an Ethernet vendor than a token-ring vendor. This is because Dr. Robert Metcalfe, the inventor of Ethernet, was a founder of 3Com Corp. Yet 3Com Corp. has moved into token ring by acquiring token-ring hub vendor StarTek. Over time, expect this MAC-layer polarization to recede if not disappear altogether.

Cabletron and SynOptics are two more examples of respected Ethernet vendors. They dominate the Ethernet hub market, though they now offer token-ring hubs, too. Conversely, Proteon, Madge Networks and Andrew Corp. sell mainly token-ring hubs.

StarTek's token-ring hub supports up to 260 users. StarTek's jitter problem solution uses a PLL and is being proposed to the IEEE 802.5 committee as the standard method to reduce jitter. Jitter is not a problem in Ethernet.

More recently, SynOptics and IBM introduced a *ringing tank* circuit that allows even low-grade UTP to support 16 Mbit/sec as far as 100 m. Used on each port, the circuit is a narrow bandpass filter that resonates at 16 Mbit/sec. Passive, the ringing tank costs one-fifth of PLL technology. It is also available in some MSAUs.

The ringing tank technology has also been submitted to the IEEE 802.5 committee for standards consideration. Along with PLL and passive filtering, standards increase interoperability between vendors and protect owners' investments.

Hubs are taking on some network-protection features. In token-ring networks, a station with a defective or improperly set NIC sends out an error alarm called a *beacon,* which can lock up a token-ring network. Some token-ring hub vendors are adding antibeaconing software to prevent a ring failure.

Reflecting the present market, there are many more Ethernet vendors around than token ring. It pays to know on which access method your vendor concentrates. If the sales person starts backpedaling on the phone when you mention token ring, look elsewhere.

Some vendors address both markets. Hewlett-Packard is a prime example. Vendors such as Ungermann-Bass and SynOptics support AppleTalk twisted pair LANs and AppleTalk bridge devices to token rings and Ethernets in the same hub.

Internetworking

Let us say that you have two different departments, one using Ethernet, the other token ring. Your boss ambles in one day and asks you to link them together. You both know this is an oil-and-water situation. What do you do?

LAN hubs offer *bridging* cards to connect different LANs of the same type together and *router* cards if they are dissimilar as in the above example. Bridging cards can also link LANs to WANs as part of an enterprise network. Thus, the solution to our problem is to simply add a router card. Since the two networks converge at the hub, what could be more logical than to link them there? With built-in bridging and routing, we save the clutter of a separate box and its associated wiring.

First and second generation hubs are located on a floor and connect a LAN to a server and a bridge. The bridge carries traffic destined to other floors to a vertical backbone, often a high-performance token-ring or fiber (FDDI) LAN ring.

As shown in Figure 4.14, by connecting these floor-based hubs to a hub instead of a ring, we collapse the backbone into the hub itself. These current third-generation *collapsed backbone hubs* will reduce the call for fiber backbones. The backbone itself is a very-high-speed backplane, a circuit board, connecting all the LAN bridges together. This is often called the *LAN-in-a-Box* approach. The problem here is that each added port divides the fixed bandwidth that much more.

Some hubs use a computer bus architecture, which while faster, is still a shared medium. What is needed is a *switched,* not a *shared* medium. That is what the fourth generation of hubs will do: They divide a

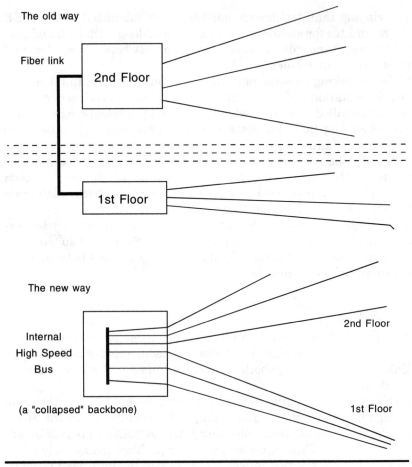

Figure 4.14 Fiber and collapsed backbones.

single LAN into segments, perhaps as small as a single user. Traffic between segments will be switched rapidly at full cable speed and without performance-robbing collisions.

From a practical viewpoint, wire your network as a star. You may change the hub and the NICs, but the wiring will stay. Buy Level 5 UTP wire that will support any foreseeable increase in speed.

Switch-based hubs

Most hubs to date are simply big buses. They are simply compact ways of sharing LAN media. Each lobe that is added divides this fixed asset one more way. While this may not make much difference on a small scale, that there is a point of diminishing returns is obvious.

Shared-media hubs will continue to be a part of LAN systems, but their scalability to higher speeds and performance is strictly limited. Conflict arises when we recognize that demands for LAN access and bandwidth will always grow. At some point we need a new approach.

That approach has proved to be *switch-based hubs* (Figure 4.15). In a switch-based hub, a short, temporary connection is established between sender and receiver(s) for as long as needed. The devices communicate; other connections occur independently. The key is that data transfer takes place at the LAN's full speed, say 10 Mbit/sec. Every new port *adds* 10 Mbit/sec of capacity to the hub, rather than *dividing* it away.

The only limitation is the backplane's speed. In some cases, they go

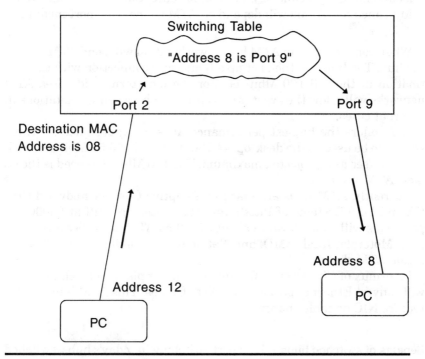

Figure 4.15 A switch-based hub.

as high as 1.7 Gbit/sec, enough to support 170 Ethernet ports. Backplanes can be linked to one another to form even larger switched hub networks.

Switching is done in several ways by different vendors. These are the basic approaches:

MAC layer switching assembles a switching table relating MAC addresses and ports. The switch uses the destination address to set up a virtual connection with the recipient's port. Using a switching backplane, frames are forwarded at full speed without buffering as would be needed in a bridge. Powerful RISC processors are used. Kalpana is one vendor who employs this approach.

Microsegmentation treats each port as a LAN segment. Segments are connected together through an internal multiport bridge. Routers may be used to connect LANs of different types, such as token ring and Ethernet. Artel, Cabletron, Chipcom, Synernetics, and 3Com Corp. use this method.

ATM parses frames into 53-byte cells. Five bytes are used for control. Extreme speed, minimal delay, and protocol transparency mark ATM as an emerging technology, not just for data, but for video and voice. Multimedia systems will depend on ATM as *the* transport medium.

When connected to an ATM hub, a workstation will send ATM cells to the hub. The hub will then set up a temporary connection with the destination at the full 100 Mbit/sec. For the long term, wide area ATM networks will allow the *exact same connection* between workstations in different cities.

ATM offers the highest performance. It is being designed for three speeds to be used to the desktop; 44.736, 100, and 155.52 Mbit/sec, with 195 Mbit/sec as a projected maximum. The 100 Mbit/sec speed is the de facto ATM standard.

Currently, ATM hubs are made by Adaptive Corp. of Redwood City, CA and Fore Systems of Pittsburgh, PA. Prices are stiff at $5000 per port. This will come down to about $1000 as ATM chips become available. Motorola, Intel, AMD, and National Semiconductor are all working on ATM chips.

Fibermux of Chatsworth, CA announced completion of a chipset that will convert Ethernet packets into ATM frames. This ATM hub will not require NIC or cable changes.

Benefits of switched hubs.   Like port switching in today's hubs, switched hubs have the inherent flexibility to accommodate the adds, moves, and changes so common in LAN management. It is even possible to create virtual workgroups, segmenting the network logically instead of physically.

Unlike physical hubs, every port in a switched hub can be used. The specific port is immaterial. Similarly, diagnostic equipment can be connected permanently to one port and dynamically switched from segment to segment as needed, remotely.

ATM technology.   One of the most exciting developments in LAN hubs is the prospect of using ATM in hubs and internetworks (Figure 4.16). The potential benefits include very high capacity, protocol transparency, microscopic delay, and seamless connections between LANs and WANs.

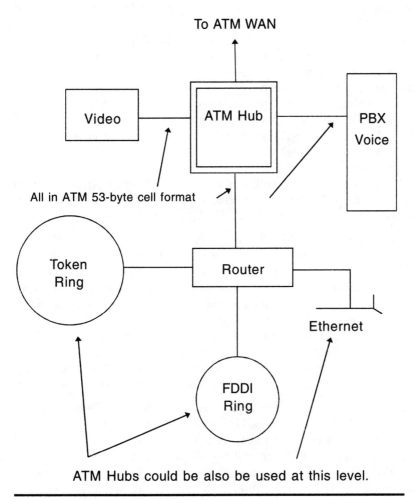

Figure 4.16   ATM hub application.

ATM, also called *cell relay,* is a cell switching technology using a 53-byte cell: 5 for control, and 48 for data. Its size supports data, video, and voice. The fixed length makes switching easier and faster.

The *asynchronous* part of the term comes from the fact that cells do not appear in the data stream at fixed intervals. They can appear or not as needed, making them untimed or asynchronous. Cells sent are guaranteed to be in the same order when received.

A virtual channel is set up from one end to the other. These can be permanent or switched. Any-to-any connectivity is allowed by use of ATM's standard identification feature. It can also carry any kind of protocol from TCP/IP to IPX.

Even so, ATM is a statistical rather than a deterministic switching scheme. Like Ethernet, there is no guarantee that congestion will not occur. Priority setting is included, but flow control has yet to be worked out by the ATM Forum.

Constant voice bandwidth is required for good quality, and minimal delay is essential for the same reason. Thus, voice applications will draw on a fixed number of cells. Data and video vary in their bandwidth needs, so they will draw cells dynamically as needed. ATM is one transport technology that suits all these types of information.

ATM bandwidth scales as needed, cell by cell. This is directly opposed to some circuits with nailed-up, i.e., dedicated, bandwidth: Up to 87 percent of such a line's capacity is wasted on a LAN because of the bursty nature of LAN traffic.

ATM has a predictable cell delivery period. There is little delay in ATM. Fiber circuits reduce the error rate to nearly zero. ATM is isochronous, meaning *self-timed,* like Ethernet or token ring.

ATM at the desktop.   ATM will arrive at your desk after 100 Mbit/sec Ethernet is in place. Desktops do not need either yet because desktop CPU buses cannot presently handle the speed. New 120-Mbit/sec PC bus architectures, such as local buses (VESA) and Intel's PCI Peripheral Connection Interface, are needed. Add a 486 or Pentium and the network capacity and CPU power are matched.

Some ATM experts think that ATM will appear first as a LAN-WAN interface using fiber backbones. Either way, the promise of a uniform LAN-WAN-voice-video technology with seamless connections and ubiquitous management is the closest to network nirvana we may ever get.

Migration strategy to ATM.   The first step for Ethernet users is to migrate to a switch-based hub at 10 Mbit/sec. The second is to go to 100 Mbit/sec Ethernet and ultimately to ATM. While NICs and hubs will change, the embedded wiring will remain the same.

To get equivalent speed in token ring, it is necessary to migrate to CDDI or FDDI. This may require a wiring change and eliminates the intermediate switching step available in Ethernet. The last change will be to ATM.

The need for 100 Mbit/sec systems will be some time coming. FDDI applications have been limited to graphics projects and other special applications such as hub backbones. Upcoming applications such as desktop video conferencing, client-server, and object-oriented programs will create more need. Some need exists now: engineering workstations and the nascent multimedia, which does not lend itself to a shared medium.

As yet, the management tools needed for these sophisticated services do not exist. It is not enough to have high speed; it has to be managed. Ultimately it is the quality of the management support built into an ATM switching hub that should determine which one is bought.

The long haul carriers are gearing up for ATM. *Switched Multimegabit Data Service* (SMDS) will run over ATM directly. Fewer parts will mean more consistent management from end to end. It is easy to conceive of the day when ATM is used for LANs and WANs, creating a truly seamless network where the LAN vs. WAN distinction loses most of its meaning.

Hub media support

Clearly, any kind of hub must support the kind of cabling you wish to use. Virtually all hubs support the two most common kinds of cabling, 10BaseT and coaxial cable for Ethernet and UTP for token ring. Shielded twisted pair and fiber are next in popularity, while support for the IBM Cabling System is the least common.

Network management

Hubs are the natural focal point for managing a star network. Since many of these hubs are remote to the network operations center, it is only logical to incorporate network management into them.

Network management is both a passive and active function. It monitors the hub for malfunctions in the network and reports them as alarms. It collects traffic statistics and reports those. In an active mode, it can turn ports on and off, switch them around as needed, and activate spare equipment such as routers and bridges.

The universal software protocol in hubs and LANs in general is the *Simple Network Management Protocol* (SNMP). Developed originally for use on the Internet, it has become the protocol of choice for LANs because of SNMP's rich features despite its relative simplicity. In one implementation, SNMP can capture up to 288 different parameters, which ought to be enough to satisfy the most analytical manager. With just one SNMP manager computer, a technician can examine an entire network: hubs, routers, bridges, and gateways. This concentrates control in one place and gives the operator a vital coordinated picture.

SNMP management is not a prerequisite if you have one hub down the hall. If you have several in a 20 story building or around the country, that is another matter.

Never build a network you cannot manage.

NICs

The NIC is the device that connects directly to the medium. It sits directly in the data path between the computer and the cable. As a result, it is a key determiner of LAN performance.

NICs (also called *network adapter cards*) have come to be considered a commodity by LAN component purchasers. Thus, the main competition has devolved to price. A closer look reveals that there are features which set cards apart from one another, and we are here to see what they are.

Here are the basics that a NIC must meet in order to be suitable in your application:

It must physically fit in your machine. One-half, three-quarter, and full size cards are offered.

The NIC must match you cabling system: UTP, STP, coaxial, or fiber. Some NICs have several connector types on one card for flexibility.

It must match your processor's bus speed. Most buses run at 8 MHz, and cards usually run at this speed. If the PC bus runs at 10 or 12 MHz, the card may not be able to keep up with the bus. Speed mismatch symptoms include a parity error message (meaning a memory error), the screen going dark, the system hanging up, or the keyboard locking up.

Software drivers must exist to support your chosen environment and NOS.

The bus width (8 or 16 bit), arbitration level, interrupt levels, Direct Memory Address (DMA) channels, and I/O addresses must be compatible as required.

Pricing, warranty, documentation and support must be acceptable.

Connectors: why are they a factor?

Most connectors are determined by the IEEE specifications. You do have the choice sometimes as to whether to use a DB-9 or an RJ-45, (Figure 4.17) as in token rings.

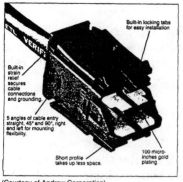

(Courtesy of Andrew Corporation)

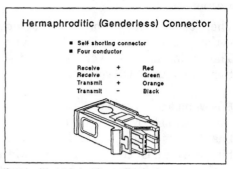

(Courtesy of Hewlett-Packard Company)

Type N Connector
for 10 Base 5

BNC T-Connector
for 10 Base 2

15-pin D BNC T-Connector
for 10 Base 2

(Courtesy of Pilgrim Electronics, Inc.)

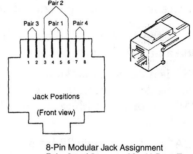

Jack Positions

(Front view)

8-Pin Modular Jack Assignment
Pairs 2 and 3 are used for 10 Base T

(Courtesy of Digital Equipment Corporation)

Figure 4.17 Connector examples.

DB series connectors are more rugged and more expensive, too. They require no special tools to make. When connections must be made and unmade often, DB-9s are less desirable than modular connectors (RJ-11 or RJ-45) . However, RJs require a crimping tool to make and are less rugged. They also increase NEXT. Coaxial media use BNC connectors for ThinNet and type N connectors for ThickNet. Both require skill to install but are quite rugged and easy to connect and disconnect.

Whatever the choice, be sure you have the support tools to maintain them: crimpers, piece parts, and hand tools. Be sure not to mix RJ-45s for stranded and solid wire.

Performance

There are two key factors which determine NIC performance. The first is the bus: how wide it is and the I/O method by which access is gained. The second is the driver software that controls the NIC and its relationship to the NOS software.

Bus width and I/O architecture.   Clearly, the number of data bits that can be transferred at a time is a performance determiner. The PC/XT bus is 8 bits wide; those in PC/ATs are 16. The 386 and 486 series is 32 bits in width. Of course, the more width, the faster the data transfer.

Most cards support 8 or 16 bits; some do both, making them ideal for AT/XT applications. Vendors such as Madge Networks, Avatar, and DCA support 32 bits.

Bus architecture plays a performance role. Three, ISA, EISA, and MCA, are in use (also see Figure 4.18):

ISA is the IBM 8- or 16-bit architecture used by XT and AT-class 8088 and 80286 machines.

EISA is a 32-bit expansion bus design developed by a group of IBM-compatible PC manufacturers. EISA was created to compete with IBM's proprietary Micro Channel Bus. It is downward compatible with ISA.

MCA is a proprietary 32-bit architecture introduced by IBM in 1987 for its high end PS/2 machines. It is incompatible with ISA/EISA but is comparable in performance to EISA.

In general, benchmark testing of EISA and MCA has found that the cards perform similarly in terms of speed. Some vendors price their cards accordingly. Other vendors believe that EISA runs faster than MCA, especially on busy machines such as servers. A vendor may therefore charge more for an EISA card than a MCA card. Still other vendors charge the same for ISA, EISA, or MCA. Perhaps your own experience should be your guide, but if you are in doubt, *test*!

PC transfer methods

Exchanging information between the card and PC is a strong performance factor. There are four basic methods (Figure 4.19), listed from slowest to fastest:

Mapped or *programmed I/O* uses the PC's I/O registers. This takes more clock cycles than other methods, so it is the slowest.

Shared memory moves data by using the PC's memory bus. Because the PC's CPU must still supervise the exchange, CPU clock cycles are used.

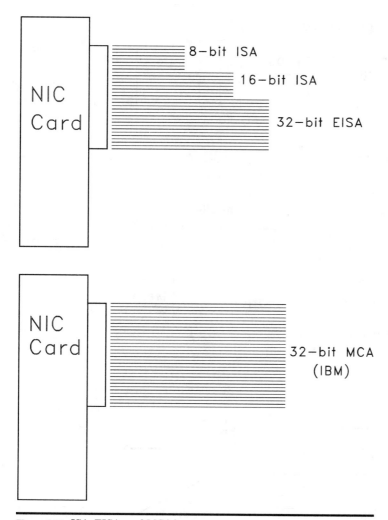

8-bit ISA

16-bit ISA

32-bit EISA

32-bit MCA
(IBM)

Figure 4.18 ISA, EISA, and MCA buses.

Direct memory access (DMA) is usually used with shared memory. DMA uses the PC's optimized DMA logic instead of the CPU for faster transfer. DMA is a two-step process: Step one moves data between system memory and the DMA controller. Step two transfers it between the DMA controller and the NIC.

Bus mastering transfers data in one step from system memory to NIC without using the CPU or *its* DMA controller. Being one step, it takes half the number of clock cycles of shared memory DMA, and so it is up to twice as fast. When used in *burst mode*, the card holds the bus for a longer time so it can transfer more data. Data can also be

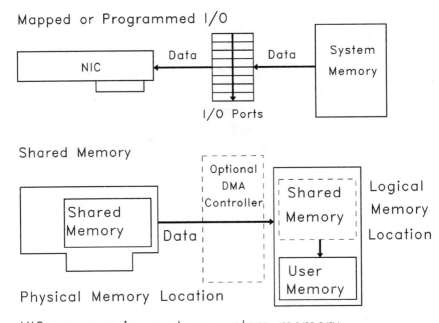

Mapped or Programmed I/O

Shared Memory

NIC memory is used as system memory.

Bus Mastering

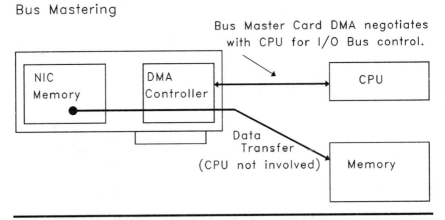

Figure 4.19 PC transfer methods.

compressed in burst mode. Small frames dilute the benefit of bus mastering, which excels in large ones.

Apple SE, SE/30, and Macintosh II NuBus all support NIC cards.

Programmed I/O and shared memory are used primarily by 8-bit cards at the low end of the performance range or by external adapters connected to the parallel port. Higher performance is gained by purchasing cards with DMA or bus master cards. Top performance is gained by using a bus master card with burst mode.

NIC chips

All NICs are built around a chip set from just a few vendors. Most token-ring cards use the Texas Instruments chip set, but Olicom and IBM (through National Semiconductor) and Standard Microsystems offer competing sets. Texas Instruments' chip sets support up to 2 Mbytes of RAM, but most other cards have 128 kbytes and are not upgradable. If they are, the upgrade is to 512 kbytes or 1 or 2 Mbytes. Usually, though, 128 kbytes is enough. RAM can increase speed on busy machines such as servers.

Ethernet chip sets are made by Intel, National Semiconductor, and others. The fact that all NIC vendors use the same few chip sets encourages commodity-style thinking. Recent consolidation of three-chip sets into two chips has made the Ethernet NIC market even more competitive than in the past.

NIC driver software

The best example of the importance of software drivers was when 16-Mbit/sec systems hit the market. Early throughput on these rings was only marginally better than 4-Mbit/sec rings and worse than 10-Mbit/sec Ethernets. What was wrong?

Vendors quickly discovered that the driver software had not been optimized for the higher speed. New drivers bumped throughputs as high as an astonishing 14.9 Mbit/sec.

The other problem was that file server performance on token rings suffered because of the inability of token-ring NICs to handle small "runt" (64-byte) data frames efficiently. Since servers get more messages than other nodes, they have to send more 64-byte acknowledgement frames. The NIC's ability to handle small frames is vital.

There are two solutions. One is to improve the drivers' data transfer between NIC and PC. The other is to process network layer protocols on the card itself. Performance improvements are *software* driven.

Throughputs of short token-ring frames have increased from the 4000 packets/sec range to as high as 30,000 packets/sec, with an average of 13,000. It's fair to say that this problem has been solved.

Typical token-ring and Ethernet drivers are:

Open Data-Link Interface (ODI) for Novell NetWare file servers

Network Device Interface Specification (NDIS) for IBM LAN manager servers and Microsoft applications

Drivers should be formally qualified to work in your system.

Management

Some NIC cards are equipped with SNMP agents making them remotely manageable. Some also have LEDs on the rear panel to give a quick idea of what is going on. Cabletron's Ethernet NICs, for example, have transmit, receive, collision present, power, and link LEDs on the rear panel.

Networking functions such as SNMP network management, and more importantly, protocol processing such as Novell's IPX and IBM's NetBIOS (see Chapter 10) are moving off the PC and onto the NIC card. This saves user system memory.

Network management lets managers collect performance and configuration data from the NIC using SNMP. However, the IEEE plans to adopt the IBM-3Com Corp. Heterogeneous LAN Management protocol, so some vendors are resisting implementing SNMP. Some vendors decry the use of the adapter for management as taking away from the adapter's processing time for user data.

Diskless workstations

Some NICS have an empty boot Programmable Read-Only Memory (PROM) socket to be used with diskless workstations. The advantages of diskless workstations are:

Save money.

Enhance security.

Prevent removing data.

Prevent introducing unapproved software into the system, perhaps including a virus. (This is the prime way viruses get into a system.)

Allow applications to be controlled by the manager.

Make enforcement of company standards possible.

Simplify support and maintenance as all configurations are the same and cannot be altered by users.

Some Erasable PROMs (EPROMs) are set up for remote booting. In remote booting, the machine attaches itself to the server during the boot process and draws a boot-disk image from the server to boot itself. In this way, upgrades and reconfigurations can be made throughout the network simply by changing the boot image file in the server.

Ethernet NICs

Ethernet NICs are available with a mix of all the above features. Some are equipped with an Intel 82586 Ethernet coprocessor or equivalent.

The presence or absence of a coprocessor is not necessarily a performance determiner. Inefficiently written firmware will create extra overhead and defeat the coprocessor's speed benefit. National Semiconductor's AT/LANTIC chip seems to be the dominant silicon. More 16-bit cards are being sold as the 8-bit market fades.

An AUI connector makes the NIC medium independent. Many Ethernet NICs come with internal baluns and RJ-45 connectors for 10BaseT and/or BNC connectors for direct attachment.

Ethernet 16-bit coaxial cards list from $100–200; 10BaseT versions vary from $50–200. Prices are negotiable and often discounted in quantities as small as 10 cards. Resellers are often heavy discounters as well, and there is even a used equipment market. (Think of them as well burned-in.)

Token-ring NICs

Some token-ring cards include an onboard media filter for Type 3 cable. It is an advantage not to have to buy a separate device for $100 or so to hang off the back of a PC. There is enough back there already.

Few buyers purchase 4-Mbit/sec cards today. Most buy 4- and 16-Mbit/sec cards that support both. Token-ring NIC cards carry IBM's TROPIC chip, made by IBM but jointly marketed with National Semiconductor. Other cards carry Texas Instruments' Super Eagle TMS380 or Standard Microsystems' or Olicom's chip sets.

In 1993, IBM announced its LANStreamer chip set that outperforms its own TROPIC chip. As yet, LANStreamer chips alone are not available for sale, but this is reportedly under consideration.

IBM is by far the dominant card and chip supplier. In an effort to gain market share compared to Ethernet's success, IBM offered its TROPIC chips for sale through National Semiconductor. Coming from IBM, they were priced higher than competing chip sets. NIC vendors bought them anyway as a way to enter the token-ring market.

Then IBM reduced its list price for NICs to make them more consistent with the actual street price. At the same time, IBM increased its TROPIC chip price. The effect has been to dampen the token-ring market after apparent initial efforts to stimulate it. For example, a third-generation Ethernet *NIC* costs as much as a TROPIC *chip*. In volume, the next largest token-ring vendor after IBM ships about a *tenth* that of a large Ethernet NIC vendor.

Token-ring cards are also sold well below retail, varying between $400 for small quantities down to $300 in volume. Prices will go lower as the new IEEE standard method for 16 Mbit/sec UTP comes out, creating demand and stiffer competition. As a result, prices will fall about linearly from $400 in 1994 to $200 in 1997.

Most people go into NIC sticker shock when they see that token-ring NICs cost twice those of Ethernet NICs. Token-ring cards *are* more expensive because they are more complex, mainly due to the more complex token-ring access protocol. This is discussed in Chapter 7.

Buyers have purchased IBM cards because they are thereby certain that all token-ring functions are included and compatible. Continued interoperability is being maintained by testing such as that at the University of New Hampshire's Interoperability Laboratory in Durham, NH, and at vendors such as SynOptics' Token Ring Interoperability Laboratory in Santa Clara, CA. Independent consulting firms such as LanQuest Group, also in Santa Clara, and InterLAB, in Sea Girt, NJ, also perform testing. The difficulty is that there are so many combinations that a conformance test suite is all but impossible.

There is also a question as to what compatibility means. To some it means communication with IBM's LAN Network Manager and IBM-compatible bridges. Standard Microsystems licensed IBM's LAN Support Program drivers, which include logical link control and NetBIOS protocols. Since these are used in the TROPIC chip, compatibility is *enhanced* but not *assured,* by definition, in Standard's NIC.

IBM compatibility has been used by vendors to differentiate their products from others. Yet there are few reports of significant difficulties when using, say, the Texas Instrument chip set.

Higher token-ring speeds?

IBM said that they planned to introduce 100 Mbit/sec token ring in 1994. It is known that 4 Mbit/sec token ring will support only 2 concurrent multimedia sessions and 16 Mbit/sec will support about 10.

The higher speed is seen as a way to further deflate FDDI, compete with 100 Mbit/sec Ethernet, and perpetuate token-ring technology. Clearly, IBM expects 100 Mbit/sec token ring to support its drive toward multimedia and other large-scale applications.

ATM is the ideal multimedia solution and is making rapid progress toward being marketed. In the meantime, a 32-Mbit/sec token ring would be a logical step in token-ring development as a high-speed backbone. Stay tuned!

FDDI NICs

Fiber NICs are available, but the demand is low. The CDDI (now renamed ANSI X3T9.5 TP-PMD) is anticipated to obviate the need for expensive fiber. However, the TP-PMD standard is not yet released, so potential users are waiting. For those who cannot wait, they can have an FDDI NIC for $995 to $40,000, depending on whether the NICs will be used in PCs, powerful workstations, or hosts. FDDI NIC prices have been falling steadily, but slowly.

Multiprotocol NICs

NICs that support Ethernet *and* token ring *on the same card* are becoming available. They give users a lot of flexibility, but at a price. If the multiprotocol NIC costs as much as a token-ring card at $600 and you use an Ethernet whose NICs cost under $200, you pay a $400 premium for the option of using token ring later. It would make more sense to buy the card with the intent of using it on token ring if the comparative price is about the same and have the Ethernet as a bonus.

Two chip vendors are making multiprotocol chip sets. Chips and Technologies, Inc. of San Jose, CA, introduced its ChipsLAN set in 1991. It supports both protocols on a variety of cabling and transmits up to 20,000 64-byte frames on token ring and 15,000 frames/sec on Ethernet. Using an Intel 82C581, it has an 8086-compatible CPU, creating an open programming environment given enough RAM.

Texas Instruments' multiprotocol chip is the TMS380C26, better known as the Super Eagle. Virtually every vendor uses Texas Instruments' Eagle chip set now. Super Eagle will also be IBM compatible and approved.

Chips and Technologies, however, rebuilt their token-ring controller, which may affect its compatibility with the IBM chipset. Both Texas Instruments and Chips and Technologies are shipping chip sets that are now being designed into products.

Server vendors are particular prospects for such chips. Compaq is reported to be interested and Tricord of Plymouth, MN, is reportedly shipping them. On the other hand, NetFrame Systems of Milpitas, CA, says that their research revealed few users running both protocols and are therefore unwilling to pay for dual-protocol support.

Onboard NICs

Some vendors are selling their machines in network-ready form, with NIC card and drivers preinstalled. They are cost competitive, save you the time and difficulty of installing them, and are guaranteed to be system compatible.

The latest wrinkle is building an Ethernet chip set directly onto the motherboard and connected directly to the bus. Ethernet chip sets are now only two chips, and their prices are falling to the point where the added cost, now about $100, will fall to about $20. This is a small price to pay for a network-ready machine that does not use a card slot. Yet the market is so cutthroat that even $20 may mean the difference between a sale and no sale. But it will happen.

Apple Macintoshes, of course, are network-ready since they include LocalTalk. High-end engineering workstations such as those from SUN Microsystems, Inc. have always included Ethernet capability, so onboard NICs are not setting any real precedent.

Chips and Technology is now suggesting its ChipsLAN on PC motherboards. Using the system bus to communicate directly with the PC's processor rather than the I/O bus could produce a four-fold performance increase.

LANs Make Strange Bedfellows

Over time, it becomes harder to see where the dividing lines are. DEC, an original developer of Ethernet, is adding IEEE 802.5 token ring to its Pathworks NOS. All DECnet Phase IV products and applications will interoperate more easily in token-ring LANs.

DEC is also adding a feature called source-routing bridge support. Source routing is IBM's (and the dominant) method for addressing, receiving, and forwarding packets in token-ring networks. Source routing will allow users to cross from one ring to another without adding a hardware bridge.

The shift is seen as an effort by DEC to become known as a LAN rather than an Ethernet vendor. The move is fortified by DEC's OPEN-DECconnect, which was an Ethernet wiring scheme and is now a "protocol-independent" wiring system.

On the other side, IBM began to offer credit-card sized network adapters for Ethernet in 1993. This was their first acknowledgement of Ethernet. In the words of Stephen C. Miller of the *New York Times,* "It's a little like SONY finally offering VHS rather than Beta." The only other acknowledgement of Ethernet had been in IBM's multiprotocol intelligent hub. Developed with Chipcom, it supports token ring ... and, oh yes, Ethernet. This trend *has* accelerated rapidly at IBM, who now aggressively markets Ethernet NICs as well as token-ring products.

Comparing Ethernet and Token Ring

Which has the bigger market share? Ethernet, by far. Based on NIC shipments, Ethernet has 67 percent, and token ring has 23 percent. For years, those needing a simple, inexpensive network went the Ethernet route.

The typical Ethernet user was non-IBM. They had minicomputers, high-powered workstations, and PCs. UNIX, TCP/IP, DECnet, Novell

IPX, Xerox Network Services, and AppleTalk reigned on Ethernets running scientific, engineering, and manufacturing applications. Most were distributed and peer-to-peer. In this environment, a technical user ran the show.

Token ring was just the opposite. MIS was IBM driven, with IBM mainframes, PCs, and midrange AS/400s. SNA was the dominant protocol, with more SNA than LAN connections. IBM LAN software, Net-BIOS, and LAN Server was everywhere. Even here, though, Novell NetWare had a presence.

In the classically hierarchical mainframe environment, transaction-oriented applications prevailed. Users were typically not technical, and applications were business oriented. AppleTalk was a nonword.

The need for both systems in the corporate world has become apparent. *Bridges* and *routers* link the two today.

Ethernet's 10BaseT is the dominant wiring scheme. Inexpensive and high in terms of performance, it and the NICs are low in cost. The problem from business' view is that Ethernet has no redundancy, has little self-management and self-healing, and does not handle heavy loads gracefully.

Contrariwise, as token-ring adapter cards do more and more processing, token-ring NIC vendors will be able to address Ethernet turf: the UNIX and Macintosh workstation users. Vendors are looking beyond their traditional DOS and OS/2 customers.

IBM is driving this by tying token-ring support to its RS/6000 workstation and pressing its competitors to do likewise. It has worked: Sun announced token-ring support for its Sparc workstations. Madge and Hewlett-Packard teamed to resell an adapter for Hewlett-Packard's UNIX workstation. Token-ring vendor Proteon released a UNIX driver.

In 1992, 90 percent of token-ring NICs shipped handled both 4 and 16 Mbit/sec. The 4-Mbit/sec users have a choice: go to Ethernet or 16 Mbit/sec. Most have stayed with token ring.

IBM's former requirement to run STP in order to use 16-Mbit/sec token ring was a major expense. When IBM approved UTP at 16-Mbit/sec, token ring began to fit the economic picture. The 16-Mbit/sec UTP IEEE standards are being finalized and may well be completed by now.

When jitter made 16-Mbit/sec token ring unusable for corporate users, that problem was solved by at least three different means: chip set changes, phase-locked loops, and ringing tank circuits.

The speed advantage of 16-Mbit/sec token ring over 10-Mbit/sec Ethernet was not that great to begin with. It was more apparent than real as network drivers at first bottled up performance. We have seen that problem resolved, too.

Today, then we have about equal wiring schemes. Token ring has cleaned up its technical act. Only cost seems to be holding token ring back.

While we have discussed all the important and some of the fine points, let us leave this chapter with one final suggestion. Most NIC vendors will loan prospective buyers a few cards for evaluation. *Do it.* All the consultants and books in the world cannot (or will not) predict everything that will happen.

5

LAN Servers

Serving Our Needs

We saw in Chapter 3 how applications and processing power can be concentrated in a server as a way of saving dollars and improving productivity. Along with the business need, the economics of a server can be compelling. Contrariwise, if your application is quite small, consider a serverless LANtastic or Personal NetWare system. These peer-to-peer LANs require no server at all—each PC can act as a server.

This chapter approaches servers from two perspectives. One is from the physical view in terms of what hardware will be used. The second is functional and views the server as a box providing a particular kind of service, e.g., file service and database service. We will look at these special-purpose servers and discuss their benefits and drawbacks.

A list of features to be checked when acquiring a server appears in this chapter. Further, a number of vendors who offer special-purpose server products and network appliances are listed at the end of the chapter.

The list below summarizes the hardware choices available in selecting a server:

No server	Use a peer-to-peer LAN, e.g., LANtastic, LAN-in-a-Can, or Personal NetWare instead.
A 286-class PC	For small, noncritical applications.
A 386-, 486-, or Pentium-class PC	Reasonable performance Not optimized as a server No redundancy Little expandability
A 386-486-Pentium chassis designed to be a server	Redundancy Expandibility Preconfigured Optimized for a particular NOS

A superserver	High powered Designed for hard use Redundant and expandable Large storage capacity
A minicomputer	Good performance High disk capacity; processing power Lacks redundancy of superservers Poor bang for the buck
A midrange machine	Can act as a server on a LAN, e.g., a AS/400
A mainframe	As part of an enterprise computing system

Recall that servers can be *dedicated,* i.e., servers only, or *nondedicated,* i.e., shared as workstations. Nondedicated servers are out of favor in the LAN community. Servers tend to be specialized platforms; workstation activities can reduce LAN performance.

This is not the only distinction we must draw based on the purpose to which the machine will be put. We must also decide if we can justify a special-purpose server to streamline our work. For instance, a file server may, at higher usage levels, begin to be used much like a database server. At this point, a specialized database server might make sense.

At the root, a server can be as simple as a 286 with a NIC, provided it has enough RAM, disk storage, DC power, and expansion slots. There is nothing wrong with a 286 if your performance, security, and reliability needs are modest.

The economics of PCs have a strong influence on server selection. Today, 386 machines cost not much more than 286s and 486-33 MHz machines are a few hundred dollars more than a 386. Clearly, for a very few dollars more, you can own a high performance server, if not a superserver. Competition is fierce and it is your market.

Typical server prices today run in the $3000–6000 range (depending on how much disk space you want) for a server capable of supporting 2–20 users with spreadsheets and word processing files. Database servers with gigabyte storage capacity and a backup facility run from $8000–17,000.

Many vendors offer preconfigured servers, with Compaq, Tricord, and NetFrame being among the best known. Dell sells servers by mail. These conveniently preconfigured machines are attractively priced, and you are purchasing a machine designed for the purpose from scratch. For example, machines from Compaq and Dell can come with NetWare preinstalled and optimized for that particular system. This packaged approach avoids incompatibilities and vendor finger-pointing.

There is nothing wrong with using a mini as a server, but it is a rather expensive solution. If you already have one, or need a very large disk system, then it may be justifiable. As a rule, a superserver will cost about the same and meet the need better. IBM even speaks of *mainframes* as servers!

While all computing platforms are potential servers and any one may be the right one in a given application, we will limit our discussion to hardware platforms based on the Intel series 286, 386, 486, and Pentium microprocessors.

Server Performance

One of the first things you must determine is your required response time, i.e., the time it takes a server to respond to a request (Figure 5.1). This is a function of the number of requests, type of requests, and number of people (workstations) asking. A satisfactory response depends on the nature of the activity of the clients. A customer service system

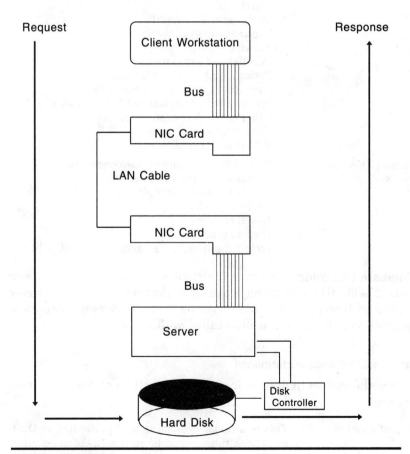

Figure 5.1 The LAN data path.

needs rapid response, while the response time for an inventory system is not quite as critical.

Performance is set by what the server is expected to do. File service makes little demand on a server's CPU, while database applications and subprograms that route packets on the fly are CPU hogs.

The following is a list of features acquiring a server. Other than distinguishing between mandatory versus optional features, the items are not listed in order of priority.

Mandatory items to check	Absolute hard-disk capacity
	Bus architecture
	BIOS version
	Processors supported
	RAM size supported
	RAM cache
	Floppy drives
	Hard-disk sizes offered
	Warranty
	Drive array availability
	Tape backup availability
	Expansion slots
	Parallel and serial ports
	Power supply capacity in watts
	Operating system(s) supported
	Preinstalled and optimized NetWare availability
	Other network operating systems
	First-year service terms
	FCC class B certification
Optional items and features	Flash PROM memory (downloads new BIOS versions via the network)
	Enclosure: tower or desk
	Cache controller
	Novell certification
	Display type
	Included software, e.g., diagnostics and utilities

Database and communications functions work better at faster clock speeds, 25–33 MHz, and perhaps call for multiprocessors. Other server functions include print, fax and server-based hubs. Servers with more than one server function are often called *multiservers*.

Factors that influence performance

Here are the factors in descending order that influence file server performance:

Disk performance	This is a major determinant of performance. Disk-head seek time should be in the 12–14 msec range

and can go as low as 9 msec. This means that the disk read-write head takes 9 msec to find the desired data on the disk in a fast disk.

Bus size   Data is sent 16 bits at once on a 286 or 386SX or in 32 bits on a 386, 486, or Pentium machine.

Processor power   Today, even the smallest server will be a 386 machine or at least a 386SX. Clock speeds are from 20 MHz upward.

Disk caching. This term relates to holding related records of disk information in RAM, since many requests often come from the same area of disk. Factors that influence performance include the size of the cache as well as the speed of the memory used to form the cache. Caching can be used for accessing the directory instead of addressing the disk directly and is used by some NOSs to hold applications programs. A default cache size is typically set and then is fine tuned for best performance. Modern NOSs, e.g., NetWare, manage disk caching internally and very efficiently.

Fast hard disk access is essential for attaining good server performance. A fast disk really excels at loading applications from the server. To do so, the drive should have a low seek time and should use a *small-computer system interface* (SCSI) drive rather than a drive based on *integrated drive electronics* (IDE).

The bus-transfer method is also a performance factor. IDE controllers have their electronics on the drive and motherboard. They will have slower performance than SCSI-2 drives. SCSI-2 type controllers have most of their controller circuitry in the drive, leaving the SCSI interface free to communicate with other peripherals. For that reason, SCSI-based drives are faster than ESDI, ST-506, or ST-412 interfaces. A 32-bit system, SCSI is recommended for all server applications. Alternatively, an optional or built-in disk coprocessor for the disk controller will speed disk access.

ST-506 controllers support two drives, but only one can be accessed at a time. SCSI lets the controller read (or write) a sector on one drive, disconnect, and then talk with another device on the SCSI bus. Then the controller goes back to the drive to see if it is done. Thus, one SCSI controller can have several drives performing I/O at once.

Disk interleave factor. This factor is calculated as shown in Figure 5.2, and it also affects performance. Disks are divided into tracks, and tracks are divided into sectors of 512 bytes each. Disk controllers are rated in terms of their ability to read consecutive sectors. If the controller can read every other sector, then it has an interleave factor of 2:1. If

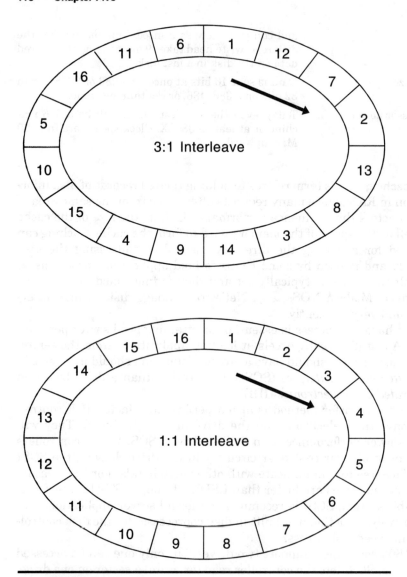

Figure 5.2 Disk Interleaving.

it can read sectors one after the other, it has an interleave factor of 1:1. Factors higher than 2:1 are not acceptable.

The network operating system (NOS). The NOS has a major effect on performance. It is important that the NOS mesh well with the operating system and that applications run properly and well under the NOS. Slow performance or the inability to use application features are the penalty for a bad match. Often the NOS comes with a set of defaults, which if fine-tuned, can substantially enhance LAN performance.

It is important to buy the right NOS for the job. One that is too large will take up more processing time and resources then its unused features justify. A too-small NOS will be overloaded with all the demands placed on it.

The network interface card (NIC). A NIC installed in the server, and thus in the serial data path, can be a bottleneck. The access method, say, Ethernet or token-ring, will influence its performance. If the NIC has an onboard coprocessor, speed can be enhanced. The bus-transfer method, ISA, EISA, or MCA, is a consideration, not unlike a disk controller. NIC driver software, to repeat, is a big performance determiner. Buffering capacity and particularly the buffer's design influence server performance.

Server capacity

Server RAM and hard-disk capacity are important. The size of server-installable RAM can range from 1–64 Mbytes, with some machines going to 96 Mbytes; 8–16 Mbytes is typical.

You can calculate the amount of memory required by NetWare 3.1X RAM multiplying the number of megabytes in the hard drive by 0.023 and then dividing by the block size, which is usually four. Then add 4 Mbytes for the NOS' overhead. That means that a 600-Mbyte hard drive needs about (7.45) 8 Mbytes of RAM. UNIX and Macintosh volumes have different factors. Heavy database server usage may need 32 Mbytes or even more.

Are there any *memory wait states?* File server memory should be fast. The CPU should not have to wait for memory access. To achieve zero wait states, access times should be 80 nsec or better; some RAM chips are as fast as 60 nsec.

RAM cache ranges from 64–256 kbytes, with an average of approximately 128 kbytes. RAM cache controllers are not needed unless the bus is too slow, since many NOSs use system memory as a cache area. If the bus is indeed too slow, a disk-side controller may help.

Hard disk drives range from 120 Mbytes to 4.08 Gbytes (in the Compaq Systempro) and higher with external storage systems. Usual sizes are 500 Mbytes to 1.2 Gbytes. The drive size is defined by the size of the applications and files and the number of expected users. Add 15 percent to the total to avoid possible file fragmentation problems, which will degrade response time.

Power supply capacity is an aspect that is often overlooked. A 200-W power supply is the minimum, with 450 W being more than sufficient for most uses. It is better to use more peripheral power connectors than to use Y-type power splitter cables. These cables have a small but measurable electrical loss, and every added connection is just one more thing that can go wrong.

Expansion is a major consideration when designing a server. It is vital that you do not lock yourself into a limited platform which cannot be expanded. (Remember that networks always grow.) *Scalability,* being able to size the system for your needs both now and later, is an important part of expansion. Servers should have a minimum of four to six 32-bit expansion slots. Since NetWare, VINES, or Microsoft's LAN Manager can support four NICs at once, it is not hard to fill up the slots. Some server platforms have as many as eight.

The same principle applies if the server is to be used as a print or communications server. It must be able to support a sufficient number of parallel or serial ports, respectively.

Bus size and type

In the last chapter, we discussed the merits of ISA, EISA, and MCA bus structures relative to NICs. Here we discuss them in relation to servers.

ISA	This is limited to 16 data bits and cannot usually transfer data fast enough. Its support for external bus mastering is poor, and it has only 24 bits of addressing (16 Mbytes).
EISA	This 32-bit bus is a good choice for low- to medium-powered servers. However, high-speed networks based on fiber and ATM will outrun it. A new, faster EISA version is being considered by the EISA consortium.
MCA	This is a 32-bit data and address bus with multiple mastering.
Proprietary buses	These are used in high-end superservers, e.g., Compaq's TriFlex with a 128-bit memory bus, 32-64 bit processor bus, and an EISA bus.

Serious servers need a 32-bit structure. Some consultants see the bus rather than the disk subsystem as the major bottleneck in a server. They reason that a fully configured server with four IEEE 802.3 NICs send the server about 30 Mbytes/sec of information. So the server's bus has to hustle! Splitting the network into four is a common way to avoid LAN cable saturation, especially when fast PCs are used. A few servers have upgradable bus structures (e.g., NetFrame), but most do not.

Processing Power

NOSs and NetWare in particular do not burden the CPU very much. Server-based applications such as *NetWare Loadable Modules* (NLMs), Value-Added Processes (VAPs), databases, network management, e-mail, UPS monitors, application meters, and routing all increase the importance of CPU power.

Most systems run quite well on 386 machines, but a 486 these days is almost the same price. Economics favor a 486 even though it may be more than you need—now.

Some platforms offer a CPU architecture that can be upgraded, such as IBM, ALR, and Zeos. Other companies offer various incremental processor-enhancing features.

Processor options

Conventional Intel processors power many servers. Most are 386-class starting with i386 SX 20 MHz chips up to i486 SX 33MHz chips. They are outperformed by the 486 DX 50 MHz and DX2 66 MHz CPUs. The next leap is into the Pentium series.

Pentium. About 80 percent of LAN applications conduct basic file and print services. These do not generally call for extremely powerful processors. Pentium-based PCs can run dedicated applications such as databases, client-server functions, and multimedia. They can use a high-performance operating system such as Windows NT or OS/2, and cable speeds of 100 Mbytes/sec are doable on Pentium-based machines.

Pentium's error-correcting RAM and CPU checking facilities will be useful in server applications. Yet Pentium's architectural improvements such as improved floating-point operation favor desktop, not LAN server applications.

Novell's focus has been to reduce processor requirements with new releases. NetWare 4.0 is the latest incarnation of that strategy. As such, a 386 33 MHz or a 486-33 MHz is a perfectly satisfactory server for up to 250 users or even more. Performance improvements will be seen on servers running heavy background NLMs for virus scanning or performance monitoring. Curiously, little or no benefit will be seen by 20–30 user LANs; the current processors are more than adequate for them.

Testing by IBM showed that servers running Pentium and NetWare on token ring could add another two rings or segments to a segmented server before performance began to suffer.

It does not make sense to upgrade simply because the power is there. Many other factors such as bus speed, disk performance, LAN cable speed, and the NOS influence LAN efficiency. In many cases, the main sources of delay are not found in the server itself. This is one reason why performance increases over 486-class machines are noticeable but not dramatic.

Some servers are upgradable to Pentium. While this is superficially appealing, simply swapping the chip is only partly effective. The server's I/O subsystem must also be upgraded to keep up with the CPU's faster speed to gain maximum benefit. The prices of upgrading can sometimes amount to half the cost of an entire server.

One strategy buyers are pursuing is buying one Pentium server and testing applications on it. Then they decide whether a further investment is warranted.

As always, price is a factor. Single-processor Pentium servers with 16 Mbytes of RAM and a 500-Mbyte hard disk cost $6000–8000. For about the same money, one can purchase a 486 DX2-66 OverDrive-based server with 16–32 Mbyte of RAM and a gigabyte of disk storage.

Users are considering Pentium machines as workstations, but the cost is presently a little high. Such a purchase would have to be justified in light of a specific application.

Reduced Instruction Set Computers (RISC).   A few vendors, notably Hewlett-Packard, DEC, and Sun offer RISC-based machines, mainly for client-server, scientific, and computer-aided design (CAD) applications. All are Unix-based, and all support multiprocessing. Broadly, RISC-based systems offer 2–3 times the performance of a 386 or 486 Intel processor.

Multiprocessing

Multiprocessing allows two or more CPUs to share the processing burden. The manner in which they divide the tasks is important. Multiprocessing is implemented in two forms:

Symmetrical	Here, multiprocessing shares the processing load evenly, regardless of function.
Asymmetrical	Here, multiprocessing dedicates processors by function, for instance, file service on one and print on another.

Symmetrical systems.   Key properties of these systems:

They are harder to find. Few operating systems or applications presently support it. For example, DOS and NetWare 3.1X do not support symmetrical processing, while Unix, OS/2, Windows NT, NetWare 4.X, and VINES do.

They are harder to design. As a result, they cost more.

They scale well. As more power is needed, processors can be added to suit the need.

They are generally better suited for databases and transaction-driven applications than for file service.

They may not be necessary if the CPU is a high-end 486 or Pentium.

Pentium CPU's promote symmetrical processing with features like *cache snooping,* which helps correlate data flow between CPU caches.

They may be a good downsizing option from a mainframe.

NOSs running under SCO Unix or AT&T's UNIX System V perform genuine symmetrical processing.

Asymmetrical systems.   Properties of these systems include:

They dedicate a processor to an application.

They are supported by many applications, such as NetWare 3.1X.

They are less effective in heavy I/O applications.

Additional processors do not add performance equal to the first CPU. Each additional CPU adds progressively less performance in a classic model of diminishing returns.

If a dedicated processor fails, only applications running on it are affected.

OS/2 can place LAN Manager on one CPU and delegate print and communications to another. This is asymmetric multiprocessing.

NetWare 3.1X is a one-CPU system, but NLMs can be distributed to run on several CPUs asymmetrically. Distributing NetWare NLMs helps NetWare performance and adds tolerance in case of a fault. Novell has said that its concept of multiprocessing is utilizing unused desktop machine cycles to provide NetWare services.

For either form of multiprocessing, there is a cost increment inherent in duplicating processors.

Superservers

Machines designed from the ground up to be servers are called *super-servers.* They are best applied in cases where the server goes beyond basic file service to processing applications. Some people call these latter machines *application servers.*

There are differences between a high-end PC used as a server and a superserver. Superservers are characterized by their capacity for multiprocessing and by a high-performance (usually proprietary) bus structure that avoids bus bottlenecking. Superservers have built-in redundancy that PCs generally lack. Superserver features include:

Capacity	At least 16 Mbytes of RAM, 2 Gbytes of storage, plus redundancy
Fault tolerance	Component replacement while on line Error-correcting memory via parity, Cyclical Redundancy Check (CRC), or *error correcting code* (ECC) Hot fix disk sector replacement Options for disk arrays such as *redundant array of inexpensive drives* (RAIDs)
Management	Remote if needed Complete diagnostics Critical error logs stored outside the operating system
Performance	Augmented by cache Disk controllers Multiple processors High clock speed
Bus type(s)	More than one bus EISA or MCA (proprietary)
Redundancy	Server mirroring
Security	Ace-style (cylindrical key) hardware locks Keyboard locks Controlled floppy access (prevents unauthorized boots)
Scale	Scalable to fit the application Highly expandable
Quality	Well-built frame (tower) Top quality components Forced air cooling

Network administrators like the performance, capacity, and expandability of superservers. They are the most bulletproof of all microprocessor-based machines. Servers of large capacity and power, not to mention those supporting critical applications, justify all the redundancy superservers offer.

The use to which they are put may well justify their acquisition. Consolidating several servers into one superserver saves cost and administration; in addition, you have all the bulletproofing you could want. They make ideal platforms for client-server applications. On the other hand, a superserver is still a single point of failure unless complete server mirroring (as in NetWare SFT IV) is used.

Be aware that proprietary superservers lock you into a given vendor. Parts, such as the supermotherboards that are often used, are hard to replace locally and are expensive. Experts are needed to configure and install them, and when their day is done, superservers are an expensive way to give someone a PC. Believe it or not though, about 15 percent of Compaq SystemPros are purchased for use as stand-alone workstations.

The superserver market is still small, amounting to about 3 percent of all PC servers sold. Of that, Compaq has about 60 percent in its ProSignia and SystemPro line. Tricord and NetFrame each have about 8 percent.

Typical superservers cost $40,000–50,000. At such prices, it is strongly tempting to buy high-end PCs instead, and about 15 percent of server buyers do just that. For those uses where price is not the first consideration, fault tolerance and disk capacity are the major factors driving superserver purchases.

Special-Purpose Servers

We mentioned in Chapter 3 that servers are often adapted for special purposes. The result is streamlined operation and a better fit to the specific application. The drawbacks include more hardware and software to support and perhaps the need for a specialist to do it.

While it is possible to adapt a server to just about any specific purpose, there are a few categories of special purpose servers that are broadly employed. They are:

Terminal servers that connect non-LAN devices to a LAN

Database servers, which speed access to and modification of information

Print servers that supervise printer allocation, priority, and document distribution

Communications servers that manage connections to dial-in users, other LANs, and other WANs

Facsimile servers to send and receive faxes without going through the paper stage

Terminal servers

The terminal server, shown in Figure 5.3, has seen a economically driven resurgence. Terminal servers connect inexpensive terminals to a LAN. Instead of $2,000 PCs, any number of dumb $500 terminals can be connected to the LAN via one connection.

Terminal users still access their applications as before; no retraining

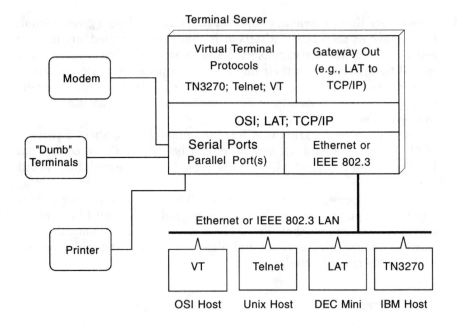

Figure 5.3 Using a terminal server.

is needed. They can also access several machines if desired, even through a WAN.

DEC introduced the terminal server in 1983 with the *Local Area Transport* (LAT) communications controller. LAT offloaded terminal handling from the minicomputer. There was an EIA-232 link between the terminal and server. Ethernet linked the server to the minicomputer using virtual terminal protocols such as TCP/IP Telnet to handle communications up through the protocol stack. Thus, software gateways could translate from TCP/IP to LAT and back, allowing LAT to be routed. (LAT is an unroutable layer 2 protocol.) Alternatively, most terminal servers support both TCP/IP and LAT, allowing users to choose whichever they prefer.[1]

Terminals servers can be small, desktop devices and may be used to

---

[1]DEC dominates the market, but Datability in NJ, Emulex in CA, Hughes LAN Systems in CA, Xylogics in MA, and Xyplex in MA are also players. Per-port prices are about $160 for 16 ports. Terminal servers are usually seen in DEC and Unix environments.

run printers and modem pools, too. They are beginning to be seen in wiring hubs, but this is generally more expensive than a stand-alone version. Terminal servers are sometimes used for simple stub routing as with a terminal pool. Adding bridging and routing to a terminal server is of limited value since LAT is not routable and most terminal servers are used by small, local workgroups. The tactic is clear: buy a stand-alone unit and do not buy built-in functions you may never need.

Database servers

Databases running on nonnetworked stand-alone workstations face certain problems. The biggest problem is that the data is unavailable or hard to get to by another workstation, i.e., sharing becomes difficult. Synchronizing updates to and from the database with other databases is equally difficult if not impossible.

Often, there is little protection of the data from corruption or erasure. Stand-alone workstation databases often lack the ability to buffer an in-process transaction so that a power failure or other disruption will not cause corruption of data. Throwing out an incomplete transaction before it can damage data is called *rollback recovery*.

Workstation users are notorious for not backing up their data. Often, workstation databases painfully built over time are totally vulnerable to loss due to a disk crash, accidental erasure, or simple theft of the machine. The very thought of rebuilding a database from scratch is one of a computer administrator's worst nightmares.

Security is a chronic problem. A stand-alone workstation or a workstation connected to a LAN containing database files is physically vulnerable to tampering or theft. Rarely is such a station physically protected or protected from a power disruption by an uninterruptible power supply.

As the database builds, it is increasingly necessary to manage it. Assuring consistency of data and eliminating duplicate entries and the like are typical tasks of a full-time professional database administrator. Few workstation users have the skill or desire to manage their database. Indeed, most are unaware of even the need for such management. If they are, they may lack the time and training to do so properly. Such a circumstance can unintentionally place precious organizational data at great daily risk.

Database processing. Database servers divide database processing into a front-end application that runs in the workstation and back-end processing that takes place in a database server or engine. In this scheme, *individual records* are downloaded and uploaded, reducing locked data and network traffic. *Structured query language* (SQL) servers operate this way in a client-server relationship as we discussed in Chapter 1.

Such a database server can be either a logical or physical entity. Logical database servers can be:

An identifiable process on a file server.

An NLM, running under NetWare. An NLM is basically a software module that plugs into NetWare.

A background process running on a LAN workstation.

Physical databases might be:

A hardware coprocessor in a LAN server, dedicated to the database application.

A hardware coprocessor in a LAN workstation.

A separate physical PC on the LAN.

It seems logical to place database service on the machine that provides file service. It does, however, create an added load for the server. This may not be noticeable at low usage levels but may become a choke point when the network gets busy.

An NLM or its equivalent tightens the link between the operating system and the application, a desirable feature which improves performance. Once again though, file service and other services may be degraded by the presence of the database NLM.

In multitasking applications based on OS/2 or Unix, a PC can carry database service as a *background process.* Here the same limitations as above apply, only the PC's power is divided between the user and the database process.

Using a database hardware *coprocessor* is possible in either the server or workstation. If it is found in the file server, it can share the high-speed bus with the file server, resulting in high speed and reduced network traffic. Regardless of where it is found, incorporating a database coprocessor is better than making the main CPU carry the entire burden.

In a workstation, coprocessing creates competition between it and the workstation processor for shared resources, specifically the data bus and NIC. Consequently, network traffic increases. If the workstation is lightly used, this may not be a factor.

In summary, a database server is easier to manage and maintain and is more accessible. As a server, it can be protected by placing it in a locked area and isolated from electrical transients by an uninterruptible power supply (UPS). Backups, access security, database administration, and all such managerial problems are carried out by a professional in a systematic way. By activating transaction tracking, incomplete transactions can be rolled back before they corrupt data. Since the data is in one place, the synchronization issue recedes in importance or disappears altogether.

Centralized versus distributed databases. There are additional concerns over whether to centralize database service in one server or distribute it among multiple servers. Some pros and cons include:

Distributed databases	Avoid the potential bottleneck of a single *database management system* (DBMS)
	Eliminate the server as a single point of failure
	Allow truly distributed database access through bridges and gateways
	Allow central database management
	Allow database corruption, theoretically, by any workstation
	Do not eliminate database updates and synchronization as issues
Centralized databases	Reduce the likelihood of corruption
	Are easier to manage
	Allow access to many database servers via LANs or WANs
	Allow lower-speed WAN links

CD-ROM readers are becoming popular for qualified database applications. CD-ROM readers are often attached to database servers or even to conventional file servers. More and more, they arrive as integrated network-ready appliances. Most are capable of supporting 8–28 CD-ROM drives. Applications can therefore range from the workgroup to the entire enterprise.

One or several can be installed anywhere on the network, and they support all the major NOSs, i.e., Novell NetWare, Banyan VINES, Microsoft LAN Manager, and IBM LAN Server. They are, of course, read-only, and the access delay is greater than may be acceptable in certain operations.

Printer sharing

Early PC users had to deal with the hard fact that the only way to get anything out of a PC was on paper. A PC at the time was a self-contained island, so the only way to get data into it was via a keyboard or diskette. The only way out was via a diskette or on paper. Therefore, a printer was needed for every PC. This became expensive fast.

PC users lacking a printer found themselves making diskettes and running down the hall to their neighbor's PC which had a printer. This was awkward, unproductive, and inflexible, but was great exercise. This form of "network" was (and is) called a *sneakernet*.

As shown in Figure 5.4, the next development was a hand-operated selector switch that connected the printer to one of several PCs. While a great improvement, it remained a manual operation. If the switch was not set correctly or if it was disturbed while printing, well, the show was over. Back up, restart, print it again.

Printer switches have become intelligent and electronic, as shown in Figure 5.5. Most include automatic printer selection via addressing, queuing, and buffering. A PC can direct print output to a buffer, freeing the PC. The printer switch buffer selects the right printer or plotter and waits in line if it is busy.

Advanced printer switches act like a mini-LAN, with basic e-mail and file exchange capability but are completely proprietary. If the above description meets 90 percent of your needs, then a LAN may be overkill for what you are doing *today*.

On a LAN, printer sharing is a basic NOS feature as illustrated in Figure 5.6. Data to be printed are passed to the server, which *spools* or buffers print jobs from users in order and prints them out in a set priority. This frees the PC and its parallel port for other things. Printer sharing allows jobs to be prioritized in order of importance (or pecking order) and to be printed on the most appropriate print device.

It is common to place several inexpensive, draft-quality printers in a workgroup and pool one or two high-quality machines. Draft and internal documents are printed on the fast dot-matrix printer, while formal

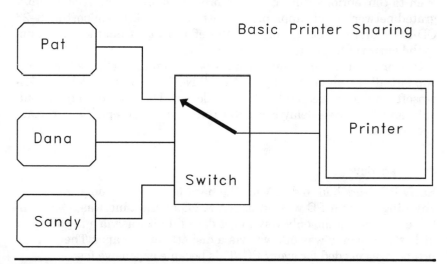

Figure 5.4 Basic printer sharing.

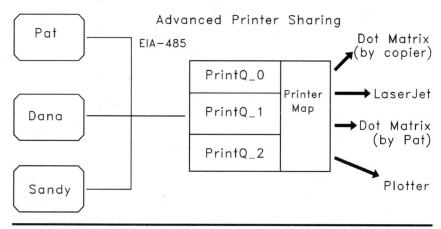

Figure 5.5 Advanced printer sharing.

outside documents are printed on the laser machine. Some firms have plotters for printing high-quality drawings, perhaps in color. These can also be shared on a LAN through the NOS. The relationship between the queue (buffer) and the printer assignment is set by printer *mapping*.

Most basically, the map takes data from a printer queue and prints it on a particular printer. To add flexibility, several queues can be created, each having a different priority. High-priority jobs will be printed first, followed by more routine ones. Conversely, several printers can work from the same high-priority queue if so mapped. Thus, several priority jobs can be printed at once.

Often, a LAN administrator or print queue operator can change a job's position in the queue, put it on hold, or even delete it. In a perfect world, people would prioritize their print jobs as something other than urgent every time. To limit potential abuse, NetWare, for example, allows the administrator or operator to specify which users are allowed to access each queue. Passwords are used to enter the queue.

Separate, specialized servers such as print and communications servers can be connected to the file server bus by an expansion chassis. This means that the print and file servers must be next to each other. Other print and communications servers have a LAN interface and are directly connected to the LAN. They can be placed anywhere on the LAN, but printing will add to the LAN cable's traffic load.

One emerging trend is to install a NIC directly in the printer and connect it directly to the LAN. Called *network-ready* or a *network appliance,* the printer can be located anywhere. For those printers than cannot accept an internal adapter, external pocket-sized versions are available. They connect the printer's parallel port to the Ethernet or

Software Print Server

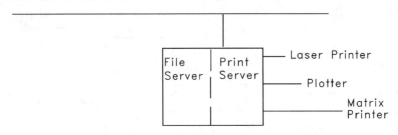

Hardware Print Servers

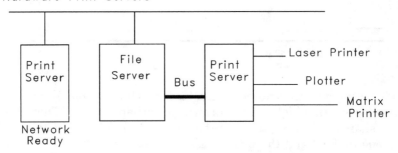

Workstation Print Server

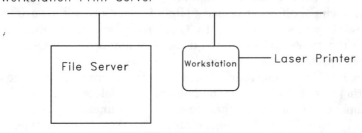

Figure 5.6 Printer servers.

token ring network as desired. This can be a very satisfactory option for those with older printers lacking option slots.

Communications servers

A communications server relieves the file server of the tasks and overhead related to communications, thereby improving the efficiency of both communications and file services. In a characteristic application, the server permits users to share a pool of modems and associated dial numbers. Outbound, a user seated at a workstation may use a modem through the LAN to call a bulletin board or MCI Mail. Another user may be on the road. They dial inbound to access the file server or perhaps their own PC.

The communications server handles each request for modem pool service. If all the modems are busy, the outbound user will be informed and perhaps queued. Inbound, the caller's authenticity will be verified before access is allowed.

From a technical view, the high interrupt rates typical in communications degrade file service. Further, the need for many ports often goes beyond a file server's capacity. Some administrators prefer to isolate communications from the file server for security reasons and to isolate the file server from communications-induced problems. All are legitimate reasons for installing a communications server.

Two key questions in considering a communications server are where and how applications processing will take place. Generally it is least desirable to do applications processing at the remote end. Reasons for this include increased remote computer requirements and rising costs. Managing remote applications software is also a problem. The link in the middle is a bottleneck, reducing processing speed.

It is more desirable to do processing at the LAN site. Here the processor could be the file server (with possible performance degradation), the user's own office PC (what if the caller is not on the LAN?), or the communications server itself. Given the last choice, there are two ways communications servers allocate their own processing power:

Multiprocessor servers (Figure 5.7) dedicate a card-style PC to each caller. This is a high-performance, but naturally more expensive, implementation. Evergreen, Cubix, and J&L Information Systems all take this approach.

Multitasking servers share one processor between several users (Figure 5.8). A "virtual server," the machine has about 750 kbytes of segmented, mapped, extended memory per user. CPUs are 386 or 486 machines running DOS and an expanded memory manager (EMM). Typically, a single NIC is shared by all users accessing the network. This can be a bottleneck and a single point of failure. Finally, the applications must be able to run in a multitasking environment. Additional users degrade the performance; up to 16 or so users are supportable this way.

A third option (Figure 5.9) is to simply use a *network appliance.* These are stand-alone devices with a modem married to a NIC. Lacking processing power, they provide only access. For this reason, they are best for retrieving and sending data but not for downloading executable applications.

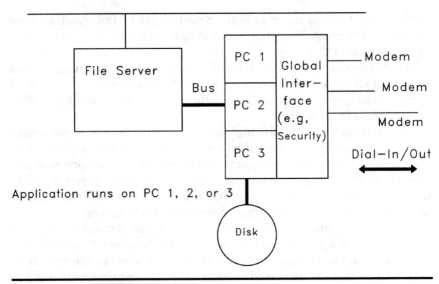

Figure 5.7 A multiprocessor communications server.

Network appliances connect the caller to the file server. For callers, usage is very simple: They use the server just as if they were in the office. These appliances can also connect a LAN to another LAN temporarily. Examples include Microtest's LANModem and Shiva Corp's Net-Modem/E.

As with print servers, multiprocessing and multitasking communications servers can be bus-connected to the file server or appear on the LAN themselves.

Multitasking Communications Server

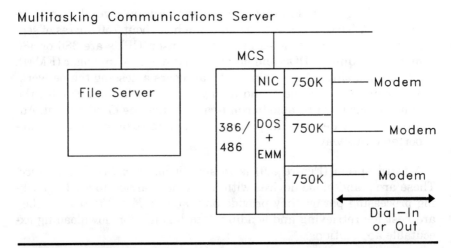

Figure 5.8 A multitasking communications server.

Self—Contained Network Appliance

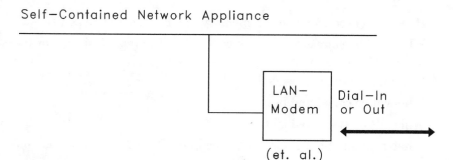

Figure 5.9 A self-contained network appliance.

Multiprocessor servers handle dial-in best. Dial-in users take over the single-board PC, and any processing takes place on that board, rather than over the link. This saves time and means that the caller's device can be a dumb terminal. Multiprocessor access is also well-suited for callers whose own PCs are not on the LAN.

A variety of PC boards are available, depending on processing requirements and range from an 8086 to a 486DX. They can even include a hard-disk controller.

There is no technical reason why a multiprocessing server cannot be used to dial-out, but the presence of a single-board PC makes it expensive, somewhere between $1,500 and $3,000 per port, not including a modem.

Simple dial-out applications are better met by self-contained appliances such as the LANModem, which provides no processing power. This is not a disadvantage if the device that is called does the processing.

Some vendors offer X.25 and shared facsimile service. All the communications server vendors listed above offer interfaces to external networks beyond the standard modem's serial EIA-232 asynchronous port. For LAN-to-LAN communication, TCP/IP or IPX/SPX support is often required. When communicating with asynchronous terminals, the DEC LAT protocol is common.

Items that need to be evaluated when assessing the need for a communication server include:

Who, exactly, are you supporting?

How many of them are there?

What do they need to do?

Are they dialing in, out, or both?

Do you need to provide dial-in users a processor?

How much processing power, memory, and disk space will be needed?

What will be your network connection, i.e., ISA bus, Ethernet, or token ring?

How many ports are needed?

Who will be called and how long will the calls be?

Will calls be staggered by time zone?

What modem options, e.g., the speed, MNP, V.42, and V.34, do you have?

What remote access communication software choices do you have?

What will be the network protocol, e.g., IPX/SPX, TCP/IP, or LAT?

Will it work with your NOS?

Do you need additional security, or is the NOS or operating system good enough?

Do you need fax, X.25, or mainframe gateway access?

Is communications mission-critical?

Can the system automatically reboot a crashed processor?

Can a defective line be "busied-out" (bypassed)?

Can processors be removed without halting the server?

Can ports be reconfigured and usage monitored?

What is the price and warranty of the server?

How about service, and on-line support?

Facsimile servers

Fax servers fall into three categories. *Software-only* packages run on a customer-supplied platform plus modems. While the packages are very flexible, you also take responsibility for making it all work together. Some people do not enjoy being system integrators.

Software and hardware packages consist of fax modem cards and software to run them. The platform may be the file server or a dedicated client workstation. While compatibility between software and hardware is assured, you cannot shift to another software package without changing the hardware, too, and vice versa. If installed in a file server, the server becomes a *logical* fax server as well (Figure 5.10).

A variation, *file-server-based software,* is fax software logically attached to the NOS. In NetWare, this is accomplished via an NLM. The added processing may adversely affect server performance, but a separate platform is avoided. This approach also reduces LAN traffic since

Logical FAX Server

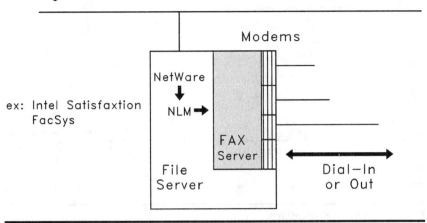

Figure 5.10 A logical fax server.

communication between the file server and fax server is via the internal data bus, not the LAN cable.

Fax server software can be used in dedicated or nondedicated file servers. Some software will allow the fax program to continue running even if the file server goes down. Another optional feature is dynamic sharing of fax loads between several servers. Not all systems offer fax load sharing.

Self-contained physical fax servers (Figure 5.11) arrive in a standalone platform and include all the modem cards and preinstalled software. There are no peripherals such as a keyboard or CRT. The only connections are to the LAN, the phone line, and to a printer. Upgradability, say to add another line, may be limited in these systems. These devices meet specific, limited, applications and are convenient only for them.

Fax server standards.   *Communications asynchronous specification* (CAS) is a quasi-standard developed by Intel and Digital Communications Associates in 1988. CAS Redirector is a *terminate-and-stay-resident* (TSR) program that resides in a client workstation. It requires a CAS-compatible fax board and software.

Many fax applications have been written by developers to comply with CAS. The next version of CAS, T.611, is awaiting approval by the Telecommunications Standardization Sector of the International Telecommunications Union, or ITU-TSS (formerly CCITT). CAS allows in-application faxing.

In 1991, a competing standard, FaxBios, was created by Hewlett-Packard, WordPerfect, Everex, and others. Hardware independent,

Physical FAX Servers

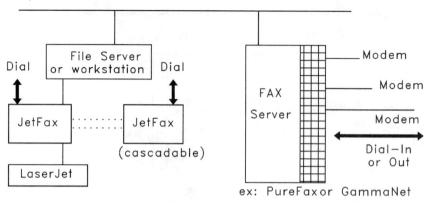

Figure 5.11 A physical fax server.

FaxBios is intended to permit faxing from word processing, spreadsheet, and database applications directly.

FaxBios is not compatible with CAS, and is generally regarded as more capable. Either the CAS or FaxBios approach is well-suited for special applications.

Sending via the fax server. Fax usage is very similar to that found when printing, which makes learning how to send one easy for most users. Sending one is a matter of building a fax from one or more files. Most fax servers will accept a variety of file formats, e.g., PCX or DCX graphic formats, transparently to the user. This ability permits graphics and text to be mixed in a single facsimile.

Once the fax is created, a "phone book" allows you to select the recipient. Broadcast faxes to groups or copies of faxes can be sent easily, and can even be scheduled for off-hours transmission.

When the user transmits the file, a TSR captures the fax and reroutes "printer" files to the fax server. Under Windows, a fax print driver must be present and selected. The necessary *rasterization* to turn a file into a fax-format document should be done in the fax server. The same server can perform broadcast fax as well.

There is usually a *logging* function which records each fax that is sent. If someone claims you did not send a fax, the log can back you up.

Sometimes a fax will not get through. Some fax server software will dial a fixed number of times and then give up. Brighter systems will retry intelligently, redialing a detected busy (as opposed to no answer) fax line until the remote machine answers. In any event, senders *must* be advised of undelivered faxes.

Receiving faxes. Faxes arriving at the fax server modem card from the outside world need to contain information telling the server how to route the fax. Conquering the inbound fax problem has been so difficult that some fax servers have been implemented for outbound faxes only. Some systems bypass the whole problem and simply print inbound faxes for manual distribution. This adds work, wastes paper, and compromises privacy.

The most reliable inbound addressing method is called *direct inward dialing* (DID). Faxes arrive at your company's telephone switch (PBX) with their own fax number. The PBX then passes this number to the server, which routes it to the right destination. While reliable, DID trunks have a cost, although it is not as high as for separate telephone numbers.

A simpler way is to allocate incoming telephone numbers to specific groups of users. This *channel-based routing* is simple but uses incoming lines with less than optimum efficiency. For instance, one group's lines could all be busy while other group's lines are idle. If the lines to a group are busy, then the fax should go to a default user for manual delivery.

Another method uses *optical character recognition* (OCR). OCR software in the fax server recognizes a routing number, perhaps inside double brackets. This requires the sender to write clearly and remember to do so in the first place. The success ratio of OCR is at best about 80 percent, so you should expect some manual intervention with the OCR method.

The least desirable method uses touch-tones tapped in by the sender to indicate the user. When the fax server's modem answers, the sender enters digits to indicate the recipient. Then the sender presses the send button on the fax. The server then route the fax as directed.

This approach means the sender cannot use a fax server but must use an ordinary fax machine. They must have a pushbutton phone that uses *dual-tone multifrequency* (DTMF), alias touch-tone. The sender must also know the code for the recipient. It is not hard to see that this approach is time-consuming and fraught with opportunity for error, such as entering an invalid or incorrect code.

The International Computer Facsimile Association has developed a standard for routing fax messages to LAN users. It works within the existing Group 3 facsimile protocol. For more information, call them directly at (617) 982-9500.

ITU-TSS is also working on a fax subaddressing standard which would place a subaddress field in a fax automatically. ITU-TSS is developing a standard called Appli/COM, which would also allow in-application transmission.

Ideally, an identified fax goes through a postmaster function that routes it to the appropriate recipient(s). If NetWare is installed, the NetWare *bindery,* which identifies users in NetWare, will often be used for this purpose. Alternately, the fax can simply be printed. Most fax

servers have a built-in plain-paper printing feature . . . but do you really want it on paper at all?

Some systems will allow a system manager to edit a fax that has just
arrived and prior to delivery to the recipient. This way, junk faxes can
be viewed and deleted without printing or forwarding them. Usually
only the cover page can be seen, but sometimes people write on cover
pages. Sometimes the editing feature is turned off (if possible) to preserve the integrity of the document.

A checklist of fax server features include:

It should be easy to install, have clear documentation, and simplify
installation via batch files, prompts, and defaults. It should not be
necessary to go to each workstation to load TSRs.

Fax modems should support the *communications asynchronous
specification* (CAS) for fax and 3270 by DCA and Intel. Group III fax
support is mandatory.

It should have 16-bit modem bus interfaces and be programmed by
EPROM, not DIP switches.

The fax process is imperfect. Therefore, the system must handle errors in a prompt, timely way. Failed faxes without notification are
unacceptable.

If you use the Microsoft Windows environment, the server should
support it.

Print features are essential, and image printing places big demands
on printers. Being able to use print queues and direct print output is
invaluable.

Security and privacy are important: Faxes should not be alterable by
a network administrator. Administrators should not be able to read a
fax except for the cover page.

Faxes in either direction should be sent and delivered automatically.
No fax czar should be needed to route incoming faxes, for instance.

It should have bidirectional logging, both inbound and outbound.

It should have either a dedicated or nondedicated server mode. Independent software is desirable in case the server itself goes down.

It should persistently redial busy numbers and retry a fixed number
of times if there is no answer. It should abort and create an error
message if answered by a non-fax device ("liveware").

It should be able to construct a single fax from different and mixed
file formats.

A variety of printers and print formats, e.g., ASCII, PCL, and Epson,
should be supported.

It should be capable of importing databases from other databases to avoid recopying phone lists.

It should be easy for clients to use. If it is not, they will revert to the old fax machine.

Fax server summary. Automating the fax process can produce long-term savings and a rapid return on investment. Yet there remains much uncertainty among administrators because the application is not necessarily simple and the first fax server products were very shaky.

As we have seen, a lack of standardization on automatic inbound routing has contributed to the problem. For that reason, fax servers have been sold primarily as senders rather than receivers.

Integration with the server NOS is very useful. For instance, copying the NetWare bindery eases management, and running the fax service on the file server increases security. As this writing, Cheyenne Software's (Roslyn Heights, NY) FAXserve is the only NetWare NLM-based product. It supports ten languages besides English.

Faxed images usually appear on the screen just as they were received. That can mean off-center or even upside down. Sometimes images will not fit on the screen and must be scrolled. Here is a new acronym: WYPIWYF (what you print is what you fax).

Properly implemented, security can be excellent if faxes are received and distributed electronically. It is much worse if faxes are printed for manual distribution, inviting inevitable eyeball leaks. Similarly, timely distribution is easy electronically, but much slower when faxes are printed. Then they can get lost or mixed up. Junk faxes (and there are many) waste paper, too.

Ideally, installation is automatic and manual fax management is unnecessary. A clue to the strength of the product, it is said, is the ease of its installation.

The rising volume of faxes are turning fax servers into strategic products. Outgoing volumes at the Fortune 500 doubled in 1992–1993, and incoming volume rose nearly 40 percent. At the same time, document lengths have doubled.

Fax machines have sprouted like answering machines in the days before voice mail, at a rate of 25 percent annually. Fax servers will do away with many of them even as voice mail did away with the cassette machines.

Not surprisingly, only 3 percent of faxes are sent at the least expensive time. When was the last time you waited until after 5 PM to send a long fax?

Fax servers can be especially useful when one realizes that most faxes are sent between two locations in the same company. This greatly simplifies the inbound routing problem. Often, the outbound convenience alone is sufficient to justify a fax server. A fax server is perfectly useful to complement a standard fax machine.

One can readily see that eliminating the paper stage is a big cost saver. There is ample room for savings when we realize that today only one fax in four is created on a computer and faxed without going through the paper stage or being initialed or signed.

Server Fault Tolerance

Because of the growing dependence on servers, engineers have developed a series of innovations that allow servers to survive several kinds of failures. Most data losses, though, are due to cockpit errors where data is deleted and then found to be unrecoverable rather than machine failures.

Memory errors in PCs are detected using memory parity to catch a dying RAM chip. Superservers go beyond parity checking by adding bits for redundant data recovery to reconstruct lost data. Cyclical redundancy checks (CRC) are used on both disk and tape to catch errors. Redundant power supplies with duplicate AC electrical cords and backup buses are all used in superservers.

Redundant array of inexpensive disks

The most susceptible device in the server is the hard disk, or single large expensive disk (SLED). Spinning at 3600 revolutions per minute, the read-write heads float just above the surface of the disk on a cushion of air while moving rapidly across the surface of the disk. Should the head touch the disk, it will score the disk and you have a *head crash*. A head crash is guaranteed to complicate your day.

In a 1988 paper, three computer scientists at UC Berkeley conceived the idea of using a *redundant array of inexpensive disks* (RAID). RAID provides three benefits: fault tolerance, reduced cost, and decent performance. There is a trade-off between redundancy and performance. Hardware-implemented RAID requires SCSI drives but reduces CPU load. Software-based RAID can use IDE, ESDI, or SCSI drives, reducing expense and performance. A RAID array is seen as one volume. All five RAID versions assure that no one disk failure will cause lost data.

The simplest answer to disk failure is a *mirrored disk array* (MDA), called RAID *level 1* (Figure 5.12). Disk mirroring means that every read and write is duplicated on a separate disk simultaneously. The theory is that both disks will not fail at the same time.

In disk mirroring, the disk controller channel is shared by both disks, creating a single point of electronic but not mechanical failure. There is no data verification: If a bad block is read from the principal drive and then written back on disk, data on both disks will have been

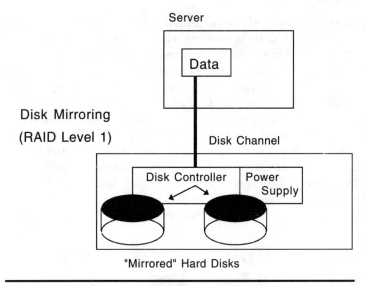

Figure 5.12 Disk mirroring (RAID level 1).

corrupted. Cynics will say that two disks double the odds of disk failure. RAID level 1 is not cost effective for disks larger than 600 Mbytes or so. It is best used in small (5–10 users) LANs.

Not a RAID configuration but commonly used in servers is *disk duplexing*. As you can see in Figure 5.13, disk duplexing duplicates the entire channel, precluding the three single points of possible failure in RAID level 1, i.e., the disk channel, disk controller, and power supply, from bringing the disk down.

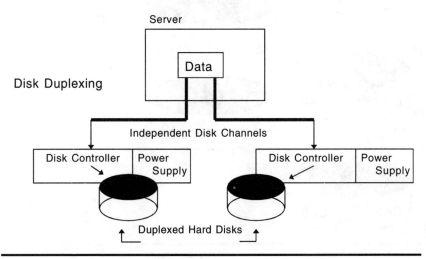

Figure 5.13 Disk duplexing (no equivalent RAID level).

Figure 5.14 shows how RAID level 2 adds *bit interleaving* and *check disks*. When a block of data is written, that block is bit-interleaved across, say, five data drives. An *error-correction code* (ECC), really a Hamming code, is also calculated and spread across, say, three remaining drives. Thus, all five drives read and write at the same time. Any single drive failure data loss can be fully recovered from the other drives. The major drawback of RAID level 2 is the cost of the extra nondata drives. RAID level 2 is used in about a fifth of NetWare SFT sites and in large systems with many large data transfers, and supercomputers. It has not been used, so far, in server-based arrays.

RAID level 3, shown in Figure 5.15, is a *parallel disk array* (PDA). A PDA is generally preferable to RAID level 2 because of its lower cost. A parity bit for each byte that is written replaces the ECC. The bit ap-

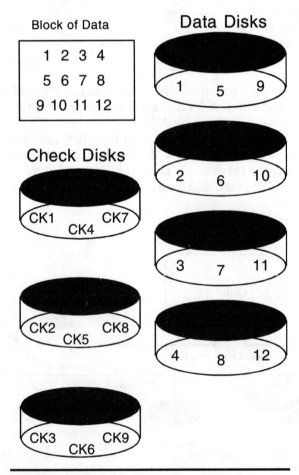

Figure 5.14   RAID level 2. Bit interleaved. (Numbers represent bits in order.)

pears on a single check disk. Data interleaving between disks still occurs. Believe it or not, RAID level 3 systems are more reliable than RAID level 2 because there are fewer disks to fail. RAID level 3 is well suited for applications needing speed and reliability.

RAID level 4 (Figure 5.16) is an *independent disk array* (IDA). It does not use data interleaving. Instead, it uses *striping,* where one block is read or written to or from drive 1; the second to or from drive 2, and so on. Like RAID level 3, there is a single parity disk.

In RAID level 4 there is a read-modify-write sequence wherein data and parity are read from disk, data is changed and parity recalculated, then written back to disk. This substantially slows down RAID level 4 and makes it better for block file manipulation than interactive transaction processing. (There is some industry disagreement on this point.)

RAID level 5 (Figure 5.17), also an independent disk array, condenses data and parity onto the data disks, doing away with the parity disk. Instead, data and parity are spread across all the disks used in the array. Again, a single disk failure still allows the other disks to re-

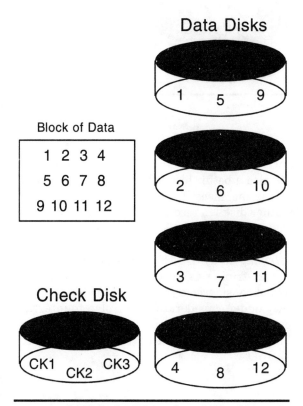

Figure 5.15   RAID level 3. Bit interleaved. (Numbers represent bits in order.)

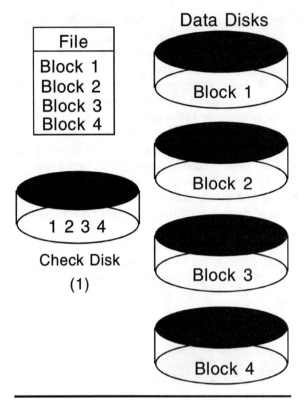

Figure 5.16   RAID level 4. Block interleaved.

cover the data. The read-write-modify sequence is the same as in RAID level 4, so RAID level 5 is also a better block than interactive subsystem. Also, the response time increases if a drive fails because RAID level 5 must read all the other disks to reconstruct the lost data on the failed disk drive. *Crippled mode degradation* results as the crashed drive's data is being rebuilt.

RAID level 0 is a *data striping array* (DSA). RAID level 0 simply provides high-performance data striping as in RAID level 4. However, it has no redundancy and is not considered a true RAID system.

RAID level 6 is presently under consideration as a plan to integrate RAID controllers in a host machine. New RAID versions 11 and 51 are being proposed. For information on the latest developments in RAID, call the RAID Advisory Board.[2]

---

[2]The RAID Advisory Board's telephone number is (612) 784-2379.

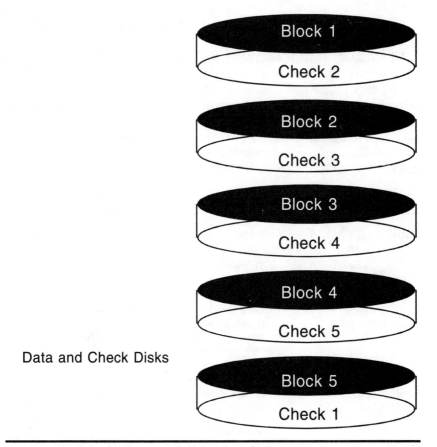

Data and Check Disks

Figure 5.17   RAID level 5. Data and check interleaved.

Merits of the different levels.   RAID level systems are expensive in absolute dollars, but they may be cheap when the cost of irretrievable data is considered. Considered in cost per megabyte of storage, RAID level 1 is more expensive than RAID level 2. But the total cost of the RAID level 2 disks, including check disks, brings RAID level 2 almost to the level of RAID level 1 in total dollars. Not many vendors have built RAID level 2 systems.

RAID level 3 is much more common and economical. Usable disk space may reach 85 percent. However, if the parity disk fails, the system must be brought down, the drive replaced, and the parity data recalculated. RAID level 4 has the same problem, but striping improves performance during large block transfers. RAID level 4 is used by Compaq's SystemPro.

RAID level 5 is the most expensive and advanced. Again offering up to 85 percent disk space, RAID Level 5 drives can be removed without bringing the system down.

All RAID systems *must* notify the operator immediately if a drive fails because there is no more redundancy. Levels other than RAID level 5 may require an off-line installation and data rebuild, including initialization, formatting, and copying. If rebuilding takes place in the background, it takes longer but affects the on-line system less. Conversely, a foreground rebuild will increase your response time. Rebuild times can vary between 20 and 3 min, respectively, for a 240-Mbyte drive.

RAID Performance versus Protection

RAID level	Cost	Recover-ability	Perfor-mance	Storage space usage	System size	Best applica-tion	I/O rate
0 (data striping)	Low	None	Very good		Servers	OLTP†; noncritical data bases	Very good
1 (mirroring)	High	Total	Good for inter-active use	Less efficient: <600 Mbytes	Servers	5–10 user LANs; SFT*	No write penalty
2 (Ham-ming code)	High	High	Data transfer is good; not good for inter-active use	Much parity data	Large system super compute	Bulk data transfers	Good for heavy data transfer; not for OLTP
3 (byte parallel array)	Low	High	Good for inter-active use	Good	Servers	High I/O and reliability; multi-media scientific	Good for heavy I/O
4 (block parallel)	Low	Very high	Good for read trans-actions	Block oriented	Servers	Very good for read-only systems	Heavy write penalty
5 (distributed striping)	Medium	High	Good for read trans-actions; cripple-mode degradation	Block oriented	Servers	Very good for read-only systems	Heavy write penalty

*SFT = system fault tolerant
†OLTP = on-line transaction processing

Not all vendors adhere strictly to a given RAID level; some cross boundaries. Compaq combines RAID levels 1 and 4. Core International shares RAID levels 3 and 4. Some vendors let users set different RAID levels within the same array, a process called *concurrent RAID*. Thus, within a master array, a RAID level 3 subarray might be used for large file transfers and a RAID level 5 might be used for small ones. Physically, RAIDs are implemented externally or internally within the server.

If all the drives are daisy-chained on one ribbon cable, the cable becomes a bottleneck as only a single transfer to or from a controller can occur at a time. Multiple drive connectors on the controller create more efficient parallel access paths. Parallel paths permit *data guarding,* a term synonymous with using a parity drive as in RAID levels 3 and 4. The performance loss in data guarding is small.

Multiple drive controllers or *controller duplexing* off-loads the CPU with the task of disk housekeeping. Like multiple access path controllers, several drives can be read or written to at the same time, improving performance considerably. RAID is well-suited to intensive computing applications such as imaging or modeling.

Operating system support.   Unix and OS/2 fully support all RAID levels. NetWare now supports levels above RAID level 1 (disk mirroring) and hot fix (where the software automatically avoids writing to bad sectors on the disk). While all RAID levels could be used with NetWare, NetWare does not indicate RAID faults or support the RAID decision-making process. There are vendor-supplied NLMs for this purpose.

NetWare *System Fault Tolerant* (SFT) III software duplicates not only the disks, but the entire server and is discussed next. Some buyers are finding this a better expenditure than buying a RAID system. The truly paranoid are even adding RAID to SFT III. Other sites find that simple disk mirroring (SFT II or RAID level 1) is sufficient, especially since SFT II comes with all versions of NetWare.

RAIDs can be configured as SLEDs. Read-request response time improves at the expense of redundancy. Several SLEDs can be set up to do split-disk seeking or spanning. Since disks typically read four times for each time they write, the performance improvement can be noticeable. Large databases spread across several drives are more quickly read this way.

Surveys show an expected quadrupling of RAID shipments between now and 1995. In view of the wide variation in application recommendations, do *benchmark testing* before buying!

Novell SFT.   As Novell expands into enterprise networking and up the hierarchy of corporate applications toward the mainframe, fault tolerance has become an essential ingredient in their mix of products. As of this writing, no other vendor provides *server duplexing* or complete duplication of a server in real time as shown in Figure 5.18.

Other NOS vendors offer disk mirroring and/or duplexing, plus other hardware fault tolerance features. These are discussed in Chapter 12 as they are mainly NOS functions employing minimal hardware such as duplicate disks.

SFT versions I and II come with NetWare 2.2 and 3.1X. SFT I/II mirror disks and controllers within a server, the equivalent of RAID level 1. While data is protected against loss, if the server fails, the network fails. Herein lies a clear example of the distinction between *backup* and *fault tolerance*.

For NetWare 3.11, 3.12, and 4.X, there is SFT III V3.11 and V4.X (not yet released). A series of NLMs, SFT III duplicates every transaction on a secondary server. Should the primary server have a hardware failure, the secondary continues with uninterrupted service. Some software failures are protected, too. In SFT III, the primary server is the

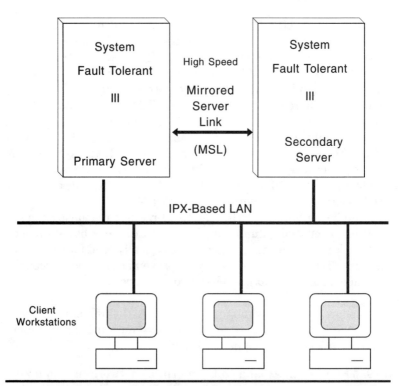

Figure 5.18 System fault tolerance: duplexed servers.

one that has been up the longest. If it is turned off, SFT toggles the other machine to become the primary server.

To do this, a link must be set up between the servers so the primary can update the secondary without using the network. This is called a *mirrored software link* (MSL). The MSL duplicates the primary server's memory and disk contents onto the secondary, and keeps them both synchronized. MSL links may be fiber (Compaq), EISA bus (Everex), coaxial, or Wave bus. Eagle Technologies, Thomas-Conrad, and PlainTree Systems are all producing MSL cards and drivers.

The virtue of using a fiber link is that the secondary server can be as far as 2.5 mi away from the primary server. This make SFT III a good disaster-recovery strategy.

SFT III servers have the same internal Internetwork Packet Exchange (IPX) numbers. If the primary fails, MSL advises the secondary server of the loss. Some inquiring clients' packets will be lost at the failure, but the client simply repeats the request. This time the secondary answers. Because the IPX addresses are the same, the client never notices the difference.

Beyond fault tolerance and disaster recovery, having the flexibility to take down the primary server for maintenance, an upgrade, or just to move it vastly simplifies an administrator's life. Any new software is automatically mirrored when the machines are linked again.

Further discussion of SFT III. Applications using hardware-specific calls cannot be mirrored, such as disk and NIC drivers, print servers, *uninterruptible power supply* (UPS) monitoring software, and routers working with hardware. Generic NetWare environments and non-NLM equipped applications servers are all that are really supported. This can be used to some advantage. One can run different print servers on each machine, for instance. However, if one of the duplexed servers fails, print services on that machine will cease. Novell recommends running PSERVER.EXE on a standalone computer.

Even some NetWare applications are unsupported, including NetWare Management Services, TCP/IP, Network File Systems (NFS), NetWare for Macintosh, and NetWare for SAA. SFT III 4.X is supposed to support these, and Novell is using this as leverage to push users into NetWare 4.X.

There have been many complaints about SFT III's documentation. Offered on CD-ROM, the documentation has been accused of being incomplete and leaving out essentials such as the order of installation. This has caused some customers to mirror the information in the secondary server (at setup, none) into the primary server, wiping out all its data. To simplify matters, Novell is working on the user interface to make it more understandable.

Another glitch was that a server failure message comes up on a server console, which may be locked up or not even connected. Novell is working on a way to notify the administrator if either machine fails.

One of the remarks in the SFT documentation stresses the importance of having identical machines, including RAM, drive sizes, video types, and processors. Some users have echoed that sentiment strongly, stressing the need for "identical twins," right down to the chips. Others have been able to run SFT III without exact duplication. SFT assumes the speed of the slowest machine, so processor speed mismatches do not preclude SFT's use.

RAM is one area where compatibility is important. Even if the RAM sizes are the same, different vendors allocate memory differently, causing problems when copying memory to the secondary. Also, if the secondary has less memory, then the primary will not be able to fully duplicate its own RAM in the second machine.

Drive sizes can be different, but the excess space on one will not be used. The NetWare partitions should be closely analogous.

SFT III supports asymmetric dual-processor operation. However the applications must support dual-processing, and Novell does not provide drivers. Instead, Novell has given third parties the specifications and left driver development to them. Ask your server and applications vendor about dual-processor support.

Some SFT III 3.11 installers have complained about quickly degrading performance. Benchmark tests noted a 15 percent decrease in throughput. Use of multiprocessing eliminates any effect of SFT overhead on performance. However, Novell claims that one installed customer installation supports 1,000 users without difficulty.

SFT III 3.11 supports only DOS and OS/2 client PCs. Unix and Macintosh users will have to wait for SFT III 4.0. The current SFT III is available only for NetWare 3.11 in the 250-user version.[3] This will force some customers to upgrade whether they have that many users or not.

If you install SFT III, purchase a UPS for each. Sharing a UPS crates a single point of failure and so defeats the purpose of SFT.

Pricing is around $19,000, about $10,000 for another server, and $2,500 or so for MSL cards, for a total of nearly $33,000.

Other solutions. There are other ways of providing fault tolerance, but most are not as clean a solution as doing so in the NOS. Totally dupli-

[3]As of this writing, NetWare 3.1X operates in unprotected mode, meaning that restricted areas of the server's memory can be accessed by the NOS, causing a system crash. Although it has not been a major field problem, ask about the status of a fix. NetWare 4.0 contains options to select protected mode operation.

cated mirroring, NOS, and applications software are often required. DOS interrupts are usually used to write the data to the secondary server and then the primary server. If the primary server fails, the secondary server takes over.

One creative solution is a 13-kbyte TSR-in-low-memory program that sends all the client's write packets to both servers. If either server fails, the software drops it and processing continues. The software is independent of the NOS and server hardware and there is no single point of failure.[4] Another solution is to have two servers share a disk subsystem as with NetGuard Systems' [Seal Beach, CA: (310) 799-5533] Failsafe Subsystem.

Maintaining Your Server

Backups

Real-life stories about backups-not-done or backups-done-wrong have a common theme: All involve a hardware error which exposed a human error during the backup process. Hardware and human errors are inevitable. While the latter are more common, we can take action to minimize both. Fault tolerant systems minimize the effect of hardware faults. Automated backup systems go a long way toward assuring that backups will be done as planned and correctly. The more automated, the more systematic, the better.

Bear in mind that backup is not the same as fault tolerance. Fault tolerance is on-line, backup is not. Fault tolerance is a step beyond backup. Backups may interrupt user service, while fault tolerant systems are designed to be nondisruptive to the user.

Storage systems for backup may be either *on-line, near-line,* or *off-line.* Their properties are:

Data is processed directly from on-line storage systems. Magnetic and optical disk typify such systems, and no human intervention is required.

Near-line data cannot be processed directly. Data are moved automatically to on-line storage first. *Grooming* moves long-unused files to near-line storage. It is a form of *virtual* storage. The media may be magnetic or optical.

Off-line storage requires manual intervention, such as mounting a tape.

---

[4]The product is *No*Stop Network* and is offered by Nonstop Networks Ltd., NY, NY.

The *hierarchical* storage concept causes the most often used files to be stored on the fastest medium, with less-often used data stored on progressively slower systems.

Backup media for LANs include:

Floppy disks	These can be used, but even 1.44-Mbyte floppies using data compression take too many disks. Floppies are not usually workable except in the smallest LANs. High-density Bernoulli cartridges are effective as secondary insurance.
Digital audio tape (DAT) cartridges	These use 4-mm wide tape. Though they are hailed as the backup technology of tomorrow, backups are slow to create and restore. Media failures do occur. DDS, from Sony or Hewlett-Packard, is the de facto standard, while Data/DAT is used in specific applications. DAT drives offer both DDS and Lempel-Ziv data compression, creating two ways to make DAT devices mutually incompatible. One benefit is that DAT drives and the tapes themselves are inexpensive.
8-mm tapes	These are available for most server platforms, making them a good way to trade data in a multivendor environment. They have high capacity (5 Gbytes) per tape and are low cost, but tend to be slow. Survivability in storage is good.
½-in VHS video tapes	These are expensive (about $33,000) but are fast, dense, and reliable. One tape can hold 14.5 Gbytes of uncompressed data. Special tapes, rather than ordinary VHS are recommended at a cost of about $20 each, and long-term storability is unclear. They may not work with all server platforms. Selective restorations are fast, but there is only one vendor at present, Metrum Information Storage. Although there is only a sole source, look at the bright side: It eliminates a compatibility problem.
½-in 3480 tape cartridges	These are made by IBM and Cipher Data Products, are expensive ($13,000), and have limited capacity (200 Mbytes). The 3490s that use compression quadruple that capacity. Backup and restoration, especially selective restoration, is nearly as good as *digital linear tape* (DLT). The cartridges need to be stored in a reasonably cool room to prevent warping.
½-in DLTs	Although DLTs are relatively new, they can store 6 Gbytes on a $45 cartridge. Drives range from $$7000–9000. DLT systems exist for DEC VAXs, Sun workstations, Novell NetWare PC platforms, and others. Backup, restoration, and selective restoration times are low. DLT cartridges seem to be quite hardy.

¼-in quarter inch cartridges (QICs)	These are widely used in Sun and Unix systems. They are respectably fast and durable.
Optical storage	This includes *write-once-read-many* (WORM) systems using an optical disk and laser. WORM systems are relatively expensive and once written, the disks cannot be changed or reused. As a permanent archive device, this is a plus.
5-¼-in erasable optical disks	These are also available and disks can be reused. These systems ($8500), and especially the disks at $200–500, are expensive, but the media capacity is high at 650 Mbytes. They are well-suited for storing images and graphics where file sizes are large. Optical systems are appropriate for archiving as the disks are good for up to 20 years. Backup rates are slow, restorations are better, and selective restorations are very fast.

Backup considerations. As you can see, there is less standardization in considering backups than, say, in disk arrays. It is important to know exactly what brands and models are supported by the NOS you have in mind. The NOS must have backup I/O device driver software, or it must come from a backup vendor. Achieving compatibility may require coordination between LAN and backup vendor.

There can also be conflicts between the NIC and backup device controller card: IRQ, DMA, and I/O port addresses should be inventoried to avoid this possibility. Any time a DOS or NOS change is made, the tape function should be tested.

Here are some backup features that need to be checked:

Will the backup attach to the file server or workstation? If the NOS does not support backups from the server, then it can downline load to a workstation equipped with the backup system. This is also viable if the server is full or if there is an *interrupt request* (IRQ) conflict. If the workstation is in another building, this becomes a form of off-site storage. Workstation backup also avoids having to bring the server down.

File selection should be flexible for backup or restoral. Items to consider are, for example, the filename, file and directory specification, and system and security files. It should be possible to specify files for inclusion or exclusion from backup. Streaming tape systems are good only for restoring entire disks.

Must you shut down the network? Clearly, you would rather not.

Is there a scheduler? If so, is it based on times, intervals, or both? Autoscheduling is one of the ways to minimize the human failure element. Off-hours backup reduces intrusion during production hours and minimizes the consequences of a slow backup method.

Error detection, correction, and unrecoverable segment bypass. This is standard.

Recovery service. Some vendors offer such a service for badly damaged tapes.

Consider a backup file server. It is expensive, but it may be worth it.

Real-time backup and restoral. NOSs on servers have a number of software protections that protect data while on line. The least sophisticated is *redundant directory processing.* Duplicate directory listings are kept so that corruption of one will not break the logical chain of directories and subdirectories. Were the chain to be broken, inaccessible files would be the result. You would have the embarrassing situation of having good files on the disk—you just cannot get to them. This would not sit well with the front office.

To prevent corrupted transactions, some NOSs have *transaction rollback recovery.* Let us say a disk failure occurs as record updates progress as part of a transaction. Since the end of the transaction has not been reached, the entire transaction beginning with the first update is undone or rolled back. Then the entire transaction must be entered anew when service is restored. Novell's SFT software does this with a feature called *transaction tracking system* (TTS).

A variation of this theme is *roll-forward recovery.* Here, a recapitulation of the database and an audit trail of transactions between summaries is recorded. In case of failure, the audit trail updates the last completed summary.

Assembling your backup strategy. Constructing a backup plan that meets your needs may be the most important contribution you make to your company's survivability. Today, data is life. Here are the basics:

Be systematic. Set a schedule. Files updated often require more frequent backup, sometimes twice daily. *Incremental* backups save only changed files. *Full* backups save everything.

How long must you save your data? When does it lose its timeliness? Typical periods are 1–2 years. Tape as a medium is good for 2–5 years, maximum. A *rotation* schedule lets you reuse media while keeping backup data current. You may have also have legal requirements to preserve data.

Keep your backups off-site. At home, in a special storage facility, or in an bank vault, the place should be dry, dust-free, cool, and earthquake-proof.

Be sure to index your backups. That way you can find them.

Do a test restoration now and then. Just to be sure it works and to make sure that you know how to do it. When the time comes for real, and it will, you will not flub it.

There is a lot more to backup strategic planning. Here is some motivation: A Price Waterhouse survey found that 60 percent of businesses would fail if their information systems are out for 4 days or more. After a month, 90 percent fail. Do not be one of them.

Power

It has been said that we are powering twentieth-century systems with nineteenth-century electrical power. There is more truth to this than you might think. Here is why:

Brownouts	These are long-term undervoltage conditions caused by heavy loads that the power company cannot meet. Its symptoms are like sags described below, but computer power supplies can fail (overheat) as they struggle to maintain proper voltages.
Blackouts	These are a total loss of electrical power due to accident, lightning, or overload resulting in a popped breaker or blown fuse. System or head crashes or file corruption may result. NetWare directories may be lost as NetWare keeps them in RAM when in use.
Spikes	These are large, short-duration pulses. They are caused by lightning, switching large electrical loads on and off, static discharges, and switching by the power utility. Effects include hardware damage, corrupted data, printer and/or terminal errors, and unit or system exception errors. Hardware damage may not be noticed for weeks afterward.
Surges	These are longer term than spikes, lasting for more than one full cycle (60 Hz). Surges are caused by utility switching or switching heavy loads on- or off-line. Their longer duration makes them a threat to delicate computer hardware and peripherals.
Sags	These are like surges but are undervoltages. Sags are caused by faulty grounding, too-small wiring, and sudden starting of heavy loads. Even lightning can cause sags. Sags cause CPU lockups and reduced disk speeds, resulting in read errors or a crash. The National Power Laboratory found sags to be the most common power problem.
Noise	This includes signals from millivolts to volts impressed on the power signal, so they are smaller in magnitude than spikes. *Radio frequency* (RF) noise

	made by switching power supplies, lightning, radars, or radio transmitters can cause unpredictable CPU errors, incorrect data transfer, and printer and/or terminal I/O errors.
Harmonic distortion	This is a change in the shape of the sinusoidal power waveform. Harmonics, or integer multiples of the base 60-Hz waveform, are reflected back onto the line by nonlinear loads (loads that draw power in other than sine waves). Computers, copiers, and fax machines are prime offenders. Symptoms are hardware damage, communication errors, and sometimes overheated transformers.

Many of these problems can be minimized by placing the server on its own AC power circuit. At the least, keep noisy machines like copiers off the line shared with a server.

Power conditioners. *Surge suppressors* reduce surges and filter RF noise but provide no alternate power source. They are passive and should be installed on every LAN workstation and server. You will need to spend about $100 per unit for adequate protection.

Power conditioners typically add voltage regulation, transformer isolation, and harmonic filtering. They are active devices but again provide no standby power.

Standby power systems perform power conditioning until power is lost, at which time they kick in to provide short-term power. This may cause a glitch and a subsequent computer problem, although transfer times are very short: 2–4 msec. Some have a cable to a server which causes the NOS to perform an orderly server shutdown. Standby power systems' batteries have a longer shelf life than the UPS below because they are only used if power fails.

UPSs provide continuous conditioning and power to the server. There is no "glitch-on-switch." The UPS may be cabled to a server serial port to trigger an orderly server shutdown and may even be accessible via *Simple Network Management Protocol* (SNMP) or a proprietary remote access software feature. Either way, the UPS must have enough capacity to allow time to shut the server down. Price runs about $1000 per kilovolt-amperes (kVA). (See below for the definition of kVA.)

Both the standby power system and the UPS should have a sine wave or quasi-sine wave output to most closely approximate the power they expect. Units with square wave or sawtooth outputs are of lower quality and may damage computer equipment. Using two ferroresonant-type UPSs in the same building can cause problems as they may interact with one another through the power line.

Sizing the standby power system or UPS. The basic problem is that computer power is measured in watts, while a *standby power supply* (SPS) or UPS is rated in *volt-amperes* (VA). If the computer gives its power usage in volts and amperes, multiply the two to obtain its VA value. Repeat this calculation for each device that will be on the SPS or UPS. Add them to get a total and multiply the total by 1.25 to add a safety and future expansion factor. The output from the SPS or UPS must equal or exceed this total VA figure. Thousands of volt-amperes are expressed as kVA. Computers and peripherals measured only in watts may be converted to VA by dividing the wattage by 0.7 (the power factor) or multiplying by 1.43 (same result).

UPS systems are sometimes rated in terms of ampere-hours: so many amperes of current may be drawn for so many hours. Within limits one can be traded for the other: a unit rated for 20 A-h can supply 20 A for 1 h or 10 A for 2 h. Generally, 10–20 min is enough to bring the system down.

UPS vendors offer help in sizing a UPS for you, so take advantage of their field experience. Get a few quotes.

Static discharge protection

Even a barely noticeable static discharge is 1000 V or more. Such voltages can ruin electronic equipment and/or cause erratic operation. Static discharge protection devices include:

Static mats under chairs and equipment conduct static charges to ground. *Antistatic carpets* and *antistatic sprays* do the same thing, although spraying must be repeated.

Grounding straps go around a user's wrist and connect to ground or a static mat. They have the unpleasant psychological effect of making users think they are chained to the machine (which might be true regardless).

Touch pads are for users to touch before working on the equipment. This is easy to forget, and the user may acquire another static charge without knowing it.

Security

Security consists of two elements: access and privacy on the one hand and virus protection on the other.

Limiting access goes without saying. This is accomplished by the use of passwords and user names. A hacker interviewed on "Dateline NBC" in October, 1992 found that first names, terms with sexual connotations, and common proper names were often used as passwords.

To confound hackers, use all the available letters, numbers, and punctuation marks. Remove all passwords that are inactive and those that come with the system, e.g., *guest* and *field service.* The "Dateline NBC" hacker called users and conned them out of their passwords! It took him less than an hour to crack a Fortune 500's security: They had given him a week to try. Staff should *never* give their passwords to anyone.

NetWare has very good access security, but even it was breached by a hacker from the University of Leiden. (It has since been patched.) This year Novell plans to introduce *keys* which a user must match to one set by the administrator. Microsoft's Windows NT will be certified at the Federal C2 level and eventually the higher B level.

Look for leaks in three places: the NOS, the file server's own file-sharing controls, and each network application's own file access controls. Some operating systems have holes: Unix, DOS, and OS/2 do. In some Unix implementations, a superuser prompt comes up if the operating system's input buffer is greatly exceeded. This reportedly happens in OS/2 also.

Install software that automatically logs inactive users off after a time, such as NetOFF for Novell systems. It will also free up applications software for others. Hubs, bridges, and routers are all gaining security features, such as limiting cross-network access. It is important to check router and bridge software for errors and viruses, too.

LANs are at the most risk from dial-ins. A separate communications server is a barrier preventing actual LAN access until the caller's identity is verified. Links to other networks via routers and bridges are also a threat. Often a network will have only one password check. Once the hacker is in, the hacker has carte blanche anywhere in the system. Read Clifford Stoll's *The Cuckoo's Egg*; it *really* happens!

Limit access to system and security files. This includes any personal files and e-mail, whose privacy should be sacrosanct. Create closed-user groups to limit browsing. Diskless workstations contribute to security and prevent introduction of viruses. Diskettes should be scanned on a stand-alone machine before they are used in the network.

Provide physical security for the server to keep a malicious user out of the system. Cabling in plain view will show improper taps immediately. Limit access to data scopes, LAN analyzers, and access to hubs where an illegal node could be attached.

Viruses

Strangely, viruses have not been the disaster that administrators expected, although LANs are the ideal medium for them to replicate in, e.g., the Internet Worm. IBM research suggests that for every 1000 PCs, a business can expect about 4 virus incidents annually. The average virus infects fewer than four PCs, and the primary transmission method has been contaminated disks, not networks. But if one hits you, it will cost you an average of $15,000 in lost data, manpower, and replacement costs.

Another study by USA Research, Inc. of Portland, OR, confirmed IBM's findings: 61 percent of infections came from disks brought in from the outside. Only 6 percent came from the LANs. But if you are one of the 6 percent, then you are 100 percent affected.

There are three basic virus antidotes: scanners, active monitors, and integrity checkers. Scanners must be invoked periodically, active monitors run all the time as TSRs, and integrity checkers check a CRC to see that a file has not been modified.

To protect yourself, see to it that employees regularly do virus scans. Automate it by loading the server with software that scans PCs each time they log on, e.g., AppMeter. LANprotect from Intel scans in real time for 400 viruses in NetWare environments. ViruSafe/LAN from Xtree learns unknown viruses and isolates them.

Macintoshes are equally vulnerable. Microcom's Virex software detects Macintosh viruses such as ChinaTalk and T4.

You can contact the International Computer Security Association's Virus Research Center for information on viruses.[5]

Server maintenance

Server maintenance mainly consists of:

Doing backups

Maintaining directories

Adding and deleting users

Setting up user groups

Print management

Performing software upgrades

Adding applications for users

Installing network applications

Defragmenting the disks periodically

Fine tuning

---

[5]*International Computer Security Association's* address is 5435 Connecticut Avenue NW, Suite 33, Washington, DC 20015; tel: (202) 364-8252; fax: (202) 364-1320; and BBS: (202) 364-0644.

Many of these jobs can and should be automated using backup software tools and automatic virus checks. These should be done during nonproduction hours if possible. Vendor of tools perform these tasks in varying network environments are listed at the end of this chapter. There are quite a few, so being an informed consumer is essential.

Novell certification

Some file servers and UPSs are certified by Novell as acceptable for their NetWare NOS. It is not necessary to buy such a certified server or UPS, as some vendors elected not to pay Novell to certify their machines. While certification is a comfort factor, it is not a buy versus no-buy decision factor in acquiring a LAN server or UPS. It tends to create inflexible configurations as even small changes to the NOS or the platform can void the certificate.[6]

Novell tracks hard-disk controller and network interface card performance in its *LAN Evaluation Report*. The report is updated periodically and is available free from Novell.[7] You can also access the Novell NetWire database on-line via Compuserve.

Server summary

Disk performance is key to server performance and reliability. From a performance viewpoint, the bus type is a close second and the processor speed is third.

Performance tests of like-equipped servers show little difference between them. The real variations are in configuration, disk and memory capacity, and vendor support. The last item includes on-site and warranty service, preconfiguring the server with an NOS, the free software that is included with the server, and telephone support.

Since most servers are a single point of failure, it makes sense to make them as bulletproof as possible, as with RAID. This philosophy includes a backup plan and hardware to carry it out. Off-site storage is a must.

Protecting the server means a UPS or at least surge protection. It means virus filtering and security provisions to limit access and assure privacy. In short, the server receives much the same protection as the glass-enclosed mainframes it is inexorably replacing.

------

[6]See *PC Magazine*, October 15, 1991, "NetWare certification: A seal of approval, but for how long?"

[7]Novell's address 122 East, 1700 South, P.O. Box 5900, Provo, UT 84606; tel: (800) 453-1267 or (801) 429-7000.

Representative Vendors

Facsimile servers

Software only
: Optus Software, 100 Davidson Avenue, Somerset, NJ 08873, (908) 271-9568.
  Offers FacSys 3.20e; works with Intel Satisfaxtion board plus Ferrari or Hayes JTFax boards, or Intel Connection coprocessor; needs NetWare 2.1.x plus Windows 3.0 and MIC DOS 3.0; mouse is recommended; Message Handling System (MHS) aware; mature product; easy to install and use.

Software and hardware
: Intel, 5200 NE Elam Young Parkway, Hillsboro, OR 97214, (800) 538-3373.
  Offers Intel Net Satisfaxtion; requires Novell NetWare 2.15 or higher; IPX 3.01 or later; DOS 3.3 or higher; IBM XT/AT with 640 kbyte plus 1-Mbyte expanded memory; 20-Mbyte free disk.

  PureData, 180 West Beaver Hill Road, Richmond Hill, Ontario, L4B 1B4, (416) 731-7017.
  Offers PureFax. Works with any LAN operating system and Windows' client; dedicated server is recommended; good Windows-based workgroup fax device; very easy to install; one phone line; one fax modem card per server; requires Windows environment.

Self-contained
: JetFax, 978 Hamilton Court, Menlo Park, CA 94025.
  Offers JetFax II; runs on any PC or file server; supports Hewlett-Packard PCL, ASCII, and three JetFax graphics formats; JetFax II is an external fax device that connects a PC or server to an HP laser printer or compatible; works with Windows.

Print server software

Fresh Technology Group, Mesa, AZ (602) 827-9971. Offers Printer Assist.

Brightwork Development, Red Bank, NJ (800) 552-9876. Offers PS-Print.

LAN Systems, Inc., New York, NY (212) 431-1255. Offers LAN Spool.

Multiprocessor communications servers

Cubix Corp., Carson City, NV, (702) 883-7611.

Telebit Corp., Sunnyvale, CA, (408) 734-4333. LAN Central System-Asynchronous Communications Server; performs both remote access and standard asynchronous communications services.

J&L Information Systems, Inc., Chatsworth, CA, (818) 709-1778. ChatterBox/Network Resource Server; many processor options; ISA interface to server.

Evergreen Systems Inc., Novato, CA, (415) 897-8888. Offers CAPserver; 25 MHz 80386SX processors; Ethernet, token ring, X.25, and fax.

Multitasking

Digi International's DigiBoard

Newport Systems Solutions, San Diego, CA, (800) 368-6533

IBM's ARTIC Adapters

Microdyne Corp., Alexandria, VA, (800) 255-3967.

Self-contained modem and NIC network appliances

Corollary, Inc., Irvine, CA, (714) 250-4040. Supports Ethernet on its CNS-1600.

Microtest, Phoenix, AZ, (800) 526-9675.

Network Products Corp., Pasadena, CA, (818) 441-6504. Offers model ACS2/SA.

Dayna Communications, Salt Lake City, UT. Offers LocalTalk-Ethernet routers.

Farallon Computing, Emeryville, CA. Offers LocalTalk-Ethernet routers; includes SNMP and TCP/IP support.

Talking Networks, Berkeley, CA. Offers LocalTalk-Ethernet routers.

SynOptics. SynOptics offers an SNMP LocalTalk/Ethernet router and Internet Protocol gateway.

Chapter

6

The Ethernet (IEEE 802.3) Access Method

What Is an Access Method?

An *access method* is a way of gaining admittance to the medium (cable) in an orderly way. Access methods are *data link layer* (DLL) 2 protocols, just above the physical layer. Both the physical and DLLs are carefully defined and standardized by the *Institute of Electrical and Electronics Engineers* (IEEE).

The IEEE standards divide the data link layer into two sublayers. The *media access control* (MAC) sublayer defines the approved IEEE methods for gaining orderly access to the cable. Just above the MAC sublayer, the *logical link control* (LLC) sublayer specifies how information will be passed between the MAC sublayer and higher layers.

Ethernet/IEEE 802.3 MACs are discussed in this chapter and token ring/IEEE 802.5 is discussed in the next chapter. MAC addressing and LLC sublayer functions are common to both access methods, so a discussion of them follows the chapter on token ring access. Both MAC and LLC functions are embedded in firmware on the *network interface card* (NIC).

We have referred to access methods many times so far: Ethernet, token ring, and Arcnet are all examples of access methods in current use. You have probably heard the terms IEEE 802.3 and IEEE 802.5 used interchangeably with Ethernet and token ring, respectively. Strictly speaking, Ethernet and IEEE 802.3 are not the same, but in practice the difference is small. These differences are:

Ethernet uses a starting *preamble,* a signal that precedes the message to ensure synchronization before the message starts, of 8 bytes of alternating 1s and 0s. IEEE 802.3 uses 7 bytes plus a *start-frame delimiter* (SFD). The SFD adds to the probability of successful synchronization.

IEEE 802.3 automatically pads, adds filler characters, to make sure the frame meets the 64-byte minimum length required for collision detection. Ethernet does not, so filler characters must be added by a higher layer.

Ethernet uses a *type* field in its data frame to indicate the type of data that follows. IEEE 802.3 uses a *length* field instead. The length field tells the receiver how many data octets follow. Further data characters must be pads.

IEEE's DLL interface to higher layers is different from Ethernet's to accommodate a variety of upper layer structures.

Some *attachment unit interface* (AUI) pin definitions at the physical layer make connections to Ethernet transceivers different from IEEE *medium attachment unit* (MAU) and therefore incompatible.

10Base2 and 10BaseT exist only within the IEEE standard.

However, the token ring as developed by IBM is enshrined as-is by the IEEE as IEEE standard 802.5.

Why are LAN standards needed?

In practical terms, standards assure *compatibility:* a NIC for IEEE 802.3 will work with anything else intended to work with IEEE 802.3. Test equipment, software, and hardware would all be otherwise incompatible. Standards make *multivendor interoperability* a given at the physical and data link layers.

The huge variety of IEEE-standard hardware and software allows *flexibility* and *adaptability* to changing needs, and *encourages information interchange* by breaking down old-style proprietary technobarriers. Network design, implementation, and maintenance are all simplified.

Standards reduce costs by making volume manufacturing possible. They give designers a framework around which to design, saving millions in *research and development* (R&D) costs. Standards *maintain investment value* and *reduce depreciation* by delaying obsolescence. Some would argue with validity that standards are *vital in a global economy* to avoid a "tower of babble." Standards can give organizations a *competitive advantage* over those who lock themselves into a proprietary system.

The hidden costs of training, support, and administration have made LANs more than three times as expensive to run than the equivalent cost of a hierarchical but homogeneous IBM Systems Network Architecture (SNA) network. Estimates by Gartner Group and Forrester Research place these hidden costs as high as $1800 per year per LAN-connected PC, excluding the user's time on the machine and training. These hidden costs are estimated to grow by 20 percent per year but will be held down somewhat as enterprise-wide central LAN management makes its way into the LAN community.

One obvious way to keep these costs down is to standardize. "Standardization" as used here applies in two senses: using industry-standard equipment and, within that domain, selecting certain vendors whose products become the internal organizational standard.

Standards bodies

"The great thing about standards is that there are so many of them!"

While this may seem true to the skeptic, the days of proprietary products are drawing to a close. Users now demand that vendors stop using their own technology as a way to lock customers into their own products.

The users are winning, but slowly. Vendors remain reluctant to see their products become commodities, differentiated only by price. Standards give users great buying leverage, whereas vendors had the advantage in the days of proprietary products. Now the shoe is on the other foot. The advantages of standards are that they:

Help control costs by creating competition among vendors

Reduce training and maintenance expense

Reduce support and administration overhead

Give owners flexibility, i.e., let them adapt quickly to change

Maintain investment value and reduce depreciation

Leverage application development

Encourage information interchange

Simplify network design, implementation, and maintenance

Simplify operation and management

Are increasingly necessary in a global economy

Can give users a competitive edge

Standards Development Groups

The primary world body for standards of all kinds is the *International Standards Organization* (ISO), in Geneva, Switzerland. An independent body, ISO is active in the creation of worldwide standards. Not limited by any means to telecommunications, ISO defines standards for everything from film speeds, e.g., ISO 200/400 camera film, to meteorological standard measurements.

The *International Electrotechnical Commission* (IEC) is the part of ISO responsible for telecommunications, including both voice and data. The IEC coordinates the activities of country-based standards group members.

Each country has an accredited body to the IEC. For example, it is the *American National Standards Institute* (ANSI) in the U.S. Similarly, the *British Standards Institution* (BSI) represents the U.K.

ITU-TSS, the International Telecommunications Union Telecommunications Standardization Sector, formerly the CCITT, is a Geneva-based advisory committee set up by the United Nations under Article 13 of the International Telecommunications Convention (Geneva, 1959). ITU-TSS's primary job is to devise standards for intercountry communication throughout the world.

In ISO's role as coordinator, ISO and ITU-TSS often work collectively on *open systems interconnection* (OSI) standards. For instance, ITU-TSS's X.700 series of management standards are also the ISO/OSI standards. Similarly, the IEEE 802.1–802.5 series of LAN standards have been adopted by the ISO as ISO 8802/1–8802/5, respectively.

ANSI coordinates standards development in the United States and represents the U.S. at the ISO. ANSI is both nonprofit and nongovernment. Over 300 standards committees, consisting of consumers, producers and general interest members, make up the higher level of the ANSI hierarchy. At a lower level, the Technical Committees and Task Groups work at the technical level. Membership is open to anyone.

IEEE is an ANSI-accredited standards development organization working with ISO through ANSI. Project 802, (the number was derived from the committee's formation date in February, 1980) has defined LAN standards. Over 125 companies and universities are involved. The project's goal is to define a LAN model and recommend specifications for interfaces and protocols. The 802.X standards are shown in Table 6.1.

The *Electronic Industries Association* (EIA) works with ANSI, but EIA, a trade group of manufacturers, focuses on hardware whereas ANSI is more procedure-oriented. EIA has over 4000 industry and government participants on over 200 technical committees. This effort has resulted in over 400 standards and publications.

The U.S. federal government has two internal standards bodies. One is the *National Institute of Standards and Technology* (NIST), formerly the National Bureau of Standards. NIST is a unit of the Department of Commerce, and drafts the *Federal Information Processing Standards* (FIPS), of which over 80 now exist.

TABLE 6.1 IEEE Standards for LANs

IEEE 802.1 (ISO 8802/1)	Describes how the later sections are related and their relationship to the OSI reference model, which was discussed in Chapter 1
IEEE 802.2 (ISO 8802/2)*	Functions and features to be used in a multiaccess, multistation environment (LAN); describes the functions and capabilities of the logical link protocol
IEEE 802.3 (ISO 8802/3)*	Broadband and baseband bus using *carrier-sense multiple access with collision detection* (CSMA/CD) as the access method plus physical interface specifications (the Ethernet standard)
IEEE 802.4 (ISO 8802/4)	Broadband and baseband bus using token passing as the access method, including physical interface specifications
IEEE 802.5 (ISO 8802/5)*	Token-passing access method with ring architecture
IEEE 802.6	Details a *metropolitan area network* (MAN) standard using *community antenna television* (CATV) or an equivalent medium

*These are the standards with which we are directly concerned. If you wish to read the IEEE standards in their original form, copies may be obtained for a small fee from the IEEE Service Center, 445 Hoes Lane, Piscataway, NJ 08855-1331, (800) 949-4333.

The other is the *Federal Telecommunications Standards Committee* (FTSC), a part of the General Services Administration. FTSC works with NIST, ISO, ITU-TSS, ANSI, and EIA to adapt and apply their standards toward federal government use. Only if there is no choice does FTSC conceive its own standards. It did so, for instance, in developing standards to assist *data encryption standard* (DES) implementation.

MAC Standards

Above the physical layer of cables and signals lies the DLL. As shown in Figure 6.1, the IEEE LAN protocols divide the DLL into two sublayers, the MAC sublayer and the LLC IEEE 802.2 sublayer residing above the MAC.

The MAC sublayer is the location of the access control method: Ethernet *carrier-sense multiple access with collision detection* CSMA/CD (IEEE 802.3) or token ring (IEEE 802.5). Whichever is used, their purpose is the same: Each controls access to and use of the physical layer—the cable.

LAN access control methods are divided into two categories according to the location of the mechanism. *Random* control allows any station to transmit without specific permission of a controlling entity. Often, the station will check the medium to see if it is busy before sending. This is the basic method used by Ethernet and AppleTalk LANs.

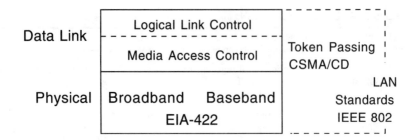

Above Layers 1 and 2, there are no LAN standards.

Figure 6.1 LANs and the ISO model.

Distributed control is embedded in the cable or medium as a *token* that is passed from station to station. Only if a token is free can a station place data on the line. Distributed control is used in token ring (IBM) and token bus (Arcnet and MAP) LANs.

The MAC sublayer is equipped with an error-detecting *frame-check sequence* (FCS). The FCS is calculated by the transmitter based on the data in the frame and placed in the FCS field. The receiver also calculates FCS. If they do not match, the data is discarded and a higher layer must ask for retransmission.

In both Ethernet and token ring, the FCS is 4 bytes long, as opposed to 2 bytes for Synchronous Data Link Control (SDLC) or High Level Data Link Control (HDLC). That makes the possibility of a defective frame being accepted as good nearly zero. HDLC and SDLC protocols automatically request retransmissions of numbered frames within the DLL. In LANs, defective frames are simply thrown away. Retransmission is left to a layer above the DLL or to the application itself.

CSMA/CD (Ethernet and IEEE 802.3)

Currently the most popular access method is CSMA/CD. It is the access method used most by bus and tree topologies and Ethernet in particular.

Carrier sense means that the station first listens for the presence of a signal voltage. If none is present, the station waits another 9.6 µsec as an interframe delay to allow other stations to recover, then transmits its message. The message is received by all stations, but address filtering by the NICs prevents action on it except by the addressed station.

The term *carrier* is a poor word choice. As we said, *there is no carrier* in a *baseband* LAN, which is what most LANs are. Formally, a carrier exists only in a *broadband* LAN. Therefore, this term is technically wrong more often than it is right.

Sometimes two or more stations will attempt to transmit simultaneously. This does not work well at all and results in a *collision*. When a collision occurs, all receivers ignore the garbled result. All the transmitters whose signals collided (as opposed to those who had no traffic to send and were therefore quiet) send a *jam* warning signal to assure that all transmitters stop. All transmitters then resort to a *backoff algorithm* that uses a random number in each machine to begin a timer. The odds of each transmitter waiting the same time to transmit again are very small, minimizing the chance of a second collision. If there is a second or subsequent collision, the backoff period increases exponentially.

Collisions are caused by propagation delay in the cable. Since it takes time to send a signal down the cable, a station at one end of the cable may begin transmitting after another one has started, causing a collision. The worst case is between the two farthest-apart stations. Doubling the length of the delay (a round trip) is called a *slot time*. A slot time in IEEE 802.3 is 512 bits, or 51.2 μsec at 10 Mbit/sec.

The backoff algorithm is designed to account for traffic. When traffic is light, the delay is minimal, becoming longer as traffic builds. The backoff delay has each station generate a random number within a range of values. If the range is small, the likelihood of another collision is greater; if the range is large, slot times may be wasted. Thus, a compromise is needed.

CSMA/CD uses *binary exponential backoff* (Figure 6.2). It is defined as the range (r) of numbers between $0 \leq r < 2n$, where n is the number of retransmission attempts made. For the first ten tries, n steps incrementally from 1 to 10. For tries 11 to 16, n's value is 10. After that, it declares a fatal error and reports it to the client layer.

The range of backoff delay that is allowed is measured in slot time increments. Beginning with a small range and expanding to a larger one only in case of multiple collisions keeps the backoff waiting time as small as possible. The maximum would therefore be 1023 slot times at 51.2 μsec each, for a total of 52.3776 msec. In human terms, this is just over half of a tenth of a second and is imperceptible to us.

Frame length

Frame length is important in Ethernet. Clearly, longer frames are more efficient than shorter ones. Further, if a station begins transmitting at one end of the cable and then another one begins later due to cable delay, the first station must transmit long enough for it to detect the collision with the second. Thus, the minimum frame length time

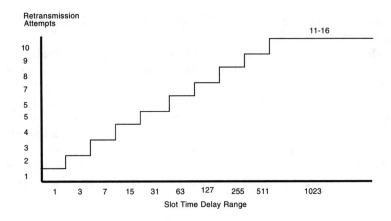

For Try Number: The Backoff Timer's range may be:
(In Slot Times)

For Try Number:	The Backoff Timer's range may be: (In Slot Times)
1	0-1
2	0-3
3	0-7
4	0-15
5	0-31
6	0-63
7	0-127
8	0-255
9	0-511
10	0-1023
11-16	0-1023

Figure 6.2 Binary exponential backoff.

must be twice the propagation delay between the stations farthest apart on the cable. Recall that this figure is called a slot time, the minimum time guaranteed not to contain a collision. In IEEE 802.3, at 10 Mbit/sec, the slot time is 51.2 μsec. The minimum frame size is therefore 64 bytes.

Frames that are too short, less than 64 bytes long, are called *runts*. By definition, *late collisions* occur after the first 60 bytes have been transmitted and are usually due to excessive cable lengths. The relationship is so strong that there is usually a 1:1 correspondence between runt frames and collisions when examined with a protocol analyzer.

Conversely, frames that are longer than 1518 total bytes are called *jabbers*. *Medium attachment units* (MAUs) that connect stations to the cable and will cut off jabbers after a fixed time-out. Otherwise, they would clog up the cable indefinitely.

The *collision domain* is the number of stations that could collide with one another. Clearly, the smaller the collision domain, the better.

In practice it is considered normal to see as many as 15 percent collisions. Greater collision ratios are abnormal and constitute cause for investigation. The usual culprit is an inadvertent violation of cabling length rules or the use of too many repeaters.

Ethernet Performance

Ethernet has virtually no delay accessing the cable under light to moderate loads. Heavy loads result in throughputs of 2–3 Mbit/sec, nowhere near the 10-Mbit/sec clock speed. Because of the increasing opportunity for collision at higher traffic loads, its performance deteriorates quickly past the 80 percent performance utilization level, the traffic "knee."

Multiple access means that each node on an Ethernet LAN has equal access to the network. There is no priority mechanism to give one station priority over another. The nearest thing to a priority-setting mechanism is that some NICs can be set for a maximum transmittable frame size. The longer the frame, the greater the time on the cable once accessed, consequently the higher the priority.

The Ethernet and IEEE 802.3 story

Ethernet standards came long before the IEEE standard. Xerox' Palo Alto Research Center (PARC) began a project in 1972 to develop a LAN to link office equipment. It failed commercially. Revised, it emerged as Ethernet Version 1.0 in 1980 under the auspices of DEC, Intel, and Xerox (DIX).[1]

In 1982, Version 2.0 was introduced as an effort to resolve differences between the now-established Ethernet Version 1.0 and the IEEE 802 Project, which had been formed in February, 1980. Version 2.0 was also backward-compatible with Version 1.0.

---

[1]The term *Ethernet* comes from the mythical ether through which radio and light waves were thought to have to travel. In 1887, the Michelson-Morley experiment sought to measure the relative motion of the earth and the ether. There was none, and so the existence of the ether came into question. Albert Einstein's theory of relativity later explained many physical events without requiring the ether premise. After 1900, the theory was discarded. But as you can see, the term has been reincarnated.

The IEEE 802.3 standard became official 3 years later, in 1985. To handle a greater variety of upper layer protocols, the IEEE changed the DLL slightly—just enough to make it incompatible with either Ethernet version.

Even so, Ethernet and IEEE 802.3 hardware can exist on the same LAN—no problem. It is just that an Ethernet card will ignore IEEE 802.3 frames and vice versa, unless the card supports both types. Many do.

Virtually all NICs support IEEE 802.3 today, but Ethernet is still found in many installations, especially if they are DEC-based.

In 1988, the IEEE published the ThinNet IEEE 10Base2 standard, using thinner RG-58 coaxial cable. The reduced cable, installation, and maintenance expense fueled the use of IEEE 802.3. The IEEE again rejuvenated the standard in 1990 with the formalization of 10BaseT as the twisted-pair wiring standard for IEEE 802.3 LANs.

The spawning of IEEE 802.3 from Ethernet, and their subsequent close relationship, has led many to refer to them synonymously. But they are not functionally synonymous. They are in fact incompatible as you will see.

Certainly "IEEE 802.3" is more of a mouthful than is "Ethernet." Therefore, it is more likely that an IEEE 802.3 LAN will be mischaracterized as Ethernet. This is especially true since the trend is to use IEEE 802.3 and away from Ethernet. The computer community's lack of rigor has led to this confusion.

In a pragmatic sense, or from a distance, there is little practical effect. But those working on LANs every day need to use the terms faithfully. Those using protocol analyzers will know immediately if the LAN they are dissecting is IEEE 802.3 or Ethernet. They should be prepared for either and understand the differences.

In this spirit, we begin our comparative investigation by noting several distinctions relating to frame structure between the two, as shown in Figure 6.3.

The Ethernet preamble is an 8-byte sequence of alternating 1s and 0s, used to synchronize the receiver and indicate the beginning of a frame. IEEE 802.3 uses seven preamble bytes but adds an SFD of 10101011 (AB_{hex}). The two ones at the end indicate the frame is about to start.

Ethernet addressing is always 48 bytes long. IEEE 802.3 originally allowed 2-byte locally administered addressing, but this option has since been deleted. Addressing, being common to both IEEE 802.3 and 802.5 token ring, is discussed in greater detail in Chapter 9.

If necessary, IEEE 802.3 adds filler characters after the data in the information field to meet the minimum frame length requirements, a process called *padding*. The *length field* indicates the length of the data

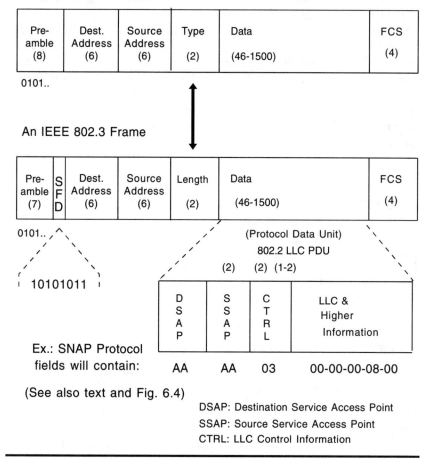

Figure 6.3 Comparing Ethernet and IEEE 802.3 frames.

field when pad characters follow. The length field has a maximum decimal value of 1500 (05DC$_{hex}$) bytes. Longer packets are invalid and are called *jabbers* or *very long events.*

There is no length field in Ethernet. If padding is required, it must therefore be provided by higher layers.

In IEEE 802.3, the data field begins with IEEE 802.2 LLC control headers that provide *destination service access point* (DSAP) and *source service access point* (SSAP) and control information. In most LANs, the IEEE 802.2 control field has no practical function unless higher layer protocols are in use.

If they are, then the type of protocol will be specified. For instance, NetWare messages using *Internetwork Packet Exchange* (IPX) protocol will contain a hexadecimal E0 in the DSAP and SSAP fields. For Banyan's VINES, it is BC in these fields.

Sometimes a LAN will use the *Transmission Control Protocol/Internet Protocol* (TCP/IP) suite for routing, i.e., IP, and end-to-end control, i.e., TCP. Using the *subnetwork access protocol* (SNAP) as shown in Figure 6.4, the LLC DSAP/SSAP then becomes AA/AA, indicating that the frame's information should be sent to IP. The control information following is an 03_{hex}, indicating that it is an unnumbered frame, i.e., the catch-all category for other than user information or supervisory messages.

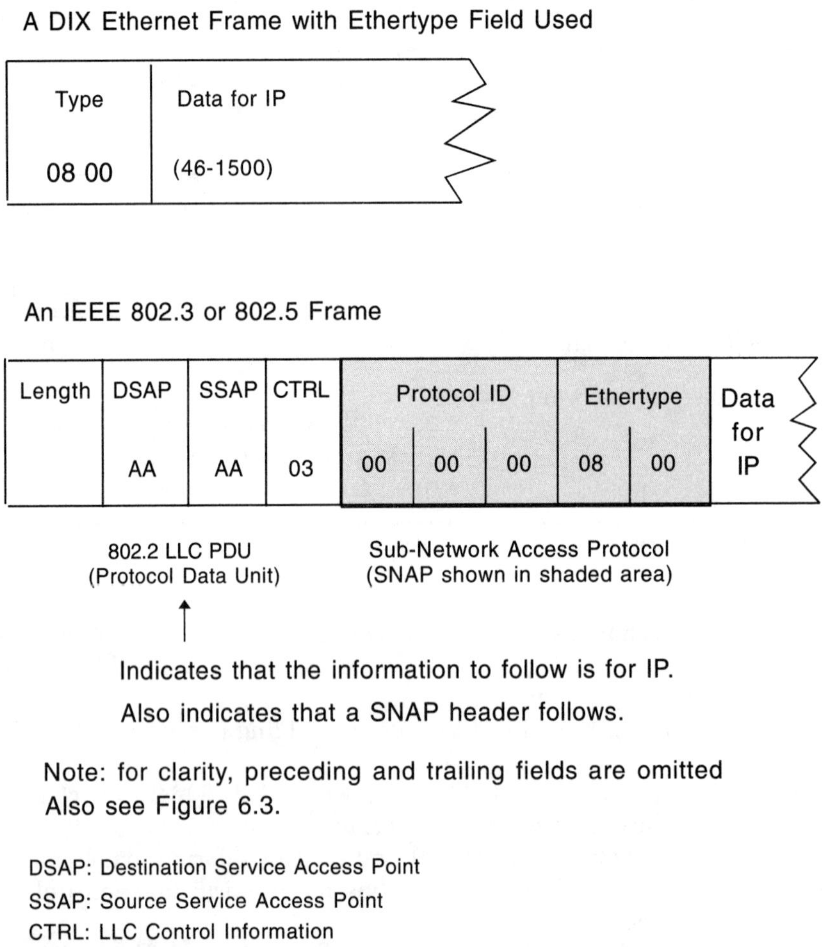

A DIX Ethernet Frame with Ethertype Field Used

Type	Data for IP
08 00	(46-1500)

An IEEE 802.3 or 802.5 Frame

Length	DSAP	SSAP	CTRL	Protocol ID			Ethertype		Data
	AA	AA	03	00	00	00	08	00	for IP

802.2 LLC PDU   Sub-Network Access Protocol
(Protocol Data Unit)   (SNAP shown in shaded area)

Indicates that the information to follow is for IP.
Also indicates that a SNAP header follows.

Note: for clarity, preceding and trailing fields are omitted
Also see Figure 6.3.

DSAP: Destination Service Access Point
SSAP: Source Service Access Point
CTRL: LLC Control Information

Figure 6.4 LLC/SNAP and Ethernet type headers.

The SNAP header follows the control field. The first 3 bytes represent the protocol identifier (ID), which is all 0s. This means that the last 2 bytes contain an Ethernet protocol type code. For IP, it is 0800_{hex}, meaning that an IP datagram follows.

Had IPX been in use, the *Ethertype* code (as it is sometimes called) would have been 8137_{hex} or 8138_{hex}. For VINES, it would have been $0BAD_{hex}$.

In Ethernet, there is no IEEE 802.2 LLC structure. The Ethernet type field simply contains the Ethertype code to indicate use of a higher layer protocol. About 30 such protocols are so defined. Using Ethertypes is optional. Even though it is used this way, the meaning of the type field itself is not defined by the Ethernet specification.

Receivers can tell an Ethertype from an IEEE length field because the highest length value of 05DC is smaller than the lowest Ethertype value, 0600 (Xerox XNS IDP).

Data must be in multiples of 8 bits but is unrestricted otherwise. If data to be sent is less than the minimum 64-byte frame size (excluding the preamble), a higher layer must pad accordingly if Ethernet is used, whereas IEEE 802.3 will do so by itself.

The IEEE 802.3 data field length is based on maximum frame size and address sizes set for a given implementation. Ethernet is less flexible: The minimum and maximum number of bytes is fixed at 46 and 1500, respectively.

Both Ethernet and IEEE 802.3 use a 4-byte FCS to detect errors. The transmitter calculates the FCS based on all the data up to but excluding the FCS itself. The FCS field contains the output of a 32-degree polynomial generator called a *cyclical redundancy check* (CRC); the same generator is used in IEEE 802.4 and 802.5

The transmitter then inserts the result of the CRC in the FCS field. The receiver performs an identical calculation. If the calculation equals the FCS value, the data is error-free. An error causes the frame to be discarded. A higher layer must detect the loss and request retransmission. Thus, for many protocols MAC communications are said to be connectionless, i.e., a "datagram."

Datagrams are sent on a best-effort basis, with no prior establishment of a session, no guarantee of delivery, and no acknowledgement of receipt. These functions are left to higher layers, often the transport layer. The logic is that it is wasteful to duplicate such checking in each layer. The higher layer, said to be connection-oriented, will establish a session and assure correct delivery and retransmission if necessary.

Both frame types can be mixed on the LAN. However, both sender and receiver must be Ethernet or IEEE 802.3. The only exception is if the receiver will accept both frame types, and some NICs do. Today, IEEE 802.3 is the predominant MAC standard. There are also some

physical pin definition differences between Ethernet transceivers and
802.3 MAUs with respect to the *attachment unit interface* (AUI) connector.

Inside the physical and MAC layers

As Fig. 6.5 shows, the allocation of physical and data-link tasks is
slightly different between the two access methods.

Encapsulation takes data packets from the *client* layer and adds the
header and trailer information, sometimes called *bookends,* to create a
frame as shown earlier. The frame is decapsulated at the other end,

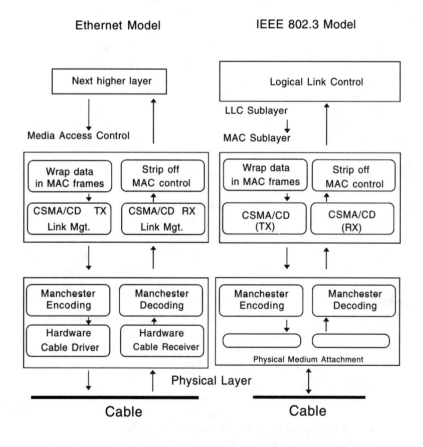

In the IEEE 802.3 Model, the MAC+LLC sublayers
comprise the complete Data Link Layer

Figure 6.5 Comparing the Ethernet and IEEE 802.3 reference models.

where the header and trailer are removed. The remaining packet is passed up to the client layer.

Link or media access management refers to the twin processes of avoiding collisions and handling collisions if they occur. For either method, *Manchester encoding* and decoding is used to guarantee a transition every bit time (.1 µs at 10 Mbit/sec). The transitions allow timing to be derived from the data sent. A transition also indicates that a carrier is present. The encoding function adds the preamble to each frame, and decoding at the receiver removes it before passing the frame on to the MAC layer. Voltage swings are between 0 V and –2.05 V (Figure 6.6).

These voltages are generated and received by the channel access hardware in the NIC if the card contains an on-board transceiver as in 10Base2 or 10BaseT. For 10Base5, the Ethernet transceiver (called a

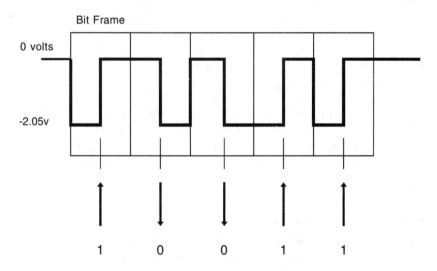

Used in Ethernet and IEEE 802.3

(Note: IEEE 802.5 Token Ring uses a variant called *differential* Manchester encoding.)
(See Chapter 7)

Positive-going transitions are 1s

Negative-going transitions are 0s

All bit positions or "bit frames" contain a transition

Figure 6.6 Manchester encoding.

MAU in IEEE 802.3 terms) is separate and connected directly to the LAN cable. The transceiver, or MAU, will be connected to the NIC through an AUI cable. The AUI cable can be up to 50 m long and makes it unnecessary to run heavy coaxial cable to a workstation. Further information concerning physical wiring can be found in Chapter 4.

Relationship to network operating systems

Because they are simple, CSMA/CD Ethernet or IEEE 802.3 NICs are inexpensive. The *network operating system* (NOS) does not know or care what access method it works with, since the IEEE 802.2 LLC software interface hides lower layers from it.

That is why Novell NetWare works with both Ethernet and token ring access methods. NetWare begins at layer 3, the network layer, with its *Internetwork Packet Exchange* (IPX). At the transport layer, the *Sequenced Packet Exchange* (SPX) protocol is used. SPX connects to the *NetWare Core Protocol* (NCP), which resides at the session, presentation, and application layers. Breaking the rules, NCP sometimes bypasses SPX for the sake of speed and speaks to IPX directly.

Above Layer 2 there are few LAN standards. That is why the Internet's IP has been drawn in to serve routing needs at layer 3, and TCP has been drafted to provide end-to-end connection control at layer 4.

IPX and SPX are both proprietary to Novell. NetBIOS is copyrighted by IBM. These are two examples of higher layer protocols, many of which are proprietary. Some have applications in LAN computing while others do not, such as the EIA RS-511 Manufacturing Message Service. To a similar extent, proprietary NOSs hook into the IEEE standard at the LLC sublayer. There is no standard NOS!

With time, standardization is migrating up the stack. Perhaps the best example is Novell's steady move toward TCP/IP and away from its own IPX/SPX.

Where Ethernet performs best

Ethernet performs well in cost-limited applications with moderate traffic loads. It is simple, readily expandable, and easy to troubleshoot if linear, as opposed to hubbed, networks are avoided. Its ubiquity gives it excellent connectivity between devices.

Ethernet has no inherent redundancy as does token ring, so it is not well suited for critical real-time applications, especially if they are remote or unattended. Nor does it have a self-healing or fault tolerance mechanism as we will see in token ring.

Ethernet is at a disadvantage in that it is a *probabilistic* access method: There is a probability that the cable can be grabbed, but no guarantee. It is therefore hard to model expected Ethernet performance. At very high traffic loads, collisions are assured and the network will slow down. Thus, Ethernet performance does not deteriorate gracefully under heavy loads. Ethernet's degradation in this way may make it unacceptable for some critical applications.

Degrading Ethernet performance can be improved by:

Making sure there are no hardware faults, such as defective NICs or cable problems.

Tuning the NOS. This is not an Ethernet problem, but it may help.

Breaking the network into smaller pieces, using a *bridge* to link them.

Using an Ethernet switch, which eliminates collisions. See Chapter 11.

Upgrading to full-duplex Ethernet (proprietary) or 100-Mbit/sec Ethernet when it becomes available, which is discussed later in this chapter.

Implementation options

To increase compatibility, options have been deliberately minimized. The former two-byte addressing option has been deleted, leaving virtually no implementation options—only Ethernet or IEEE 802.3. Addressing, though a MAC-layer function, is discussed in Chapter 9 since it is common to both IEEE 802.3 and 802.5.

There is a practical difference for NetWare 3.X and 4.X users. Novell calls its Ethernet_II software NIC driver "802.3," which you now know is a contradiction. It is in fact the Ethernet frame format with the Type field. Novell calls the IEEE format the "802.2" format, which is semilogical since only the IEEE version uses the IEEE 802.2 LLC sublayer. Novell now ships both drivers for both NetWare versions.

Some newer NetWare options and fixes reqire the IEEE 802.2 frame format, such as NetWare Core Protocol (NCP) Packet Signature and IPX checksumming. Packet Signature makes sure IPX packets are not forged, spoofed, or altered. Checksumming verifies that an IPX packet is not damaged on receipt.

Bridging Ethernet frames to token ring can cause problems. These are mostly eliminated if the IEEE 802.3 frame format is used since both IEEE 802.5 token ring and IEEE 802.3 frames contain IEEE 802.2 LLC sublayer headers. A common sublayer makes source-route transparent bridging possible (see Chap. 11) and eliminates the need for an IPX router to send Ethernet frames.

Both Ethernet and IEEE 802.3 drivers can be loaded; this is the default for NetWare 4.X servers. This way, the server can handle both frame types. However, if there are other servers on the network, Net-

Ware's Service Advertising Protocol (SAP) and Routing Information Protocol (RIP) traffic will double since two frame types are in use. This adds network traffic and can also cause routing troubles. Accordingly, it is best to load as few frame types as possible and migrate off the Ethernet format as quickly as can be managed. Lastly, if routing is used, be sure the router can handle the IEEE 802.3 format.

Common Ethernet errors

Too many collisions cause network delays. A collision rate of 15 percent or less is considered normal. Collisions tend to increase in direct correlation to server utilization and traffic on the cable. If there is no correlation, a fault exists. Faults may be reported as collisions when in fact an equipment failure is the real culprit.

Collisions may be *local* or *late*. Local collisions occur on the same segment and usually indicate that the segment is too long. In a too-long segment, the cable appears clear at one end, when in fact a packet is coming from the other end. A collision results. Check the cable lengths to make sure that the cable specifications are met. Local collisions often happen after recent cable additions to the segment.

Late collisions occur later in the transmission (after 60 bytes); this should not be possible. Late collisions meet the 64-byte minimum, but the CRC does not check and the collision-detection pair within the AUI cable (if used) is tripped. Defective cabling or topology-rule violations can also cause late collisions. Electromagnetic interference that clobbers a packet and creates the appearance of a collision between two frames can also be reported as a late collision.

It is useful to "ping" each station in the collision pair. If a station does not answer, check it for proper length packets (64–1518 bytes). Also check to see if its reply packet passed the CRC check. If one does not respond to the ping, replace the NICs, one by one. One of the receivers may be unable to hear traffic on the LAN and so prevent a collision.

CRC errors are caused by corrupted data packets in transmission. The packet is thrown out, and a higher layer must request retransmission. Faulty or illegal cabling or *electromagnetic interference* (EMI) is a common cause of CRC errors. If one station has chronic CRC alignment errors, replace the NIC.

Jabbers, frames longer than 1518 bytes, should never occur. Jabbers fail the CRC check and can be detected by a protocol analyzer or by the simple expedient of shutting one station off at a time until the errors decrease. Jabbers are most often caused by a defective NIC or NIC drivers, a congested transceiver, or a malfunctioning repeater.

Runt frames are the opposite of jabbers: They are less than 64 bytes long, but have good CRCs. Runts and jabbers are often due to bad NIC software drivers in the transmitter. Reload, or update, the drivers.

The NIC itself can malfunction and cause collisions. Using a protocol analyzer's station or traffic monitor, observe the stations, see if one in particular is associated with the collisions, and then replace the NIC and/or drivers.

Cable faults are responsible for nearly 80 percent of LAN problems. Be sure that the simple things are covered, i.e., that the terminators are in place and are not accidentally grounded, that all connectors are firmly secured, and that there are no intermittent or frayed wires. Mismatched coaxial cable and use of nontwisted silver-satin cable in 10BaseT systems invites trouble.

Is there a common denominator? If several stations report similar problems, something they have in common has changed. Seek a common denominator, e.g., the cabling, a repeater, or the same hub. Did you recently add a segment or change something in the file server? Here, as in every area of LAN activity, an accurate and updated administrator's log can be your best troubleshooting tool.

Ethernet design goals

These goals are declared in the Ethernet specification:

Simple	There should be no more complexity than necessary.
Low cost	It must be low in cost relative to the devices attached to it.
Compatible	Fewer options mean fewer incompatibilities.
Flexible in addressing	It should be able to address single stations, multistations, or all the stations.
Fairness	All the stations have equal network access.
Progress	No station should prevent the progress of another.
High speed	It should run at 10 Mbit/sec; CSMA/CD will run between 1–20 Mbit/sec.
Minimal delay	CSMA/CD minimizes delayed access to the cable.
Stability	The network should be stable regardless of the load.
Maintainable	Never build a network you cannot manage.
A layered architecture	Layering isolates the physical medium from the logical data link portion of the network.

Ethernet and IEEE 802.3 Enhancements

Full-duplex Ethernet

Full-duplex variants of Ethernet exist today. The ability to send and receive at the same time is touted as the equivalent of bumping Ethernet speed up to 20 Mbit/sec. This is not true in a strict technical sense, but clearly the throughput rises substantially. Existing 10BaseT cabling remains unchanged but a full duplex hub is required. For example, Seeq Technology's Kodiak subsidiary offers full duplex 8- and 16-bit ISA NICs. This is a nonstandard, proprietary implementation.

On-board Ethernet

Today, some vendors, e.g., Hewlett-Packard, Compaq, and Dell, offer PCs with preinstalled NICs. The trend will be to streamline this process and build Ethernet directly onto the PC motherboard. Engineering workstations today all have this capability, much the same way that AppleTalk is part of every Macintosh (see below).

Right now, the added cost of an on-board NIC, about $100, is too high to include Ethernet as a built-in feature. Variables in the networking environment, e.g., operating systems, NOSs, and cabling, are also a concern.

Some of these variables are becoming constants. The acceptance of 10BaseT has made *unshielded twisted pair* (UTP) a common denominator for cabling. Ethernet semiconductor makers continue to add features that will make an on-board chipset as flexible as a stand-alone card.

Ethernet is used today by about 56 percent of networked PCs in business and is expected to grow to 66 percent in the next few years. In this decade, Ethernet's growth rate has been more than double that of its nearest competitor, token ring. Even with an Ethernet-ready PC, those needing token ring or any other LAN access method can simply add the appropriate card as they do now.

Current predictions are that the value NIC-makers add to a chip set will decrease as the chips become more self-contained. For instance, software drivers are provided free of charge by NOS vendors such as Novell and Microsoft. Ultimately, a chip set will cost about $20 and become as standard as a parallel port.

100 Mbit/sec Ethernet

Since the CSMA/CD specification is written in terms of bit times, although we refer here to bytes for convenience, rather than nanoseconds, scaling it to 100 Mbit/sec is thought to be relatively easy. In fact, this has already been done once, as early Ethernet ran at 1 Mbit/sec. When it was scaled to 10 Mbit/sec, the MAC layer remained unaltered. Retaining the MAC would also mean that existing LAN analyzers and management systems using SNMP MIB II would require no changes.

Users have generally rejected existing 100-Mbit/sec *fiber-distributed data interface* (FDDI) technology to the desktop as too expensive at

$2500 per workstation. Even *copper digital data interface* (CDDI), using copper instead of fiber, will cost $1500 per node and is yet unproven. Vendors believe that users really want an inexpensive solution that will let them run at 100 Mbit/sec at twice the price of 10BaseT.

For example, Thomas-Conrad of Austin, TX, and LAN Performance Laboratories of San Diego, CA, offer a 100-Mbit/sec Ethernet NIC operating on UTP. MicroAccess of San Jose, CA, offers a similar NIC for fiber. None of these products is standards-based as none exists as of this writing.

At this writing, a consortium consisting of Hewlett-Packard, AT&T Microelectronics, Ungermann-Bass, and others has proposed a 100-Mbit/sec standard called 100Base-VG to the IEEE 802.3 (Ethernet) Higher Speed Study Group. It would use inexpensive IBM Type 1 UTP, fiber, or Level 3 UTP cabling; however, the standard would require a new access protocol, called Quadrature Signaling and Demand Priority Protocol.

Workstations would use all four pairs of wire in Level 3 10BaseT cabling to exchange data over an unrestricted radius. The workstation would request bandwidth, prioritized and allocated from a hub, so that time-sensitive multimedia applications could have rapid access.

MAC frame size and format would not change. In principle, the NOS and application would not be affected, being insulated by the LLC sublayer. Cards would be priced around $200 that support both 10 and 100 Mbit/sec. Under the consortium's plan, 10- and 100-Mbit/sec segments could communicate via a bridge; a more expensive router would be unnecessary. The consortium's proposal minimizes physical layer disturbances and is robust, but the access method is so different that it really is not Ethernet anymore.

Another consortium, consisting of 3Com, SynOptics, and others has proposed using Level 5 cable called 100Base-X. It would retain the existing IEEE 802.3 MAC. A 100Base-X card would cost $600–700.

Yet a third proposal from start-up Grand Junction Networks, Inc. would substitute the ANSI Physical Media Dependent (PMD), from FDDI, layer for the physical layer and retain the Ethernet 802.3 MAC. Their argument is that FDDI is established and known to work at 100 Mbit/sec. Grand Junction Networks, Inc. cannot be dismissed—Ethernet's father, Robert Metcalfe, is on its board of directors.

As of this writing, the Hewlett-Packard/AT&T proposal, backed by 30 or so vendors, is under evaluation by a newly created IEEE 802.12 subcommittee on the basis that their proposal does not use CSMA/CD. The 3Com/SynOptics proposal remains with the IEEE 802.3 subcommittee, which must decide whether to retain developmental control or delegate it, too, to a new subcommittee.

For users, the probable outcome will be a choice between the two standards. Like VHS and Beta, the winner will be chosen in the marketplace.

Today, few applications short of multimedia or imaging need Fast Ethernet's 100-Mbit/sec speed, but mainframe links, graphics, computer-aided design/computer-aided manufacturing (CAD/CAM), medical/document imaging, and Windows applications might need it.

Established functional requirements for Fast Ethernet include:

Multiple hub support

A distance of 100 m from the workstation to hub

Support for EIA/TIA-568 categories 3, 4, and 5 UTP, plus shielded twisted pair (STP)

Use of RJ-45 connector for UTP

A medium-independent interface

Switchable 10 to 100 Mbit/sec adapters

Detection and isolation of 10-Mbit/sec adapters accidentally plugged into a 100-Mbit/sec hub

FCC Class B emission conformance

European EN550-22B emission conformance

IEEE 802.3 frame format, packet size, and error detection

IEEE 802.3—equivalent error rates

The current thinking is that CSMA/CD will be retained. Delays in setting standards will swing more users toward ever cheaper FDDI and CDDI. Perhaps some will wait for high-speed *asynchronous transfer mode* (ATM) as their ultimate high-speed solution. While ATM will be more expensive and will require an active hub, Fast Ethernet will cost around $500 per node and need no hub. We can conceive of a high-performance network using Fast Ethernet to the workstation and incorporating an ATM backbone. Applications such as graphics, CAD/CAM, and software engineering could benefit from this kind of speed and still be cost-effective.

Carrier-sense multiple access with collision avoidance

A non-IEEE, non-OSI variation of CSMA/CD is *carrier-sense multiple access with collision avoidance* (CSMA/CA). In CSMA/CA, all stations listen to a transmission in progress. Afterward, all stations begin individual timers whose setting is different for each. Timer expiration with no data to send gives the next station with a longer delay an opportunity to send, and so on down the chain, until one times out who has data.

What happens if no one has data to send? One system uses the highest priority station to send a dummy packet, triggering a new time-out period. Another lets anyone transmit and uses collision detection to resolve any conflicts.

Setting priorities is easy: the station with the least delay gets the highest priority. Another option is to give the station that just received a message first opportunity to respond. A third enforces a delay on the last transmitter to give others a chance.

An example of CSMA/CA is AppleTalk. AppleTalk is a proprietary access method loosely based on the OSI model. It is not a de jure standard. AppleTalk uses a variation of CSMA/CA in which the sender looks to see if the cable is busy. If it is not, it waits for an additional pseudorandom interval. If the cable is still free, it sends a request-to-send frame. If the receiver responds with an affirmative clear-to-send frame, the sender transmits its message. Otherwise, the sender tries again.

Collisions are possible even with pseudorandom timing, but AppleTalk has no way to detect them. It relies on higher layers to make sure frames are not lost.

The proprietary physical layer of AppleTalk is called LocalTalk. LocalTalk uses EIA-422 *differential balanced transmission* over STPs. In differential balanced transmission, the receiver detects only voltage differences between the two wires in the pair. Noise spikes appearing on both wires have the same electrical voltage and so are ignored.

Optical fiber and plain old telephone wire is also used. A network cannot be more than 300 m long (990 ft). Up to 32 devices are supported at a comparatively slow 230.4 Kbit/sec. The topology is, like Ethernet, a bus or tree.

LocalTalk circuitry and AppleTalk client firmware is included in every Macintosh and devices like Apple laser printers. AppleTalk is also supported in the operating system, so all the hooks are present to build a peer-to-peer and printer-sharing LAN by adding a few cables. Apple's NOS is called AppleShare.

Third parties have substantially extended AppleTalk's functionality. Bridges and routers allow longer distances and links to other networks. IBM, Hewlett-Packard, and Sun machines can be connected to an Apple network. Servers of various types are also offered for file sharing, print servers and communications servers. Cards inserted in the Apple will let it work on frame relay networks or even at 100-Mbit/sec FDDI speeds.

There are also Apple-based NICs that let an Apple machine participate in an Ethernet, using EtherTalk access, or a token ring network, using the TokenTalk link access procedure. Arcnet cards are also available.

Conclusion

Though the differences are small, the use of the terms Ethernet and IEEE 802.3 are not strictly interchangeable, although in daily use it happens all the time. The networking professional should be aware of this distinction between usage and reality.

We have seen that Ethernet and IEEE 802.3 provide a random yet organized way of accessing the cable. Inexpensive and efficient, the method is the single most popular access method in use today, and it is expected to grow at a rate well ahead of its nearest challenger, token ring. Enhancements such as 100-Mbit/sec operation will extend its utility well into the next millennium.

Even so, Ethernet and IEEE 802.3 are less well-suited for high-performance applications where self-healing and graceful performance under load is mandatory. For these applications, token ring is the access method of choice, and we explore its intricacies in the next chapter. You will also find a concise comparison of these two most popular access methods at the end of that chapter.

Chapter

7

The Token Ring (IEEE 802.5) Access Method

In this chapter, we continue our discussion of *media access control* (MAC) methods with a focus on the second most popular method, token passing. If you have not yet read about the purpose, role, and function of a MAC method, go back to the previous chapter and read the introductory sections. You need not read the later part of the chapter focusing on Ethernet. Then return to this chapter. You will then have the necessary underlying knowledge to get the most from the following discussion.

Although at first glance, a ring might seem a poor way to architect a LAN, it is in fact a very good way. Physically wired as a star, it has hubs that simplify installation, troubleshooting, and maintenance. A hub can be unpowered or highly intelligent; either way it can handle any station that is disconnected or unpowered and could therefore potentially break the ring. Furthermore, a token ring has an alternate path between hubs that gives it a measure of redundancy lacking in Ethernet. For further details concerning token ring wiring, see Chapter 4.

As is customary in the industry, we refer here to token ring, token passing, and IEEE 802.5 as synonymous terms, even though they are slightly different things. Token ring is an architecture, whereas token passing is an access control method and the subject of the IEEE 802.5 standard.

In the last chapter, you saw that Ethernet and IEEE 802.3 use a *random* control method. The access control mechanism is embedded in each *network interface card* (NIC), and there is no signal on the shared bus cable to act as a green or red light to the data. Access in Ethernet is *probabilistic:* There is always a probability that a given station can seize the cable but never a guarantee.

For some applications, that is not good enough. They need a guarantee of access after no more than a certain period of time. That is what token-passing provides: It is a *deterministic* access method under which eventual access is assured. Let us see how this *distributed* (as opposed to random) mechanism works.

Token Ring Performance

Token passing (IEEE 802.5)

Networks using a ring topology, shown in Figure 7.1, take a different approach to access control than Ethernet's linear bus and random control method. Rather than looking to detect an absence of a carrier, ring stations look for a small message on the network called a *token*. If the token is free, the station absorbs the token and begins to send data.

A message, now called a *frame* because it contains data, then circu-

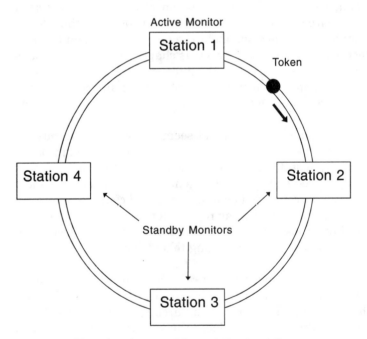

The token is passed from station to station.
A station may capture the token and transmit data.
If there is no token available, it must wait.

Figure 7.1 A token ring.

lates through other stations unaltered. When the message reaches the destination station(s), bits are set, indicating that it has been received. When the frame gets back to its originator, the station places the token back in the ring. Only the originator can release a token as a way of verifying successful transmission. Free once again, the token goes back into circulation.

Normally, all frames go around the network just once. Since only the sender frees the frame, there is an inherent ability to perform broadcasts. Token ring uses broadcasts heavily for administration and control. In reality, the token is just one of many IEEE 802.5 MAC frame types.

Various error conditions can cause a sending station to fail to recognize its own message and thereby restore the token to circulation. To prevent this, an *active monitor* station on the ring watches frames go by and detects frames that are going around for the second time. In a typical ring, all other stations are passive standby monitor backups that can take over this responsibility if the primary monitor is turned off, is disconnected, or fails.

Unlike Ethernet, the token ring approach *guarantees,* short of ring failure, every station an opportunity to transmit within a given time. Thus, token ring access is called a deterministic access method. Station priorities can be set by giving some stations more access to transmission than others.

Multiple frames can usually be sent using a single token. When this happens, they are marked as intermediate frames, by setting the *intermediate* (I) bit in the ending delimiter to a 1, indicating that more will follow. The final frame contains a 0 in this position to indicate the end of the sequence. The net effect is to reduce overhead and delay.

If there is only one frame, it will also be marked as final with a 0. Note that bridges copying the frame for passage to another network will not copy the I-bit.

In contrast to Ethernet, there is much complexity in monitoring the ring. Consequently, there is a need for an active monitor in a much more intelligent NIC.

Token ring systems are common where high-volume traffic is present and/or high performance is required. Token ring networks operate at 4 or 16 Mbit/sec with 150-Ω *shielded twisted pair* (STP) or 100-Ω *unshielded twisted pair* (UTP) cables. Token rings are perceived, rightly or wrongly, as the "Cadillac" of LANs.

Token passing is not restricted to rings; it can be used in bus and tree wiring configurations, too. The *Manufacturing Automation Protocol,* used in automated manufacturing and developed by General Motors, uses a token bus, as does Arcnet, a long-standing LAN scheme developed by Datapoint Corp., that runs at 2.5 Mbit/sec.

In the *token bus* scheme, the token is passed from the highest address station in the network to the next lower address. This station can transmit for up to a predefined time. Then the token must be passed to the next station. Stations receiving a token but having no traffic pass the token on immediately.

Monitors

The active monitor.   In any token ring network there will be one *active monitor*. The active monitor is the usually the first station powered up on a ring. Since this function occurs in the NIC, *the workstation user is unaware* that their machine is the active monitor. The active monitor changes automatically if that station is turned off or unplugged from the network. The active monitor:

Issues tokens. Typically, there is one token per ring.

Looks for a token to pass through it every 10 msec using the *Good-Token Timer*. The average time to traverse a 4-Mbit/sec token ring network with 100 stations is 60 μsec, so this is quite generous. In other words, the token has 166 opportunities to reset the timer before the timer expires.

Monitors for and detects the absence of a token.

Performs a *ring purge* of tokens and restarts the ring using a *claim token frame*.

Provides master timing and jitter compensation which are embedded in data transitions. All the other stations synchronize themselves with the active monitor since it is the master timer. *Jitter*, or undesired changes in phase of the signal as it traverses the cable, are smoothed out by the active monitor.

Ensures sufficient ring latency, buffer delay, to hold a token. The latency must equal or exceed the length of time needed to transmit 24 bits. An additional elastic 6-bit buffer maintains constant latency. The result is a 30-bit buffer, which is usually initialized to 27 bits.

Controls the issuing of tokens and transmission priority.

Queues reservation requests from stations and servers.

Sends *active monitor present* (AMP) frames every 7 sec.

During startup, the first station to attach to the ring becomes the active monitor. Thereafter, the first station whose Good-Token Timer expires will initiate the claim token process and become the active monitor if the current active monitor is turned off, disconnected, or fails.

When the active monitor sends the AMP frame, each *standby moni-*

tor, all the other stations, sends a *standby monitor present* frame. This is called a *ring poll* and lets each station identify its *next active upstream neighbor* (NAUN).

From the ring poll, a function called the *configuration parameter server* (CPS) learns the physical order of devices on the ring. Stations are allowed to report soft errors to the *ring error monitor* (REM) function, and each station learns the address of its NAUN. The NAUN address is needed in a *beacon frame* if a hard error occurs.

Beacons are needed because each downstream neighbor monitors its upstream neighbor for proper operation. If a downstream neighbor suspects its NAUN is ill, it sends a beacon frame to tell that specific machine to go off-line and test itself. The beacon frame must therefore contain the address of the suspect machine.

The standby monitor. Every other station on the network is a standby monitor. If the active monitor is not working, a new active monitor will be selected. The active monitor is declared dead if there is no token for 2.6 sec and no AMP frame for 15 sec.

Active monitor contention begins when a standby monitor sends a claim token frame (Figure 7.2) into the network. The first station to send a claim token usually becomes the new active monitor. This sta-

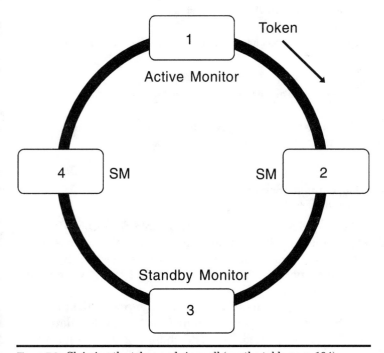

Figure 7.2 Claiming the token and ring poll (see the table on p. 194).

tion is also usually the first *downstream* neighbor of the old active monitor. Standby monitors

Back up the active monitor.

Send "I am here" messages every 7 sec.

Expect to see AMP frames from the active monitor.

Initiate a claim token if the AMP frame is not seen on time.

Compare the claim token frame address with the station address. If the station has a higher address, it initiates claim token, and the process continues until the highest station address is found. When the station that sent the claim token copies three of its own claim tokens, it becomes the new active monitor.

Determine the physical order for the CPS by using standby monitor present (SMP) frames. SMP frames also allow soft error reports to be sent to the REM. NAUN identification is also performed via standby monitor present.

1. Station 1, the active monitor, is powered off or disconnected from the ring.

2. Stations 2–4 see the absence of AMP frames every 7 sec.

3. Downstream, station 2 starts sending claim token frames.

4. Stations 3 or 4 can substitute their own if their address is higher, but this does not usually happen.

5. When station 2 copies three of its own claim token frames, it becomes the active monitor.

6. Station 2 sends a ring purge, clearing the ring of tokens.

7. Once the purge has gone around the ring, station 2 issues its own new token.

Remember all this happens in the NIC and is transparent to the user and the user's workstation.

Error monitoring, configuration control, and parameter distribution

Soft and hard errors described below are acquired from the NICs and are counted by the REM. The REM evaluates errors and reports them, along with threshold violations, to the *network operating system* (NOS). Not all rings necessarily have a REM, but the NICs do have REM collection capability.

Configuration control is provided by the *configuration report server* (CRS). The CRS collects configurations and station status data, and sets ring parameters as directed. The CRS changes ring configurations by requesting stations to remove themselves, a useful security tool. There will be a CRS on each ring in a multiring system. A *ring parameter server* (RPS) allows central management of operational parameters, usually from a bridge. The RPS receives and responds to request initialization frames from stations seeking entry to the ring. These responses include the ring number, ring station soft error timer value, and physical location information.

Note that use of the term "server" does not mean there is a separate server box for the REM and CRS. Data is gathered on the NIC card and then given to management function software incorporated into the file server.

MAC's role in token rings

MAC processes manage token creation, circulation, and ring purging. They also control neighbor notification and govern station insertion and removal, beaconing, and error reporting. The NICs detect soft and hard errors, and often they recover from both kinds automatically. There may be some degradation of service and intermittent disruptions, but recovery is usually spontaneous. The next sections in this chapter define and describe the most common and important MAC functions.

The token ring MAC sublayer. As Figure 7.3 shows, *logical link control* (LLC) frames are wrapped by MAC frames with a MAC header and a MAC trailer. For this reason, MAC frames are sometimes called *bookends*. MAC frames protect the LLC and its data as the frames travel the network. At the receiver, the frame check sequence (FCS) is checked to make sure the data is error free and the MAC bookends are stripped off. The LLC sends the data to higher layers and ultimately to the correct application.

MAC frames are created, received and acted on by the NICs, which ensure that the ring is running properly. They fix minor problems, via self-healing procedures, identify the *fault domain* of bigger problems, and indicate the location of such problems. All this takes less than 1 percent of the network's capacity, so the administrative overhead is minimal.

There are a core of 25 MAC frame types which fit into 6 categories:

1. Media control frames let the ring recover from most errors.

2. Station initialization frames let stations get into and out of the ring gracefully without disrupting other stations. Examples include the *duplicate address test* (DAT) frame, the request initialization frame

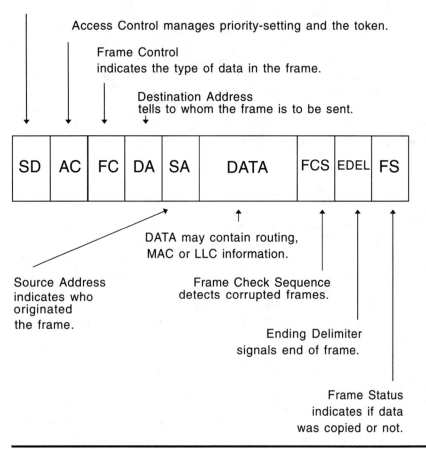

Start Delimiter indicates the beginning of a frame.

Access Control manages priority-setting and the token.

Frame Control
indicates the type of data in the frame.

Destination Address
tells to whom the frame is to be sent.

| SD | AC | FC | DA | SA | DATA | FCS | EDEL | FS |

DATA may contain routing,
MAC or LLC information.

Source Address
indicates who
originated
the frame.

Frame Check Sequence
detects corrupted frames.

Ending Delimiter
signals end of frame.

Frame Status
indicates if data
was copied or not.

Figure 7.3 The IEEE 802.5 MAC frame.

to the RPS, and the ring poll, which allows stations to find out who is upstream from them.

3. Error monitoring frames report errors from stations to the REM. The errors include defective cyclical redundancy checks (CRCs) in the FCS field, misframes, beacons, and the like.

4. Network management frames let the network manager control the configuration of each station, including controlling ring access and modifying parameters. These frames are used by the CRS and RPS.

5. Token frames control access.

6. Information frames carry an applications's data management software.

Media control frames. Accessing and controlling media control frames requires a NOS located in a server or other intelligent device. The five media control frame types can *detect and isolate* soft errors such as:

Line errors	Manchester code errors and defective frame check sequences.
Internal errors	Recoverable errors inside the NIC.
Burst errors	Errors that indicate a lack of transitions on the ring. Transitions are needed to maintain synchronization between NICs.
A and C bit errors	Errors that indicate faulty neighbor notification.
Abort delimiter sent	Count of frames that are ended prematurely. The aborting station sends an *abort delimit,* a 2-byte message consisting only of a start and end delimiter, described shortly.

Media control frames can report, but not isolate, these errors:

Lost frame errors

Receiver congestion

Frame copied error

Token error

Soft errors are a symptom of ring degradation, but they do not stop the network. The ring will self-recover from the above soft errors and from the following hard errors:

Faulty wiring

Frequency errors

Loss of ring signal

Typical token ring problems

Recall that *MSAUs* are Multistation Access Units, used to create the ring. These connect to workstations through two twisted-pair wires called *lobes.*
These problems include:

Defective or miswired connectors	These cause intermittent operation or complete failure.
Too-long cables	These may violate cabling specifications and cause errors.

Noisy cables	These caused damaged frames, hence CRC errors. Cable testing and thorough documentation are required to find these flaws.
Noisy MSAUs	They often appear as excess phase jitter.
Stuck MSAU ports	These are problems if they do not close when a station is removed from the ring. Conversely, ports can stick closed when stations apply phantom voltage to open the ports.
Defective or marginal NICs	These cause repetitive beaconing.
Intermittently defective NICs or cabling problems	These are indicated by beaconing rings.
Ring or station speed mismatches	These can bring down the entire ring.
Marginal cabling	This causes the ring to work at 4 Mbit/sec but not 16 Mbit/sec. Is it the entire ring, or is it a lobe? This effect can also be due to excessive ring jitter.
Excessive broadcast traffic	This can tie up the ring, especially where heavy source routing is in use.
Too much traffic or ring errors	This can cause slow response time. Properly running rings should never beacon. Self-correcting soft errors can also mask latent problems so periodic health checkups are mandatory.
Lobe not inserting into ring or frames so badly damaged that station and server cannot communicate	This results in the inability to find a file server.
Overloaded servers	These may be dominated by one or a few stations, or may have internal problems which increase response time.
Duplicate local or remote addresses	These can be very difficult to find, as the symptoms can come and go. A LAN analyzer is often required to spot such malfunctions.
Misconfigured stations, bridges, or routers	These can cause delays due to poor routing, insufficient buffer space, or excessive traffic on one or a few servers.

Ring poll (neighbor notification)

The purpose of a ring poll is to identify each station's NAUN. The NAUN is used in *beaconing,* which is described in a moment.

For this discussion, refer to Figure 7.2, which illustrates the claim token process. The steps in the process are:

Station 1, the active monitor, sends an AMP frame. Its destination is all the stations.

Station 2 reads the source address of the frame, its *upstream neighbor address,* (UNA) and saves it. The frame status is set to 11xx11xx, meaning that the frame has been copied.

Stations 3 and 4 see that the frame has been copied by reading the frame status byte and pass it along unchanged.

The active monitor sees that the token frame has come back and that it has been copied. It then frees the token.

Station 2 sends a SMP with an all-station broadcast address.

Station 3 copies the source address and saves it as its UNA.

Stations 4 and 1 see the frame and pass it along.

Station 2 sees its frame come back and frees the token.

Stations 3 and 4 do the same thing.

If any station saw a change in its UNA, it reports to the CRS.

Beaconing

Beaconing results from detection of a hard error: a wire fault, frequency loss, or ring signal loss. Beacon frames indicate which type of hard error has occurred. The frame also contains the NAUN.

A downstream neighbor may detect what it believes to be a fault in its NAUN. It sends eight beacon frames with the NAUN's address. When the NAUN sees its address, it removes itself from the ring and does a *lobe test.* If it passes the test, it reattaches itself to the ring without doing the full reinsertion process.

The original beaconing station may still perceive an error after 26 sec of NAUN reattachment. It then disconnects itself for a lobe test. The test is comprehensive and if the station passes, it is probably fully functional. If the problem continues, manual intervention is required to resolve the *streaming beacons* problem. The usual result of a hard error is removal of one station from the ring, which results in a change in ring configuration or an inoperative ring requiring intervention.

Station insertion

Let us say a station powers itself up on the ring. How does it insert itself into the ring? The process has five steps:

Lobe media test   Recall that the station is looped to itself through the
                           multistation access unit (MSAU). At power-up, the
                           NIC transmits a Lobe-Media-Test MAC frame. If it

is successfully received within three tries, it goes to the next step.

Physical insertion   The station applies *phantom voltage* to the MSAU relay. The relay changes state and the new station is now physically in the ring. The station looks for an AMP, SMP, or purge MAC frame. If it sees none within 18 sec, it is likely to be the only station on the ring and it starts sending claim token to become the active monitor. However, if it sees an AMP, SMP, or purge, it sends a DAT frame.

DAT   The station sends itself a DAT frame, where the destination address is itself. If the frame comes back unread, it is the only station on the ring with that address.

Neighbor notification   The station takes part in the next ring poll to learn its NAUN.

Request initialization from the RPS   The station sends a request initialization frame to the RPS. If the RPS does not answer within four frames, the station uses its own internal default parameters.

In case the station passes a beaconing self-test, the station reattaches to the ring. Only physical insertion takes place. There is no need to repeat the other tests.

Token Ring Bit by Byte

The previous discussion is a summary of the essential token ring functions. We continue now with a more detailed discussion of token ring frame structures, showing how some of the above functions are implemented at the bit and byte level.

Part of the ensuing material discusses some features unique to token rings: priority setting, bridge-routing, and addressing.

Inside the token

As shown in Figure 7.4, the token is a 3-byte message. It consists of a starting delimiter, access control byte, and an ending delimiter.

The starting delimiter is a unique 8-bit warning telling all stations that a transmission is coming. It contains deliberate and unique Manchester code violations[1] (Figure 7.5) that never occur in the transmis-

---

[1]As shown in Figure 7.5, in differential Manchester coding, the lack of a transition during a bit frame is a code violation. If there is no transition as the bit frame starts, it is a J violation. If there is a transition, it is a K violation. Js and Ks are always paired to avoid accumulation of a DC component, an electrical imbalance caused by the use of one without the other.

A Token Frame

Priority
Token
Monitor
Reservation

Intermediate Frame Bit
Error Bit

Start Delimit	Access Control	End Delimit
JK0JK000	P-P-P-T-M-R-R-R	JK1JK1IE

An Information Frame

CRC Protected

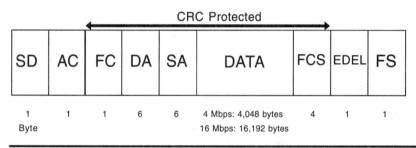

SD	AC	FC	DA	SA	DATA	FCS	EDEL	FS

| 1 | 1 | 1 | 6 | 6 | 4 Mbps: 4,048 bytes | 4 | 1 | 1 |
| Byte | | | | | 16 Mbps: 16,192 bytes | | | |

Figure 7.4   A token and an information frame.

sion of data. This way, data and control cannot be mistaken for one another. The code violations are JK0JK000, where J and K are the specific violations and 0 is a binary zero.

The access control field contains 8 bits. The P bits indicate the priority level, and the R bits are used to make a priority reservation. A frame is a token if the T bit is a 0. If the T bit is a 1, it is a frame containing either data or control information.

M, the monitor bit, is normally a 0 and is set to a 1 by the active monitor the first time it encounters a data frame. If the active monitor sees a 1 again, it removes the frame and issues a new token. All the other stations simply pass the M bit along. The rationale behind removing the frame is that the originator was unable to recognize the corrupted frame or that the originator failed. The same method is used to detect a constantly nonzero priority token. As with recirculating frames, this frame is detected and removed.

Eight levels of priority are possible, from 000, the lowest, to 111, the highest. When the token is received, a NIC compares the token's priority to the priority of the frame it has to send. If the token's priority is the same or less than the frame to be sent, the NIC sends the frame. If the token's priority is higher, the frame must wait.

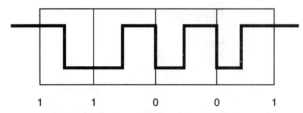

1   1   0   0   1

A transition at the beginning of a bit period is a 0.
No transition at the beginning is an 1.

The *direction* of the transition does not matter.
A noise pulse would have to change the signal's polarity
both before and after the anticipated transition in order to escape detection.
A missing expected transition indicates an error.
Having no DC component, transformer coupling is feasible.

Manchester coding is used because it includes the
necessary bit transitions to make timing recovery possible
from the signal itself.

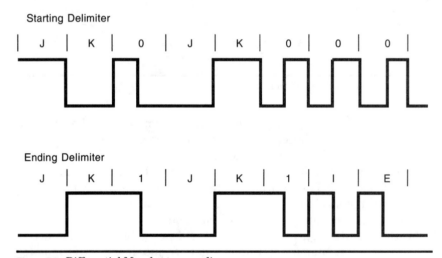

Figure 7.5 Differential Manchester encoding.

There are also eight reservation levels using the same format as the priority bits. When a station passes a frame, it can set the reservation bits if they have not already been set to a higher value by another station.

You may infer correctly from Figure 7.4 that the originating station removes its data from the ring by absorbing the frame and releasing the token. As part of the release process, shown in Figure 7.6, the station copies the reservation bits or its own frame priority bits, whichever is higher, into the priority field and saves the original priority value. This gives the station that made the reservation the ability to send its data, unless an intervening station has an equal or higher priority frame waiting. When the station that copied the reservation into the priority field sees the token come around again, the NIC restores the token's priority bits that it saved earlier if the priority was lower. Priority setting, not always implemented, provides a mechanism for

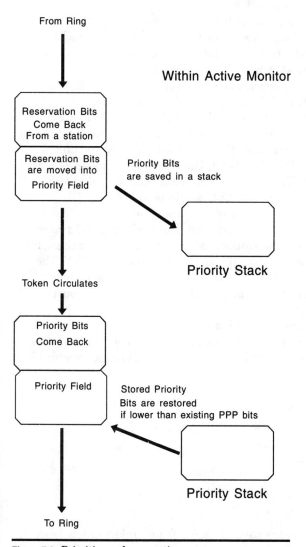

Figure 7.6 Priorities and reservations.

ensuring that the data in low-priority frames (ultimately from and to user applications) will be sent.

The ending delimiter is located at the trailing end of the token. Again, deliberate but different Manchester code violations shown in Figure 7.4 are used. Using the deliberately code-violated token means that stuffing zeros into the data stream as in SDLC/HDLC is unnecessary to avoid the possibility of mistaking data for a delimiter.

The Ending Delimiter code is JK1JK1IE. If I is set to 1, it means that this is an intermediate (more data to follow) frame, and if E is set to a 1, it means that an error was detected.

As you can see, there is no addressing in the token. It is passed in what is called *physical attachment order*, i.e., serially by machine, going endlessly around the ring until data is to be sent. Then the token is replaced by a frame as shown in Figure 7.5.

When the token is replaced, more control plus data is inserted between the access control and ending delimiter octets. The first of these is a single octet called *frame control* (FC) (Figure 7.7). The FC octet indicates whether the frame contains control information or a LLC plus data. If the first 2 bits are 00, the receiver knows that this frame contains MAC information. If it is 01, the frame contains a LLC protocol data unit (PDU). Thus, the *subnetwork access protocol* (SNAP) header (from Chapter 6) with its LLC would be coded 01.

A third possibility is 1X, indicating an undefined format. The frame control field also specifies any buffering required for MAC frames in the remaining 6 bits. All the stations will decode and act on these bits.

In a LLC frame, the six control bits are designated rrrYYY. The rrr bits are set to 000 on transmission and ignored at the receiver. The YYY bits indicate the priority of the LLC PDU from the source LLC entity to the destination entity.

In MAC control frames, the third and fourth bits are presently unused. The four remaining bit positions are called the *physical control field*. They contain six essential attention codes, also called vector identifiers. These are:

0010	Beacon frame
0011	Claim token frame
0100	Ring purge frame
0101	AMP frame
0110	SMP frame
0111	DAT frame

Any other code indicates that all MAC frame information is in the information field. The six codes also indicate the presence of additional

MAC, LLC, or Undefined Frames may be sent as shown.

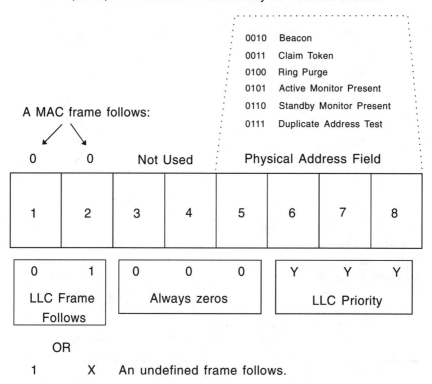

Figure 7.7   The frame control field.

MAC data in the information field, called *vectors*. Each vector may contain subvectors, which carry data or modifiers. Subvectors may be nested and contain other subvectors and vectors.

If the frame contains LLC information (higher layer data), that data will start at the beginning of the information field. The destination *service access point* (SAP) directs the data to the correct protocol stack. The source Service Access Point (SSAP) tells which stack the data came from. Hexadecimal examples of SAPs include E0 for Novell NetWare, F0 for NetBIOS, or AA for TCP-IP's SNAP protocol. LLC is discussed in greater detail in the next chapter.

Addressing

Addresses are 6-bytes long. As in Ethernet, both the destination station and source station addresses are given (Figure 7.8). Destination addresses can be individual, groups, or broadcasts, but all source ad-

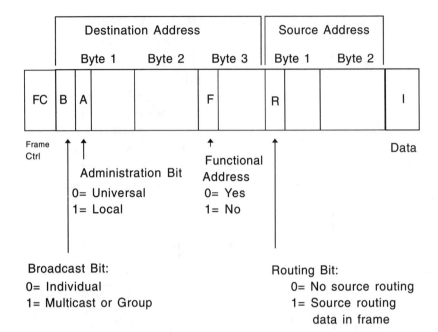

Figure 7.8 Addressing.

dresses are individual. Broadcasts can be sent in either of two forms. All Is (16 FFs) indicates that all the stations on all the rings in a multiring network should receive the frame. Sending a destination address starting with C0 00 FF indicates that all the stations on the same ring should receive the frame.

For destination addresses, a 0 in bit 0 of byte 1 means that the address that follows is to an individual. A 1 indicates a multicast or broadcast using the format above.

In a *source* address, this bit position is used to indicate that *source routing* information is found in the frame. Source route bridging is defined by ANSI/IEEE 802.1d-1990, MAC Bridges. In addition, IEEE 802.5M contains the SRT Operations Addendum to IEEE 802.1d.

Again in destination addresses, bit 1 of byte 1 indicates that the address is universally assigned (set to 0) or locally assigned (set to a 1). Universal administration invokes a guaranteed unique address burned into the NIC's ROM. Local administration is assigned locally and is often used in token ring and internetworks.

At this time, IEEE is considering a scheme that would split the 6-

byte address into a 14-bit ring number consisting of the remaining 6 bits of byte 1 plus all of byte 2. The last 32 bits would be used as station subaddresses. You may hear this referred to formally as the "Hierarchical Structure for Locally Administered Addresses."

In byte 2, bit 0 indicates a *functional* (0) or *nonfunctional* (1) address. Functional addresses speak to a network *function* rather than to a NIC. Sometimes they speak to a bridge. Here are a few examples:

Functional address	Functional network entity
C0 00 00 00 00 01	Active monitor
C0 00 00 00 00 02	Ring parameter monitor
C0 00 00 00 00 08	Ring error monitor
C0 00 00 00 00 10	Network manager
C0 00 00 00 00 80	NetBIOS
C0 00 00 00 01 00	Bridge

Routing

In the strict sense, layer 2 routing is not part of the IEEE 802.5 standard. Consequently, provisions for routing constitute an extension to the IEEE 802.5 frame format.

Routing methods. Under *source routing,* a sending station—the source—tells the network how to route the frame. Routing tables are not used. Under *network routing,* routing of the frame is left to the network, and neither the sender nor receiver has anything to do with it. Token rings use *source routing.*

The interconnection of rings is performed by bridges. Bridges *filter* frames on a ring, looking for frames addressed to stations not on the ring. Bridges *forward* these frames to an adjacent ring. Bridges may be as simple as a PC with two token ring NICs and bridging software. They may also be incorporated in a server. The highest performance bridges, those with the highest filter and forward rates, are dedicated machines designed specifically for bridging. Products from vendors such as Cisco and Wellfleet fall into this category.

Bridges may be able to load-share traffic among several paths. Most bridges can be configured to pass or reject the *discovery frames* that find routing paths. This ability provides a security mechanism and through proper configuration, can reduce the likelihood of a "frame explosion" in which frames are broadcast and then rebroadcast until the network is flooded with them.

Figure 7.9 shows that source-routing paths are described by a sequence of ring and bridge numbers. To find a route, a sending station first tests the waters by sending a test or *exchange identification* (XID)

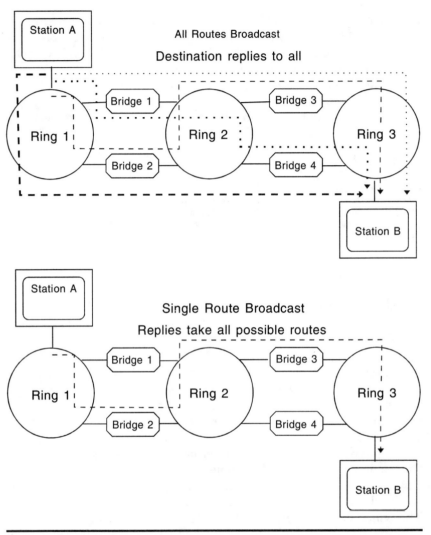

Figure 7.9 Source routing.

discovery frame around its local ring with its desired destination address attached. If there is no response, it sends another test or XID discovery frame to all the rings.

These are referred to as "query," "explorer," or "discovery" frames and include the originating ring number. The explorer frames take all possible routes until the destination is found. Ring and bridge number information is added as the frame goes from one ring through a bridge to another ring.

Eventually these frames find their destination. The destination replies in the same sequence as the received explorer frames, reversing the route taken by the explorer frame. The destination also includes its ring number.

At the source, these frames begin to arrive, each containing a different route. The originator chooses one, usually the first one that is received, as it was the quickest to respond. Just because a route was selected does not mean that it was the cheapest, most efficient, i.e., the least number of hops, only that it was the quickest. Frames are now sent using the selected route. If the destination has traffic in reply, it uses the same route as the sender, but in reverse.

A variation on the theme is the single-route option. Here a *single-route broadcast* (SRB) frame is sent, and the destination replies with an *all-routes broadcast* (ARB) frame. The best route is usually chosen based on the one with the smallest number of hops. This greatly reduces network traffic, which can be expensive on a WAN segment.

Route discovery is used only once per logical session between devices. For instance, once logged into a remote server, the route is established and is used unchanged.

Ethernet uses a different routing method, called the transparent *spanning tree protocol*. The term "transparent" means that the routing process is transparent to the workstation. It is incompatible with source routing. For this reason, many vendors offer a bridge called a *source-route transparent* (SRT) bridge.

This bridge links Ethernets and token rings by looking for a *routing indicator* (RI) bit (Figure 7.10). If the bit is present, it uses source routing and looks for source routing information in the frame. Otherwise, it uses the spanning tree protocol. Being a hybrid bridge, the SRT bridge combines "source routing" and "transparent" in its name.

Of great concern in any routing algorithm is the amount of traffic it creates. While source routing uses discovery and reply frames, it does not have the traffic inherent in updating routers' routing tables throughout the network. Furthermore, the continuity established between the source and destination is established through actual use, not some routing table that may not reflect a failed link. In this sense, source routing is a very empirical and pragmatic way to do routing. It can also provide some performance advantages, especially in 16-Mbit/sec LANs.

Source routing at the bit and byte level. As mentioned above and as shown in Figure 7.11, if bit 0 in byte 1 of the source address is set to a 1, routing information will be present after the source address field. This bit is used by an SRT bridge to determine which routing method to use in routing the frame.

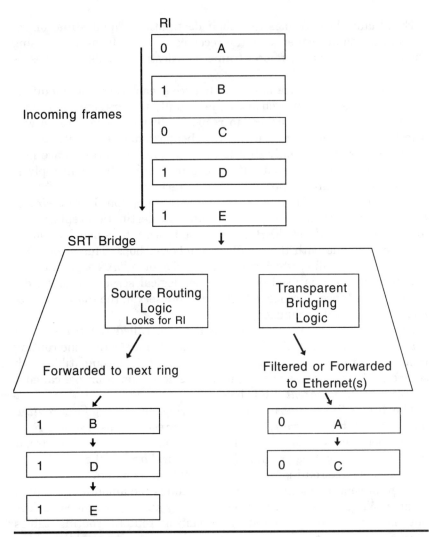

Figure 7.10 SRT bridging.

The first piece of routing information is the *routing control* field. It consists of 2 bytes, but at present, bits 1 and 2 of the first byte and the last 7 bits of the second byte are not used. This is often done to allow room in the structure for expanded functions later. The routing control field is followed by segment numbers that identify each traversed bridge and ring segment "hop." Let us look at the routing control field first.

Bit 0 is the broadcast bit. If it is a broadcast frame, the bridge checks all the segment numbers (ring and bridge numbers) attached to the

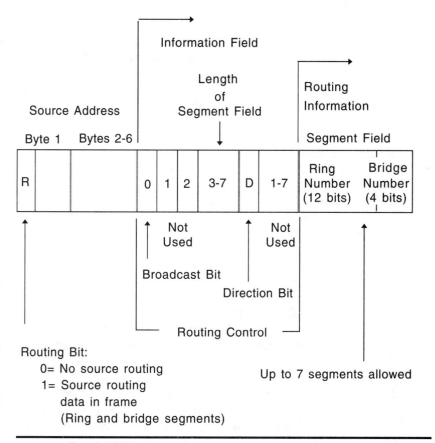

Figure 7.11   Detail of SRT bridging.

frame. If its own segment number is missing, the bridge adds it. If it finds its own segment number, the bridge discards the frame because it has already been through the bridge.

A nonbroadcast frame uses the segment numbers to route the frame to its destination. If its segment number is in the frame, it copies the frame to the segment number to its left or right as indicated by the direction bit in bit 0 of the second byte of the routing control frame. This is how the bridge handles outbound messages that already carry routing information versus reply frames going back to the source. If its segment number is absent, it is not in the route and so it does not copy the frame.

Bits 3 to 7 indicate the length of the routing information field. Since the routing information field intrudes on the early part of the information field and since there is no delimiter between them, the NICs need to know where MAC or LLC information begins after the routing information.

Bridges use the length information to know where to add a segment. After it is added, the bridge increments the length field. Bridges also update the routing control frame to indicate the largest frame size that can traverse the route.

Recall that segments consist of a ring and bridge number, and are contained in 2 bytes. These numbers are assigned by hand to assure that they are not duplicated by accident. Ring numbers come first and are 12-bits long. Bridge numbers follow and are 4 bits long, for a total of 16 bits.

The routing control field can support up to 7 segments or hops. It is common to have many more bridges and rings than the hop count can support. The effect is simply to limit the distance that can be traversed by a frame.

The information field follows any routing information. It is a variable-length field, whose maximum length[2] depends on the ring's speed. At 4 Mbit/sec, the maximum length is 4048 bytes. At 16 Mbit/sec, it is also four times as large, i.e., 16,192 bytes.

There is no limit on data format and no bit stuffing to avoid control aliasing (mistaking data for a control code). The information field must, however, be sent in multiples of 8 bits or else a misframe error will be declared.

As discussed above, the information field may contain routing information, MAC information, or LLC information plus application data. Similar control field headers that are necessary at higher layers are also considered data.

The *frame check sequence* (FCS) field shown in Figure 7.12 is a 4-byte field containing the result of a cyclical redundancy check as defined by IEEE 802.5. Everything from and including the frame control field to the FCS field itself is used to perform the calculation at the transmitter. The result appears in the FCS field.

The receiver performs the same calculation on the data. If the result matches the content of the FCS, the data is free of error. Otherwise, the frame is discarded. In that instance, a higher layer must request retransmission.

A 4-byte CRC-32 is a very thorough *cyclical redundancy check* (CRC) indeed; SDLC and HDLC use a 16-bit CRC on transmissions that are sent via leased telephone lines and satellites—very imperfect media. The cleaner nature of shielded or even unshielded wire reduces the

---

[2]The maximum lengths vary slightly as they depend on the allowed token-holding time.

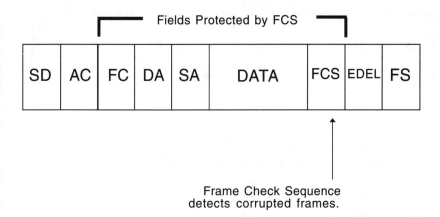

Frame Check Sequence
detects corrupted frames.

The FCS is computed using the data in binary form
from the fields indicated.

If any bit is incorrect, the FCS computed by the receiver
will not match. The frame will then be discarded.

Figure 7.12 The frame check sequence.

probability of error even more. LAN traffic is as close to error free as
you can get.

As mentioned earlier, the ending delimiter follows JK1JK1IE. If the
I bit is a 1, then the frame is an *intermediate* frame, meaning that
more frames will follow within the token. Frames continue to be sent
until there are no more to send or the token holding time expires. The
last frame is indicated by setting the I bit to 0.

The E bit is an *error* bit. If a forwarding station senses an error during retransmission, the station sets the E bit to a 1. This tells the sending station that the frame or token was sent incorrectly. Such errors
might include a defective CRC, a frame that is not a multiple of 8 bits,
or a code violation sensed somewhere else than in a delimiter. The ending delimiter will be recognized regardless of the setting of the IE bits
or even if they are not sent at all.

Frame status field

As Figure 7.13 illustrates, the frame status is set by the receiving station to let the sender know what happened. The form of the 8-bit field
is ACxxACxx. Both A bits are set to 1s by the receiver when it recog-

A	C	X	X	A	C	X	X

A=1: The destination address was recognized by the receiver.
A=0: The destination address was not recognized.

C=1: The frame was successfully copied.
C=0: The frame was not copied.
X: Don't care.

A and C bits are duplicated for safety
as the Frame Status field is not CRC protected.
The bits must match to be accepted as valid.

Figure 7.13 The frame status field.

nizes one of its addresses (e.g., an individual, group, broadcast, or functional address). When it is set to 1, the C bits indicate that the frame was copied.

Therefore, a properly received frame should have both A and C set to 1s when the frame is returned to the sender. Anything else indicates a problem in recognizing the address, copying the frame, or a combination of these. The redundant bits are used to minimize the possibility of bit error(s) in this field, since they are not under the CRC's protection.

Here are the possible frame status codes:

00xx00xx	This code indicates an inactive station.
10xx10xx	The station exists, but it did not copy the frame.
11xx11xx	The frame was copied successfully.
01xx01xx	This code is not possible since it indicates that the address was not recognized yet the frame was copied.

Early token release

Ordinarily, when a workstation sends a frame, the LAN is tied up until the frame circulates back to the station. This ties up the entire LAN and is called *ring latency* time. Typical latency times are 50–100 characters in a 4-Mbit/sec LAN and up to 400 characters on a 16-Mbit/sec LAN.

When IBM released its 16-Mbit/sec token ring product, it included an optional feature called *early token release* (ETR). Using ETR, the originating station sends a new token just after sending its data frame. This gives downstream stations a chance to send their own data. Thus, the LAN is busily passing tokens and data frames instead of a string of idle characters.

ETR makes sense when frame sizes range from 50–100 bytes and network utilization is under 80 percent, which is typical. Workstation frames are almost always aimed at the server that is requesting parts of a file. These requests take only a few bytes, so ETR usually improves performance.

The negative side of ETR is that it compromised IBM's priority scheme. Each new token created by ETR has the same priority and reservation bits as the previous token. So a downstream workstation might not get to use the token if it is seized first by another node, regardless of its own reservation request.

Where Token Ring Is Headed

There are rumors that IBM plans to unveil a 100-Mbit/sec token ring with faster NIC, more RAM, and perhaps an onboard processor. The medium of choice, fiber or wire, is unclear. However, since fiber is well suited to token ring networks and 100-Mbit/sec UTP is not a tried-and-true technology, many observers suspect that fiber will be the chosen medium, at least at first.

Other sources report that IBM has tested a 64-Mbit/sec token ring and might introduce a 32-Mbit/sec UTP-based token ring. IBM touts these as backbones, but LAN designers and managers will surely use them to connect clients. Watch for these developments.

IBM has its own version of Ethernet, called EtherAND. EtherAND was designed to connect IBM's token ring gear to IEEE 802.3 LANs. However, IBM's own machines, e.g., AS/400s, only support token rings despite EtherAND and IBM's support of Ethernet-based zero-slot adapters, NICs, and the Ethernet hub that IBM codeveloped with fellow vendor Chipcom.

IBM's power within the IEEE reportedly forced the IEEE to make token ring a standard along with the already-accepted IEEE 802.3. The creation of the LLC sublayer, in effect a buffer, ensured that implementation of either access method would not be perceptible to any higher *International Standards Organization* (ISO) layer.

While the MAC and LLC are published and open, network management is not part of the IEEE 802.5 specification. This has forced competing vendors to reverse-engineer IBM's LAN Network Manager protocols, including the REM we just discussed. Although the vendors have done well, by definition there is no way that they can be fully IBM compatible.

Bridge and router makers, hub manufacturers, and NIC card vendors therefore cannot claim total IBM *network management* compatibility. The goal of having a single network management station manage all the LAN components on several ring segments is not fully attainable while these protocols remain proprietary. Clearly, the trend toward LAN networking will only exacerbate the present problem.

A guaranteed IBM-compatible device fetches extra money. In 1992, National Semiconductor, a major supplier of Ethernet chip sets, began selling IBM's token ring chip set. At the time, National Semiconductor's token ring prices were reported to be 10 times higher than chip sets from competitor Texas Instruments. The speculation is that some customers will pay double for NICs with guaranteed IBM compatibility. The alternative is trying a Texas Instrument set, and National Semiconductor is gambling that prospective customers will pay the extra money instead.

The foregoing does not necessarily mean that you should purchase only IBM gear. It does mean that you should be aware that the network management system you purchase may not fully control the LAN elements we have discussed.

Choices in Token Ring Implementation

At the MAC layer, the choices are few. They center mainly on speed: either 4 or 16 Mbit/sec. This is more a cable than a NIC function as most NICs today support both speeds. The claim token method contains an implementation option for deciding which NIC will become the active monitor. Implementation of the REM, ETR, and use of the priority mechanism are all options.

The choice of local or universal address administration must be made. While we have discussed token ring addressing here—it is a MAC-layer function, after all—we will discuss addressing as applied to Ethernets and token rings in Chapter 9. Both addressing and LLC apply identically to IEEE 802.3 and 802.5 LANs. Access method characteristics for both are given in the following table:

Comparison of Ethernet and Token Ring Access Methods

Characteristics	Ethernet and IEEE 802.3	Token Ring IEEE 802.5
Developer	DEC, Intel, and Xerox (1978)	IBM (1984)
Speed	10 Mbit/sec	4 or 16 Mbit/sec
Access protocol	CSMA/CD	Token passing
Topology	Bus/tree or star	Physical star; logical ring
Media	Thick or thin coaxial or UTP cable	UTP or STP cable
Maximum number of nodes	1024	With UTP, 72 and 9 *multistation access units* (MSAUs); with STP, 260 and 33 MSAUs
Packet size	64–1518	With 4 Mbit/sec, 4,048; with 16 Mbit/sec, 16,192
Relative expense	Lower	Higher
Redundancy	No	Yes
Self-healing	No	Yes
Reliability	Good	Better than 802.3
Priority mechanism	No	Yes
Complexity	Less	More
Access	Probabilistic	Deterministic
Traffic load handling	Sharp traffic "knee"	Gradual degradation
Expansion	Good	Fair
Troubleshooting	Easier in hub systems; Harder in linear networks	Good
Future projected speed	20 Mbit/sec (proprietary full duplex [FDX]) and 100 Mbit/sec	32 and 100 Mbit/sec

Chapter

8

The Fiber-Distributed Data Interface

What is the *fiber-distributed data interface* (FDDI)? In short, it is a local area network where the medium is fiber instead of wire. As a result FDDI is virtually error free, and very fast.

FDDI uses a ring topology, consisting of point-to-point fiber connections between stations on the ring, as shown in Figure 8.1. While only one ring is required, often a second is added for redundancy, in much the same way that token ring *multistation access units* (MSAUs) are connected.

In order to create a backup, the rings carry traffic in opposite directions, i.e., they "counterrotate." In one configuration, unless there is a ring break, the arbitrarily designated backup does not carry traffic. However, its continuity is verified periodically. In another configuration, certain types of FDDI stations *do* use the backup ring to carry traffic plus back up the ring. This doubles the capacity of the ring.

The analogy to token ring can be extended further since FDDI and token ring use the same token-passing concept to regulate access to the ring. However, the details vary between them.

FDDI's operating speed is 100 Mbit/sec, and it operates over a maximum circumference of 100 km (200 km if just one ring is used).

As shown in Figure 8.2, two types of fiber strands may be used with FDDI. *Multimode* fiber allows light to take multiple paths down the fiber. The resulting losses make multimode fiber suitable only for shorter distances. Accordingly, FDDI allows up to 2 km between stations.

Singlemode fiber is designed to allow only one path for light to

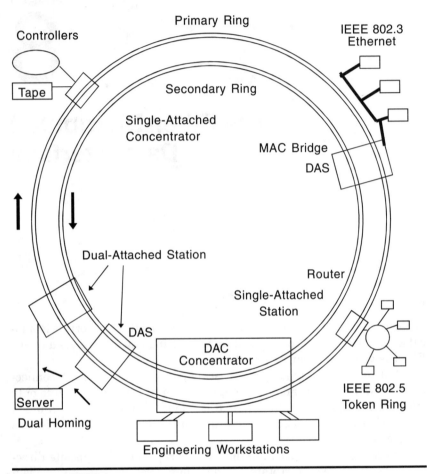

Figure 8.1 A FDDI ring.

travel, and so it can go longer distances. Using singlemode fiber, up to 60 km is allowed between stations.

Modes can be mixed between stations but not within a station-to-station connection. Up to 500 directly connected nodes or stations[1] can be supported. FDDI can easily handle this load since thousands of connections are possible using fanout devices, much as multiport transceivers are used in Ethernet.

One virtue of using FDDI is that it has standards endorsement. Working at the bottom two layers of the *open systems interconnection* (OSI) model, namely the physical and data link layers, FDDI is de-

---

[1]As we will see later in this chapter, nodes and stations are slightly different in FDDI.

scribed by *American National Standards Institute* (ANSI) standard X3T9.5 and is also *International Standards Organization* (ISO) compliant. All the standards are complete except for the *station management* (SMT) component, which should also be final by now.

FDDI as well as IEEE 802.3, 802.4, and 802.5 support the same IEEE 802.2 *logical link control* (LLC) standard. Now we can see the value of IEEE 802.2—any protocol stack running atop IEEE 802.2 does not need to worry about the underlying media. *Network operating systems* (NOSs) and all higher layer protocols, including IPX/SPX, TCP/IP, and NetBIOS, can run on FDDI without modification.

Interoperability of FDDI equipment from different vendors, as demonstrated at Interop shows, in testing laboratories[2] and at vendor demonstrations, is excellent. There are some 40 FDDI vendors purveying products and services in the marketplace.

FDDI finds itself most often in these three applications:

1. As a backbone connecting multiple LANs, especially between floors and buildings in a campus or even a multicampus environment

2. As a back-end network in a data center or computer room, connecting high-speed devices, e.g., mainframes to superservers, with runs of approximately 50 meters

3. As a front-end LAN directly connected to a user's high-powered workstation

In this chapter we begin with a discussion of FDDI's technology, illustrating how fiber works and especially drawing out its unique terminology. Then, we discuss the current state of developmental work on using copper instead of fiber, commonly called *copper digital data interface* (CDDI).

Market trends are important when discussing FDDI. FDDI got off to a slow start. The basic problem was cost. Since the *network interface cards* (NICs) alone are priced at $1500 and up, the total per-port cost to the desktop is sometimes prohibitive. These costs are becoming more reasonable.

FDDI's evolution to FDDI-II plus its relationship with emerging *asynchronous transfer mode* (ATM) and 100-Mbit/sec Ethernet technologies help us obtain a more complete perspective of FDDI, the fastest LAN technology on the market. Finally, the chapter concludes with some profiles of FDDI applications.

---

[2]An interoperability test laboratory has been established at the University of New Hampshire, (603) 862-4519, and at the Advanced Network Testing Center (ANTC), (408) 749-3510. The one at ANTC is vendor supported.

Basics of Fiber Optics

First conceived of in 1966 by Kao and Hockham, fiber optic technology has come into its own in the last 5–8 years.

Fiber offers virtually unlimited bandwidth, and capacities in the 3–4 Gbit/sec (gigabit/sec; 10^9; billions of bits per second) range are not at all unusual. This is fast enough to send the entire Encyclopedia Britannica, all 45 books, in *one-half of a second*. Nor is that pressing the limits of fiber technology, which is now around 40 Gbit/sec.

As a medium, glass fiber is relatively inexpensive. It is so transparent that you could see clearly through a 9-foot-thick block of fiber optic glass!

Because it is not electrical, fiber is immune to electrical noise, magnetic fields, and radio interference. That makes the error rate nearly zero. It also means that fiber is very difficult to tap. It is ideal for military TEMPEST applications. By the same token, fiber is electrically immune to lightning strikes, ground loops, and many of the other electronic impedimenta to error-free communications. Fiber can be safely buried near water or power lines without risk.

Because of its great bandwidth, an increase in capacity is easily achieved by upgrading the equipment at the fiber's ends while the fiber itself remains unchanged. Although it is expensive to install fiber cable, improved electronics can result in continually improving return on the initial investment. Consider also the following:

Fiber is a natural medium for digital transmission: Simply turn the light on and off.

Using single-mode fiber and a laser transmitter, unrepeatered distances of over 160 km are routine.

Fiber has longevity. A satellite lasts about 10 years. A laser for fiber use has a *mean-time between failure* (MTBF) of over a *million hours* or *114 years.*

The economics of fiber are good: While copper costs rise, fiber and fiber electronics costs continue to fall.

Some negatives of using fiber are:

Some older cables, those that are about 15 years old, have become cloudy because of absorption of the cable's cladding into the core of the fiber where the light travels (Figure 8.2). As a result, the long term viability of cable is under close scrutiny.

Splicing and connecting optical fiber, while easier today, still calls for special training and equipment.

Testing and repairing fiber links calls for a *time domain reflectometer* to find breaks and poor connections. This is not an item found at too many mall electronics stores.

Proper selection of fiber media, loss calculations and sheathing (the outer jacket of the fiber) call for the services of an expert.

Fiber is more brittle than wire. Therefore, it can handle bends of only limited radius.

It has less utility. While wires can be switched from a phone to an *unshielded twisted pair* (UTP) LAN, fiber can only carry light.

Fiber cables should be part of a comprehensive cabling plan. They are relatively expensive to buy and more expensive to run.

Single-Mode and Multimode FiberOptics

For longer distances, a type of fiber called *single-mode* cables shown in Figure 8.2, is preferred. Light propagates down the center of the fiber, thus minimizing the contact with the outer edge. As the name infers, it travels in one path or *mode*. This is readily attained using the narrow beam of a laser or light-emitting diode (LED) at a wavelength of 1300–1500 nm (a billionth of a meter). The core of a single-mode fiber for FDDI is 8.7 µm (a millionth of a meter) in diameter, with a 125-µm cladding. It is referred to as *single-mode fiber at the physical layer medium dependent* (SMF-PMD) sublayer.

Usually, the laser operates in the infrared region and is invisible to the eye. Shorter distances allow the use of *multimode* fiber, also shown in Figure 8.2, where the light bounces off the edges of the fiber and so zigzags its way down the fiber. This means more loss, so multimode fibers are most often used locally for distances of up to a few miles. Multimode fiber is ideal for LANs or local networks.

Figure 8.2 shows that for both types, the cladding has a different density than the glass. Therefore, when light strikes it, it bounces back, i.e., is *refracted,* back into the core.

If only two densities of glass are used, the fiber is called a *step index* cable. Some multimode cables vary the density within the core itself, resulting in an eye-shaped light path as shown at the bottom of Figure 8.2. Known as *graded index* fibers, they have somewhat better performance than step index versions. Both are used widely.

Multimode fibers are usually driven by an LED with a wavelength of 1325 nm rather than a laser. They also use a *positive–intrinsic-negative* (PIN) diode as a sensitive photocell receiver.

LEDs avoid OSHA's safety issues implicit in using a laser. The FDDI MMF-PMD *multimode fiber at the physical layer medium dependent*

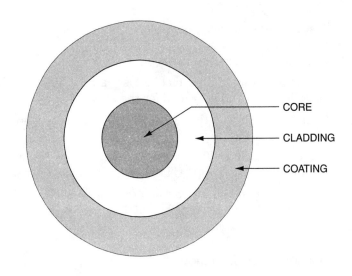

TYPES OF FIBERS

Figure 8.2 Single-mode and multimode fiber core and cladding.

sublayer (MMF-PMD) specification calls for a 62.5 μm core surrounded by a 125-μ-thick cladding, often abbreviated as 62.5/125. Other acceptable alternatives for FDDI are:

50/125 fiber for high bandwidth and low loss. The fiber is used in longer distance multimode applications in private premises networks as well as feeder and loop portions of telephone company outside plants.

85/125 fiber for international broadband applications.

100/140 fiber for short distances where inexpensive optics are used.

There is even a plastic fiber called *low-cost fiber at the physical layer medium dependent* (LCF-PMD) sublayer. The LCF-PMD sublayer is physically very flexible and is meant for short distances of up to 100 m. This can be a very cost-effective cabling solution.

The Technology

FDDI is among the most complex technologies ever devised for use in LANs. Its complexity is a direct result of years of hard-earned experience with broken cables and devices, high facility error rates, and lack of management tools.

Intended for a campus or similar area, FDDI takes advantage of the high speeds and low error rates found in fiber. Accordingly, it uses a "turbocharged" token-passing protocol. FDDI defines only the physical and data link layers within the OSI model.

Principal FDDI features include:

Data speed of 100 Mbit/sec

Fault-tolerant, dual counterrotating rings

A deterministic token-passing access method

Scalable distances between adjacent stations

All the benefits of fiber, including an extremely low error rate

Built-in station management

Insensitivity to routing, transport, and higher protocols

Transparent compatibility with IEEE 802.2-based NOSs

Compatible with existing Ethernet- or token ring-based applications.

Relationship to the OSI model

As shown in Figure 8.3, the physical layer is divided into two parts, the *physical media dependent* (PMD) sublayer and the *physical layer protocol* (PHY). The *media access control* (MAC) and LLC reside above them at the data link layer. SMT is melded into PMD, PHY, and MAC.

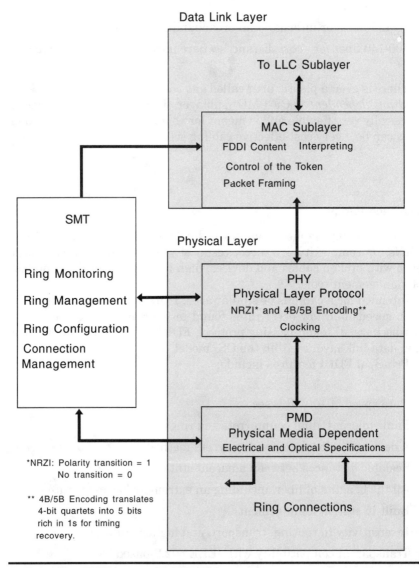

Figure 8.3 How FDDI maps to the OSI model.

The PMD sublayer

PMD sublayer specifies the following details of the cable to be used:

Shielded twisted pair or STP, sometimes called SDDI, or CDDI* using unshielded twisted pair (UTP) as specified by *twisted pair* (TP)-PMD. TP-PMD is designed for connections between concentrators on the ring and single attachment devices (explained shortly). Copper is *not* under consideration for the ring itself. The idea here is to reduce the cost of FDDI by using copper for short runs of up to 100 m.

Fiber cable, usually 62.5/125 MMF-PMD or 8.7/125 SMF-PMD.

Connector styles, i.e., polarized dual connectors for both rings.

Optical link parameters, including optical frequency (1325 nm) and signal levels.

Distances of not more than 2 km for MMF-PMD or 60 km for SMF-PMD between nodes on the ring. The maximum ring circumference is 200 km for one ring or 100 km for two rings. (The secondary backup ring is optional.)

The PMD sublayer includes cables, connectors, power, and optical bypassing of failed units.

Many companies are moving toward hierarchical-structured wiring systems such as EIA/TIA-568. FDDI is well-suited for connecting buildings together in such systems.

Station types

Nodes and stations are not the same.   A *node* in FDDI parlance is a general term denoting an active component on the network. Nodes can repeat incoming transmissions but may not be able to perform error recovery tasks at the data link layer. Nodes contain at least one PMD and one PHY entity, completing the FDDI physical layer as shown in Figure 8.3. They may or may not contain one or more MAC entities.

A *station* is also a node, but it is addressable. It always contains at least one PMD, PHY, and MAC entity. As a result, a station can send and receive error recovery information. All stations are nodes, but not all nodes are necessarily stations.

Classes of stations.   The FDDI standard ANSI X3.166 (ISO 9314-3) defines three classes of stations, dual and single attached stations and

---

*CDDI includes unshielded twisted pair and shielded twisted pair sometimes called SDDI.

concentrators. Stations may be connected to one ring, both rings, or indirectly via a concentrator. (Figure 8.4). *Dual-attachment stations* (DASs) connect to both the primary and secondary rings. If DASs are equipped with multiple ports, they are called *dual-attachment concentrators* (DACs) because they can connect several *single attachment stations* (SASs) to the ring.

For critical applications, one DAS will sometimes cascade into another DAS on the ring. One port will be attached to one DAS and the other port to a second ring-connected DAS. Should either ring-con-

Dual Attached Stations and Concentrators

Port Type A: Primary Ring IN and Secondary Ring OUT
Port Type B: Primary Ring OUT and Secondary Ring IN

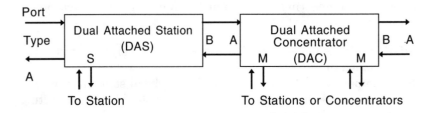

S Ports appear on and connect only to Stations
M (Master) Ports appear only on Concentrators.
They may connect to either concentrators or stations.

Single Attached Stations and Concentrators

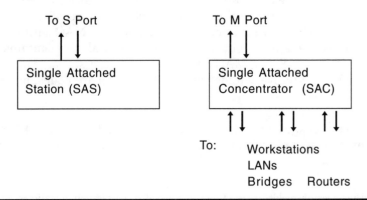

Figure 8.4 Station connection methods.

nected DAS fail, the cascaded DAS will be unaffected. This is called *dual homing* and is shown in Figure 8.5.

When concentrators are cascaded, the configuration is called a *dual ring of trees*. (Figure 8.6). Workgroup concentrators are often organized this way. Often, such concentrators will connect to workgroup Ethernets and token rings.

DASs with dual PMD, PHY, and MAC entities can use both rings to pass traffic, resulting in a doubling of the raw speed to 200 Mbit/sec.

SASs attach only to the primary ring. SASs also connect to concentrators on the ring or to single-attachment concentrators, which in turn connect to a DAS on the ring.

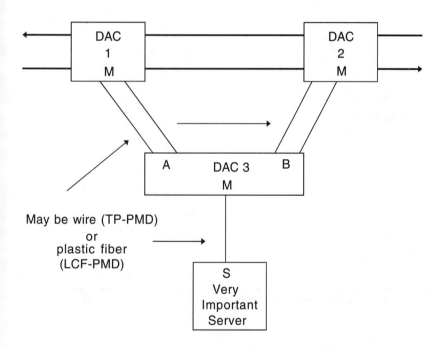

Dual Homing protects the server against failure of DACs 1 and 2
DAC 3 protects the network against a server malfunction.

S ports are always single connections
M ports may be single or dual
A and B ports are always dual

Figure 8.5 Dual homing.

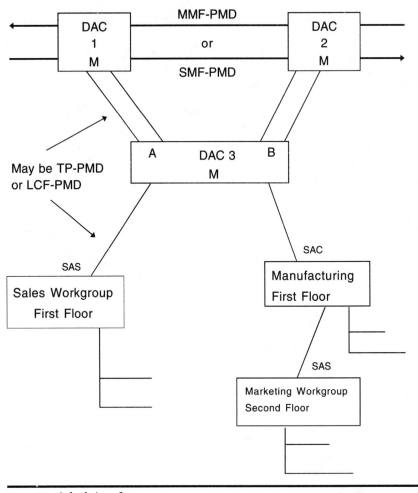

Figure 8.6 A dual ring of trees.

The number of direct connections to the ring is limited to 1000. Since each device has an input and output, no more than 500 *stations* can be directly on the ring. However, there is no limit to the number of devices that can be tied to a *concentrator* that is connected directly or indirectly to the ring.

A station becomes a concentrator when it has ports beyond those it needs to attach to the network. Concentrators have multiple PHY entities (ports) to accommodate multiple SAS connections. These connections can be either fiber or copper and this is where TP-PMD can save significantly on cost.

Much of the cost of FDDI comes from the optical portion of the PMD sublayer. That is why the use of copper cable for short-distance runs, up to 100 m, will reduce the cost per workstation below the psychologically significant $1000-a-port barrier.

There is an inverse relationship between the number of stations and the ring's circumference. Fewer stations permit a greater circumference and vice versa according to rules published in the FDDI standard.

TP-PMD and CDDI

TP-PMD is the ANSI term for using twisted pair at the PMD layer. TP-PMD is designed for connections between concentrators on the ring and single-attachment devices. Copper is *not* under consideration for the ring itself. The idea here is to reduce the cost of FDDI by using copper for short runs of up to 100 m.

Here are some specifics about TP-PMD:

TP-PMD is upward compatible with PHY functions, which are cast permanently into silicon chips.

Both Type-1 150-Ω STP and Level-5 100-Ω UTP are supported for distances of up to 100 m. The UTP and STP elements are known collectively as CDDI.

TP-PMD meets the FCC and EN55022 Class B emissions standards.

TP-PMD must not affect signal delays or error rates, or restrict the range of usable port types. In short, it must perform just as well as fiber. (It is tempting to say "transparent" here. However, what is more transparent—a copper wire or the purest glass ever known?)

The TP-PMD working group has adopted *multilevel-three level* (MLT-3) encoding. MLT-3 uses *nonreturn-to-zero-inverted* (NRZI)-like encoding plus stream cipher scrambling to reduce emissions and spread them over a broader spectrum. It also uses a digital and analog postsignal compensation technique to obtain better signal purity and noise immunity. The familiar DB-9 and RJ-45 are expected to be used as connectors.

De facto copper standards

There are two de facto standards in use. SDDI (FDDI over STP) was created by five vendors, and it was then endorsed by IBM; IBM, in turn, expanded on it. SDDI seems to dominate the other de facto standard, TP-FDDI. SDDI is the "green book" standard, so named because it was published as a pamphlet with green covers.

Both standards will give way to TP-PMD once TP-PMD becomes sufficiently well developed for vendors to build products. Virtually all the vendors have promised to support TP-PMD.

Existing UTP and STP media will accelerate the use of CDDI, especially to the desktop computer. With copper wires already in place, a UTP or STP standard provides an ideal migration path from a 4- or 16-Mbit/sec token ring to CDDI and hence to FDDI.[3]

PHY

The PHY sublayer has the following functions:

Defines symbols	The smallest transmission data unit in FDDI is the 4-bit *symbol*. These symbols are converted into 5-bit patterns rich in 1s, a process called *4B/5B coding*. Therefore, the actual bit rate of FDDI is 125 Mbit/sec, but only 100 Mbit/sec is usable.
Encodes and decodes data	Under NRZI coding, a transition is a 1 and no transition is a 0. NRZI keeps the light intensity fairly constant. NRZI coding occurs after 4B/5B symbol translation.
Handles clocking	By sending a sufficient number of 1s, the transitions can be used to recover timing. PHY assures that there will never be more than three 0 bits in a row and therefore no more than 3 bits sent without a transition to maintain synchronization.

The data link layer: MAC

FDDI's MAC is similar to the token-passing IEEE 802.5 token ring protocol. There are differences, however, in the priority, management, and token-handling mechanisms.

Synchronous and asynchronous transmission classes. The MAC offers *synchronous* service to applications that require a guaranteed bandwidth. Providing synchronous service in a FDDI system is optional.

Asynchronous service is the remaining bandwidth, which is allocated dynamically as needed. Optionally, up to eight priority levels of asynchronous service can be implemented.

Nonrestricted and restricted tokens. Typically, tokens are *nonrestricted,* meaning that any station may send asynchronous data if the capacity is available. A *restricted* token will allocate all the asynchronous bandwidth to a station that needs to send a large burst of data. A higher layer protocol decides which mode will be used.

---

[3]If you are interested in this development effort, contact the ANSI X.3 secretariat at (202) 737-8888.

Token handling.   The handling of the token is based on three timers:

1. During initialization, all the stations agree on a *target token rotation time* (TTRT), which is the average time between appearances of the token at a station. TTRT includes an allowance for latency, delay, in propagating around the ring.

2. The *token rotation timer* (TRT) monitors the time between token arrivals at the station. It is initialized to equal TTRT.

3. The difference between the TTRT and TRT is the *token holding time* (THT). If the token arrives early, the station may transmit asynchronous frames until THT runs out. If the token is late, it cannot send any asynchronous frames.

As in IEEE 802.5 implementation with early token releases, the station releases a new token after its packet is sent. Frames returning to the originator are removed by that station. In FDDI, early token release is standard.

A long TTRT lets stations send more data but reduces overall station access. Conversely, a short TTRT improves access at the expense of throughput. Typically, TTRT is about 8 msec. As discussed above, it is set by agreement between the stations during ring initialization. TTRT cannot normally be set by the network owner.

Error recovery.   Hard failures, such as a broken ring, are resolved using a process called *beaconing*. In case of a ring break, beaconing works this way:

1. A station's *valid-transmission timer* (TVX) runs out, indicating an inactive ring after the break. The station's MAC layer software begins the process of error recovery by sending a claim token frame.

2. If the station attempts token origination, i.e., claim token, and cannot complete it, then the station begins sending out beacon frames. If it receives beacon frames, it stops sending its own and repeats what it has received.

3. Eventually, the beacon originator is the station just past the break, and the network wraps (loops) there. Should the station receive its own beacon frames, it considers the ring restored and starts the claim token process to resume normal operation.

FDDI frame format

The framing format shown in Figure 8.7 follows the IEEE 802.5 standard, with some modification. The framing format uses symbols of 4

PRE*	SD*	FC*	DA	SA	DATA	FCS	EDEL*	FS
12 min.	2	2	12	12	0 to n	8	1	3+

All units are in symbols (4 bits)

*Indicates a field used as part of an FDDI token.

The **preamble** precedes the SD field. Consisting of at least 12 4-bit I or Idle symbols (all 1s), the preamble synchronizes the station's clock with each transmission.

SD, or Starting Delimiter, consists of two nondata symbols (J:11000 and K:10001 in five-bit form) to identify the start of the frame.

FC, Frame Control identifies the frame type: restricted or unrestricted token; station management, SMT, MAC or LLC. The field takes the form CLFFZZZZ:

C (Class) indicates an asynchronous (0) frame or a synchronous (1) frame.
L (Address Length) indicates 16 bit (0) or 48 bit (1) address length.
FF (Format) indicates whether a MAC (00) or LLC (01) frame follows.
(10) is reserved for implementers and (11) is reserved for future versions.
ZZZZ consists of control information needed by MAC frames.

Destination and Source Addresses are 48 bits long. Destinations may be individuals, groups, or broadcasts to all stations. Source addresses must be individual stations.

Data, or the **Information Field,** may range from 0 bytes upward. As with other frame formats, higher layer headers, control and data may be in this field.

The Frame Check Sequence, FCS is a CRC-32, or 32 bits long. It is computed on all bits starting with Frame Control through the FCS itself.
If the receiver does not calculate the same number, the frame is in error.

EDEL, the Ending Delimiter, marks the end of a frame. One four-bit T (for Terminate) symbol is used for all frames other than tokens, which use two.

FS, or Frame Status, consists of at least three symbols of the form EAC.
E indicates whether an error was detected. **A** is the Address Recognized Indicator.
C means a frame was copied.

For E, A, or C, an R symbol in that position means ON or TRUE. An S symbol means OFF or FALSE.

Additional frame status symbols may be appended if so implemented. A Terminate **(T)** symbol follows any such added symbols.

Figure 8.7 The FDDI frame format.

bits, called *quartets,* rather than 8-bit octets. Tokens consist of a preamble, starting delimiter, frame control field and an ending delimiter.
The following frame types are defined:

LLC	LLC header, and optionally, higher layer protocol data.
Control	Tokens, MAC frames, and station management

Reserved for   For implementation-specific purposes
implementer

Reserved for future   For future versions
standardization

FDDI frames can range between 17–4500 bytes. The link between the MAC and LLC is also very similar but not quite the same as the IEEE 802.2 LLC standard. However, the LLC to network layer interface *is* the standard IEEE 802.2 LLC format.

SMT

FDDI includes SMT. It is one of the few LAN standards to include a comprehensive set of management capabilities.

SMT is the supervisory entity within a station that controls and monitors station activity. Some vendors add *Simple Network Management Protocol* (SNMP) to FDDI.

As shown in the FDDI-OSI map, SMT resides alongside the PMD, PHY, and MAC layers. There are three parts to SMT:

1. *Ring management* (RMT), which discovers and fixes ring faults

2. *Connection management* (CMT), which manages station insertion and extraction

3. *SMT Frame Services,* which creates frames for use by higher level programs to monitor and/or test the network

RMT. Just as in IEEE 802.5 token ring, FDDI can suffer from continuous, "stuck" beaconing. In token ring, manual intervention is usually required, but in FDDI, RMT will find and squelch a stuck beacon.

Duplicate addresses plague all LANs, and FDDI is no exception. The addressing, 48 bits, is identical to that used in IEEE 802.3–802.5. Under universal administration, the first 24 bits are assigned by IEEE to each vendor. The vendor is then responsible for the remaining 24 bits. Local administration, where the network manager assigns the addresses, is allowed but is implemented less often in FDDI networks.

A station is expected to remove itself from the ring upon detecting its own address. If it does not, the RMT in the stations on either side of the offending station will wrap the ring on both sides to isolate the station.

CMT. There are three elements to CMT:

1. *Configuration management* (CFM) provides data, such as which ring is active, to the PHY and MAC sublayers to run the ring correctly.

2. *Entity coordination management* (ECM) controls any optical bypass devices. These devices are simply mirrors that swivel into place to bypass a station whose power goes off. While they avoid wrapping the ring, the associated light loss can be substantial.

3. *Physical connection management* (PCM) manages connections between stations. It ensures the quality and correctness of the connection according to FDDI's rule table.

SMT frame services.   SMT frame services permit inspection of the network and external control. These include a link error monitor, neighbor notification frames, and status report frames. Neighborhood information frames give the station address, device type, manufacturer, and connection type. Station information frames indicate the current health of a station and are used in the link error monitor function. These SMT frame services allow a great deal of flexibility in drawing out information and constructing uniquely useful services.

Dedicated SMT management devices are as yet hard to find. It is easier to use the FDDI SNMP Management Information Base, which is quite comprehensive and vendor independent. It will run on Sun Microsystems and other vendors. It has become the most popular way to manage multiple FDDI LANs.

Inherent Reliability

Ordinarily, FDDI operates on two counterrotating rings, one of which is active, in FDDI terminology, *primary,* and the other one of which is a backup, *secondary.* The second ring is optional, not normally used for traffic unless DASs are used as mentioned earlier. If the backup ring is not carrying traffic, its continuity is checked regularly.

If the primary ring breaks, i.e., there is a ring fault, the stations on either side of the break wrap one ring to the other and so restore continuity. The same happens if a station fails, i.e., a station fault. FDDI is automatically self-healing. It will even unwrap the ring if it sees that a fault has disappeared.

Recovery times vary between under a second to about 6 sec. This is rapid enough that established sessions, especially time-sensitive Systems Network Architecture (SNA) and *Local Area Transport* (LAT) sessions, will not be broken. While multiple failures can create multiple segmented rings, most networks and network protocols will not work this way, especially if a server is on one segment and the workstations are on another!

Optionally, to avoid wraps, simple optical bypass devices (*nodes,* as defined earlier) are available to restore continuity around a failed or powered-off station (Figure 8.8). A bypass device is often used with a

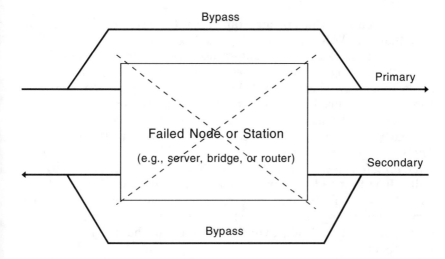

Optical bypass devices go around a failed component. This avoids having to wrap the ring.

They are especially useful for servers and other devices, such as bridges and routers not designed for FDDI.

Their drawback is that the light loss can be substantial.

Figure 8.8 Optical bypass.

Dual-Attachment Station connected to a server, because the DAS card may be inside the powered-off server. Without the bypass device, if the server is turned off, the ring would loop.

PMD specifies these devices to enhance reliability. Optical bypass switches are used most often with dual-attached stations and concentrators. They bypass the station should the station be turned off or fail. This avoids a wrap because the bypass device completes the serial path again.

Wiring concentrators create a physical star even though the structure is a logical ring, just like a token ring *multistation access unit* (MSAU). They can bypass ring breaks without invoking the FDDI wrap procedure. As a last resort, there is the dual ring structure itself.

Internetworking

FDDI is internetworked like any other LAN, using bridges and routers. The router approach is generally preferred because routers detect and eliminate corrupted packets from Ethernet, token ring, or other LAN subnets. These packets could cause disruption in WANs. They also provide flow control, which is important when the FDDI LAN's speed outruns that of a WAN link by roughly a 100 to 1.

Larger networks call for routers because routers keep broadcasts from propagating throughout the network. Often, routers have FDDI cards that allow them to be DAS devices directly on the ring. This eliminates the need for a concentrator, although concentrators have the effect of isolating attached-device failures from the ring.

Clearly, only very stable devices should appear directly on the ring. These include concentrators, routers, and bridges. All should have *uninterruptible power supply* (UPS) backup and perhaps optical bypass units. It is best to keep servers and specifically workstations off the ring. These should be connected through concentrators. In the case of servers, there may be a small performance decrease because the concentrator acts as a bridge. On the other hand, the benefit is greater ring reliability.

Ethernet or token-ring frames are not directly compatible with FDDI framing. To bridge them together, two bridging techniques, *encapsulation* and *translation,* are used.

Encapsulation places an Ethernet or token ring frame within a data "capsule" that is proper for FDDI transmission. While encapsulation is fast and easy to implement, it is often proprietary. This means that decapsulation can only be done by equipment from the same vendor.

Translating bridges convert the frame into FDDI format directly. Then the FDDI frame can be read by any bridge device.

FDDI adapters

NIC chips for FDDI are expensive, but prices are falling. There are two reasons for this: integration of older four-chip FDDI chipsets into two chips and use of copper instead of fiber to the desktop. Since as much as 40 percent or more of a FDDI NIC chip's cost is in the optics, eliminating this cost results in a large savings.

Industry Standard Architecture

ISA bus interfaces are too slow. Extended ISA (EISA) and Microchannel buses are better, with EISA having a slight advantage because EISA cards are large enough to carry the chips needed for a complete FDDI implementation. In terms of bus access, bus mastering is preferred with burst-mode direct memory access as an alternate. Emerging local bus architectures such as from *Video Electronics Standards Association* (VESA) or Intel are suitable as well. Novell, Crescendo Communications, and Eagle Technology are working on FDDI and CDDI cards that will be sold by Novell.

NICs for non-PC machines such as Macintoshes are becoming available. It is important to verify their availability, which may be spotty. Some NICs come with internal modules that allow users to change the card between TP-PMD, SDDI, and FDDI.

With the completion of management standards for SMT, SMT on the card must be implemented using a general-purpose CPU running SMT. The alternative is to load SMT into the NIC software driver. If it is done in this way, SMT loads the main CPU and more ominously, takes up system RAM. While SMT is usually not that busy except during reconfigurations and faults, it may affect application performance. SNMP agents can also run on FDDI cards.

The implications for computer memory are more fateful. Since system RAM is precious, user applications may be limited when using DOS. All told, it is better to spend a few extra dollars for card-based SMT to avoid possible performance and memory conflicts.

FDDI-II

As it stands presently, FDDI is not designed for voice or video, just for data. This is in part a function of its maximum frame size, which is too long for either of these delay-sensitive applications. FDDI-II will divide the network bandwidth into as many as 16 time-division-multiplexed channels of up to 98.304 Mbit/sec each. All of them will be equal and full duplex.

Given that ATM[4] will become functional by about 1996, it seems that the relative rigidity of FDDI-II will be supplanted by the much more flexible and dynamic ATM. With time, users will replace backbone FDDI rings with an ATM switch, in the same way that switches are used today with Ethernets. The result will be gigabit-class switching capability without the disruption of existing bridges, routers, and workstations.

Comparison with 100-Mbit/sec Ethernet

Since people think that FDDI is synonymous with speed, they assume that 100-Mbit/sec Ethernet is competitive with FDDI. This is not so. Both 100- and 10-Mbit/sec Ethernet have the same access control problems, no redundancy and no management dimension. Thus, the role of 100-Mbit/sec Ethernet remains relegated to the desktop, whereas

---

[4]ATM (Asynchronous Transfer Mode) is a high-speed cell-switching technology that divides data, voice, or video into fixed 53-byte cells: 48 carry traffic payload, and 5 are used for control. ATM is discussed in Chapters 4 and 11.

FDDI excels in the backbone. In brief, they are two high-speed technologies intended to solve different problems. Note that 100-Mbit/sec Ethernet is a very new idea, while FDDI is a long-established technology.

Related Fiber Standards

Fiber optic interrepeater link (FOIRL) is an IEEE 802.3 standard and links repeaters over distances of up to 1 km. That is the standard, but many vendors go further.

10BaseF is the standard that implements Ethernet over fiber optic cable. It has three parts:

1. *10BaseFL* is a transceiver or *medium attachment unit* (MAU) for an Ethernet fiber link. It offers a 2-km maximum link length between devices, including workstations to transceivers. 10BaseFL is required to be backward compatible with FOIRL transceivers.

2. *10BaseFB* is a synchronous Ethernet fiber backbone system that is used in lieu of FDDI, for instance. Up to 20 repeaters are allowed as opposed to the usual 4. It includes link diagnostics but is not backward compatible with FOIRL.

3. *10BaseFP* is an unpowered, fiber star Ethernet hub. It is very reliable and is intended for inaccessible locations and/or high reliability applications.

Applications

FDDI is useful in networks with outstripped capacity. Ethernet, for example, becomes clogged when about 35 percent of its bandwidth is utilized, or 3.5 Mbit/sec. By contrast, FDDI does not approach saturation until 80–90 percent of its bandwidth is used, or 80–90 Mbit/sec. This is a ratio of nearly 28 to 1, and is a result of FDDI's speed and its efficient, deterministic token passing access method.

Tests have shown that loading one intensive application atop another on FDDI barely affects each application's throughput until nearly 90 percent of FDDI's capacity is reached. Similarly, FDDI's ability to replace a token ring backbone has been demonstrated. FDDI preserves essential source-routing information needed by source-routing bridges.

FDDI networks tend to be very horizontal as in campus-area networks. This is because FDDI can support so many stations and has the traffic-carrying capacity to make segmenting unnecessary. Aside from a simpler network to manage, fewer hops mean smaller transaction times.

Greater speed is usually not required to handle individual applications. Rather, the problem is combinations of them running at the same time. Similarly, individual objects in an object-oriented system are not high-traffic items, but when linked together, they become high-traffic items. For example, at IBM a prototype desktop videoconferencing system runs fine on a 16 Mbit/sec token ring—for one to three sessions. For anything higher, FDDI is needed.

Some good applications for FDDI in a nutshell are:

Where traffic demands exceed the capacity of slower LANs. Object-oriented processing will aggravate traffic problems.

While interconnecting of high powered computers, such as back-end processors.

While serving as a backbone for other LANs. As a rule of thumb, the backbone carries 20 percent of the traffic and the LANs 80 percent.

In applications requiring a great deal of data from a single source. These include document and medical imaging.

For preserving data synchronization, such as videoconferencing and mirror image processing for backup processing centers. FDDI can be used to link duplicate servers in Novell's SFT III, for instance.

In real-time applications where guaranteed access time is mandatory. It is well suited for workstations, computer-aided design and engineering, and publishing.

FDDI will find more applications as the need for speed grows. In particular, imaging, cooperative processing, and dual-operation systems will expand FDDI's installation base.

The collapsed backbone

One of the more clever applications is to use a concentrator as a collapsed backbone hub. SAS workstations connect to the hub through TP-PMD, fiber, or SDDI. The result is a 100-Mbit/sec FDDI LAN, perhaps without any fiber in it at all.

FDDI as a metropolitan area network

Finland, France, and Italy are using FDDI as a metropolitan area network (MAN). In the U.S., telephone companies unwilling to wait for *switched multimegabit data service* (SMDS) are resorting to FDDI. They include United Telephone of Ohio and Centel Telephone Co. of Florida. In addition, independent companies such as Metropolitan Fiber Systems, Teleport Communications Group, and NYNEX are considering FDDI as a way of selling high-speed service.

There are a number of challenges in using FDDI this way. FDDI has no billing mechanism, and security is a potential problem since data from every user passes through every site. The large circumference also adds to latency. ATM has none of these problems. Nonetheless, the installed applications are working well.

A high-level application

We have discussed LANs, WANs, and MANs. But how about a mobile local area network (MLAN)? In this case, mobile means inside a Boeing 777 moving along at about 600 mph. That's moving data . . . fast.

Plans are being made to equip Boeing's new aircraft with two FDDI rings, one in the cockpit and one in the cabin. The cabin ring will connect to three bridges, one for first class, business class, and coach customers. Airlines may choose either token ring or Ethernet to connect to displays located at each seat.

Laptop computers will be connected via a modem into the seat's telephone connection to access *electronic mail* (e-mail) and the like. Charges would be via credit card the same way that airborne phone calls are charged today.

The cockpit ring will provide graphics-based instrumentation as well as all charts and graphs that the pilots might need. These high resolution files, 8–10 Mbits in size, will reside on an airborne server. Response time must be 1.5 sec or better, even if several crew members pull up files at once. The servers will be multiple-redundant, flight-critical systems.

Since airline costs are highly maintenance driven, the system will collect real-time data for storage in logs or for transmission to the ground. Problems, especially intermittent ones, can be detected while airborne and repaired on arrival. Serious inflight problems can be diagnosed by ground-based experts in real time.

Interestingly, there is a router between the cockpit and cabin rings. Could its purpose be so the captain can send you an e-mail message asking you to fasten your seat belt?

Chapter

9

Logical Link Control

What Is It?

Logical link control (LLC) is the sublayer residing above the *media access control* (MAC) sublayer. In IEEE-based LANs, the MAC and LLC sublayers comprise layer 2, the data link layer of the ISO model. IEEE 802.2 LLC is common to IEEE 802.3 Ethernet, IEEE 802.5 token-passing and FDDI access methods, so the ensuing discussion applies to all.

What LLC Does

For the protocols discussed in this book, the LLC's primary job is to identify the correct protocol stack to use since several stacks can exist in parallel in a system.[1] The LLC also

Insulates higher layers from any network tasks or problems.

Provides a standard software interface for use with higher layer protocols such as *Transmission Control Protocol/Internet Protocol* (TCP/IP) and Novell's *Internetwork Packet Exchange* (IPX).

Makes sure that outbound application data can be passed to the local MAC. This is a function of the sending station's LLC.

Makes sure that the received data is sent to the correct protocol stack. This is a function of the receiving station's LLC.

---

[1]SNA (Systems Network Architecture) also uses the LLC to create a reliable, connection-oriented link.

Maintains a peer-to-peer relationship with the LLC at the other end.

Sends data using *connectionless* service.

Starts, maintains, and ends a logical relationship with the LLC at the other end. It does this using *connection-oriented* service. The LLC also provides error detection, retransmission, and flow control.

Although the MAC sublayer below the LLC adds addresses, the addressing scheme is common to both token ring and Ethernet MAC sublayers, so it will also be discussed in this chapter.

The LLC in the middle

Figure 9.1 shows the LLC's direct interface to the network layer above it, the MAC layer below it, and implies a logical peer-to-peer link to the

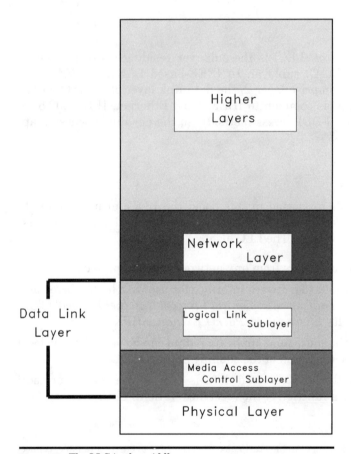

Figure 9.1 The LLC in the middle.

LLC at the other end. The details of these interfaces are precisely defined by the IEEE 802.2 *Service Interface Specification* (SIS). There is an SIS for the services that interface the network layer to the LLC and the LLC to MAC. The peer-to-peer relationship is also defined.

How it works

Let us say you have typed an *electronic mail* (e-mail) message to Ed on your PC. How does the message reach him?

Your e-mail message enters the stack at the application layer. After all, e-mail *is* the application. It progresses down the protocol stack. Each layer adds *header* control information in front of your message, then passes it down. By the time it reaches the LLC, it looks like a five-car freight train and your data is the caboose.

The message is passed from the network to the LLC sublayer through a *service access point* (SAP). This is the pipe through which outgoing and incoming data must pass. There can be several SAPs, one per protocol type. In this way, different applications can reach the cable, and the SAP tells the receiving station which network layer entity to send the data to.

The LLC assembles an LLC *protocol data unit* (PDU). The data unit contains the individual, group, or global *Destination Service Access Point* (DSAP) and the *Source Service Access Point* (SSAP). Control information is followed by the message itself.

The LLC PDU is passed down to the MAC sublayer. The MAC adds an identifying header, labeling the PDU as an information frame and including the destination station address of the recipient as well as its own source address. The MAC trailer includes a frame check sequence to detect errors as we discussed in Chapter 6.

Note that SAP addresses and station addresses are two different things! A SAP address could be, e.g., 06 (hexadecimal) for the Internet stack, E0 for Novell, or F0 for NetBIOS. Often the SAP will tell you the entire overlying stack, e.g., NetWare, TCP/IP, or ISO. In contrast, station addresses identify *network interface card* (NIC) hardware. As Fig. 9.2 shows, the *DEC-Intel-Xerox* (DIX) Ethernet frame type used in NetWare's IPX protocol does not use SAP fields in its frames, but the IEEE 802.3 version does use SAP fields. DIX, however, can carry many different protocols. DIX identifies the protocol carried in its TYPE field.

When the cable is free in Ethernet, or when the token is captured in a token ring, the message is passed down from the MAC layer to the cable, the physical layer. At the receiver, the MAC layer recognizes its station address in the frame and accepts the message.

The MAC layer in the receiver checks to see if the frame is correct or not by recomputing the *frame check sequence* (FCS). If the FCS checks,

IMPLEMENTATION OF NOVELL'S UPPER LAYERS

ETHERNET FRAME

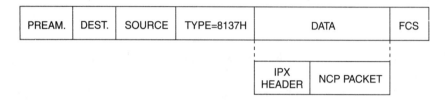

IEEE 802.3 FRAME

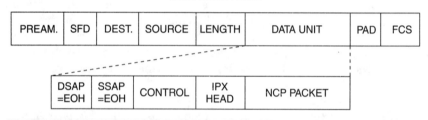

Figure 9.2 Ethernet and IEEE 802.3 SAP implementations.

the message is then checked to see if it contains MAC information or LLC data going up the stack. If it contains user data, the message is stripped of the MAC header and trailer, then passed to the LLC as an LLC PDU (Figure 9.3). It progresses up the stack until the message winds up in Ed's mailbox.

If the FCS check fails, the frame is thrown away. If the frame contains MAC control information, the information is used and not passed any higher. Remember, one purpose of layering is to insulate higher layers from things they do not need to know.

People get upset when they hear that a frame is thrown away if it is bad. In *Synchronous Data Link Control* (SDLC) or HDLC, the receiver asks for retransmission. In a LAN, this is not the case unless the Type 2 connection-oriented class of service, which is explained below, is being used. It then becomes the responsibility of a higher layer to verify that the message has been received. Note, however, that Type 1 connectionless service, which does not perform acknowledgements, is far more common. Since LANs have such low error rates, they do not need to perform acknowledgements as in WAN protocols. LANs, therefore, do not waste cable time on this overhead.

This symbolic layer:

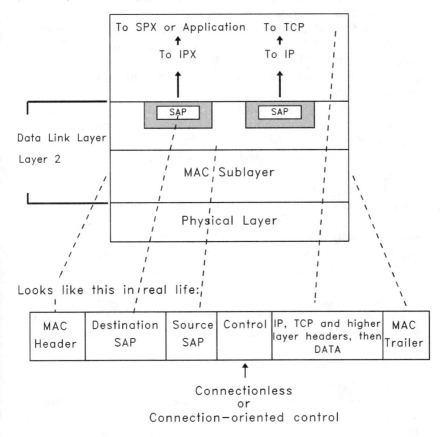

Looks like this in real life:

MAC Header	Destination SAP	Source SAP	Control	IP, TCP and higher layer headers, then DATA	MAC Trailer

Connectionless
or
Connection−oriented control

The LLC sends data to the right place,
in this case, IPX or IP.

Figure 9.3 The LLC PDU.

Station addressing. As we said in Chapter 6, station addressing (administration) was developed by IEEE Project 802. There are two forms of station addressing.

The first form, *local administration,* has the organization set the source addresses. The organization is responsible for avoiding duplication. Addresses are 48 bits long. Local administration is used for separate, isolated networks where there is no chance of duplication with another network or in a system of subnetworks where part of the address will consist of the higher network, e.g., DECnet, and part of it will consist of the lower network address.

The other form of addressing is *universal addressing*. The universal addressing uses a 48-bit field and can therefore contain 281,475 trillion possible addresses. (Will that do?) Multilevel networks use universal administration. In very large networks, it is really the only way to guarantee nonduplicate addresses.

Blocks of addresses are assigned to vendors, who "burn" the addresses into their NICs. Nonduplication is therefore assured. In actuality, the IEEE assigns the first three octets as a vendor ID. The vendors then add three arbitrary address bytes. As a result, it is possible to identify vendor components such as NICs. For instance, Hewlett-Packard's identification number is 08-00-09.

Vendors also provide the means to override universal addresses if you wish. Your organization must decide which form of address to use; you may use both if you like. Chapter 14 discusses the pros and cons of universal and local administration, and offers suggestions as to how to track these addresses in a typically dynamic LAN environment.

The *source address* is used by IBM in the token ring to indicate if source routing data is included in the frame. Token-ring addressing and source routing is discussed in Chapter 7. Chapter 11 shows how token rings and Ethernets can be linked to form an enterprise-wide network using the power of addressing.

Types of service connections. Data delivered on a best-effort basis is called a *connectionless* service or Type 1 operation. The control byte following the SSAP indicates whether Type 1 or Type 2, a connection-oriented service, is being used. Type 1 is far more commonly used in LANs. Type 2 is discussed primarily for the sake of completeness.

In connectionless Type 1 service

A preexisting logical connection ("build a session") between the sender and receiver is not needed. Each data unit is sent independently.

Sequence checking to ensure that data is received in the correct order does not exist.

The receiver does not acknowledge receipt of a data unit.

Flow control to avoid overrunning the receiver does not exist.

Error *detection,* but not error *recovery,* is implemented.

Data units can be sent to individuals or groups of addresses.

Connectionless service is also called *datagram* service. Examples include the Internet IP and RIP protocols and Novell's IPX.

Connection-oriented or Type 2 service is just the opposite of Type 1 service. A logical session must be built before data can be exchanged. The logical session must then be maintained while data is transferred and broken down when the exchange is complete. Sequence checking, acknowledgements, flow control, and error checking take place. Contrary to Type 1 service, *data can be sent to only one address at a time.* Connection-oriented protocols are exemplified by IBM's SDLC and SNA LLC 2.

In the LLC specification, all stations must support Type 1 service. Supporting Type 2 is optional. Stations that support only connectionless operation are called Class 1 stations; those supporting both are called Class 2. The implementation of Class 1 or 2 is at the network/LLC layer interface. Virtually all LANs use connectionless service except those supporting IBM's SNA-SDLC.

The LLC to MAC interface.   The LLC to MAC interface lets communicating LLCs exchange data. To do that, a peer-to-peer relationship must be set up using either a Type 1 or 2 connection.

As discussed above, Type 1 connections deliver unacknowledged datagrams. There are only three commands:

1. *Unnumbered information* (UI) sends a data unit to an individual, a group, or every destination.

2. *Exchange identification* (XID) lets two stations trade information about the services they can provide without resorting to Type 2. XID can be used in various ways and is left to vendors as an implementation option. Recall that XID is used in token ring as a discovery or explorer packet.

3. *Test* simply stimulates the opposite-end LLC for a response. The purpose of Test is to check that the LLCs have a communication link. Test datagrams are also used as discovery packets.

Type 2 protocols are a little more complicated. They have to do with:

Setting up the session, ending it, and rejecting invalid data

Transferring information

Link supervision

Acknowledging data

Providing flow control to prevent overrunning the receiver

Setting up and ending sessions, and rejecting invalid data.   Unnumbered frames, which are the same as Type 1 UI frames, are used to:

Start a session by sending *set asynchronous balanced mode extended* (SABME). The receiver returns an *unnumbered acknowledgement*

(UA). Transmission then begins. However, if the receiver returns a *disconnected mode* (DM), the receiver cannot make the connection for some reason.

End a session by sending *disconnect* (DISC). Either end can disconnect. Receiving a UA or DM also causes a disconnect.

Reject invalid data by sending a *frame reject* or FRMR. FRMR is used to tell the other end that an error occurred which cannot be fixed by retransmission. The receiver can DISConnect or start a new session using SABME. (Save Me!)

Unnumbered frames are also called *U-format* frames.

Transferring information.   The information transfer command (I-format) transfers information. I-format frames are numbered and sequenced. The procedure is identical to the frame count sequence used in HDLC or SDLC. The procedure ensures that frames are neither lost nor reassembled out of order. Up to 127 frames, also called the *window size* or *modulus,* can be sent before an acknowledgement is needed.

The size limits for an information field are:

46–1500 bytes for Ethernet, plus 18 bytes of overhead

0–4048 bytes for 4-Mbit/sec token ring, plus 21 bytes of overhead

0–16,192 bytes for 16-Mbit/sec token ring, plus 21 bytes of overhead

The maximum frame size may vary somewhat for either token ring speed as it depends on the token-holding-time parameter set in the NIC.

Supervision.   Supervisory frames are called S-format commands. They are very similar to SDLC and have the following characteristics:

Receive ready (RR) acknowledges received data and tells the sender that it is ready to receive more data.

Receive not ready (RNR) acknowledges received data but asks the sender to stop sending, perhaps because its buffer is full.

Once cleared, the receiver may send a RR to tell the sender to continue. This is an example of *flow control.*

Reject (REJ) tells the sender to retransmit data units (I-frames), beginning with a specified number.

Acknowledgements.   Acknowledgements can be requested by the sender. By setting a bit called the *poll-final* bit to 1, the transmitter can request an immediate acknowledgement.

Once the sender has sent 127 frames, it stops sending until they are acknowledged. Sender and receiver can negotiate a smaller window size (the maximum number of unacknowledged frames) by using the XID command. In addition, the window size can be decreased by the user. This is only done if many errors appear on the cable or to limit congestion on the cable. The trade-off is that it takes longer to complete an exchange.

If the sender transmits less than the agreed-upon maximum number of frames, the receiver waits for more data. It will wait until the *acknowledgement timer* runs out, then the receiver will send an acknowledgement.

The sender also starts a timer when it begins sending data units. If the sender completes its transmission and receives no acknowledgement, the sender will wait until its timer runs out. The sender will then send a supervisory command with poll-final set to request acknowledgement. If an acknowledgement is received, transmission continues. If a REJect occurs, the sender will resend data. If no response is received, it will reset using SABME. ("Save Me!")

Flow control. We have seen that there are two flow control mechanisms: a RNR transmission by the receiver and the 127-frame window size limit. The latter can be set by hand or negotiated by the systems.

Summary

Understanding the operation of the LLC is important, especially if you need to understand the output of your protocol analyzer. In this chapter, we have discussed the function of the LLC sublayer, i.e., the LLC places data on the LAN and once the data is off the LAN, the LLC delivers the data to its correct destination. In addition, important terms such as SAP were introduced.

We also discussed the pros and cons of Type 1 connectionless service and Type 2 connection-oriented service and the procedure by which Type 1 and 2 data are exchanged. Generally, the application software is written to use Type 1 or 2.

In connection-oriented applications, the window size is often started at 127 frames. You may find that tuning this figure produces an improvement in performance if a WAN is involved and is prone to producing errors. Of course, windowing is automatic in some applications, such as NetWare applications using Burst Mode Protocol.

The next chapter on LAN protocols discusses the layers above the LLC that are needed to run a LAN at the enterprise level.

Chapter

10

LAN Protocols

What Protocols Do

The problem with the word "protocol" is that it is used to refer to dozens of different protocols, of which we have discussed but two. Which protocol do we mean, or do we mean some or all of them? It is no wonder that of the top nine internetworking challenges faced by network professionals, managing multiple protocols was cited *first*.

Protocols, or rules, have three major elements:

1. *Syntax,* which defines the protocol fields
2. *Semantics,* which gives those fields meaning
3. *Timing,* which makes sure that each protocol stays in step with its partner(s)

Here we look above the *logical link control* (LLC) to the network layer protocols and higher protocols. In terms of frames, these protocol characters trail the LLC fields we have just discussed. Would it not be nice to finally send some user data? In this chapter, we do!

The difference between the protocols we have studied so far and those in this chapter is that until now we have had the IEEE to guide us. Now we enter uncharted territory. Except for the Internet's *Transmission Control Protocol/Internet Protocol* (TCP/IP), and the *International Standards Organization* (ISO), there are no more standards, only vendor implementations.

The reason this chapter is important is because functions essential to LANs, such as routing and end-to-end transport reliability, are not defined by IEEE standards. Something else is required to fill the vacuum. As a result, the always-enterprising vendors have championed their own proprietary solutions.

Other members of the LAN community have turned to already developed protocols to plug the void. In large measure, they adopted TCP/IP for routing and end-to-end reliability. Mature, tested, and public, these protocols have proved a good choice.

The *Internet Engineering Task Force* (IETF) returned the compliment by creating an informational document illustrating how Novell's IPX (Internet packet exchange) protocol can be carried via WAN media. It is embodied in *Request for Comment* (RFC) 1362, the *Novell IPX Over Various WAN Media* (IPXWAN). The RFC gives developers a specification against which to create products designed to work with NetWare over WAN networks.

TCP/IP has become so popular that major vendors are moving toward these protocols as replacements for their own proprietary protocols. This is most clearly evidenced by Novell's slow but perceptible drive to separate IPX/SPX (*Internetwork and Sequenced Packet Exchange*) from its own NetWare Core Protocols and adopt TCP/IP as well. NetWare-IP, supporting both TCP/IP and IPX, is a clear example of Novell's long-term direction.

In a similar vein, IBM has embraced TCP/IP and supports it in the *Systems Network Architecture* (SNA) environment, though not without some difficulty. Accordingly, we will discuss the issues of *Synchronous Data Link Control* (SDLC) and TCP/IP encapsulation.

IPX/SPX are by far the most popular Layers 3 and 4 protocols for LANs; it is used in 44 percent of them. For that reason, it is also worthwhile examining the workings of these protocols.

Another popular protocol and interface, *Network Basic Input/Output System* (NetBIOS), is used at the Session Layer 5. Understanding this popular protocol-interface, conceived by IBM and Sytek and widely emulated, is essential to an in-depth understanding of LANs.

Where Do They Fit?

We have already looked at two layers of the LAN protocol stack, the physical layer and the *data link layer* (DLL), consisting of the *media access control* (MAC) and LLC sublayers. In this chapter, we examine the higher-layer protocols that open a communications channel and establish a session. These layers also specify how data should be divided into smaller pieces for transmission, a process called *fragmentation* (at Layer 3) or *segmentation* (at Layer 4).

As with the data link sublayers, our user's data is preceded by additional precisely defined headers at each layer. (Remember our earlier analogy about the freight train where the data is the caboose.) These include the network layer (Layer 3), transport layer (Layer 4), and the session layer (Layer 5). These are all worth knowing and have strong relevance to a LAN's operation.

The presentation and application layers, Layers 6 and 7, are called *service protocols*. They determine how programs handle data and how clients ask for network services such as printing. *Network operating systems* (NOSs), for instance, operate at the application layer but have few if any presentation layer functions.

Another way to categorize the layers is to say that the lower four layers provide *connectivity* and the higher three layers offer *interoperability* between applications.

Layers 3–7 handle the following LAN requirements:

Routing (Layer 3)	Routing is not defined by IEEE
Transport (Layer 4)	With internetworks, end-to-end transparency is essential.
Session (Layer 5)	Synchronization of process dialogues and data management is a function of this layer.
Presentation (Layer 6)	Data format conversions, for transmission across a network, is a function of this layer.
Application (Layer 7)	Application-to-application links are handled at this layer.

Many of these functions are handled by the various NOSs such as VINES, NetWare, or LAN Manager.

It is tempting to force-fit the protocols that will be discussed into the *open systems interconnection* (OSI) stack. Some fit better than others. Many predated the OSI stack, and others have made little or no effort to comply with OSI. Therefore, the portions of applications belonging to a particular stack may be hard to separate. The point is that all or most of the OSI functions are accounted for even though the boundaries are often indistinct.

Most of the protocols in this chapter operate at the network, transport, and session layers. The protocols share many traits by layer. We will first review the functions of these layers and then discuss the protocols in functional terms.

Layer 3

Layer 3, the network layer, has the following characteristics:

The network layer performs *routing,* i.e., directing a message from source to destination through a network.

Routing is by no means a standard process on many LANs.

Routers build routing tables, which contain information about the networks connected to the routers and directions to get from one network to another.

Routers from one vendor will not work with those from other vendors if proprietary protocols are used. Internetworking based on generic protocols works well.

Routers that use the *Routing Information Protocol* (RIP) or a protocol similar to RIP contain a *hop count,* which is the number of routers a packet must pass through to get to its destination. The usual RIP hop-count limit is 15.

Routers that use RIP take the path with the smallest hop count on the *assumption* that it is the shortest, least expensive path.

Under RIP, routing tables are updated often, typically every 30 sec. The updates can create a large amount of overhead traffic.

Host machines and servers can also copy and use routing tables.

A problem associated with routing is that a route can loop on itself. In that case, the packets will circulate forever unless they are stopped.

Current popular routing algorithms are RIP-IP, *RIP-Xerox Network Services* (RIP-XNS), RIP-IPX, *Open Shortest Path First* (OSPF), and OSI's *Intermediate System to Intermediate System* (IS-IS). There are approximately 17 in all.

Transmissions, e.g., routing-table updates, sent at the routing layer are *unreliable* datagrams. They are neither acknowledged nor sequenced, i.e., no response action is performed and no session is created. However, they are connectionless, have very low overhead, and are also fast.

Within this layer, group and broadcast addressing, such as for table updates, are common functions.

Layer 4

Layer 4, the transport layer, ensures correct end-to-end communications. Characteristics of Layer 4 are the following:

Connection-oriented transport layer connections are *reliable:* A session is established and transmission acknowledgements are used.

Point-to-point addressing only is used often.

Acknowledgements, sequence counts, and window sizes are all used.

The transport layer often includes a naming-service directory. A naming service allows users to find resources on the network.

TCP is a transport layer protocol and the TCP/IP protocol suite includes an *unreliable* transport layer alternative called the *Userable Datagram Protocol* (UDP). UDP is used with the *Simple Network Management Protocol* (SNMP).

Layer 4 communications are full duplex: They can talk both ways at once.

Layer 5

The *Session Layer* resides at Layer 5. In essence, the Session layers in both machines negotiate the terms under which communication will take place. It would be just as valid to call the Session layer the Moderator layer, because the Session layer:

- Initiates a session by "shaking hands" with its partner.

- Negotiates terms of the information exchange: Shall we operate in full duplex or half duplex? How much data can you accept at a time? If something goes wrong, shall I fix it, or will you?

- Monitors and manages the exchange of information under the terms just negotiated.

- Initiates corrective action if needed.

- Closes a session gracefully and completely once the information exchange is done; this is sometimes called "breaking down" a session.

In summary, the Session layer works just as people do when they have a conversation. One person says, "Hello," followed by the other person's "Hello" (the handshake). Then they negotiate terms: "The reason I called you . . . " or "Which of us shall speak first, since we both have information to convey?" During the ensuing exchange, both people are—or should be—active listeners (correcting if needed). At the end, they close gracefully by saying, "Goodbye."

Observations on layers 3–5

Layers 3–5 have the following interesting properties:

Several frame types can exist within one protocol. Novell's IPX protocol has *three* possible frame types. A *network interface card* (NIC) software driver associates a frame type, protocol, and a NIC together.

Until recently, a different NIC and driver were needed for each protocol to be used, and only one could be used at a time. Now the *Open Data [Link] Interface* (ODI) from Novell and other vendors allow a NIC to handle several protocols in full-duplex mode.

Protocols are often mixed together on a LAN cable at these layers. For example, network layer IPX and XNS packets can coexist, but each is ignored by the other.

Ports and *sockets* are common terms that are used at these layers, but they have different meanings, depending on the protocol (Table 10.1).

Table 10.1 illustrates how different terms are used by different protocols at the same layer. The concept, though, is always the same: Whether it is called a port, socket, or *service access point* (SAP), the field always contains a higher-layer source or destination for data.

Some protocols combine terms from different layers. TCP/IP has a *socket address,* which is a combination of an IP address and a UDP or TCP port number. The socket address includes all the information needed to send data from one process to another. Similarly, XNS combines the socket address at Layer 4 and its network and host addresses at Layer 3 to form what is simply termed an *address.*

LAN Protocols

TCP/IP

TCP/IP did not begin life as a LAN protocol. It was borne by the Defense Advanced Research Projects Agency (DARPA) and led to the creation of ARPANET and MILNET, both of which evolved into the Internet. The Internet is the world's largest network, with millions of devices connected to it.

TCP/IP is really *two* protocols. TCP is used for end-to-end data transport at Layer 4. IP's main function is *routing* at Layer 3. We begin our discussion with IP.

IP addressing. Internet addresses are doled out by the *Internet Network Information Center* (InterNIC) Registration Service.[1] InterNIC

TABLE 10.1   Upper-Layer Terminology

Layer	TCP/IP	XNS	NetBIOS	IPX	AppleTalk
			Protocol		
3	IP address	Network and host addresses		Destination network and node	
4	Port	Socket	Session partner	Socket	Socket

---

[1]InterNIC can be reached at 1-800-365-3642 or call vendor PSI at 1-800-827-7482.

will give you a main network address large enough to identify every node on your network.

If you have your own network, you may set up your own network information center. You need not contact Internet's NIC unless you plan to be connected to the Internet, in which case you will need certified addresses. Nevertheless, even if you are not connected, the NIC* will still help you set up your own network address scheme. It is wise to use the class conventions below if you think you might one day connect to another TCP/IP network such as Internet.

You have probably seen a 32-bit IP address. It uses *dotted decimal* and looks like this: 128.101.4.9. A dotted decimal address is a lot easier to work with than 10000000 01100100 00000100 00001001. Wouldn't you agree?

There are five classes of Internet addresses (also see Table 10.2 and Figure 10.1). They are as follows:

There are 127 *Class A* network addresses, occupying the left-most octet. The high order-bit (0) identifies this class of address, so this bit cannot be used as an address bit. The three octets to the right provide addressing for over 16 million nodes. About one-third of these addresses have been allocated, and they are very hard to obtain.

Class B addresses use the two left-hand octets for network addressing. The two high-order bits (10) are used for identifying this class of address. This leaves 14 bits for network addresses (16,000-plus networks) and 16 bits for network nodes (65,000-plus nodes). About 5000 Class B addresses are already assigned.

Class C addresses are the most common class of Internet address. Less the three high-order bits (110) the three left-hand octets are

TABLE 10.2   Address Classes and Their Equivalent First-Octet Values

Address class	First-octet decimal value
A	000–127
B	128–191
C	192–223
D	224–239
E	240–255

*Do not confuse the Internet Network Information Center (NIC) with the identical acronym used to refer to an interface card!

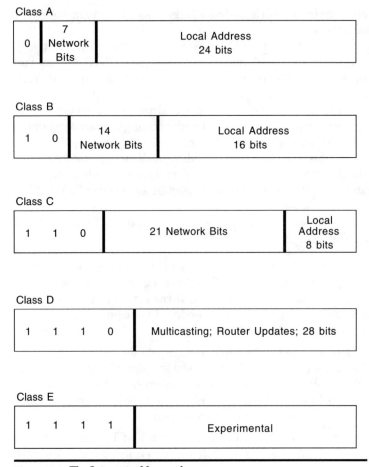

Figure 10.1 The Internet address scheme.

used for addressing. Over 4 million networks of less than 255 nodes can be identified. Over 2 million Class C addresses are so far in use.

Class D addresses are fairly new. Its address recognition header is 1110 (of 32 bits). Class D is used for *multicasting*, e.g., for router updates.

Class E addresses are reserved for experiments. Their recognition header is 1111 (of 32 bits).

Network software and routers use a *subnet mask,* as shown in Figure 10.2, to identify whether a message is to stay within the network, or be routed elsewhere. Also called a *netmask,* the presence of 1s in a field indicates that a field contains all or part of a network address. Zeros

Subnet Address Mask:
A 1 indicates the presence of a network address bit.

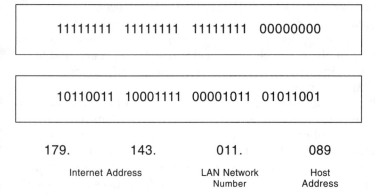

| 11111111 | 11111111 | 11111111 | 00000000 |

| 10110011 | 10001111 | 00001011 | 01011001 |

| 179. | 143. | 011. | 089 |
| Internet Address | | LAN Network
Number | Host
Address |

Figure 10.2 Subnet masking.

indicate the host address location. For instance, a Class C address, which is the most common, uses the first three octets to identify the network and the last one to identify the host. Thus, the subnet mask is 255.255.255.0.

Masking can also be used to create subnets. Let us say you apply to InterNIC for a Class B address, and you are given 179.143.*XXX.XXX*. If you have 11 LANs with 89 workstations each, you can attach them all to the Internet with only this one Class B address. (Internet addresses are getting scarce. At the current rate of usage, they will all be in use by 1996. However, several address extension schemes are under consideration.)

Create an address mask of 255.255.255.0. Assign a fixed number to each LAN in the third cell, say 1–11. Use the last cell for the workstation (the "host" in TCP/IP parlance) addresses on each LAN. Then your addressing will look like: 179.143.(1-11).(1-89). How you select the addresses in the last two octets is completely up to you. There is no need to be sequential beyond whatever innate passion for order you possess.

Going outbound, hosts look in a *name server,* which performs name-to-address translation, for the address of the appropriate router along the path to the destination. It is the network administrator's task to build these routing tables. Internet routers can also converse with each other using a protocol called RIP-IP to find a destination and update their tables.

IP connects subnetworks in order to from an internetwork, called an *internet* in TCP/IP phraseology. IP routes data. In our example from Chapter 9, where you are sending an e-mail message to Ed on another network, the message would be handed to TCP, which would then pass it to IP for routing. IP adds a header to make it an internet datagram. Then it is passed to the LLC, if IEEE 802.2 is being used.

IP datagrams are connectionless, like Type 1 service at the LLC sublayer. They are called *unreliable* in TCP/IP jargon, which sounds worse than it really is. Unacknowledged transmission is acceptable because the overlying TCP protocol provides reliable (acknowledged) connection-oriented service.

Connectionless services are easier to specify in a multivendor environment, and upgrading them is easier, too. It is inefficient to have layer protocols duplicate one another's functions.

Datagrams can take different routes each time and need not be delivered in sequence. Datagrams can be thrown away if they are damaged or if there is no place to store them, i.e., the buffer is too small. In addition, links can be out, hosts and gateways can be congested, and misrouting or defective headers can be created because of incorrect implementation.

Because of all these unpleasant possibilities, a second protocol called *Internet Control Message Protocol* (ICMP) is always implemented with IP. ICMP tells the originating host of the problem and expects the host to fix it.

IP's secondary function is to divide a datagram into *fragments,* if necessary, to traverse a network with a smaller maximum packet size than the source used. IP hosts must accept datagrams of up to 576 octets. Fragmenting is normally done at a gateway router and always at an 8-octet boundary. The originating upper-level protocol can prohibit fragmentation, but a gateway or router may throw the segment away if the router or gateway cannot handle the larger frame.

IP routing.   Believe it or not, there are no unequivocal routing standards in IP. The closest is RFC 1058, which defines RIP-IP. RIP-IP is a *distance-vector protocol* based on *hop counts.* IP in the sender decides whether the destination address is on the local network or not. If it is, IP sends the datagram directly. Otherwise, IP sends the datagram to an appropriate router using routing tables. Then it is up to the router. An IP datagram header is shown in Figure 10.3.

Router tables are updated manually or automatically by other routers periodically. The table has an entry for each network accessible by the router. It also contains the address of the destination network and of the next router in the shortest path to the destination.

Routing information traded between routers includes destination network, subnetwork, host and router addresses, and the number of hops (intermediate networks) required to reach the destination via a given router. The hop count indicates the shortest distance, and table updates from other routers keep the receiving router's routing table

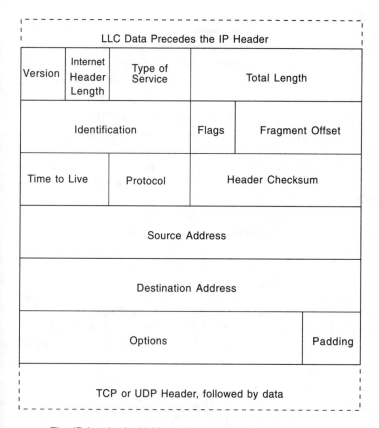

The IP header is 32 bits wide, in 8 and 16-bit segments.

Figure 10.3 An IP datagram header.

current. Updates have sequence numbers to ensure that only the latest version of the routing data is used to update the routing table, e.g., a lower number cannot replace a higher one.

IP also supports host source routing from the TCP layer or higher. Source routing is rarely used except for high security applications. In source routing, addresses of networks and routers to be traversed are specified. Even when source routing is specified, it is useful for the sender to have current routing data. This is because routers have multiple addresses, for data going out and coming in. A packet traversing the network saves router addresses along the way. The receiver must use the same path in reverse to return a message.

RIP-IP.   R.I.P. is just the right acronym for Routing Information Protocol; it is that old. It can only pass through 15 intermediate networks or *hops,* which is too small for today's internets. A hop count of 16 means the destination cannot be reached. Routing updates require sending the whole table, not just the changes. Lost links or routers show up as slowly increasing distances. After a change, traffic may fall into a loop for a period of time. (This is a chronic problem in distance-vector protocol routing.)

OSPF. OSPF has been proposed to replace RIP-IP. OSPF was proposed as a standard in 1990. In OSPF, the network domain is broken down into *areas*. Every router in an area knows all the routers and links. Only routing *changes* are sent, not the entire table. And once a change has been made, the whole network starts using the correct routes very quickly—within 3 sec.

OSPF supports traffic splitting via multiple paths, routing based on the type of service, and authentication for routing updates. The equivalent OSI routing protocol is called *Intermediate System* [a router] *to Intermediate System* [another router] or IS-IS routing.

TCP. Overlying IP is TCP at the transport layer. Connection-oriented, TCP makes sure that the data is accurate, in sequence, complete, and free of duplication. Data passed from higher layers down to TCP is broken into pieces. As shown in Figure 10.4, a TCP header, including a sequence number, is added to the message, now called a *segment,* which is then passed to IP.

At the receiver station, TCP reassembles the segments in the right order, throws out any duplicates, and acknowledges receiving the transmission. TCP also performs flow control. The window size (number of unused bytes in the receive buffer) can be changed dynamically if network congestion is present.

TCP is a full-duplex protocol. When messages are sent back, an acknowledgement of past received segments is included. Duplicates, however, are possible because an unacknowledged segment causes the segment to be sent again.

TCP/IP based products abound: Terminal emulations use Telnet for VT100 dumb terminals and 3270, called TN3270, which makes a dumb terminal act like a 3270 using TCP/IP. This is commonly used to remotely access IBM hosts. Other services include the Simple Mail Transfer Protocol and File Transfer Protocol. Modern versions of Unix, both those from Berkeley and AT&T, bundle TCP/IP inside them.

Ports. TCP has *ports* that are functionally similar to the *source service access point* (SSAP) and *destination service access point* (DSAP) in IEEE 802.2. Ports let TCP/IP handle several communications processes at once.

The connection-oriented nature of TCP/IP requires that ports at both ends be able to communicate. The software port is a two-octet binary

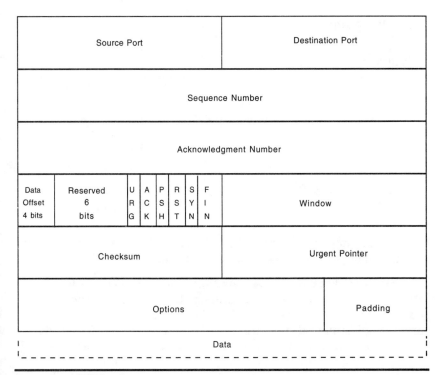

Figure 10.4 A TCP header.

number. When combined with the network address, we wind up with a *socket address*.

Security. Because of its Department of Defense origin, TCP contains security mechanisms to limit transmissions to trusted machines; the transmissions are then passed along to IP. This means data is kept out of unsecure systems and unauthorized applications. Commercial TCP/IP versions often omit these features.

UDP. An alternative to TCP is to use UDP, whose header is shown in Figure 10.5. Like IP, UDP is a connectionless datagram service and is also *unreliable* with no delivery guarantee. The only error checking is done with the *checksum* function. Received packets with mismatching checksums are jettisoned. UDP is used by TCP/IP's management proto- col, the *Simple Network Management Protocol* (SNMP). SNMP is widely deployed in LAN devices of every kind such as hubs, bridges, and routers. Even uninterruptible power supplies have SNMP, and soon workstations will too.

UDP is suitable for management and noncritical functions such as interactive directory service. Applications that must broadcast or mul-

UDP Datagram

Source Port	Destination Port
Length	Checksum
Data	

Figure 10.5 A UDP header.

ticast datagrams can also use UDP, whereas TCP, being connection-oriented, cannot perform broadcasts or multicasts.

Address Resolution Protocol. *Address Resolution Protocol* (ARP) translates IP addresses into media addresses. Installed on a host, ARP lets the host build an address table. The host broadcasts an ARP request carrying a destination IP address. The target recognizes its IP address and responds with its hardware (NIC) address. The target also adds the host's IP and physical address to its own routing table.

Reverse ARP has the host broadcast a query with its own physical address. The server responds with the host's IP address. This is used when hosts initialize themselves by using server configuration information. Of course, the server must have the IP addresses to begin with.

Proxy ARP lets a host query a remote destination. Instead of the destination, a router to that destination responds, giving its own physical interface address. The router is a *proxy* for the remote destination.

TCP/IP summary. In the absence of other higher-level protocols to support LAN internetworking, TCP/IP has filled the gap well. The IP layer is similar to the OSI network layer because the latter was based on the former. TCP/IP has been accepted as a standard by the federal government although the plan is to migrate to OSI. However, TCP/IP is widely implemented today and is built into most versions of Unix. Its modularity, having a rich set of optional protocols at each layer, has not hurt its popularity. Furthermore, its small shell program size, usually about 20 kbytes, makes it suitable for even the smallest PC.

NetWare Version 3.1X supports TCP/IP for server-server and server-host applications. Novell also supports Network File System for file and print services to Unix clients through three *NetWare Loadable Modules* (NLMs) called Flex/IP. Novell also supports SNMP.

Novell's LAN Workplace currently supports TCP/IP and IPX on

DOS- and Windows-based workstations. Novell will soon support TCP/IP and AppleTalk on Macintoshes used as NetWare clients.

An NLM for NetWare 3.1X (and planned for NetWare 4.X) is called IPTunnel. IPTunnel encases an IPX frame inside a UPD/IP packet in a process called *tunneling*. However, the processing time involved in tunneling plus the continued use of IPX perpetuates the efficiency problems inherent in using IPX on a WAN.

NetWare nodes tell each other who they are and what services they offer through the Service Advertising Protocol (SAP). SAP broadcasts information about network nodes through the network. If tunneled UPD/IP is being used, broadcasts are not allowed. This means that servers must update each other one-by-one, causing congestion in the system.

NetWare-IP avoids this problem by using two more NLMs: a *Domain-Naming Service* (DNS) and a *Domain Server for SAPs* (DSS). These can reside on a server or another station.

DNS is found in any TCP/IP network. The DNS keeps host information, name tables, and internetwork addresses in it.

The DSS is the data bank for SAP information. Rather than broadcasting SAP data to all the nodes, it is kept in the central DSS. When a user logs in, a connection is set up with the naming service to find the nearest domain service for SAPs. The user then logs onto the DSS to get to the desired NetWare services.

OSI's HDLC and IBM's SNA/SDLC

These two Layer 2 DLL protocols are virtually identical, so we treat them as one. They are in fact compatible and are used together. The only difference is that the data field in HDLC can be any number of bits whereas those in SDLC must be a multiple of eight. An SDLC header is shown in Figure 10.6.

A transmission begins with a *flag*, which is a hex 7E, i.e., a pattern of 01111110. This is the *only* time six 1s in a row can be sent. The flag is the starting and ending delimiter.

The flag is followed by an 8-bit address field. This can be modified to permit extended addressing as far as it is needed. Control information follows the address field. This is where the poll/final bit is buried, the same as in the IEEE 802.2 LLC.

An HDLC or SDLC frame ends with a 16-bit *cyclical redundancy check* (CRC) called a *frame-check sequence* (FCS), followed by the closing 7E flag delimiter.

To prevent *aliasing,* an invalid detection of a flag, any five 1s in a row will have a 0 inserted after them, even if the next bit is already a 0. The receiver always deletes the 0 following five 1s. This applies to the en-

FLAG	ADDRESS	CONTROL	INFO.	FCS	FLAG
01111110	1 or more 8-bit chars.	1 or 2 8-bit chars.	0 or more chars.	16 bits CRC-CCITT	01111110

For ADCCP or HDLC, any number of bits may be used in the Information field.

For SDLC, the I-field must be a multiple of 8 bits.

CRC accumulation and zero insertion applies to all fields between but excluding Flags.

Figure 10.6 A HDLC-SDLC-ADCCP (ANSI Advanced Data Communication Control Procedures) header.

tire frame starting with the address, including the FCS. Similarly, the FCS protects the same fields, even itself.

HDLC and SDLC use the same kinds of controls as in Type 2 connection-oriented service in IEEE 802.2. Even the terms are the same: I-format frames, U-frames, and S-frames. HDLC and SDLC are connection-oriented, reliable, *link-by-link* services. Also, since HDLC and SDLC are DLL protocols, they contain no routing information, such as network layer addresses.

One routing solution is to *tunnel* HDLC and SDLC through a network using TCP/IP. The other is to convert HDLC and SDLC frames into token-ring frames. Conversion boosts performance while tunneling degrades it.

To complicate matters, an IBM front-end processor will cut off an SNA/SDLC session in approximately 10 sec if it does not get a response to a polling request. So speed of routing, tunneling, and untunneling is of the essence. IBM customers also object to having to add TCP/IP solely for the purpose of routing.

In a test of both approaches, *Data Communications* magazine investigated each in its May 1992 issue. Conversion throughput was 99 percent, and tunneling's throughput was 70 percent. The strategy becomes clear: Continue tunneling only if you already have it. If not, go the conversion route. IBM's *Advanced Peer-to-Peer Networking* (APPN) is intended to resolve the SDLC routing problem.

All this explains why the most popular protocol for internetworking is TCP/IP with 45 percent of the market: It is well-known, and many products that can use it already exist. Novell's IPX follows at 34 percent of the market, due to NetWare's popularity, and IBM's SNA trails at 21 percent.

Novell's protocols

Figure 10.7 shows the six native protocols used by NetWare. The first two that are discussed, IPX and *sequenced packet exchange* (SPX), derive their names in part from the XNS protocol suite upon which they are based.

IPX. IPX dominates the network layer. This point is essential: IPX is the delivery mechanism for *all five* of the other protocols that are used. As a result, IPX is involved in routing using RIP-IPX and in distribut-

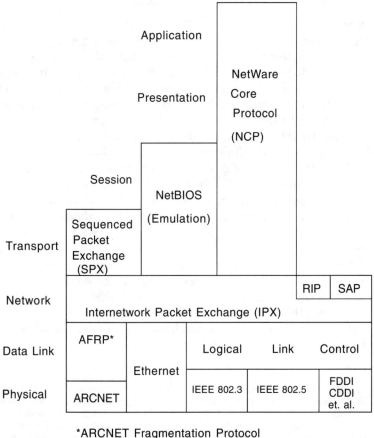

Figure 10.7 NetWare relative protocols.

ing SAP broadcasts. NetWare servers use SAP to issue messages announcing their presence.

IPX is a fast, low-overhead, connectionless, half-duplex protocol. In and of itself, no acknowledgements are required, although higher layers may encapsulate a message in IPX requiring an acknowledgement. For example, SPX and the *NetWare Core Protocol* (NCP) do this.

IPX works fine on high-speed LANs but gets bogged down once WAN-size network delays and lower speeds are introduced. This, among other things, has limited NetWare's applicability to enterprise-wide environments.

The reasons for IPX's difficulties have been two-fold. First, the packet size, normally 512 bytes, is too small for efficient use over a WAN. Second, the routing protocol for IPX, call RIP-IPX, is based on RIP, an older and less-efficient routing algorithm. Novell has addressed both problems by introducing a feature called Burst Mode Protocol and *NetWare Link Services Protocol* (NLSP).

Burst Mode Protocol. If NCP or SPX uses IPX and an acknowledgement is required, then a 64-kbyte message will decompose into 128 blocks of 512-byte messages, each one acknowledged in sequence. On a WAN with a 0.5 sec delay each way, the time to send the message will be just over 2 min. This alone is unacceptable, and on a packet network, the traffic charges will build up very quickly. One company found itself paying $17,000 a month just for the Service Advertising (especially) and NCP background protocols carried by IPX.

To alleviate the problem, the Burst Mode Protocol allows packets of up to 64 kbytes (128 blocks of 512 bytes each) to be sent in one *burst* under certain circumstances. For instance, burst mode streams fragments of large transmissions, not small ones. "Large" means larger than the maximum MAC frame size: 1500 bytes for Ethernet; about 4 kbytes for 4-Mbit/sec token ring, and about 16 kbytes for 16-Mbit/sec token ring.

Accordingly, burst mode will not improve application performance where small packets are used, such as during logging on. In fact, testing has shown a slight negative effect with records that are longer than 512 bytes but less than the maximum frame size.[2]

Novell claims a 5–300 percent throughput increase over large multi-

[2]Thomas, Richard: "Burst Mode Boosts NetWare's Wide-Area Acumen," *Data Communications* 63–70, September 21, 1992. Novell now recommends DOS Requester Virtural Loadable Module (VLM) instead of BNETX.COM due to reported, but nonduplicated, data corruption problems when using BNETX with XCOPY. Experiment with pb buffer sizes (start at 3) to optimize response time. Microsoft Windows-based applications may show a performance decrease when using BNETX.COM.

segment networks when using burst mode. Burst mode performance depends on:

The number of bytes in the frame

The number of bytes in the transaction

The end-to-end network latency (delay)

The number of routers or bridges to be traversed

The network window capacity, e.g., X.25

Potentially, bridges or routers could be overloaded by such long messages. The solution here is to adjust window and buffer sizes. However, making the window size too small will just recreate the problem.

In some cases, routers will fragment large messages into 512-byte chunks because that is what the original XNS protocol demanded. Such fragmentation is inefficient over WAN links, so Novell now offers a router to support adjustable frame lengths. Other vendors offer similar flexibility.

As implemented by Novell, burst mode sends a large block of data, internally fragmented into 512-byte packets. If the receiving application finds one or more damaged packets, only they need to be resent. The receiver inserts the good packets in the right place and hands the block to the application. Thus, burst mode starts with a window size of 128 bytes and works down and up again as line conditions warrant. This is what Novell means when they call burst mode a "modified" sliding-window protocol. Conventional sliding-window protocols such as HDLC have a fixed window size (usually 7) regardless of the link's error rate.

Burst Mode Protocol will work with non-burst mode IPX workstations, servers, bridges, and routers. It is offered for NetWare versions 3.1X and 4.X.

RIP-IPX. Novell has its own routing information protocol, RIP-IPX. In RIP-IPX, a station simply sends a broadcast seeking the router that can forward the packet. The router with the shortest hop count is selected. A similar protocol, SAP, is used for printers and other peripherals.

RIP-IPX and SAP are "chatty," set to broadcast routes and services every 30 and 60 sec, respectively. Routers filter SAP and RIP-IPX traffic, except for router updates, to keep them off WANs.

IPX routing is based on RIP, which was described earlier. RIP-IPX is limited by its 15-hop count limit, and complete (rather than updates-only) routing information is sent out every 30 sec to adjacent neighbors. RIP-IPX also does not necessarily pick the best path.

A newer version of IPX routing software called NetWare Link Services Protocol or NLSP is based on the OSI IS-IS algorithm. Using IS-IS, data can take several paths to distribute the traffic load. NLSP sends routing *changes only as needed.* With NLSP, NetWare is expected to be able to support several hundred to a thousand or so routers, whereas the current practical limit is a few hundred. Before implementing a large network, ask routing vendors whether they support NLSP. NLSP also contains a new addressing hierarchy capable of addressing almost 4 billion network addresses.

The Novell Network Registry.   Unlike IEEE universal addressing, administrators select their own IPX addresses, which could duplicate those used elsewhere. This becomes a problem as more networks are connected together. Unpredictable results can include sending the message to the wrong place, sending half to one place and half to another, or simply causing a string of error messages. Sometimes a program or device will hang or freeze, or an entire LAN or segment will go down.

To avoid possible address duplication, Novell has set up the Novell Network Registry. It is an optional service under which NetWare administrators can register the IPX addresses they use or plan to use. If the addresses are unused, they are simply registered. If any are already in use, the administrator has to change the duplicated address(es) in their system.

The registry operates in synchronization with the Internet's existing registry to the extent that IPX addresses can be derived from existing IP addresses. The registry will therefore be of particular importance to those who plan to operate NetWare/IP. Registration fees start (as of this writing) at $100 and increase based on the number of addresses requested or registered.[3]

An IPX header.   An IPX header is shown in Figure 10.8. Recall that this header is used with all the Novell protocols, whose own information appears in the data field.

SPX.   SPX is the nearest Novell equivalent to TCP. SPX is connection-oriented and guarantees delivery. As its name says, packets are delivered in order once the connection is established. Some applications require that packets arrive in order, which is why developers might use SPX and IPX instead of IPX alone. SPX uses IPX as its delivery mechanism just as TCP uses IP.

You may have used SPX if you have ever used NetWare's *remote console* (RCONSOLE) command. In RCONSOLE, the server mirrors key-

---

[3]The Novell Network Registry can be reached at (408) 321-1506; by fax at (408) 956-0463; and by e-mail on the Internet under REGISTRY@NOVELL.COM.

strokes entered at the remote station. Clearly, all the keystrokes must be seen in the proper order, and thus there is the need for SPX's guaranteed and orderly delivery.

One alternative to using burst mode IPX is to use SPX instead. SPX allows more than one outstanding request, but most applications are not written to use SPX. As shown in Fig. 10.7, SPX sits atop IPX and comes with NetWare server and workstation software.

SPX is used for critical applications. Recent database servers from Oracle and Gupta use SPX, despite its additional overhead. Some

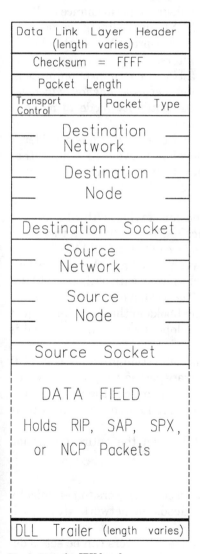

Figure 10.8 An IPX header.

mainframe gateways, tape backup systems, and third-party programs also use it. On WANs, these applications have correspondingly fewer response-time difficulties.

The down side is that SPX has a little extra overhead that cuts performance for short transmissions while improving it for long ones on mesh-type WANs. Accordingly, NetWare Shell bypasses SPX on a LAN to get all the speed possible.

SPXII.   In NetWare 4.X, a version called SPXII is included and is intended to be a better-performing version of SPX. SPX uses requests-responses to guarantee delivery, which can degrade performance on WAN networks. Like Burst Mode Protocol, SPXII uses sliding windows to send optimally sized packets through an error-prone WAN. Also, larger packet sizes can be negotiated across routers.

The new SPXII is also enhanced by a two-stage connection process, option negotiation, orderly release, and *negative acknowledgement* (NAK) support. It also has a special compatibility mode to make it work with conventional SPX.

The down side is that SPXII adds packet overhead and is considered by some to be too ponderous. Many developers avoid SPX altogether and use their own checks to assure delivery while retaining the speed of IPX.

Transport layer interface.   Another reason for staying with SPX is that the *applications programming interface* (API) for SPXII is the Unix-based STREAMS *Transport-Layer Interface* (TLI). STREAMS TLI is a higher-level network API that sits between SPXII and the application.

Some applications cannot be modified to work with TLI, and TLI applications themselves are uncommon. The burden of placing one bulky layer atop another that lacks application hooks in the first place is just too much, especially for DOS-based developers where the overhead is simply too high.

TLI is a transport-layer protocol. It is connection-oriented as is TCP. Yet TLI resides atop SPXII, another transport-layer protocol. While this has little practical significance, it does point out the vagaries and the occasional futility of trying to fit software functions into neat little pigeonholes.

If NetWare goes wholesale to TCP/IP, then the entire discussion above will be moot!

SAP.   SAP is also a user of IPX. SAP is used by servers to periodically broadcast their existence. As such, SAP floods the network with repetitive information every 60 sec.

The overhead from SAP can be minimized. Routers can be set to delete SAP traffic. Novell's multiprotocol router passes SAP traffic only if it has changed since the last broadcast. Cisco routers pass SAP traffic at intervals specified by the user, typically 30 min. NetWare servers look for SAP traffic every 60 sec. Accordingly, Novell and Cisco routers send "spoofed" SAP frames to locally connected stations. The problem is that if a server fails between broadcasts, a Cisco router will still present it as active.

A better solution is to solve the problem at its source. Novell has introduced an NLM for NetWare 3.1X called SAP Restrictor. Using this NLM, users can change the 60-sec period to anything they like.

NCP. NCP has functions ranging from the transport to application layers. In brief, NCP sets the rules for workstation-server communication. As with SAP and all the other protocols, NCP uses IPX to carry its traffic.

Like the other protocols, NCP was optimized for LAN usage. NCP also carries a substantial amount of overhead. Using burst mode with NCP has only partially offset the inefficiency of NCP in a WAN environment. This is because NCP still permits only a single message to be outstanding between a workstation and server at one time. At least burst mode can bundle them together.

Customers who wish to use NetWare 2.X or 3.1X in an internetworked environment can tune their systems as we have discussed. Even so, NCP's origin as a LAN-optimized protocol is deeply embedded in these NOSs, and there is no changing that.

NCP is the heart of NetWare. As a result, specifications for NCP have not been released until recently and then only under license to developers with genuine NetWare interoperability needs.

There is a clear trend to separate NCP from IPX. The general consensus is that Novell does not wish to perpetuate a large, proprietary structure that will drain resources for years as the industry moves toward an open protocol such as TCP/IP.

Novell's NetBIOS. Since NetBIOS is not unique to Novell, the next section contains a discussion of this interface. However, Novell's NetBIOS emulation uses IPX in NetWare systems.[4]

---

[4]NetWare protocol references (all published by Novell) include (a) NetWare 386 Theory of Operations, V3.0 and 3.1, 479-000042-001, August, 1989; (b) NetWare System Interface Technical Overview, 100-000569-001, 1989; (c) NetWare V2.1, Internetwork Packet Exchange Protocol (IPX) with Asynchronous Event Scheduler (AES), 100-000405-001, February, 1988; (d) NetWare V2.1, Sequenced Packet Exchange Protocol (SPX), February, 1988; (e) Turner, Paul: "NetWare Communication Processes," *NetWare Application Notes* pp. 25–81, September, 1990; (f) Stevenson, Dave and Duncan, Sandra: "An Introduction to Novell's Burst Mode Protocol," *NetWare Application Notes* pp. 45–93, March, 1992; and (g) ARCNET Packet Header Definition Standard, 100-000721-001, November, 1990.

Where IPX is going.   Novell has the credo that it is "the Switzerland of networking—we don't choose sides." In fact, outside of NetWare, Novells's biggest seller is LAN Workplace for DOS, a TCP/IP-based product.

Bit by bit, Novell has signaled that IPX is on the way out, especially in medium to large networks with WAN links. Drew Major, chief NetWare architect, has said that IPX and WANs do not mix. In 1989 he stated that a transport-independent architecture built on a Unix-based network API (STREAMS TLI) had replaced IPX/SPX as the firm's strategic platform. Deeds were matched with words with the release of SPXII in NetWare 4.X (see above), and in 1992, Novell issued a press release indicating that it was making IPX specifications public.

It is known that within Novell some technologists have been pushing to move NetWare away from proprietary IPX/SPX toward a more transport-independent architecture, but others, apparently a minority, have objected, probably for fear of losing customer control. The scenario envisioned by many analysts is that by 1996 half of Novell's IPX users will have migrated to TCP/IP. By 2000, there will be no IPX. Incidentally, the same prediction is being made for AppleTalk, as being just too lightweight and insufficiently robust for use in enterprise WANs.

For a time, Novell will have both TCP/IP and IPX stacks, perhaps running side by side and supporting both at once. Novell seems to be encouraging the trend toward TCP/IP. Even so, in non-WAN local environments, IPX is fast and efficient, so migration to TCP/IP does not necessarily make sense for all systems.

BIOS and NetBIOS

NetBIOS is a widely used interface for getting application data into or out of the protocol stack. It is used by every Microsoft DOS- and OS/2-based application and NOS.

The main purpose of NetBIOS is to make it possible for local programs to access the network without having to change them. In fact, the program does not even realize that an external communication has taken place.

While its popularity makes NetBIOS a de facto standard, it is not a de jure standard. In fact, as an interface, it is slowly being replaced by other APIs such as LU6.2. (More about this shortly.)

Today NetBIOS is used as an interface between applications software and network interface cards, and is not used as a protocol stack in new applications anymore. Originally, NetBIOS *was* a full protocol written by Sytek and sold by IBM.

Because NetBIOS is copyrighted, all other implementations are emulations. NetBIOS was originally a ROM chip on the NIC, but may also be implemented in software.

For example, other vendors such as Phoenix have written NetBIOS emulations that reside in ROM. Applications programmers can write to this de facto interface and know that it will work on the LAN. NOS vendors like Novell modify NetBIOS so that network requests go to its own IPX protocol.

As an interface, NetBIOS helps ensure that applications and NICs will work together. This means that the two may be independent of each other. Network designers are therefore largely freed from a possible constraint. For example, even though a token-ring NIC requires its own interface, TOKREUI.COM, IBM provides another program, a software emulation of NetBIOS called NETBEUI.COM, to make the NIC application compatible. The two functionally constitute a NetBIOS interface.

What NetBIOS does.   When a user makes a request of an application program, the program goes first to DOS, which routes it to BIOS ROM firmware. BIOS controls physical devices, such as disk drives. The flow is shown in Figure 10.9.

Network calls must not go this route. They are filtered by a *redirector, requester,* or *shell* program that screens requests to see if they are local. The program runs as part of the operating system and is invisible to the user. It knows what requests are network-related.

If the request is network-related, it is passed not to DOS but to Net-BIOS. As shown in Figure 10.10, the request enters the protocol stack below it, i.e., IPX or TCP/IP, and ends up on the cable. Alternatively, the request may go directly to the IEEE 802.2 LLC if no higher-layer protocol is used. Directly or indirectly, NetBIOS is a way of getting application data to the LLC layer.

NetBIOS is to LAN hardware what BIOS is to local hardware. It is the link between applications and hardware.

NetBIOS Protocol: Nonroutable.   The NetBIOS protocol is not considered an internetworking protocol because its abilities are very limited at the lower layers. As such, NetBIOS frames must be preceded by TCP/IP, IPX, or equivalent headers in order to be routed. Alternatively, Net-BIOS may be preceded by an IEEE 802.2 LLC plus an IEEE 802.3 or 802.5 MAC (or their equivalent) in order to be bridged. NetBIOS alone cannot be bridged, although its sister LAN protocol, NETBEUI, can.

NetBIOS as an API.   NetBIOS is the de facto LAN-to-applications program interface. As a function call to an applications program, the application does not need to know what happens within NetBIOS and below.

In NetWare, applications writers can use DOS' BIOS and let the redirector intercept network requests. Alternatively, they can use Net-BIOS requests and go straight to IPX. Their third choice is to go to IPX directly and bypass NetBIOS altogether.

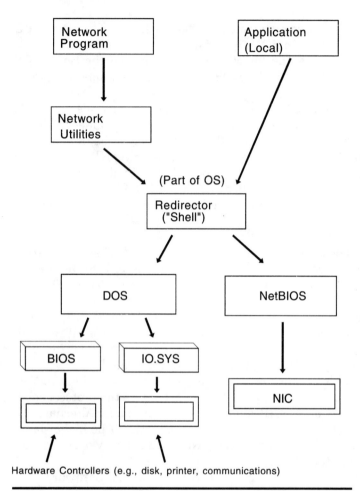

Figure 10.9 BIOS and NetBIOS data flow.

While NetBIOS is a de facto *input/output* (I/O) interface, applications communicating with each other must use the same communications protocol, e.g., NETBEUI or IPX. Incompatible protocols may be mixed on the same medium, but they will not communicate even if both are based on NetBIOS.

NetWare does not depend on NetBIOS, but its emulation is there for applications that require it. You will see them as NETBIOS.COM and INT2F.COM. IPX.COM writes directly to the NIC, and NETx.COM is the redirector. Novell is also supporting emulations of IBM and Microsoft APIs.

NetBIOS in detail. NetBIOS turns operating system requests into a formatted *Network* [sometimes called *message*] *control block* (NCB) with

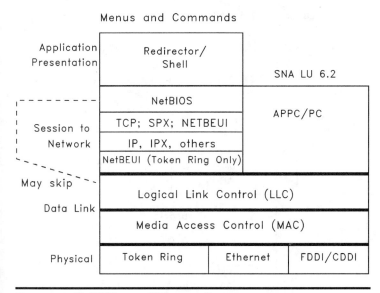

Figure 10.10   NetBIOS as an LLC connection.

certain data in a certain format. The NCB then performs the necessary operation in NetBIOS. The NCB contains information in its initial byte as to whether NetBIOS (going down the stack) or the LLC (going up the stack) performs the function. This way, programmers can use the standard NCB format to set the LAN as an I/O device. The resulting NetBIOS frame header format is shown in Figure 10.11.

Controls.   Commands exist to reset the NetBIOS interface, cancel commands, get its status, make it compatible with earlier versions, and trace commands issued to NetBIOS, including transmissions and receptions.

NetBIOS protocol and TCP/IP.   TCP/IP network utilities are not adequate on their own to support the full NetBIOS protocol. Accordingly, the IAB formed the NetBIOS working group. At the IAB's behest, the group, formed mostly of vendors, came up with the additional protocols needed to support NetBIOS. These are contained in IAB RFCs 1001 and 1002, which are pertinent to those using NetBIOS with TCP/IP.

These efforts to date have met with only partial success. The RFCs tried to provide applications compatibility across the TCP/IP environment, which includes not only PCs but minis, mainframes, and supercomputers as well. Many of these systems lack the RFC 1001 and 1002 protocols.

Some of the features inherent in NetBIOS protocol are very inefficient when used on a WAN. This includes the dynamic naming and group and broadcast datagram capabilities. There seems to be no easy

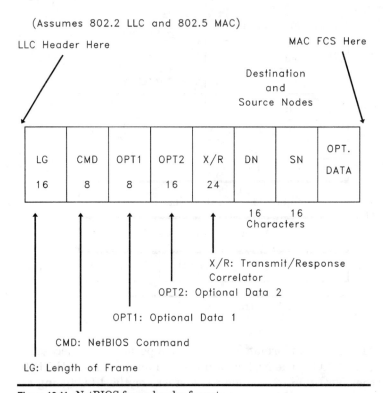

Figure 10.11 NetBIOS frame header format.

way to make a LAN-optimized protocol work equally well in a WAN environment, and we have seen that Novell's IPX, SAP and NCP, and Apple's Routing Table Maintenance Protocol (RTMP) share this difficulty.

NetBIOS and OSI. Like TCP/IP, the OSI protocols are inadequate— meaning, too slow—to support NetBIOS protocol. In a similar fashion to the IAB, the *Manufacturing Automation Protocols and Technical Office Protocols* (MAP/TOP) user groups formed a NetBIOS-migration *special interest group* (SIG).

MAP/TOP sees NetBIOS as a vehicle to migrate applications toward OSI. Understanding the enormous investment in NetBIOS, the MAP/TOP NetBIOS interface is a way to use OSI to carry NetBIOS protocol.

Neither the MAP/TOP or NetBIOS SIG carries any weight at the ISO level. Thus, the ISO is free to accept other parties' recommendations, which is seen as unlikely.

Some interesting parallels have occurred between the independent efforts of the TCP/IP working groups and the MAP/TOP SIG. The two specifications greatly resemble each other, and they share the difficulties of using dynamic naming and group and broadcast datagrams on WANs. Furthermore, some NetBIOS functions may not be available where a WAN is involved, and platforms other than PCs will need interface software to converse with PCs using NetBIOS.

NetBIOS limitations. As an *I/O interface,* NetBIOS is in wide use, but as a *protocol* it is obsolete. IBM's OS/2 LAN Server and Microsoft's LAN Manager plus many third-party applications use NetBIOS as an interface.

NetBIOS protocol is fine in LANs. However, they create problems in internetworks because the broadcast datagrams used in name discovery take up a lot of network capacity.

Functionally, NetBIOS is not effective at the lower layers and is unroutable by itself. Even using TCP/IP or OSI to make up the difference is difficult. They are both inadequate in terms of functionality and speed to handle the NetBIOS protocol without additional protocols such as RFC 1001 and 1002, or the MAP/TOP NetBIOS interface.

The NetBIOS interface is becoming a little dated. Because it does not support true distributed processing, IBM and Microsoft are slowly replacing NetBIOS with other API services. One example is LU 6.2. Because LU 6.2 is part of the SNA architecture, it is easy to use LU 6.2 as an entry point to the LAN for SNA devices. As an entry point to the LLC sublayer, LU 6.2 is used widely for applications as well. A specific version called *Advanced Program-to-Program Communications/PC* is used for this purpose.

Conclusions

You can see from the foregoing that a discussion of higher-layer protocols can seem daunting at first. You have also seen the common threads and the variations that occur in each protocol. Once you understand the basics, these protocols all fall into place.

People who will not use internetworking need not worry about the higher layers too much. But since most subnetworks become internetworks sooner or later, this chapter may have significance for you at a later time.

Our next chapter makes use of what you have learned about routing and expands upon it. We also discuss bridges, routers, and gateways as ways to create internetworks.

Chapter

11

LAN Internetworking

Core Concepts

You have already obtained a hint of what is in this chapter from our discussion of higher network layers in Chapter 10. Here we focus specifically on bridging, routing, and linking LANs through WANs.

Physically extending a LAN calls for a discussion of repeaters and bridges. Performance problems in overgrown LANs may also necessitate bridging.

Over three-fourths of American firms consider LAN internetworking an essential dimension of their overall information strategy. *Routers* are the workhorse of LAN internetworking.

Like every other area of LAN activity, internetworking is a rapidly moving field. This is especially true regarding the latest developments in link protocols and routing algorithms. The routing protocol can have a major effect on network performance and administrative overhead. In this chapter we discuss routing concepts and applications.

This chapter also contains a discussion of the many WAN options available, starting with voice-grade speeds and extending into the megabit per second range. Internetwork designers have more options today than ever. We itemize each one, discuss how it works, and note its status in the industry and when it makes sense to use it.

Internetworking Devices

In increasing order of capability and complexity, LANs use the following devices:

Repeaters   These are signal regenerators that extend cable distances, work at the physical layer, and have no intelligence.

Bridges	These connect LAN segments, have limited intelligence, and work at the *data link layer* (DLL).
Routing bridges	These combine the functions of bridging and routing. They are a router and a bridge in a box.
Routers	These have a lot of intelligence, are the centerpieces of interconnected LANs, and work at the network layer.
Gateways	These match totally dissimilar networks. They are designed for connectivity but do no routing.

Repeaters

A repeater is a device that recreates the signal so it can go longer distances as shown in Figure 11.1. It is often used in bus-type LANs such as Ethernet to extend the reach of a cable. Token-ring cards repeat the signal inherently, so every token-ring card is a repeater. Repeaters are often built into token-ring hubs.

Repeaters are inexpensive but cannot be used indiscriminately. Ethernet can have no more than four *interrepeater links* (IRLs) between any two stations, *regardless of whether they communicate or not.*

When a repeater joins two Ethernet segments, the *collision domain*

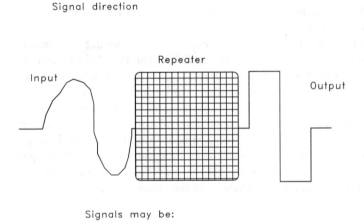

Signal direction

Repeater

Input

Output

Signals may be:

Electrical to electrical,

electrical to optical,

or optical to optical.

But *always* at the physical layer!

Figure 11.1 A repeater at work.

is extended. If the repeater adds 4 devices on a segment to 8 on another, the number of machines that can bump heads is increased to 12. A maximum of 30 devices are allowed on a ThinNet segment, and 100 devices are permitted on a ThickNet segment. No device that is added can duplicate an existing address, or havoc will result.

Repeaters can link similar or dissimilar cables such as *unshielded twisted pair* (UTP) and fiber. In this case, to communicate, both data link sublayers *must* be identical, e.g., IEEE 802.2 and 802.3. The repeater is indifferent to protocols above Layer 2, i.e., those for network, transport, session, etc.

Ethernet repeaters often have multiple ports to facilitate building a tree from the bus. They make a convenient connecting point for adding a number of users.

Repeaters generally cannot be installed in air plenums because the power cable must exit the plenum. However, being outside the plenum facilitates maintenance and troubleshooting, and simplifies access to AC power.

Do not confuse an Ethernet *transceiver* with a *repeater.* Transceivers connect to *attachment unit interface* (AUI) ports on computers and contain collision detection and antijabber circuits. Repeaters do not. Some repeaters have *segment isolation* that will isolate a malfunctioning Ethernet segment from another one. Some also have front-panel diagnostic *light-emitting diodes* (LEDs).

Repeaters are active devices and require AC power. Since repeaters are largely transparent, some have LEDs, but few have management capability such as *Simple Network Management Protocol* (SNMP).

Bridges

Bridges used for Ethernet differ from those used in token ring. Ethernet bridges use only MAC sublayer addresses for bridging, whereas token-ring bridges look for specific routing information in the MAC layer. This is called *source routing.* Both methods are described in the discussion to follow.

Ethernet-IEEE 802.3 bridges. The term "bridge" is apt because an Ethernet data bridge passes traffic from one LAN segment to another the same way cars pass over a suspension bridge from one land mass to another. Figure 11.2 illustrates how bridges are used.

Ethernet data bridges seize frames whose destinations are not on the segment and pass them through the bridge to another segment. This is the equivalent of an automobile whose destination is across a real bridge but does not know it.

Imagine posting your destination (the frame's destination address)

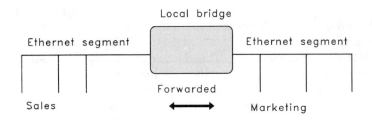

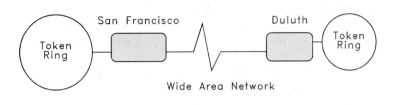

Figure 11.2 Bridging two LANs: local and remote.

in your car window. A kindly state trooper (the data bridge) examines each car's destination and directs it to take the bridge exit (pass to another segment) or not (its destination is on the local segment).

The state trooper knows only that the destination is not local, so it must therefore be somewhere else. Other state troopers (bridges) down the line, working on the same principle, keep passing the frame until it reaches its destination. It sounds like LANarchy, but it works.

Like the state trooper, an Ethernet-IEEE 802.3 bridge watches for *media access control* (MAC) frames (destination addresses) that do not reside on the segment. Knowing that they do not belong on the segment is sufficient to pass them to another segment where they *might* belong.

> In terms of cable access, bridges are treated just like any workstation or server. They must obey all the same access-control rules.

A basic bridge cannot see anything higher than the MAC sublayer. This is another way of saying that both networks must use Ethernet or token-ring access if a simple bridge is to be used. Higher layers, such as *Transmission Control Protocol/Internet Protocol* (TCP/IP) or *Internetwork Packet Exchange* (IPX), are ignored, i.e., they are "transparent."

The simplest form of bridge (shown in Figure 11.3) has an address filter that checks the MAC destination address to see if it is on the same network as the source. If it is, it does nothing with the frame in Ethernet (or passes it along in token ring). If it is not destined for the local network, the frame is forwarded to another port on the bridge and onto another network.

You can see then that bridges are *store-and-forward* devices. The frame enters the new network when the bridge senses the network is available. A bridge looks like any other station on the network, complete with its own address.

Local bridges segment traffic to reduce congestion. For example, if the Marketing Department's Ethernet LAN is connected to the Sales Department's Ethernet, the collision domain increases. A bridge installed between the two segments reduces traffic yet permits communication.

For this reason, thoughtful location of a bridge will improve LAN performance. Thought*less* location, say in the midst of the Sales department, will create a bottleneck. You should have a clear idea of who is communicating with whom before siting a bridge. You do not need a protocol analyzer—just common sense.

Remote bridges work the same way, but half the bridge is in one place and half in another with a WAN link in between. The link may use the

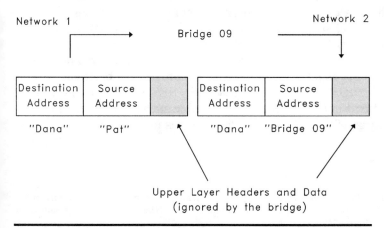

Transparent Bridge Frame Forwarding

"Dana is not in the address table
for Network 1"
"So forward this frame to Network 2"

Network 1   Network 2

Bridge 09

Destination Address	Source Address		Destination Address	Source Address	
"Dana"	"Pat"		"Dana"	"Bridge 09"	

Upper Layer Headers and Data
(ignored by the bridge)

Figure 11.3 MAC layer bridging.

Internet Engineering Task Force's IETF's *Point-to-Point Protocol* (PPP), High-level Data Link Center (HDLC), or a proprietary variant. Frame relay is now being used, too. Both PPP and frame relay are described later in this chapter. Some bridges will multiplex non-LAN traffic such as IBM's SDLC or DEC's DDCMP along with LAN traffic as a way of sharing the expensive WAN link.

Bridges "learn" the MAC addresses of stations on each network. This way they learn which traffic will stay on the LAN and which must cross to another LAN. The bridging table is built from traffic and from tables entered manually, or the bridge can poll the network. Typically the table can hold at least 2000 entries, with expansion to about 8000 entries.

Filtering rates run between 2000 and 25,000 packets/sec. *Forwarding* rates can be lower, in the range of 1500–15,000 packets/sec. To put these numbers in perspective, the maximum Ethernet packet rate is 14,880 packets/sec.

Packets can usually be protocol-prioritized by the bridge to minimize timeout problems in time-sensitive *Synchronous Data Link Control* (SDLC) or *Local Area Transport* (LAT) protocols. However, some bridges and routers have chronic difficulty in prioritizing two or more such time-sensitive protocols in the same network.

Some bridges compress data to get the most out of a WAN link. Compression may quadruple the performance of a WAN circuit, a traditional bottleneck. The trade-off is a slight latency delay at the beginning of a transmission versus faster message transmission and better link utilization. Stand-alone compressors are also available.

A bridge can be a dedicated device or a properly equipped PC. Sometimes a bridge is built into a server or a hub. Stand-alone bridges designed for the task yield the best performance and expandability.

Many bridge and router vendors artificially inflate their filtering and forwarding rates by using abnormally small packets of 28–32 bytes. This is not realistic, because the smallest legal Ethernet packet is 64 bytes. A 250–270 packet size is closer to the real world.

A "brouter" or bridge-router examines a packet's protocol and decides whether to act as a bridge in the case of nonroutable protocols such as LAT or *NetBIOS Extended User Interface* (NETBEUI) or a router if the protocol turns out to be something routable such as IP or DECnet.

A checklist of transparent[1] bridge features include:

---

[1]Used in this way, *transparent* means that the frame contains no specific routing information. The source is ignorant of any bridging done to the frame and so is said to be transparent to the bridging process.

The filtering rate (at your packet size).

The forwarding rate (at your packet size).

The filtering criteria: source and destination address, and protocol type.

An adaptive learning routing table plus manual entry.

The table size; 3000 entries or more is a good figure.

The ability to downline load software from a network parameter server.

Network management such as SNMP MIB (Management Information Base) I and MIB II, or SNMP Version 2.

Spanning-tree protocol support: IEEE 802.1d.

Media support: UTP, *shielded twisted pair* (STP), ThinNet, or Thick-Net.

The packaging: stand-alone, rack mount or in a card cage. If it is in a cage, is the bridge card hot-swappable without disrupting other cards or networks?

The service and support terms.

The price and delivery terms.

The documentation.

A checklist for remote bridges includes:

The supported WAN links: analog, digital, T-1, and frame relay (all of these are discussed later in this chapter).

The supported WAN protocols: PPP, HDLC, others, or proprietary.

Data compression, if any.

Configuration flexibility, e.g, parallel load-sharing bridges.

Bridge-routers (Figure 11.4) combine two functions in one box. They *bridge* using DLL information. They *route* using network-layer information if it is found in the packet. If the router can route several protocols, it is called a *multiprotocol* router.

Sometimes serial or cascaded bridges are used, passing a message from LAN to LAN. Cascading creates a logical-tree structure, which is generally necessary to keep a message from reaching the same point by two different paths. The result would be a duplicate or out-of-order message.

Token-ring bridge differences.   Token-ring bridges are different in some respects. The major difference is that Ethernet-IEEE 802.3 bridges use

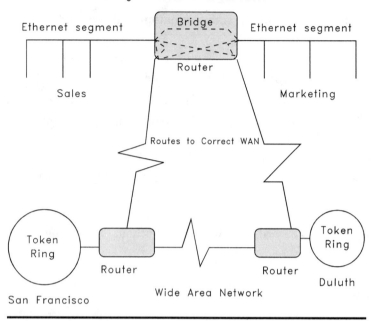

Figure 11.4 How a bridge-router is used.

a table to decide whether to forward a frame while token-ring bridges look for the *routing indicator* (RI) bit followed by routing information in the frame's source address field. Hence, the term *source routing* since the source of the frame obtains and provides routing information. The use of the term *routing* is a little imprecise because source routing is mixing a Layer-3 function, routing, into IEEE 802.5, a Layer-2 protocol.

Since IBM token ring places source-routing information in the source-address field, there are no tables to update. Instead, the end stations provide routing information. Source routing and *source-routing transparent* (SRT) bridging was discussed in detail in Chapter 7.

SRT bridges permit a combination of the IBM source-routing technique and the IEEE 802.1d transparent bridge standard. The result is a way to connect IBM source-routing networks to transparent ones such as Ethernet-based LANs.

SRT bridges check for source-routing information or the lack thereof (transparent frames) in the packet and filter or forward it as necessary. An address table is required for the transparent portion of the bridge.

Token-ring bridges are in the serial-ring path and again must obey all token-ring access rules. A frame is copied, marked, and then returned to the originator who then places the token back on the ring. Incoming frames from other networks must wait in the token-ring bridge until a token can be seized.

Local token-ring bridges are becoming a commodity. For the most part, token-ring bridges are plug-and-play devices.[2]

Token-ring bridges are distinguished somewhat by their ability to handle a mix of frame sizes. Some work better with short frames and some better with long ones. File transfers use frames that contain about 2000 bytes, such as Novell's NetWare and IBM LAN Server, both of which often use 2–4-kbyte frames. (This parameter can be manually set.) Yet 3270 emulations typically use 270-byte frames. It is thereby incumbent on the buyer to understand the environment in which a prospective bridge will be placed.

As with Ethernet bridges, token-ring bridges are available as dedicated devices or in PCs. This is a good way to use the hardware that is available and still get reasonable performance. However, the PC approach is somewhat limited in its ability to add ports and interfaces by the size of its platform.

Pros and cons. Bridge technology enhancement consists of adding larger address tables, customized filtering, load balancing (passing data by two or more paths), and network management. Fault tolerance and redundancy are becoming common features.

Bridges alone are generally not appropriate in larger environments. For instance, bridges use the token-ring route discovery process that floods the network and chokes slower WAN links. Well-suited to routers and bridge-routers, the PPP has been found to be less useful in bridge connections.

Finally, bridge costs are presently $1000–2000 below router prices, and their respective functions are being consolidated into a single box. You should, therefore, seriously consider obtaining more-efficient routing if the costs are equal.

Bridges are well-suited to:

Operate in simple, single-site internetworks.

Link different media types, such as UTP and fiber.

Handle concurrent upper-layer protocols such as IPX and TCP/IP. Bridges cannot see above the MAC layer.

---

[2]Tolly, Kevin: "Speed and Simplicity Make Smart Shopping a Snap," *Data Communications,* p. 94, August, 1992.

Handle unroutable protocols such as SDLC, LAT, and *Network Basic Input / Output System* (NetBIOS).

Operate in networks where staff expertise or technical skill are not available.

Operate in networks where minimizing cost is an absolute requirement.

Address table size and performance. Ethernet bridges are considered *transparent* as they do nothing but filter and forward packets. Their capacity to do so hinges on the size of their address tables. Most tables today have 2000–4000 entries, but the size depends more on whether it is a local or remote bridge. A local bridge table may range from 512 to 56,000 entries. Remote bridges start at around 8000 entries and go up to 40,000 entries. *Fiber-distributed data interface* (FDDI) bridges handle 16–22,000 table entries, but they are also filtering half a million frames a second.

Too large or too small a table can hurt performance. If it is too small, the bridge cannot learn all the active station locations. Too large a table means it takes too long to look up a specific entry. Lookups done in hardware take about 10 μsec, which is faster than a software algorithm for a large number of entries.

Filtering and forwarding rates and performance. Filtering and forwarding rates are not the sole criterion of performance. Real-world rates depend on the packet length and the mix of frames that your system must filter or forward. If you do not know your own traffic sizes, laboratory test reviews are the best judge of performance.

User-definable filtering is a mixed blessing. User-defined filters add flexibility, WAN-use efficiency, and security.

Logical filtering, e.g., not forwarding any LAT frames off a particular segment, allows physical LAN segments to be treated as separate logical segments. The penalty is that filtering adds processing time. With too many parameters to filter, the packet latency time increases. At this point, a router makes more sense.

Other bridging features. *Load sharing* creates multiple paths between bridges but does not work with Ethernet. Load sharing is often a proprietary algorithm, so it probably will not work between different vendors. The IEEE 802.1d spanning-tree algorithm is used to create dormant backup paths between networks, which is not to be confused with load sharing.

Fault tolerance, card-based bridges, and RISC-based machines are found in current leading-edge technology. *Multiport* bridges look like a hub and allow a user to subdivide LANs yet link them into a single unit. (The classic "collapsed backbone.")

Switching. Some vendors such as Kalpana and Artel both switch and bridge in one box. Here, a high-demand device such as a server is given its own 10-Mbit/sec switch port. Any work group can contend for it directly. Rather than having to travel up a hierarchy of bridges to get to several servers, the switch permits parallel conversations within workgroups, between clients and servers at the same time. Latency is reduced since the device only switches packets, not processes them. Switches are semiexpensive in absolute terms but the cost per packet is low. The various forms of switching are discussed in Chapter 4.

There are at least 50 bridge vendors and over 100 models, so take your pick. Low-end prices start at around $2000. Competition has pressed prices down a little, but vendors add functions to keep prices firm. In some cases, prices have gone up.

Hi-tech, multiport bridges cost about 20 percent less than a router, but a router adds complexity, which turns into staff-time demands. On the other hand, a router tolerates network failures better and supports redundant network paths based on speed or cost.

Spanning-tree capability in a bridge uses a redundant path only if the primary path fails, a two-for-one cost. But a spanning-tree bridge is better than a basic learning bridge, which has no intelligence at all.

Bridges run faster than routers because routers work at the network layer and must know more about the packets they are switching. An SRT bridge or router is better suited to linking mixed media networks such as Ethernet and token ring. In like media, transparent bridges are cheaper and faster.

Bridges are growing in capability while routers are being scaled up and down. Pretty soon, they will *all* be bridge-routers! Bridges are inexpensive and fast, but lack port capacity and expandability into the routing realm.

Routers. In WAN internetworks, multiple paths are possible. The need for an intelligent router arises because of the rapid decisions that must be made in order to route data efficiently and economically. Since links go down and up and there is the risk of routing loops, devices called *routers* are needed in LAN internetworks. By 1995, about 60 percent of enterprise-wide networks will use 50 or more routers. Routers also join dissimilar technologies so they will work together.

As Figure 11.5 shows, routers forward packets based on the packet's destination address, its routing information content, if any, and their own routing tables. The difference is that they do it at the network layer, making them protocol-dependent. A router receives a packet, dis-

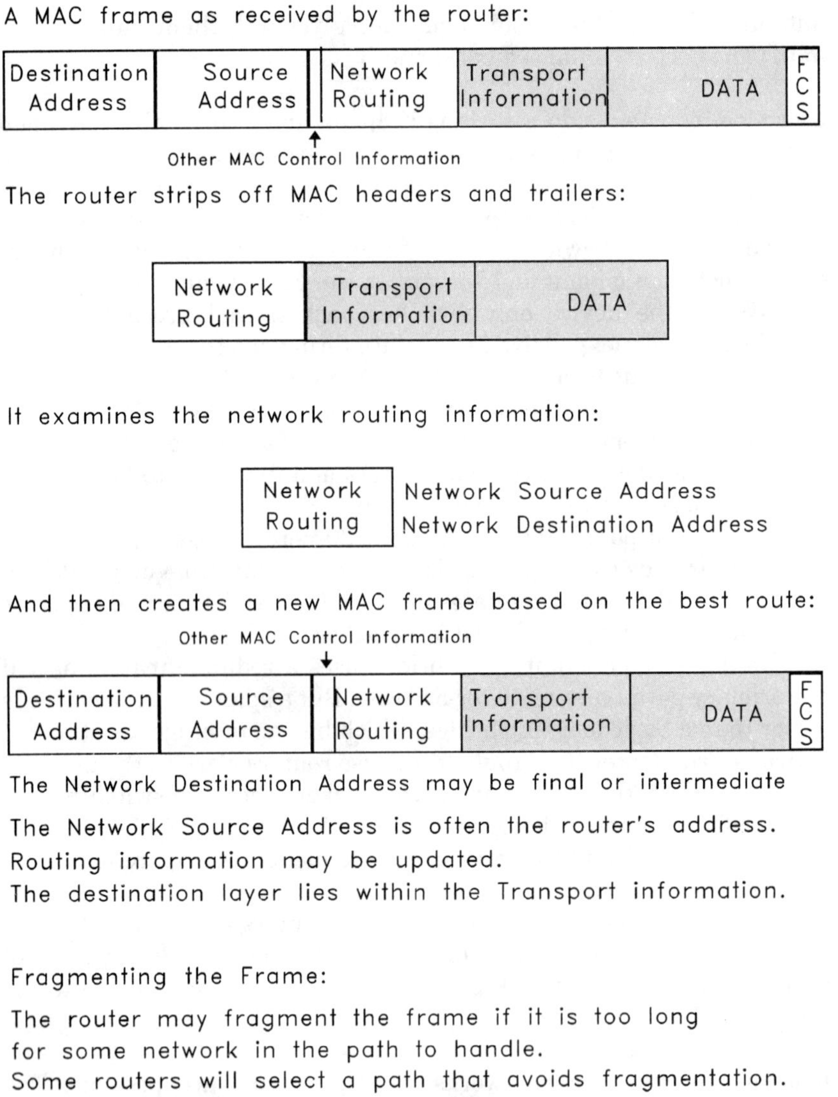

A MAC frame as received by the router:

Destination Address	Source Address	Network Routing	Transport Information	DATA	F C S

↑
Other MAC Control Information

The router strips off MAC headers and trailers:

Network Routing	Transport Information	DATA

It examines the network routing information:

Network Routing	Network Source Address Network Destination Address

And then creates a new MAC frame based on the best route:

Other MAC Control Information
↓

Destination Address	Source Address	Network Routing	Transport Information	DATA	F C S

The Network Destination Address may be final or intermediate

The Network Source Address is often the router's address.
Routing information may be updated.
The destination layer lies within the Transport information.

Fragmenting the Frame:

The router may fragment the frame if it is too long
for some network in the path to handle.
Some routers will select a path that avoids fragmentation.

Figure 11.5 Routing from the packet's point of view.

cards the MAC information, and checks the network layer destination address. Consulting its routing table, the router decides where to route the message. Creating a new MAC frame, the router sends it off, either to a destination network or to another router.

If the message is passed through another router, then the *intermediate* address will change, perhaps several times. But the *final* destination address stays constant. Each succeeding router must know the best path for the message to take. The routing path could be manually defined, automatic, or specified by the source or destination.

Routers, then, make efficient use of narrow and expensive WAN links by intelligently selecting traffic to pass over them, whether the link is LAN-to-LAN or LAN-to-WAN-to-LAN.

Minimizing the size and expense of WAN circuits is the key to effective internetwork cost control. *It is always better to purchase a device that will save circuit dollars than to pay for extra circuit capacity every month throughout eternity.* Large initial hardware costs can be readily justified when these never-ending (and rising) charges are considered.

As a network layer function, routing is not defined formally by LAN standards. The networks may all be different at the physical layer and DLL, but must be compatible at the network layer and up in order for routing to work. This is one reason why companies tend to buy from one vendor.

Another pair of reasons is to get better price and support. While it is possible to mix and match routers successfully, surveys show clearly that users do not want more than one vendor's routers in their internetworks.

Since several nonduplicated paths may be used, a message may arrive out of sequence. The transport layer must be able to reorder and assemble them in their correct order at the destination.

A router can also *fragment* frames for certain protocols such as TCP/IP or IPX. It breaks them into smaller pieces to work with LANs with small maximum frame sizes.

Routers are hardware-independent. They do not forward packets, only the data within the packets. They are, therefore, protocol specific, such as *IPX-Sequenced Packet Exchange* (IPX/SPX) or *Xerox Network Services* (XNS). Some routers handle multiple protocols. A router can be a stand-alone platform, an equipped PC, or even hardware and software located within a server. For instance, Novell's NetWare has an internal bridge (really a routing) function that links different LAN hardware types. However, it can only handle NetWare IPX/SPX or IP frames. The moral is that, as with bridges, the best performance is gained from a device designed for routing.

Many routers also perform data compression to squeeze the last bit of value out of a WAN link. Vendors also offer data compression as a separate device. Typical compression ratios run in the four-to-one range for text, source code, or assembly language. Binary data is less compressible, and encrypted or previously compressed traffic yields little, if any, effective compression. As is always the case with compression, it works best on file transfers and bulk data and is less effective on shorter interactive exchanges.

The march of time shows that routing is the wave of the future and that bridging is on the way out. By 1995, routers will dominate internetworks as pictured in Figure 11.6. Since routers can bridge as well as route, and their prices are nearly the same as a bridge, there is no point in buying a bridge unless the need falls within one of the criteria discussed under bridging. Even if the router does more than is needed

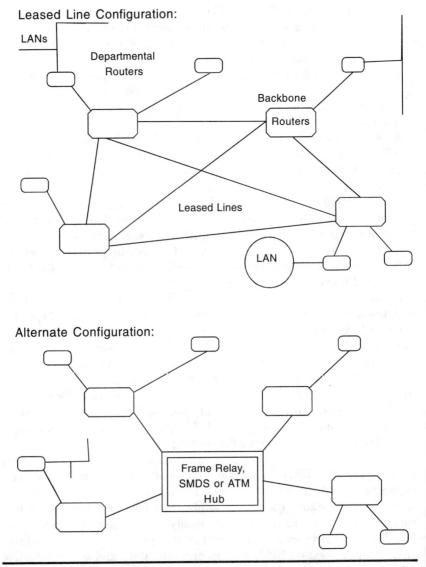

Figure 11.6 Routers in a LAN internetwork.

today, the network may need its added capability tomorrow. *Networks always grow; they never shrink.*

Router prices are falling about 20 percent per year, and the low-end machines are becoming commodities. Even these machines, used mainly at the departmental level, can process some 12,000 packets/sec and cost under $3000.[3]

A checklist of router and bridging router features includes:

Filtering and forwarding packet rates

WAN link interfaces: frame relay, X.25, and fractional and full T-1

Network management via SNMP or alternative protocols

Media support: UTP, STP, coaxial cable or fiber

Access method support: *carrier-sense multiple access with collision detection* (CSMA/CD), token ring, FDDI, or any other support

Ability to work with other routers

Vendor experience, customer base, and support

Priority-setting for LAT and SDLC time-sensitive protocols

Latency delay, measured in microseconds

Aggregate throughput: packets/sec multiplied by the packet size in bytes

Ability to handle broadcast storms

Subnetwork support configurations

Protocols routed: TCP/IP, IPX, AppleTalk, or SNA/SDLC

Bridging capability, if needed: IEEE 802.1d spanning tree

Transparency to upper layer protocols

Routing protocol support: *open shortest path first* (OSPF), *Routing Information Protocol-IP* (RIP-IP), RIP-IPX, and *Service Advertising Protocol-IPX* (SAP-IPX)

Protocol translation capability

---

[3]A sampling of PC-based router vendors includes Basic Networks Corp. (MA), DEC (MA), Eicon Technology, Network Application Technology (CA), Clearpoint Research Corp. (MA), and Novell (UT). PC-based routers are intended for less than 100 users and support single-to-multiprotocol networks (except SNA). The main feature of the PC approach is price. A standalone multiprotocol router costs from $5000 to $10,000. A PC version costs $1000 to $3500.

Evaluating routers.   In evaluating a router:

Use the most appropriate device for the job. Multifunction devices are appealing but may not be sufficiently powerful for your specific application.

Test the device. Try out new functions, but make sure that basic ones work, too.

Ask router vendors if they have licensed protocols from manufacturers such as IBM, Apple, or DEC. Reverse-engineered software or emulations avoid licensing fees to the vendor but are less acceptable to the buyer.

Talk to vendor references. Also post inquiries on Byte magazine's *Bix* bulletin board, Usenet, Compuserve, NetWire, etc. Vendor references are naturally slanted toward their best customers.

Test the vendor's willingness and ability to offer support while you are evaluating the device. You will invariably require this support during the evaluation period.

Local service and perhaps on-site systems engineers may be needed to build a new network. Routers are difficult to configure, although some vendors include a simplified step-by-step program. Some software even includes a "novice configuration mode." Because of their complexity, router-technician certification programs are common.

Bridge and router management.   Internetwork management approaches using SNMP often come up short because the SNMP "set" command is not widely implemented for security reasons. This weakness is corrected in SNMP Version 2. *Fault management* in multiprotocol routers is a potential problem because the routers' management agents can conflict with each other.

This problem begs for a solution because routers are in an ideal position to monitor traffic, detect inefficiencies, and alert us to bottlenecks. However, for the time being, the only viable option is remote monitoring (RMON) probes, which listen to each LAN and detect hard and soft faults.

Interoperability.   Routers from different vendors do work together. Of course, data link protocols must match, such as PPP. They must also use the same routing protocols. Routers must carry transport protocols over the data link pipe in the same way; the only current standard for this is *Request for Comment* (RFC) 1293.

Link protocols.   Bridges and routers are tied together via *link protocols*. We have already mentioned two: ITU-TSS's HDLC and DEC's DDCMP, an HDLC variant. Here we focus on the IETF PPP.

IETF-PPP.   PPP connects multiprotocol routers and works at Layer 2. PPP is a workhorse for remote users, modest workstations, and any router-to-router connection. PPP can manage and set up links between these devices. Implementation is straightforward for routers. PPP presently provides basic connectivity between bridges.

PPP is intended to replace the *Serial-Line Interface Protocol* (SLIP). PPP can encapsulate TCP/IP, *open systems interconnection* (OSI), DEC-net, and AppleTalk frames, all specified in the PPP specification. Most vendors have so far written code only for TCP/IP. However, Novell's IPX is supported by PPP using NetWare WAN Links 2.X. IPX is the second most popular routing protocol behind the IP portion of TCP/IP.

PPP can authenticate senders and receivers to prevent fakes from getting into the network. It lets routers exchange their identities and compress data. PPP is a private-line service, as opposed to frame relay, which is shared.

Gateways.   Gateways are the most sophisticated internetworking tool, matching totally separate networks. A gateway is used when two protocol stacks are completely different. The gateway takes data from one physical layer and progressively removes each layer's header until it has raw information at the application layer. Then it creates a new set of headers, layer by layer, until the physical layer is again reached.

Gateways require a lot of computing horsepower. A gateway must convert code types, message formats, and sizes from one protocol type to the other and back again. If the addressing between the networks is different, and it usually is, the gateway must be able to translate them. All control functions such as frame sequence counts must be converted from one protocol to the other without information loss.

Since conversion must occur at every protocol stack layer, the conversion process is a complex one. Typically, gateways are used as shown in Figure 11.7 between well-defined networks such as a DECnet network and an SNA/SDLC network. Multiple sessions are generally supported.

Gateway features to look for include:

Compatibility with protocols at Layers 2 and 3

Upper-layer support: TCP/IP, LAT, and TN3270 format

WAN link options

LAN media and access method support

Multiple session capability

Transparency

Standards-based software-loading options

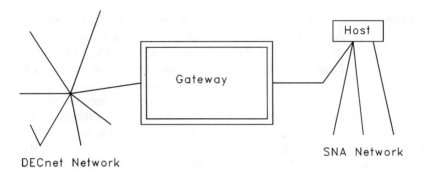

DECnet Network

SNA Network

Two completely independent protocol stacks
They meet at the top: at the Application layer

Used mainly in well-defined network architectures

Figure 11.7   A gateway in use.

Floppy disk entry

Automatic connection capability, e.g., routing ITU-TSS X.25 calls to a specific LAN address

Network management via SNMP Version 2

No external converters

Documentation

Packaging: either stand-alone, rack mounted, or in a card cage, in which case, it should be hot-swappable without disrupting other cards or networks

Redundant power option

Service and support terms

Price and delivery

Routing Algorithms

Types of routing

There are two types of routing, *static* and *dynamic*. Static routing is fine for small areas, but the routing table is manually configured. A failed link will cause an alarm. The failed link will not, however, compensate with a network reconfiguration.

Dynamic routing is used with WANs. Reconfiguration is performed automatically, using the routers' own table and taking the least expensive path. *Convergence,* or reconfiguring the table, must be quick, or packets will be routed incorrectly into nowhere. Some routers can also load-balance traffic by sharing it over several paths.

Protocol-dependent routers have to ask the computer where to send a packet. Unroutable protocols such as NetBIOS, SDLC, or LAT can be encapsulated within TCP/IP for routing transmission. If the router detects an unencapsulated NetBIOS, SDLC, or LAT frame, it will bridge the frame to another network but is unable to route it.

Routing protocols

The older but well-established distance vector algorithm is used in RIP, DECnet Phase IV, HELLO, and proprietary routing protocols. Using a *metric,* the algorithm creates a network map by talking to other routers to "learn" the network. It is simple to implement but uses a lot of bandwidth. Convergence takes a long time (several minutes) in larger networks, and temporary loops may occur until it is complete. It does find the best path, but the hop count is limited to 15 (for RIP). The distance vector algorithm is similar to the *Bellman-Ford* algorithm. Distance vector algorithms know only distances, not the network's real topology.

Link-state protocols (LSPs) are newer and are used in *Intermediate System to Intermediate System* (IS-IS) and OSPF. Link-state information periodically floods the network, including cost and line speed information. In OSPF, the data builds a table of routers and net connections. Each router then converges on the shortest path from itself to any other router. There is no hop count limit. LSPs are based on the *Dijkstra* algorithm, and contain a logical model of a network's true topology.

LSPs inherently resist loops, adapt to network changes rapidly (on the order of a few seconds), make sure each router is legitimate, and have low overhead. LSP-based authentication plus rules-based routing increases the security of an internetwork.

Interdomain routing divides the entire network into domains. The virtue is that changes in one domain do not affect the others, and global routing tables remain unchanged. The vice is that network management becomes harder when the network is logically divided.

Spanning-tree protocol.   This is the nearest thing to a routing protocol in the IEEE 802 standards. Implemented as IEEE 802.1d, the spanning-tree protocol is used by many bridges; it is the one protocol that can be used by bridges made by different vendors. Under the spanning-tree protocol, bridges negotiate with each other. The one with the best path is in the *forwarding* state, while the other is said to be *blocked.* If the open path degrades, the other bridge will open and the first one will close. This prevents duplicate packets from being sent to the same destination.

The protocol's simplicity has made it popular among low-end bridges. It can connect Ethernet, token-ring, and FDDI LANs.

There are two versions in the field: One is the IEEE version and the other comes from DEC. They do not work with one another, but some bridges support both.

Source routing.   IBM is the major proponent of source routing in token-ring networks. Source routing has been accepted by the IEEE as the routing method of choice for token-ring networks.

In source routing, the outbound frame contains information about the desired route, hence the term *source* routing. Routing tables are not needed. A detailed discussion of source routing is found in Chapter 7.

Routing information is gained using the *logical link control* (LLC) test or XID (*exchange identification*) command described in Chapter 9. Source routing, therefore, works at Layer 2, not Layer 3.

Source routing uses two methods. The *shotgun* approach sends an explorer packet via all the possible routes. The destination replies to each packet received by the reverse of the path each took. The first one back is by definition the "best" route. This method uses a lot of packets and can cause a "frame explosion" since every bridge copies discovery packets from every other bridge.

The *single-route* approach sends a single discovery packet. The destination sends one back via all the routes. The first one back is the best route. Traffic is much lower and the likelihood of a frame explosion is greatly reduced.

SRT.   SRT bridges link Ethernets and token-ring LANs in one bridge. SRT is being worked on by the IEEE 802.5 token-ring committee and appears in the IEEE 802.1d SRT Bridging Appendix.

An SRT bridge is a source-routing device on the token-ring side and a transparent bridge on the Ethernet side. The word "transparent" is used to indicate that the bridge is transparent to end stations on the LAN. They learn device locations and store them in the bridging, routing, or forwarding table; all these terms are used.

SRT bridges filter both source- and nonsource-routed traffic. The bridge forwards source-routed traffic and looks up the destination for transparent packets.

Networks using only token ring or Ethernet do not need an SRT bridge. SRT *is* a connectivity option in mixed networks or in those networks using FDDI with token ring or Ethernet.

Token-ring frames have a *routing information field* (RIF) and a *routing information indicator* (RII) bit within the frame. The route established from the source-routing procedure is in the RIF. The RII is a single bit in the source address header of the frame. A 0 indicates no RIF, so the bridge treats the frame as nonsource-routed. A 1 causes the SRT bridge to look for the RIF and so source-routes the frame throughout the network. This is a very schizophrenic bridge because both source and transparent routing exist within its MAC layer.[4]

Internetwork Links for LANs

We have said much about bridges and routers, but less about the physical links between them that carry all that traffic. These physical links account for *two-thirds* of the cost of LAN internetworks; the equipment cost accounts for the other one-third.

This aspect of internetworking breaks down into two subtopics:

1. Fixed-capacity circuits that are basically data pipes
2. Intelligent circuits that supply bandwidth as needed

For the sake of perspective, we examine each of these options in increasing order of complexity and hence capability.

Leased circuits

You may require full-period leased service. In heavy-demand applications, such circuits may be justified. Here are the choices:

Analog service   This service uses modems. Speeds of up to 28 kbit/sec are possible. It is available everywhere and is easy to back up. It can, however, be a bottleneck.

Digital service   *Digital Data Service* (DDS) is an example of this service. It is characterized by extremely high quality and very low error rates. Its availability is greater than 99 percent. Speeds of 2.4, 4.8, 9.6, 19.2, and 56 kbit/sec are possible. While it is still slow, 56 kbit/sec may be enough. It is slightly more expensive and not as available as analog service.

Fractional T-1 service   This service divides a 1.544-Mbit/sec T-1 into 24 blocks of 64-kbit segments, of which 56 kbit is usable. It can be used to tailor the speed to satisfy your

---

[4]Vendors supporting SRT include Andrew Corp. (IL), Cisco Systems (CA), CrossComm, FiberCom, IBM (NY), Microcom (MA), Netronix, North Hills Electronics, Proteon (MA), Wellfleet, and Vitalink.

requirements and can be used with BONDING devices, which will be discussed below. *Integrated Services Digital Network* (ISDN) at 128 kbit/sec is also being used and can be cost-effective if analog service speeds are inadequate.

Full T-1 service

The speed of this service is 1.544 Mbit/sec. It is fairly expensive but is generally available. It has a low error rate and automatic telephone company backup. The break-even point is about 10–12 analog lines.

T-3 service

This service runs at 44.736 Mbit/sec and is for heavy hitters only. It is very expensive and is hard to back up. (It equals 28 T-1s.) The cost of a T-3 is about equal to 10–12 T-1s. The *high-speed serial interface* (HSSI) is used to link routers to the T-3 span.

Native LAN speeds service

These are being considered by the *Regional Bell Holding Companies* (RBHCs), notably BellSouth. Running at 4, 10, 16 or 100 Mbit/sec, it would replace private lines and complement other services such as frame relay or *switched multimegabit data service* (SMDS). Operating over a metropolitan area network (MAN), it is expected to be offered in 10–15 BellSouth-served cities under a general tariff as opposed to a special assembly. Other RBHCs may follow BellSouth's approach.

Dial circuit services

Lower-traffic intensity, mobile callers, and applications that require varying circuit speeds typically justify using dial-up services. These services connect users into the LAN or connect LANs to one another. These services can take several forms:

Remote access service

This service accesses a LAN using dial-up lines through a communications server. It is ideal for light, interactive, mobile traffic and intermittent, periodic use.

File-transfer protocol service

These can be used with ITU-TSS V.34 (formerly V.fast) modems to get very high transfer rates, as high as 96–115 kbit/sec. It is not effective for interactive users where traffic levels are insufficient to make full use of the data compression.

Dial DDS or switched 56-kbit/sec service

This service is often used with BONDING devices. A dial DDS circuit may also be connected to a bridge or router to set up a temporary LAN-to-LAN connection. Analog circuits may also be used this way to save the expense of a leased line.

| Switched fractional T-1 service | This service works like the dial DDS service, but uses ISDN instead. |
| Full switched T-1 service | This is the dial-up version of regular T-1 service. It requires an on-site T-1 circuit and may require a reservation with the telephone company. |

Some of these dial services and *bandwidth on demand interoperability group* BONDING devices make fine backups for full-period circuits that may fail. Some managers use several carriers to further insulate their networks. The key qualifier is the length of time the link must be up. If it is less than 10 h/day, BONDING may be right for your network. Using time-of-day calling, you could connect a remote office to your LAN during office hours, then hang up at night.

Some vendors offer a feature that triggers a bandwidth dial-up based on a figure given to it by the application. This way, the multiplexer does not have to dial incrementally; it simply dials whatever speed is called for by the application.

Most inverse multiplexers connect to routers or bridges. Some offer a direct token-ring card interface, placing the multiplexer right on the ring.

As we will see, BONDING is not as elegant or dynamic as frame relay or SMDS. But if frame relay service is unavailable or the other options are too expensive, BONDING begins to make sense.

BONDING devices

BONDING devices make use of an old data communications technique called *inverse multiplexing* in a new way. One technique to create a high-speed link is to take several lower speed links and tie them in parallel as shown in Figure 11.8.

Ordinarily, multiplexers are used just the other way, i.e., to share bandwidth on a single fast circuit on the principle that one fast link costs less money than several slow ones. So an inverse multiplexer takes a fast user port and divides it into several slower data channels, hence the term *inverse* multiplexer. But why do this?

The reason is that we want to use the bandwidth *incrementally*. If the application calls for only 56 kbits, then the multiplexer *dials* that much, using switched 56-kbit circuits. If more is needed, another one is called, and so on. As the load drops, circuits are dropped too.

Inverse multiplexing is being used for T-1 backup and for transferring data, such as file transfers. Some now support several simultaneous applications and provide access to different carrier services. BONDING is becoming a multiapplication technology.

Bandwidth on demand was originally created for video conferencing,

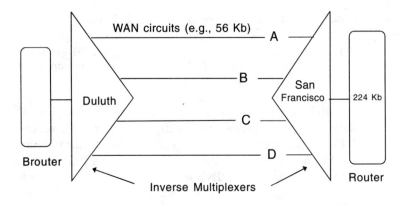

Inverse multiplexers combine several low-speed circuits
to present the appearance of a high-speed circuit
to a bridge or bridging router

This is exactly the *inverse* of what a multiplexer
is designed to do: that is, *reduce* the number of circuits.

Figure 11.8 Inverse multiplexing.

which is still its primary market. However, it also has utility for LAN internetwork owners as well.

Vendors. A BONDING box should have a variety of application and network ports, dynamic bandwidth allocation, built-in *channel service units* (CSUs), BONDING-compatibility certification with other BONDING devices, network management, and certification for use outside the U.S. if that is important for the application. A BONDING box can be purchased from a variety of sources.[5]

Inverse multiplexers can also be purchased from an original equipment manufacturer (OEM) and resold by other vendors. So be sure to ask if your vendor buys or makes their own device. OEM arrangements may affect the price, service, and support.[6]

---

[5]Some principal inverse multiplexer vendors include Ascend (CA), Teleos (NJ), Promptus (RI), Digital Access Corp. (CA), and Newbridge Networks, Inc. (VA).

[6]These are among some of the vendors that purchase and relabel inverse multiplexers for sale under their own name: Larse (CA), Network Express, Racal-Datacom (FL), and Telco Systems' Network Access Corp.

ITU-TSS X.25. BONDING and dial-up techniques are forms of *circuit* switching to meet connectivity and traffic-load requirements. Systems exist to switch individual data *packets,* and these systems are more dynamic than BONDING and dial-up techniques.

Packet switching, largely synonymous with ITU-TSS X.25 packet-switching standard implementations, has been around a long time. It is available everywhere and is well-understood. The standards are stable. Figure 11.9 shows a packet-switching network.

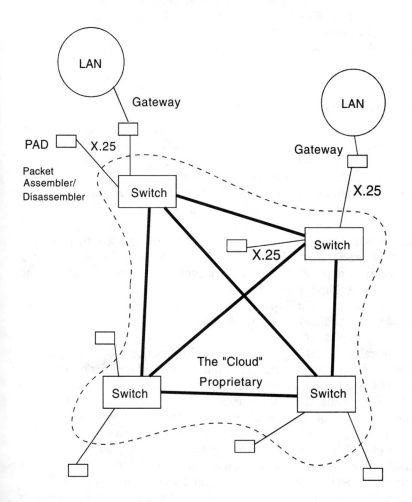

X.25 is an *Access* Protocol
Switches and WAN Link Protocols are Proprietary

Figure 11.9 ITU-TSS X.25 packet-switching network.

The problem is that packet switching is mainly suited for low-speed data, i.e., under 64 kbit/sec and has excessive and unpredictable delays, making it largely unsuitable for LAN-to-LAN use. This is why ITU-TSS X.25 service vendors such as BT Tymnet are working so hard to upgrade to frame-relay service.

This is not to say that ITU-TSS X.25 is not used between bridges and routers. It is. If traffic loads are light and the applications can tolerate delay, then ITU-TSS X.25 may be a suitable link. However, polled systems such as SDLC and systems that rely on broadcasts to work such as routers and NetWare's SAP will chew up kilopackets at an alarming and expensive rate.

For further discussion of LAN protocols in the WAN environment, see Chapter 10.

Frame-relay service

Frame-relay service is a streamlined form of ITU-TSS X.25. It deletes ITU-TSS X.25's error-correction function in favor of speed, taking advantage of the fact that the digital facilities it uses have very low error rates. Error *detection,* not correction, is done only at the end points, not at intermediate stations as in ITU-TSS X.25. Nor are there sequence numbers, frame acknowledgements, or *automatic repeat requests* (ARQs) for incorrect received data.

Frame relay concentrates on delivering data quickly to the right destination and simply throws away incorrect data. The simplicity of frame relay is dependent on today's largely error-free data paths and the greater intelligence in today's user devices.

Frame relay is unforgiving. Incorrect data of any kind is discarded without notification. Even network congestion in the absence of errors can cause loss of data.

Frame relay is a DLL protocol and is connection-oriented. There is no Layer 3 for routing. As such, permanent virtual circuits must create a session between the sender and receiver. Switched virtual circuits using ISDN signaling are in the works.

One advantage of frame relay is that a single connection to a frame-relay switching office can support several independent sessions, saving the cost of multiple lines. In frame relay, these multiplexing functions, normally a Layer 4 activity, are drawn into Layer 2. Typically, a link to a frame relay switch will be a 56-kbit/sec DDS link or fractional T-1.

It is said that frame relay is an *access technology* in that it connects the user to a frame-relay switch as illustrated in Figure 11.10. This connection is a fractional T-1 circuit or is part of a full 1.544-Mbit/sec T-1. Typical fractional speeds in frame relay are 64, 128, 256, 384, 512, or 768 kbit/sec.

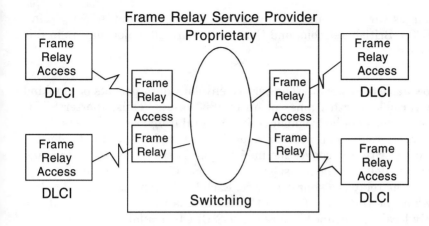

Figure 11.10 A frame-relay network.

Bellcore now offers the *SMDS Interface Protocol* (SIP) relay service, which allows access to SMDS via 56- or 64-kbits frame relays. This is expected to propel both technologies forward.

The frame-relay approach suits the burst-like nature of LAN data. In a leased line, sufficient speed must be purchased to support the highest burst rates that can occur. In fact, LAN traffic on a T-1 link is estimated to be at peak usage only 15–25 percent of the time.

Although frame relay handles data packet-by-packet, it can run (and be paid for) at a lower aggregate speed but still have the flexibility to handle short bursts of heavy data. This feature is making frame relay very cost-competitive.

Frame-relay billing. Billing is usually based on three components: a port fee for access to the network, a fixed monthly charge based on access speed, and a traffic component based on the number of kiloframes sent. This makes the payment scheme usage-based since the greatest expense is for kiloframe usage. Usage billing is generally more cost-effective than paying for a full T-1, whether it is used or not.

Typical kiloframe rates run in the 50-cent or less range. Billing charges vary tremendously by carrier, so shop around. AT&T, Sprint, WilTel, British Telecom, and Compuserve are all major players in this market.

How frame relay works. The service envelops data packets of any kind in variable-length frames of up to 1600 octets. Thus, shorter SDLC frames need not be fragmented into several frame relay packets.

Frame relay then adds an explicit route address, content information, priority, and congestion information. There is almost no store and forward delay as the message follows a specific virtual route.

Frame relay is a shared service. Each local circuit is assigned a *data link connection identifier* (DLCI). A DLCI is not an address as it has only local significance. There are 992 DLCIs available on a switch for subscriber use. The switch statistically multiplexes users' data packets in a city and sends it via high-speed technology, perhaps *synchronous optical network* (SONET). This gives users very high speed and significant economies of scale.

Much ado has been made of the way frame relay handles congestion. The network can discard data if it encounters congestion in either direction.

To warn the receiver of this, the frame-relay header contains a *forward explicit congestion notification* (FECN) bit telling the receiver that it encountered congestion delay. A *backward ECN* (BECN) indicates that the path back to the source is congested. The attached device is expected to throttle itself back until the congestion is cleared.

Frame relay will look at the *discard eligibility* bit to see if the application has made the frame a high (0) or low (1) priority. If it is low priority, the frame may be discarded in case congestion is encountered.

Usage. Intended for remote internetworking, frame relay is well-suited for peer-to-peer communications, especially in intracompany applications.

Frame relay is becoming more widely deployed, but service may not be available from some vendors in certain cities. Both value-added-network carriers such as Compuserve and the RBHCs are vendors.

Frame relay is not implemented consistently by every seller of frame relay service. This includes carriers, frame relay multiplexer vendors (usually selling a card in a high-speed multiplexer), and bridge and/or router vendors.

The broad definition of the specification, competitive factors, technical reasons, and a variety of frame-relay vendors have all contributed to the problem. The bottom line is that there is no standard implementation of frame relay by all the carriers, especially with respect to billing plans and congestion management. Nor do the bridge, router, or multiplexer manufacturers meet any common standard.[7] The implication for you here is obvious. Make any acquisitions contingent on satisfactory end-to-end performance and write clauses into contracts that make the vendors responsible for working out any differences between them at their own expense.

Despite slow acceptance and incompatibility bugs, frame-relay service is a proven technology. Compared to LAN speeds, its relatively low data rate may be all some users ever require, and it is available today.

Relationship to SMDS and asynchronous transfer mode. The use of frame relay does not lock a customer out of SMDS or *asynchronous transfer mode* (ATM). In fact, frame relay can be used to access SMDS via the Bellcore DXI or SIP relay specification. Frame-relay access to ATM backbones has already received standardization attention from ITU-TSS, and this option is being promoted by AT&T, Cisco Systems, and Stratacom. For the many customers who cannot justify SMDS' 1.544-Mbit/sec minimum access rate, lower speed frame-relay access may be just the ticket.

SMDS

Description. Frame relay was a proprietary, vendor-driven LAN internetworking scheme derived from ITU-TSS X.25 standards. Standards for frame relay are being developed. In contrast, SMDS is not proprietary. SMDS was developed by *Bell Communications Research* (Bellcore), the research arm of the RBHCs. Such powerful and ubiquitous backing makes SMDS a de facto standard from the start. An SMDS network is shown in Figure 11.11.

There had been some question as to whether frame relay or SMDS would win out in the user community. The RBHCs short-circuited this contest by embracing both frame relay and SMDS. As a result, they have placed themselves, and by inference their customers, in a no-lose position.

This is well-exemplified by the SIP relay service, which allows access to SMDS via 56- or 64-kbits frame-relay circuits. For customers who cannot afford T-1 or T-3 SMDS access, SMDS may become affordable because of SIP relay. Another standard, *data exchange interface* (DXI) is also available but is less flexible than SIP relay.

SMDS is more complex than frame relay but can do more and will

---

[7]See "Routers May Test Frame Relay Users' Patience," *Network World* p. 35, May 25, 1992.

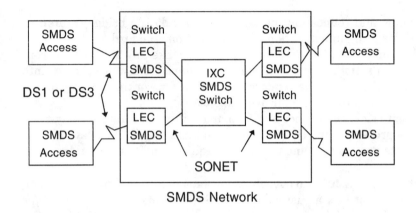

SMDS Network

SMDS is a higher speed access technology
It is backed by the Bell operating companies
It is designed to work with ATM one day

Figure 11.11 SMDS.

greatly exceed frame relay's speed limit of 1.544-Mbit/sec. SMDS is being initially tariffed at 1.544 Mbit/sec and can go up to 45 Mbit/sec.
Extensions up to 155 Mbit/sec are also possible.

SMDS has been fully defined by Bellcore, in contrast to the vendor-
orientation of frame relay. There are no proprietary elements to SMDS.
In fact, SMDS is based on the IEEE 802.6 MAN standard and is compatible with *broadband ISDN* (BISDN) ATM.

Support services are equally well-defined. These services, including
circuit provisioning, network switching, maintenance, and operations
procedures, are required by demanding commercial users. SMDS billing software lets customers pay based on usage.

Data packets or *cells* in SMDS are very small. Each cell consists of 53
bytes, of which the first 5 are for control and the last 48 contain data.
They can be carried easily by SONET or as broadband (600 Mbit/sec)
ISDN. Their fixed length makes them easier to manage than variable-
length frame-relay packets.

SMDS is *connectionless*. There is no requirement to establish a connection with the receiver before data transfer begins. This contrasts
with frame-relay service, which requires a call to be set up before data
can be sent and a tear-down afterward, in much the same way that we
make a telephone call.

The heart of SMDS is the *fast packet switch* (FPS). The FPS at the
central office will handle all SMDS services and is capable of switching

millions of cells per second, much faster than frame relay. Data sent between offices will be handled by SONET.

At the premises of each customer, an SMDS access device will be required unless frame-relay access is used. Incorporating not only the CSU monitoring and testing functions, the access device will also encapsulate packets into a *protocol data unit* (PDU), which adds the destination address and other overhead information. The PDU is then segmented into cells of equal length with still more overhead. The now thoroughly encapsulated packet is finally mapped into a DS-1 (1.544 Mbit/sec) or a DS-3 (45 Mbit/sec) signal via a *physical layer convergence protocol* (PLCP). As with frame relay, delays are very short and there is no link-layer error correction.

The future of SMDS. Development of the SMDS access device and of the complex software for the SMDS switches is ongoing. Local and long-distance carriers must figure out how to hand off data between themselves, an ongoing issue since only MCI to date has committed to offering interexchange SMDS service. Customer-based network management remains an issue.

It is expected that regional Bell operating companies will deploy SMDS first in large cities on an *intra-local access and transport area* (intraLATA) basis. From there they will extend wide-area connections across LATA boundaries into the interexchange carriers' realm. Since SMDS is an RBHC creation, we can expect SMDS to be deployed at least on a regional basis.

Frame relay and SMDS appear to be complementary because frame relay stops where SMDS begins. However, customer surveys show that users will do one or the other and not both. Either one was gauged as satisfactory for their needs. Customer ambivalence seems to guarantee a shakeout.

The reception by the RBHCs has been equally lukewarm. The initial cost of SMDS development and deployment will be high, as will marketing and service costs. These costs can be offset somewhat if the same central office switch is used for all three: frame relay, SMDS, and ATM. Given decreasing access rates, this may well be practical.

With marginal user and *interexchange carrier* (IXC) interest, there is a real question about SMDS' viability. Though five of the RBHCs offer SMDS, Nynex placed plans to use SMDS on hold in favor of developing ATM. Southwestern Bell presently does not offer SMDS either.

The carriers still need to do more educating before either frame relay or SMDS is implemented on a large scale. More than anything else, a general lack of knowledge may be the greatest impediment to the growth of either service.

A redeeming feature of SMDS is that it has a clear migration path to higher speeds and a high degree of compatibility with other standards. The SMDS cell is closely aligned to the IEEE 802.6 cell, which in turn is like the ITU-TSS and T1S1 (U.S.) cell for ATM, also called *cell relay*. This basic format maps closely to broadband ISDN at 600 Mbit/sec.

Most significantly, the economics remain unclear. Some RBHCs think that SMDS will be an alternative to the leased line networks of the past. Expensive leased lines, they say, will be eliminated, bringing a new set of users into the WAN market. These users are profiled as needing high-speed intercompany connectivity between dispersed regional locations.

SMDS access costs are considered a make-or-break item. If they can be held low, many more applications will use SMDS. Higher rates will limit SMDS to specifically cost-justified uses.

ATM

SMDS and ATM are very similar to one another as shown in Figure 11.12. However, they are at different sublayers. The duplication is deliberate to give users an upgrade path from SMDS to ATM. What is more important to customers is that SMDS is closer to delivery than ATM.

What we are discussing here is the same ATM technology that is being applied to LAN hubs. The potential exists, then, to create a seamless ATM network where the WAN and LAN elements both use ATM as the transport medium for voice, data, or video. In such a scenario, the terms WAN and LAN lose their meaning. In such a scenario, the complex and sometimes awkward devices we have conceived to marry these two, such as bridges and routers, disappear.

The goal of ATM is not just to support LAN interconnections, but to carry voice, data, images, and video on one high-quality medium. The network planner will at last have the universal transport medium.

Bellcore conceives of ATM as being the technology to carry SMDS and frame relay internally. At a higher level, ATM will be extended to the subscriber's premises and will become a multiservice communications interface. In this model, "network utopia" will become possible by using cell-by-cell multiplexing, mixing voice, data, and video cells among each other on a high-speed path.

That is where ATM gets it name. Cells from different input paths contend for cell space in the output stream. The ATM switch can only switch one at a time, so the others are queued. The queuing adds a variable delay to each cell, so cells are considered to be transferred *asynchronously* across the switch.

Cell relay is connection-oriented but supports many connection-oriented *permanent virtual circuits* (PVCs) and connectionless *switched*

IEEE 802.6:

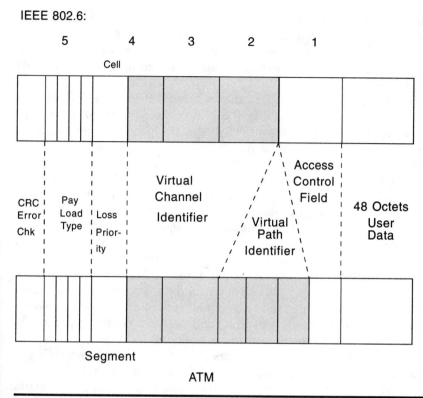

Figure 11.12   Comparing SMDS and ATM cells.

virtual circuits (SVCs) within the connection. *Virtual channels* (VCs) can be grouped into a *virtual path* (VP) for network management, where a VP represents a customer. Since these channels are not of fixed bandwidth, only the average bandwidth need be purchased rather than the peak bandwidth, provided that any "burstiness" is random.

If any congestion occurs, the cell relay "loses" cells until the congestion is cleared. Which cells are lost is based on cell priority. This is functionally similar to frame relay, and losing cells clearly affects the quality of service on that channel.

ATM is defined by the *American National Standards Institute* (ANSI) and ITU-TSS, and has been chosen by both for use in BISDN at 600 Mbit/sec. Specifically, the ATM switching and multiplexing techniques at Layer 2 will be used by BISDN to carry traffic from the originator to the recipient.

There are three layers involved in this process. First, the *Physical* layer defines how ATM cells are transmitted by a physical medium. It also provides a uniform interface to the next layer up. The *pure ATM* interface sends a constant stream of ATM cells. Alternatively, the *SONET-SDH* (Synchronous Data Hierarchy) interface option transports ATM cells within a concatenated payload of the SONET-SDH frame (90 bytes).

Second, the *ATM* layer does the switching. It uses the VC and VP identifiers, monitors usage, is the billing mechanism, and manages overloads by discarding low-priority cells. Its "policing" medium keeps services from exceeding their negotiated bandwidth limits.

Third, the *ATM adaptation layer* (AAL) segments user traffic into cells. When the information field is full, it adds the VC and VP data. At the receiver, it uses the VC and VP data to extract cells from the cell stream, removes the user data, smoothes it, and presents it to the user.

ATM is being set up to operate at 45, 100, and 155 Mbit/sec. The 45-Mbit/sec speed is the first priority as existing T-3 (or DS-3) circuits can be used.

Like SMDS, data is multiplexed into fixed-length 53-byte cells. There is a 5-byte header plus 48 bytes for data. The header carries control information such as cell routing and type of connection. It takes a slightly different format, depending on whether it is carrying network-to-network information or user-to-network data.

ATM's major benefit to LAN users is its minimal delay, which is the result of the small, fixed-length cell. If data, voice, video, and "bursty" LAN traffic are to be mixed, the sudden entry of a LAN burst should not affect the other services. The small cell size allows all the traffic to be interleaved and reduces the tendency of a LAN to "hog" the line.

The minimal network latency will also meet some heavy-duty bandwidth applications such as multimedia with its simultaneous voice, data, and video needs. ATM will deliver as much bandwidth as is needed much more dynamically than is presently feasible using ITU-TSS X.25, BONDING, or frame relay.

Networks are simplified by sharing transport technology between LANs, WANs, and MANs. The medium becomes *seamless:* The medium is the same regardless of traffic type. With only one medium, network management also becomes seamless.

Frame relay, SMDS, and ATM

Between frame relay, SMDS, and ATM, we can see the clear leapfrogging of one emerging technology by another before the ink is dry on any of them (Table 11.1).

Pragmatically, frame relay is the most available because it is the oldest of the three. Even so, it has been slow to gain popularity for a variety of reasons, including its cost and complexity, its lack of standards

TABLE 11.1   Comparison of Frame Relay, SMDS, and ATM

Feature	Frame relay	SMDS	DLL
Protocol layer	DLL	DLL	DLL
Connection type	Connection-oriented PVC or SVC	Connectionless	Connection-oriented PVC and SVC within VC and VP
Speed	64-Kbit/sec channel with increments to 384-kbits	1.5, 45, and 155 M-bit/sec	45, 100, and 155 M-bit/sec
Packet type	Variable length	Fixed cells	Fixed cells
Cell size	1600 octets	53 bytes	53 bytes
Standards supported	Vendor-oriented ECSA T1S1 for ANSI ITU-TSS I.233	Bellcore after IEEE 802.6	ANSI and ITU-TSS
Migration path	None	ATM or BISDN	BISDN or SONET

among suppliers, and the natural reluctance of communications managers to buy a technology they may not understand. Its proprietary nature and limited top end speed do not help, either.

Still, frame relay is expected to grow from about 21,500 ports in 1994 to nearly 100,000 ports in 1996, a 5-fold increase. Revenue will show about a 4-fold increase in the same time frame. Its use as an access technology to SMDS will multiply its deployment by a factor of three to five.

SMDS and frame relay revenues are expected to be even by 1998, the watershed year in which SMDS and frame relay will be about even in revenue terms. At that time, ATM will be in a strong third place and gaining. By 2003, ATM is expected to have some 60 percent of the market. In the same 5-year period, BISDN will eclipse both frame relay and SMDS to take second place. [8]

SMDS has no meaningful high-end speed limit, and it is backed by the RBHCs. In addition, it has a clear migration path to ATM, which LAN managers know is coming soon to a LAN near them. Some have elected to make do with less capable technology such as dial-up or frame relay until SMDS is fully deployed. Some plan to wait for ATM.

However, SMDS's deployment by IXCs is lagging behind the RBHCs. Thus, users are limited to intraLATA turf until the IXCs get on board.

---

[8]The source for these predictions is Electronicast Corp., San Mateo, CA.

ATM products, much less applications, do not exist yet in volume anyway.

ATM's future, or at least its broad utility, seems assured because it directly addresses the needs of emerging applications for very high bandwidth, dynamic switching, low delay, and low cost. ATM's ability to carry different forms of information such as voice and data will save users money. Sharing ATM switches among hundreds if not thousands of customers makes the economics that much more attractive.

From the customer's standpoint, a single link to the switch is a lot easier to manage than several and is far less expensive. Customers can also look toward reducing the number of protocols and routers they need to support. A decline in administrative and technical overhead is probable.

We also have to look at the long term. Frame relay is increasingly perceived as short-term technology. It and SMDS will peak in the late 1990s. It may not make sense to invest in a short-term technology knowing that it will be soon supplanted by a more permanent system, most likely ATM.

To stay abreast of these developments, it is necessary to have periodic briefings by the carriers and router vendors. Watch the trade press to get a sense as to where the technology is going and how quickly it is moving.

12

Network Operating Systems

What a Network Operating System Does

The functions of a *network operating system* (NOS) are similar to the functions of the operating system of a computer except that they are being applied to a network. The NOS does the housekeeping, manages files, and ensures a smoothly running network. The NOS contains the necessary control functions, such as printer queues and security functions, that make a network practical in an office setting.

In this chapter, we discuss what a NOS does and compare representative NOS software packages. While each has its relative vices and virtues, the real criterion is whether the package fits your needs. For instance, a large enterprise-wide network can use Banyan's *Virtual Networking System* (VINES) or NetWare 4.X, but is simply too large for NetWare 3.1X, LANtastic, or a peer-to-peer style LAN. Conversely, in a small office setting, a peer-to-peer LAN is ideal and VINES is overkill.

Trade press-based LAN evaluations, declaring one NOS better than another for all time, must not be regarded as absolute arbiters. Different test regimes yield different results, and once again, the objective is to acquire the best system for your needs. These criteria will vary for each user: One LAN's meat is another LAN's poison.

LAN performance depends on many factors, not the least of which is the type of traffic to be carried. One NOS may excel carrying interactive traffic and another may excel carrying batch traffic. Most NOSs can be tuned to more closely match the type of traffic that is being carried.

Some NOSs allow the host server to be used as a workstation, too. This is called a *nondedicated* (to the NOS) *server.* Other NOSs do not permit this, so the server is *dedicated* to the NOS. Some NOSs permit the server to be configured either way, but server performance may suffer intermittently as workstation processing starts and stops. LAN professionals much prefer dedicated servers.

Static performance measures such as the maximum number of users and features such as fault tolerance are easily compared. Intangibles such as vendor and product stability, service, support, training, and availability of third-party applications supersede small performance differences, and are unlikely to be perceived by a user. These intangibles affect the long-term viability of a LAN much more than raw performance.

Evaluating NOSs is like shooting at a moving target. They are constantly being upgraded and enhanced. Therefore, attempting a detailed evaluation of each would involve a mass of detail and obscure the forest for the trees. So our approach here is to cite the most useful features, and let you select the important ones in your application. Then, we compare each NOS in these terms and identify the general setting in which each excels and falls short.

It is difficult to make a really bad choice because all of them do the job. The choice is really between adequate and best.

Selection Criteria

Table 12.1 itemizes the key criteria to consider, in approximate top-down order. In this section, we expand on the most important of these criteria.

Performance

Performance is what keeps users happy. If network delay, *latency*, is high, files take too long to upload and server-based applications run too slowly. You know something is wrong when users start relying on their own hard drives, applications, and printers.

File and print services are the bread-and-butter of NOSs. They are the essence of low-end peer-to-peer systems such as LANtastic. Many users need little more.

There is a trend toward using mail and client-server database systems to replace file-service-dependent products. The most time-consuming task is finding the right document, not downloading it.

Some NOSs are better suited to some applications than others. Since NetWare usually downloads data in 512-byte chunks, it excels at short, interactive transfers. NetWare's performance declines in batch processing, though, compared to Microsoft LAN Manager and VINES. This is because NetWare transfers only 512 bytes or so at a time and requires an acknowledgement for each frame. LAN Manager's *NetBIOS extended user interface* (NetBEUI) uses a 2-kbyte block and VINES

TABLE 12.1   NOS Selection Criteria

Performance

Support and service availability and terms

Fault tolerance

Ease of administration

Server platform requirements

Application compatibility

Access control and security

Ease of use by clients

Client support types

Server and client memory requirements

Mass storage requirements

Utilities available, i.e., third-party support

Expansion options and migration path

Shared printer and plotter support

Other shared device support, e.g., fax, scanners and CAD-CAM

Internetworking and mainframe access capability

Network naming support, e.g., global naming and NetBIOS

Backup and archiving capability

Price, product direction and vendor viability

---

uses a 1500-byte (default) block; VINES can further improve performance with sliding windows, which was discussed in Chapter 10.

Speed in processing file requests is the other big performance determinant. With its outstanding file caching, NetWare is fastest at handling small files. NetWare optimizes all hard disk activity. Thus, the heads move in sequence and in a linear fashion, not at random, for all read and write requests. LAN Manager is slightly optimized for larger files, and VINES performs about the same with any file size.

The size and speed of the processor counts. Most NOS vendors prefer at least a 386SX processor for decent performance. Only VINES presently supports true symmetrical processing on server platforms, such as Compaq's SystemPro, that support several CPUs. Asymmetric processing sends specific tasks, such as printing, security, or file access control, to a designated CPU. Symmetrical processing, discussed in Chapter 5, is a near-term future need.

The operating system also affects performance. After booting up under DOS, NetWare becomes its own operating system on a server. As an operating system, NetWare handles data files operations in 4-kbyte segments instead of DOS' usual 512 bytes. As discussed above, Net-Ware's caching stores megabytes of data in memory, allowing nanosecond access times.

VINES runs atop of Unix, which lets VINES run on fast, powerful platforms, even minicomputers, and takes advantage of Unix' multitasking power. Microsoft LAN Manager runs on OS/2, which is also capable of multitasking. Microsoft LAN Manager will migrate to Windows NT, which is designed for symmetrical processing.

Most NOSs will support up to four *network interface cards* (NIC) in the server platform, all under the same NOS. This makes it possible to divide the network and, thereby, reduce each segment's traffic. This strategy works especially well in Ethernet LANs where contention is an inherent problem. Network speed and the access method, plus the NIC and especially its driver, all affect performance, too. Recall that a token ring degrades more gracefully under load than Ethernet, which hits a "knee." (Some would say a wall.)

Basically, networks create, find, read, and write files. We said before that file and print service do not press a CPU very hard. Hard disk access and pushing data to and from NICs are the major delay sources. However, adding functions to the server, such as network and database management, can adversely affect server performance. The new Pentium-class CPU will minimize these effects.

There is also a trend to port NOSs to RISC-based machines. For example, NetWare is being ported to the DEC Alpha processor, Hewlett-Packard's PA-RISC, and Sun Microsystems' SPARC. VINES is being ported to Hewlett-Packard's PA-RISC.

Tuning also affects performance. Many default parameters in the NOS can be changed to match the hardware platform, the applications, and the sizes of files that are up and down loaded. Tuning can make a noticeable difference in the way a LAN operates.

Fault tolerance

Different operating systems support varying types of fault tolerance. NetWare's SFT II supports disk mirroring (same disk controller) and disk duplexing (separate controllers), plus hot fixing (to fix bad disk sectors), transaction tracking, and automatic shutdown on command by an *uninterruptible power supply* (UPS) (with a user warning message).

Server duplexing allows two servers to run in parallel. If one fails, the other continues seamlessly. It is often implemented by running a 100-Mbit/sec link between the servers to update them both rapidly. If a NIC or power supply fails, processing continues on the other server. Product support varies as follows:

NetWare supports this with *System Fault Tolerance III* (SFT III), an add-on to NetWare 3.1X and intrinsic to NetWare 4.X.

With third-party software, VINES allows backup of some services to another server, but VINES itself is not very fault tolerant.

Microsoft LAN Manager has good fault tolerance features similar to NetWare's; they are, however, harder to initialize and manage.

Peer-to-peer packages have few fault tolerance hooks. However, since each PC is usually also a server, thereby eliminating that particular single point of failure, you can consider this an intrinsic fault tolerance hook.

Even AppleShare systems can get in on the act via fault tolerant hardware and software additions from third parties. Server hardware can help, too, such as Compaq's SystemPro fault tolerant hardware.

In their quest for nonstop application platforms, some customers have even resorted to fault tolerant Tandem or Stratus machines. This is an expensive solution to be sure. However, since true server duplexing has only become recently available, users have had little alternative.

Application compatibility

Clearly, your application(s) must be LAN compatible. What does this mean?

Single-user software will often run on a LAN, but the server copies the application software in it to each user's workstation. Files cannot usually be shared. There are licensing issues. More workstation power is needed, and extra network traffic is created.

Multiuser software lets several users run at once on the same software and share files using file, record, or field-locking. Accounting and database systems are multiuser.

Networked software makes full use of all network resources: modems, printers, etc. Networked software directs output to and receives input from shared resources without being told. The server often keeps user-customized software, a major convenience. Today, some shrink-wrapped application software comes in a networkable version.

Bulk data transfers are easily handled by LAN Manager or VINES while NetWare is better with interactive applications. If you have both, deciding which NOS to buy based on the bipolar nature of the applications is a schizophrenic experience and usually means that other factors will ascend in importance.

Some applications simply will not work with a given NOS. If they do work, not all of its features may be usable. The question is not just, "Is it compatible?" It is really *"How* compatible is this NOS with my applications?"

To the extent possible, retain your applications software as you move into a networked environment. New LAN client users have enough to learn without starting over with new applications. Leave that for later.

LAN client software occupies precious DOS RAM space to the point where other applications may be crowded out. Typically, about 110 kbytes is required. Applications needing 512 kbytes or more may not work.

Many memory management games are played. Some client software will be loaded in extended memory, with only a little in base memory. Sometimes it will be loaded or unloaded, depending on whether the application request is sensed by the redirector as a network request. Peer-to-peer LANs often have very small RAM requirements, as small as 2 kbytes in low memory.

Security

A LAN is a double-edged sword. It is designed to give more users access, but it simultaneously creates the risk of abuse.

The problem is not the NOS; most NOSs have flexible and scalable security. *The problem is that administrators fail to use the features they have.*

Account locks prevent brute-force efforts to find a password by limiting the number of logon attempts allowed. Limiting *access privileges* keeps improper users out of a file, directory, or a LAN device such as a server, gateway, or application.

Some NOSs include *audit trail* capability to track usage, logons, and illegal entry attempts. Some, including NetWare, also encrypt passwords. NetWare uses a *NetWare Loadable Module* (NLM) for those customers wanting audit trails. Auditing is not native to NetWare.

VINES encrypts server-client data to foil wiretappers with LAN analyzers. LAN Manager uses OS/2-based security features such as its limited audit trail. In LAN Manager, security domains can be set up giving a group of users the same privileges in that domain.

Future NOSs will automatically detect and expunge viruses, which usually show up on workstations. Doing this from the NOS makes eminent sense as it gives the administrator the power to protect each network station. Some metering software, such as AppMeter, also performs this function as an added-value feature.

In AppleShare, a new Macintosh on the LAN cannot do anything until the administrator creates a user account for it. Server documents can be copy-protected to prevent copying. Folders can be locked. To limit browsing, the number of simultaneous sessions can be limited. If all else fails, the manager can arbitrarily log off an illicit user.

VINES' StreetTalk is a *global naming service* that includes security. One server handles security for all the servers in its domain. By contrast, DOS LAN-like NetWare 3.1X requires users to log on separately to each network resource and/or server.

Supervisory utilities should let an administrator create user names and a bindery of security-related data. (NetWare has these features.) A supervisor should be able to replace a user's password and override it if necessary.

The system should force users to change their passwords periodically. A list of resources allowed for each user should be presented at logon. The supervisor should be able to see at any time a list of active users, resources in use, and a record of suspicious logon attempts.

Manageability

The ability to implement and run security features daily is the first aspect of manageability. The ability to change, create, and expedite print queues is another commonly used daily feature. Can you work with this thing? Do you prefer a Microsoft Windows *graphical user interface* (GUI) or is a text-based presentation okay with you?

Installation of a LAN operation system used to be a complex affair taking a day or more, and often requiring an expert. Recent improvements have allowed the installation time to be shortened to a few hours in many cases.

A major element of manageability has to do with the extent to which the system is internetworked. Controlling remote resources such as servers can be a real problem. This is an area where VINES excels and NetWare has classically been weak until the introduction of NetWare 4.X.

In an effort to strengthen NetWare management, Novell offers an NLM called *NetWare Management Service* (NMS), which uses *Simple Network Management Protocol* (SNMP) to draw maps and control devices such as hubs and wiring concentrators. Apple, Banyan, and Microsoft as yet have nothing comparable for *devices,* not *servers.*

Last year, Novell introduced the *Hub Management Interface* (HMI), which places wiring hub management inside the server. While this gives better control, the server also becomes a single point of failure. From a cost and configuration view, though, it has advantages. Other vendors, mainly the hub manufacturers, are expected to follow with HMI products.

Third-party vendors have augmented LAN management. Frye Computers (Boston, MA) offers software to document a complete NetWare

LAN. Blue Lance (Houston, TX) tracks and logs network alarms for several NOSs. Cheyenne Software (Roslyn, NY) offers NetWare network management software, and Trellis Software (Hopkinton, MA) does the same for VINES. The latter two both use graphic maps.

Major NOSs support SNMP. SNMP has become the hook for managing everything in a LAN from bridges to routers, gateways, and hubs. SNMP is now in workstations, too. SNMP had some weaknesses, especially in security, that have been addressed in the son of SNMP, SNMP version 2. Look for SNMP version 2 in forthcoming products.

SNMP is an Internet Engineering Task Force (IETF)-based de facto standard. Some NOSs also support the *Common Management Information Protocol* (CMIP). Based on *open systems interconnection* (OSI), CMIP is potentially more functional, and its cost is accordingly higher. The response to CMIP has been tepid, but it has been used to connect IBM mainframes using NetView and in those using heavy-duty integrated management solutions such as OpenView and AT&T's Accumaster.

At the very least, an NOS should support SNMP. Virtually all do except perhaps the peer-to-peer products, and they are mostly for local use anyway.

Ease of use by client "liveware"

In this case, we mean client in the sense of the person using the workstation. Any NOS should be easy to use, with simple access to needed applications, files, and resources such as printers, modems, and fax cards. It should have enough latitude to let thumb-fingered users make a typing mistake without evil consequences. It should not present so many options as to confuse or lose a user.

A GUI such as Microsoft Windows is appealing to many users, but others prefer text. The bottom line is that users will not accept a hard-to-work-with NOS, no matter how flexible it is. Virtually all NOSs meet this criterion, but knowing your user community, ask yourself which one is the most compatible.

A good user interface insulates the user from network faults and background operations. Conversely, the interface protects the network against unintended changes or incorrect operation that might harm the network's operation.

Client support types

Today, most NOSs client software supports every manner of PC and Macintosh. You may need to support transient notebook, laptop users, or dial-ins. The NOS software suite should handle any of these conveniently.

Client software should not impose stringent performance or capacity requirements, such as having a hard disk in the client. Ideally, NOS client software is indifferent to the nature of the processor, operating system, speed, bus type, etc. This may seem impossible but current software drivers do a fair job. One thing is certain: The moment you lock yourself out of a whizbang 186, someone will trudge one into the office. The more client software choices, the better.

Memory requirements

Server RAM requirements are typically 12–16 Mbytes. NetWare in particular uses memory for caching but allocates it unusually well. This accounts for much of its speed.

Client RAM may limit the kind of client that can be used. NetWare needs about 100 kbytes, LAN Manager need 94–111 kbytes, VINES needs typically 110 kbytes, and AppleShare typically needs about 100 kbytes. This may stretch 286 machines, but 386s will have little trouble.

Placing the client software in high memory is okay, but it must be contiguous. Some users install memory management packages such as Compaq Expanded Memory Manager (CEMM) or Quarterdeck Expanded Memory Manager (QEMM) to find such a memory segment. When Windows is used, memory management is mandatory.

Utilities

NetWare leads hands down in the availability of utilities, called NLMs (Figure 12.1), for NetWare 3.X. Earlier versions of NetWare used *value-added processes* (VAPs) in NetWare 2.X operating systems. It only makes sense for developers to concentrate on the NOS with 64–67 percent of the market.

This is not to say that VINES lacks third-party support; it does have utilities for management and fault tolerance, for example. Other NOSs such as Microsoft LAN Manager, IBM's LAN Server, NCR's StarGroup, and DEC's Pathworks are not as aggressively addressed by developers.

Generalizing does not work here. If you need a specific utility, search the market for it in the LAN magazines and the *Computer Select* CD-ROMs published by Ziff-Davis and others such as Faulkner Research (NJ). By all means ask the NOS vendor. If it is important, the existence of your needed utility may influence the choice of your NOS.

Availability of support

NetWare in particular has become easy to support. It is ubiquitous, and Novell has a formal training program in place, the *Certified NetWare Engineer* (CNE), Technician, Administrator, and Instructor program. There is now an enterprise-wide network program.

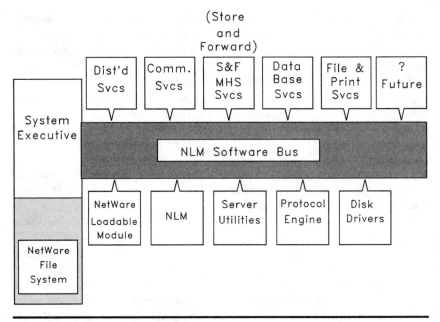

Figure 12.1   NetWare Loadable Modules.

In contrast, direct Novell support seems harder to come by. Novell relies heavily on its dealer network for fulfilling the support mission.

CNE certification has become a rite of passage for network technicians; it is a quantifiable qualification on a resume. Unfortunately, it is not a legitimate yardstick. Some CNEs have hardly touched a Novell system; some non-CNEs have lots of experience but lack $6000 to gain certification.

CNEs are both employees and self-employed, but they are not usually Novell employees. You must look to the employer for satisfaction if the individual is not satisfactory to you. CNEs do not have access to internal Novell documentation, but they do have access to NetWire, Novell's Compuserve-based *bulletin board system* (BBS).

You can buy *telephone support* on an incident basis. An "incident" is defined as resolving one specific NetWare product-related issue, regardless of the number of phone calls it takes to (800) NETWARE. An incident purchase is good for 1 year, and is available 24 hours a day. *Support contracts* guarantee on-site 2-hour response by Novell employees.

The NetWare users group is *NetWare Users International* (NUI). User groups can be very beneficial.[1]

---

[1]NUI can be reached at (800) 288-4NUI or by fax at (801) 429-3056.

Banyan offers a Certified Banyan Engineer program for end users and support organizations, but it is offered through Banyan rather than resellers. Training is offered year-round at four Banyan Education Centers in the U.S., one in Canada, and one in the U.K. They can also be presented on-site. Nine courses are presently offered.[2] Banyan has its own User Group, the *Association of Banyan Users International* (ABUI).[3]

LANtastic has support offices around the country. They support LANtastic primarily via telephone. Support is free for registered purchasers. LANtastic is also supported locally by its reseller network in the U.S., the U.K., Europe, and Mexico. Artisoft has no certification program, but training is offered through resellers. Whichever NOS you consider, ask about these support options.

Expansion

There are several limits here. If you use Ethernet ThinNet with a limit of 30 connections, that is a limit. An NOS that supports 50 users cannot make use of its additional capacity until a repeater is added. Some LANs differentiate between a maximum number of users and the number of simultaneous users. Be sure to ask.

Your major limit may be something else, perhaps the maximum number of concurrently open files per server. In Novell 3.11, that is 100,000—no problem. In LANtastic, it is 5000. But in NetWare 2.2, it is 1000. Since NetWare 2.2 can have up to 100 users, this could prove to be a limitation.

The migration path is really more of a problem in peer-to-peer LANs. If you suspect you might hit a limit in the peer-to-peer realm, consider the small version of NetWare (version 2.2) or its equivalent so that you have an assured upgrade migration path.

Internetworking capability

This is more of a problem at the peer-to-peer level than anywhere else. Both the LANtastic and PowerLAN packages are beginning to offer internetwork options. But they still cannot touch the server-based NOSs.

When considering internetworking, you must look at the network both from the outside as a user would see it (the logical view, in both senses) and from the inside as a network architect. We discuss the logical aspect first.

---

[2]Call Banyan Educational Services at (800) 832-4595 for details.

[3]ABUI can be reached in Massachusetts at (508) 443-3330.

The logical view: global naming. Using global naming, the network is one big, seamless logical entity. Global naming allows a client to log in once. With a lookup service, resources are easy to find. The user interface is in simple English, not awkward computer syntax. Global naming is mandatory in an enterprise-wide network.

NetWare 2.2 and 3.X is fully capable of being internetworked, but they require additional packages such as global naming to be really useful. For NetWare 2.X and 3.X, *NetWare Name Service* (NNS) is used, although it is not a full-blown global-naming system on a par with Banyan's StreetTalk. NNS permits users to access resources or several servers with one login. NMS is also needed to make NetWare 3.X globally workable. Novell's true enterprise-wide NOS is NetWare 4.X.

Functions such as global naming were incorporated into VINES from the outset, and VINES includes a lookup service to find a specific resource. VINES, while slower than NetWare in client-server communication, excels in server-server linkages. VINES is designed specifically for LAN internetworks.

For VINES and NetWare 4.X, a single logical domain allows all the servers to be accessed and managed as one. Some other NOSs such as LAN Manager and LAN Server create several domains, which is less desirable since each can only support a certain number of servers in a given domain.

Microsoft LAN Manager fits in the middle between NetWare 3.X and VINES. Its naming service is stronger than NetWare NNS but not as strong as Banyan's StreetTalk.

In summary, VINES and NetWare 4.X have the edge here. To a user, all the network resources look like *one* network.

The physical view: internetworking protocols. Support for routable protocols depends on whether the NOS has a network layer built into it. NetWare has *Internetwork Packet Exchange* (IPX), and VINES has VINES IP (Internet Protocol), making them both routable. Add-on software allows them to be routed using TCP/IP instead. LAN Manager and LAN Server (Advanced) use *Network Basic Input/Output System (NETBIOS) and NETBEUI*. Since these are unroutable, they must either be bridged or encapsulated in a routable protocol, which entails delay.

The AppleShare NOS is for small workgroups. AppleTalk does have a network layer protocol, the Datagram Delivery Protocol. Even so, AppleTalk must be carefully networked because of its routing table overhead, possible routing loops, and other factors such as its requirement for zoning in large networks.

Price

As they say, with such a range of NOSs (see Figure 12.2), there is one to suit every budget. NetWare is considered slightly overpriced for what it is, a reflection of its stature as the de facto standard. But price is the least significant factor. NOS prices range from a few hundred dollars for a peer-to-peer starter kit to $8000 or so for NetWare 3.1X or VINES. NetWare 4.X for 1000 users costs (at list) nearly $48,000.

If it does what you need, the price is right. If it does not, then any price is too high.

Novell's NetWare

Founded in 1983 with just 14 employees, Novell has grown to a 3200-plus employee company with nearly $1 billion in sales and 64–67 percent of the LAN NOS market.

The introduction of the PC/XT, breaking the NOS out from LAN hardware, and working with other vendors' hardware, proved to be Novell's keys to success. Novell does not make servers, but it does offer NICs as the NE2000 series, considered better-than-average performers. Most recently, the NE3200 for 32-bit Extended Industry-Standard

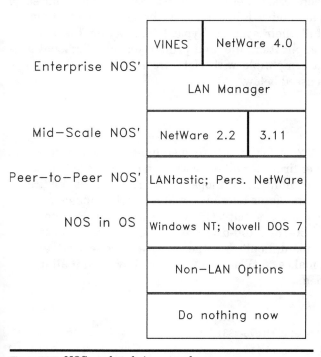

Figure 12.2 NOS market choices at a glance.

Architecture (EISA) and NetWare 3.1X was introduced, a high performance NIC for Ethernet.

NetWare is currently offered in four versions: *Personal NetWare,* NetWare 2.2 and 3.1X, and the high-end version 4.X. A complete description of each is beyond our scope, but an overview is given here. For those interested in knowing more, call Novell[4] and ask for a free copy of the *NetWare Buyer's Guide.* It is also available on diskette if you prefer to save the tree.

Personal NetWare*

Many small offices do not need the power, complexity, or the expense of a full Novell system. Vendors such as Artisoft (LANtastic) and Power-LAN stepped in to offer an alternative. Novell responded with Personal NetWare.

Novell's smallest NOS was introduced to preserve Novell's eroding position at the low end of the market. It is a *peer-to-peer* NOS, which is another way of saying it does not use a server and all the stations are workstations.

Personal NetWare supports 2–50 users, though the average office usage is about 10 users. Basic network features are included, but some security functions are omitted. It is designed for new PC-network users who will self-install their system. Typical installation takes a few hours and allows application, file, and printer sharing. Personal NetWare is somewhat compatible with NetWare 2.2. Peer-to-peer LANs are more fully discussed below.

NetWare 2.2

NetWare version 2.2 is for small- to medium-sized businesses and workgroups in larger firms. Small networks can use a nondedicated 16-bit server, while medium-sized shops would run best in dedicated mode. Internetworking, fault tolerance, and network management are included for up to 100 users, but TCP/IP support is not. Packages are available in 5-, 10-, 50-, and 100-user sizes. Migration to the next level of NetWare is not too difficult, but the relative price of NetWare 2.2 compared to 3.1X makes NetWare 3.1X a better buy, even if all its features are not needed.

---

[4]Novell may be reached at (800) 873-2831.

*NetWare Lite has been replaced by a newer and more refined product called Personal NetWare.

NetWare 3.1X and 4.X

At the higher end, NetWare 3.1X is a full-featured 32-bit NOS supporting 5, 10, 20, 50, 100, or 250 users, depending on the package purchased. There is a special NetWare 1000 version for up to 1000 users.
DOS, Windows, OS/2, Unix, and Macintosh workstations via AppleTalk
are all supported. The maximum disk storage is 32 Tbytes (*trillion
bytes*). Will that do?

Most recently, Novell introduced its enterprise-wide NOS, NetWare
4.X. NetWare 4.X's chief feature is its NetWare Directory Services,
which provides for the seamless traversing of an enterprise-wide network. Another major feature is the SFT III (see Chapter 5), which
allows real-time duplexing of servers. NetWare 4.X supports the automatic transfer of data to near-line and off-line storage.

NetWare 4.X also includes a number of refinements from NetWare
3.1 such as packet signature security to verify the authenticity and
source of a message. Another refinement, packet burst mode, adapts
IPX for more efficient transfer of large amounts of data through WANs.
Most importantly, NetWare 4.X contains the all-important management tools needed to administer an enterprise-wide LAN.

Common NetWare features

All NetWare systems share some common features:

Except for Personal NetWare, they all have a multitasking, mul-
tithreaded kernel. NetWare servers are truly multiuser, and their
performance improves under load. (NetWare takes over as its own
operating system in the DOS environments.)

NetWare sorts incoming read requests in order based on the disk
head's current position. This *elevator seeking* greatly reduces head-
seek times.

We have already mentioned that NetWare has disk caching. Large,
often-read blocks of data are stored in memory for faster access.

Disk writing takes a back seat to disk reading. Writes are saved in
memory and written to disk during reading lulls. This is called *background writing*.

NetWare can seek on several disk channels at once. This keeps all
the disks busy instead of forcing one disk to be idle when the other is
active. You will hear this feature referred to as *overlapped seeks*.

NetWare uses the standard disk *file allocation table* (FAT) to locate
data on network hard disks. Files larger than 2 Mbytes cause the

FAT to be indexed (TurboFATs), allowing NetWare to search it quickly and so improve the speed of disk reads.

Every disk write is then read and verified as readable.

The root directory structure is duplicated in RAM. The copy ensures file access if the directory structure is corrupted.

Similarly, FATs are duplicated in RAM. A contaminated FAT does not render a disk's data inaccessible.

The hot-fix feature detects disk defects and stores data elsewhere on the fly. This is not implemented in Personal NetWare.

SFT includes disk mirroring, disk duplexing, and transaction tracking. (SFT and Transaction Tracking System (TTS) are not implemented in Personal NetWare.)

In the client, the *Open Data [Link] Interface* (ODI) allows third parties to write NetWare drivers for their NICs.

Security.   Security is a principal feature of the NetWare server itself. It is not implemented in the workstation. NetWare's proprietary file structure prevents access via DOS, OS/2, Unix, or any other operating system.

NetWare imposes its own security even on a privileged operating system user. For example, a superuser Unix system administrator still cannot access NetWare files without NetWare authorization.

NetWare security includes:

Account security

Password security

Directory security

File security

Internetwork security

User names and passwords are well-understood security mechanisms. But Novell introduced the concept of a user profile, which lists the resources a user account can access and the rights it has while using the resource. A supervisor can dictate the date, time, and location from which a given user can access the network.

NetWare includes intruder detection and a lockout feature to inform a supervisor of improper access attempts. Passwords are encrypted on the network hard disk and on the cable. A supervisor can require users to change them periodically.

A student at the University of Leiden breached NetWare 3.11 security. The program, HACK.EXE, watches IPX data packets traveling between a NetWare server and a workstation. Registering the details in the packets, it then forged packets to the server as if it were the workstation. The server, not knowing the difference, gave the "spoofer" program the workstation's rights. HACK.EXE even allowed spoofing of the network supervisors' security rights.

This weakness has been patched by Novell in an NLM called *NetWare Core Protocol* (NCP) Packet Signature. The software patch adds an 8-byte digital signature to an IPX packet. The signature indicates who sent the packet, as would a signature on a letter. The server validates the signature and then grants rights as stored in NetWare's bindery. Since the signature is different for each packet sent, according to a pattern known only to the workstation and server, the packet cannot be spoofed.

Administrators can configure servers to initially accept both authenticated and nonauthenticated packets, then move to a fully authenticated system. A NetWare utility called WSUPDATE lets administrators install new client software that modifies the client shell across the network from a single server. The effect on performance is said to be negligible.

While the breach occurred in NetWare 3.11, NetWare 2.X is equally susceptible. The same fix method will apply although the exact software will be different.[5]

File access rights, secure network console operation, and encryption are all strengthened in NetWare 4.X, including packet signature and frame encryption.

Any data access must pass through NetWare security. Therefore, access through a nondedicated server is not a back door route of entry. The user must log in regardless of location. This applies regardless of the workstation type or operating system. Even NLM's pass through NetWare security user profiles or as determined by the NLM application.

Operating system support.   NetWare is a cross between a proprietary product and industry standards. Novell supports the following operating systems in workstations for file service:

DOS, Windows, and OS/2

Apple Macintosh System 7

Sun Microsystems Solaris

---

[5]Those needing further information can call Novell at (800) 638-9273. The patches are free.

For client-server service, NetWare supports:

DOS-, Windows-, and OS/2-based clients

Macintosh OS and Unix as client platforms

OS/2, Unix, DEC's VMS, and other operating systems through licenses with *original equipment manufacturers* (OEMs) as server platforms

Even though client and server operating systems may be different, client-server applications use *interprocess communications protocols* (IPCs) to link client to server. NetWare supports the following:

Sequenced Packet Exchange (SPX)

IBM NetBIOS

IBM *Advanced-Program-to-Program Communications* (APPC), also known as LU6.2.

Microsoft's Named Pipes

AT&T's *Transport Level Interface* (TLI) library

Berkeley Software Distribution (BSD) sockets library

Communications standards.   Communications standards are divided by Novell into media, data transport, and client-server protocols. In terms of the physical media, NetWare supports more than 100 different types of network adapters (NICs). Supported data transport protocols include:

Novell's IPX-SPX

Apple's AppleTalk

Standard TCP/IP

Standard OSI data transport protocols

Workstation connectivity.   Novell supports file and print services for OS/2, Macintosh, and Unix workstations. OS/2 workstations run as clients on a NetWare network using NetWare Requester.

NetWare for Macintosh 3.0 is client-server software that resides in the server and provides NetWare file, print, and routing services to Macintosh workstations. Under NetWare 3.1X, Macintoshes are supported via NLMs. Similarly, Macintosh support in NetWare 2.2 runs as a VAP.

NetWare's *Network File System* (NFS) allows Unix workstations to run as clients on NetWare 3.1X. Actually, NetWare NFS consists of several NLMs that add NFS server capability to the NetWare server. The server can share files between NFS and other NetWare clients and print to NetWare printers.

Database services. NetWare offers two database products: Btrieve and NetWare SQL (*structured query language*), and supports third-party databases such as ORACLE as well.

Btrieve runs on the server. It is a key-indexed record manager designed to provide efficient data handling. Btrieve is the de facto LAN record management system and has been used by many developers.

NetWare SQL allows direct access to Btrieve from various desktop platforms and/or applications. Since NetWare SQL relies on Btrieve for data handling, applications written to either one can share data with the other one.

Messaging. *Message-Handling System* (MHS) was originally created by Action Technologies in the mid-1980s. Novell bought MHS in 1991 for use with NetWare.

NetWare Global MHS runs as an NLM. It uses network resources only when receiving or sending messages. MHS can connect to ITU-TSS X.400, IBM PROFS, Unix systems, DEC All-In-1, VMS Mail, MCI Mail, Western Union's (WU) EasyLink, telex, fax, and voice mail. MHS is supported by more than 600 application, gateway, and utility developers.

NetWare Messaging CONNECT links NetWare MHS-driven applications on NetWare LANs to IBM mainframe and midrange messaging products. This gives mail access to users of SNA networks and the LAN.

Bound by the bindery. As Figure 12.3 illustrates, NetWare 2.2 and 3.1x servers contain a *bindery,* a naming system for recording users, disk resources, and printers *by server.* The bindery requires the administrator to manage each server individually. Similarly, each user communicates with each server separately, through a separate login script.

For a user to have access to several servers, the administrator must create a user profile on each server to be used and grant the user access. Users must log on to each server separately (up to eight concurrent sessions are allowed in 3.1X). This is cumbersome for both users and the administrator, and is the big reason why VINES administration is easier than NetWare 3.1X in multiserver networks.

Banyan has in fact capitalized on this weakness in NetWare by offering its StreetTalk naming system repackaged as a NetWare NLM called *Enterprise Network Services* (ENS). Administration in VINES and NetWare 4.X is now comparable.

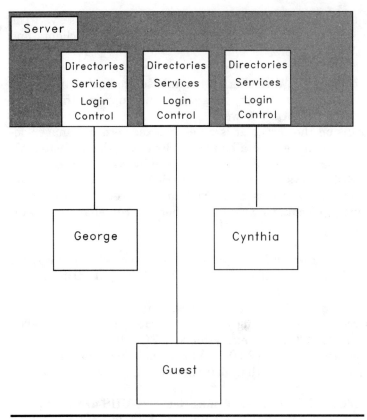

Figure 12.3 The NetWare bindery concept.

If a printer or file volume is moved from one server to another, every affected user's login script may need to be changed. You can see how complicated this can get. In 1990, Novell grouped a set of utilities together, called *NetWare Name Service* (NNS), to alleviate (but not solve) the problem. NNS copies bindery information to all the servers in a domain. While NNS automates bindery management, it does so for disk volumes and printers only. It is not a global directory as is StreetTalk.

Discussion

NetWare has excellent interactive capabilities on small- to medium-sized LANs. Its client memory and hardware requirements are modest. NetWare optimizes server performance by virtue of its caching and delayed write features. It supports multiple protocols and has fine print service (up to 16 printers) and security features. As the most popular NOS, thousands of third-party programs exist and support is ubiquitous.

Entry-level NetWare 3.1X can run on a 386SX with 4–6 Mbytes of memory, but larger user groups (over five or so) will need a full 32-bit 386 with 6 Mbytes of RAM or more.

NetWare's architecture is shown in Figure 12.4. The figure shows how NLMs can be plugged into NetWare, even on the fly. NLMs communicate with TCP/IP, AppleTalk, OSI TP4, and NetWare's own IPX-SPX. Complete applications, such as ORACLE, Ingres, and Sybase can be run as NetWare NLMs.

NetWare 3.1X had difficulty in meeting growing enterprise-wide LAN connectivity needs. Three problems, however, chipped away at the sterling performance of NetWare 3.1X as a local LAN:

1. It lacked an internal global naming service and network management.

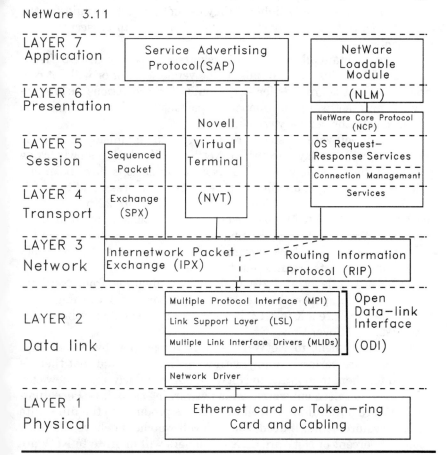

Figure 12.4 NetWare: layer by layer.

2. TCP/IP tunneling to connect servers degraded performance.

3. It required a small packet size.

These issues are addressed in NetWare 4.X. A ITU-TSS X.500-like directory service, internal management, and full routing under Net-Ware using WAN-streamlined protocols make NetWare 4.X very competitive at the enterprise level.

Some observers consider NetWare too pricy, but many users disagree. Taken as a whole, over 90 percent of NetWare customers would recommend it to others.

A vendor who quotes an unusually low price may be selling a bootleg copy of NetWare. Isolated LANs with the same NOS serial number will not experience problems until someone calls Novell for support or unless one NOS is linked up with another NOS with the same serial number. Then operation stops and a warning appears.

Purchasers are legally liable if they cannot prove they paid for the software. Novell has demonstrated its willingness to prosecute copyright violators.

Be sure to obtain all the original diskettes, especially GEN.DATA or SERVER.EXE, plus the manuals. If the vendor cannot or will not provide them, that is grounds for suspicion. Other protections include receiving new software in unopened packages and registering the software with the vendor *yourself.*

Since four software versions are an ordeal to administer, it is likely that Novell will one day discontinue NetWare 2.X, which is slowly losing popularity but is widely installed. Novell's intentions have been signaled is various ways: unofficial hints to the trade press, addition of 5- and 50-user versions of NetWare 3.11 so that NetWare 2.X users would not have to upgrade to 100-user NetWare 3.11, and simplified upgrade tools in NetWare 3.12 to make migrating easier. They are needed because the two versions have incompatible file structures. Add-on applications and products are different between the versions, too.

NetWare 3.12 is basically a maintenance upgrade from NetWare 3.11. It includes packet burst, packet signature, and the migration tools from NetWare 2.X to 3.12. It also includes some 80 patches made to NetWare 3.11 over time.

The enhancement to NetWare 3.11 is recognition by Novell that many users are perfectly happy with what they have and that there is no need for them to upgrade to NetWare 4.X. Similarly, many new customers will not need enterprise-wide networking capability. Perpetuating NetWare 3.XX allows Novell to tailor its products to the full strata of NOS requirements. Indeed, some Novell-watchers believe that only about 10 percent of NetWare 3.1X customers will migrate to NetWare 4.X.

The enterprising NetWare 4.X

These shortcomings were addressed with the introduction of the long-awaited NetWare 4.X. NetWare 4.X is the first enterprise-wide NOS from Novell.

Since NetWare 4.X is object-oriented-based software, there will be a big learning curve as the NetWare community relearns NetWare from scratch. Being aware of this, Novell has conducted an aggressive training campaign to get the latest information into the hands of its training organizations. For the most part, consultants and integrators have been satisfied with the quantity and quality of the training.

The centerpiece of NetWare 4.X is its *NetWare Directory Services* (NDS). NDS is

Hierarchical	Up to 15 tree layers let the software match the hierarchy of a large organization. However, as in large organizations, the number of layers can become cumbersome to administer and may prevent access to users who do not know their full directory string.
Distributed	Each server in the network maintains all or part of the management database. One change causes all the servers to be updated.
Replicated	Saving part of a directory across several servers protects against local outages. NDS contains a synchronization mechanism to keep them in step.

NDS is based on the ITU-TSS X.500 directory services standard.

NetWare 4.X includes SFT III, which allows server duplexing. If one server fails, the other picks up the load transparently to the users (see Chapter 5). This feature is available for NetWare 3.1X as well.

On-the-fly disk compression saves disk space in servers and is invisible to the user. In another innovation, installation directions come on CD-ROM. While this makes it easier to find information, migrators to NetWare 4.X will need a CD-ROM reader before installation can proceed. Also, recognizing the vulnerability of WAN links to tapping, on-line encryption is offered.

Planning the installation, especially with respect to directory structure, is absolutely mandatory. At present, once a directory is named, the name cannot be changed. The paper-and-pencil upgrade approach that Novell espoused has been widely criticized. For an upgrade of this magnitude, thorough knowledge, a strategy, and automated tools are a necessity. Doing things in the wrong order or incorrectly can result in an unwieldy system at best or irretrievable data loss at worst. The devil is in the details!

WAN performance is enhanced by NetWare 4.X's use of sliding windows. IPX normally routes packets in 512–1500-byte chunks, expecting an acknowledgement for each one. In burst mode IPX, multiple packets are sent before acknowledgement, up to 64-kbytes at once (see Chapter 10). Novell is also modifying IPX to accept larger packet sizes (up to 16 kbytes) on 16-Mbit/sec token rings.

Burst mode IPX is also available for NetWare 2.X and 3.X. A new version of NetWare Shell, BNETX.COM goes in the client. (Novell now recommends DOS Requester.) It takes an additional 6–8 kbytes of RAM. An NLM goes in the server. Burst mode-equipped devices are compatible with unequipped ones.

NetWare 4.X will not work with NetWare 2.2 or 3.1X seamlessly. While NetWare 4.X will include bindery emulation to let NetWare 2.2 and 3.1X servers communicate with the directory, those services cannot be accessed or managed by NDS. All servers have to be using Net-Ware 4.X for that feature.

If server duplexing is not essential, consider using Banyan's ENS for NetWare, discussed below. It combines Banyan's powerful directory services with all the features of NetWare 3.1X, including NetWare support and third-party programs. ENS is even available for NetWare 4.X.

Why do this? The chief reason is that ENS brings all NetWare versions under a single directory. As mentioned above, NetWare 4.X presently provides bindery emulation in NDS but not true integration.

The old-think logic of upgrading just to stay current, or worse, just to stay up with the Joneses, is bankrupt when considering an upgrade to NetWare 4.X. If it is really needed—fine. Otherwise, assuage yourself with a NetWare 3.12 upgrade if you must.

To stay current with developments in NetWare, various subscription publications are available. These can be useful both for current LAN administrators and those seeking information for acquisition purposes.[6]

Banyan's VINES

Overview

VINES is also intended for large, multiserver enterprise networks. Banyan's VINES makes using multiserver resources simple through its own global directory service, StreetTalk (see Figure 12.5). It has fine between-sites security, reliability, and interoperability. VINES (SMP) can fully realize the power of multiprocessing hardware platforms such as the Compaq SystemPro or ALR PowerPro DMP. However, the application itself must support multiprocessing as well.

---

[6]For those who are serious about NetWare, contact The Cobb Group at 9420 Bunesen Parkway, Louisville, KY 40220 and ask about subscribing to their monthly journal, *Inside NetWare*. It is aimed at NetWare administrators.

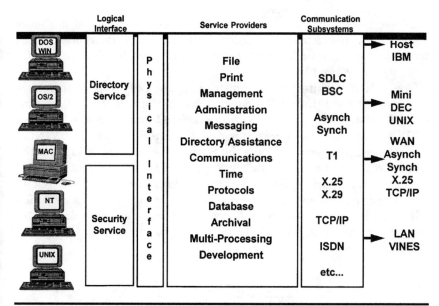

Logical Interface		Service Providers	Communication Subsystems	
DOS WIN		File		Host IBM
	P h	Print	SDLC	
OS/2	Directory Service	y s	Management	BSC	Mini
	i c a l	Administration Messaging	Asynch Synch	DEC UNIX
MAC		Directory Assistance Communications	T1	WAN Asynch
	I n	Time	X.25	Synch X.25
NT	t e r	Protocols Database	X.29	TCP/IP
	Security Service	f a c e	Archival Multi-Processing Development	TCP/IP ISDN	LAN VINES
UNIX			etc...	

Figure 12.5 VINES services. (*Courtesy of Banyan, Inc.*)

Be sure to check for hardware compatibility if you are considering using VINES. VINES lacks the hardware ubiquity of NetWare. For instance, VINES server software supports Proteon 1990 cards, but its client software does not. In VINES 5.0, the Compaq *Intelligent Drive Array-2* (IDA-2) card is supported. The IDA card lets eight disks look like one 4-Gbyte drive, but VINES will not support it. Instead, two 2-Gbyte drives must be created.

VINES excels in server-to-server communication performance. Large packet sizes and sliding windows make volume transmissions quick and efficient. The down side is that it is slower than others in client-server exchange. Periodic flushes of the cache force incoming client transactions to go directly to disk, resulting in a temporary slowdown of the server.

Considering its capability, VINES is reasonably priced and is certainly not overpriced. Its disadvantages include less market penetration (7 percent) with less third-party support and fewer Certified Banyan Engineers around than CNEs. It is also too much for a small-to medium-sized LAN, especially if the LAN is not internetworked. However, if internetworking is a looming possibility, then it makes sense to look at VINES.

VINES' large packet sizes favor bulk data transfer applications as opposed to interactive exchanges. Being Unix-based, "DOS heads" will have to make a transition, although once they are in VINES, they will not have to deal with Unix. The platforms that are needed are more powerful and hence more expensive. An enterprise network also brings WANs into play, an unfamiliar area for many, but this would be true for any internetworked NOS.

The VINES architecture is shown in Figure 12.6. Applications have two ways to get into VINES: via the *NetRemote Procedure Call* (NetRPC) and then to *VINES Interprocess Communications Protocol* (VIPC) or through the *Server Message Block* (SMB). Note that VINES' own file and print services take the SMB route. Instead of VIPC at the transport layer, these services use *Sequenced Packet Protocol* (SPP).

The network driver for NetWare is *Open Data Interface* (ODI); its VINES equivalent is the *Network Driver Interface Specification* (NDIS), which was written by Microsoft. Banyan supplies drivers for most LAN adapters, but this is something to verify before purchase.

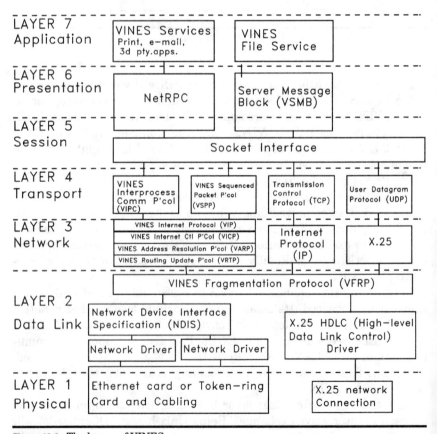

Figure 12.6 The layers of VINES.

Both VIPC and SPP use NDIS, making it possible to use several protocols at once. These layers add flexibility but cost more time than their NetWare equivalent in the client-server exchange. The problem is compounded by Unix' file-handling system, which is reported to be better in VINES 5.X.

VINES features

Client support. Banyan ships client shells for DOS, OS/2, Windows, and Macintosh System 7. You can stay in Windows while attaching to a server. For Macintoshes, the VINES Option for Macintosh is needed in the server when VINES 5.X is running and costs about $2000. Installation of VINES is reported to take about an hour after the necessary drive formatting is completed. Macintoshes can use the power of StreetTalk without giving up the Macintosh's user interface.

Print management capability in VINES is about equal to that of NetWare. Jobs can be deferred, killed, or moved to a different queue.

Global naming. The centerpiece of VINES is StreetTalk. Every server has a copy of the StreetTalk database, and the servers update each other periodically. The database contains:

The name, location, and attributes of every user and resource

Shared volumes, printers, lists, and nicknames

Host gateways and installed third-party software throughout the network

In an all-VINES network, naming is easy (see Figure 12.7). To link to other LANs, Banyan plans to link StreetTalk to ITU-TSS X.500 Directory Services software as a gateway to other NOSs such as NetWare. Another avenue for linking to NetWare is via Banyan's *ENS for NetWare,* a Banyan NLM that links StreetTalk to NetWare.

ENS for NetWare. ENS for NetWare runs on a separate, dedicated server and provides directory, security, and management services. It is logically connected to NetWare 2.X, 3.X, and 4.X servers through a VAP (2.X) or NLM (3.X and 4.X), respectively. Physically, it is connected to the same network. The ENS server can also be equipped with messaging and SNMP management for servers in its domain containing SNMP agent software.

Recall that each NetWare server contains a *bindery.* ENS for NetWare maps the bindery to a StreetTalk directory. StreetTalk is then used to manage the network. When a user is added or deleted, the

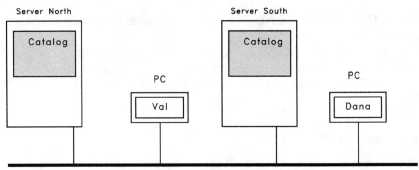

Catalog Content for Server "South":   Catalog Content for Server "North":

Server South @ Mfg @ Widget   Server North @ Mfg @ Widget

Val @ Mfg @ Widget   Dana @ Mfg @ Widget

Catalog entries are not duplicated.

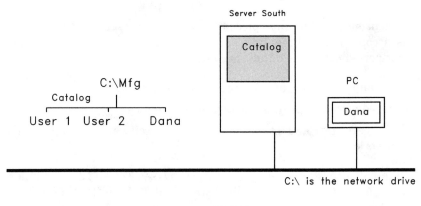

Catalog Content:

Server South @ Mfg @ Widget
Mfg @ Mfg @ Widget

Figure 12.7 VINES global naming via StreetTalk.

change is made in StreetTalk, which then updates all the affected ENS for NetWare binderies.

ENS for NetWare has several advantages. It can be applied to NetWare 2.X, 3.1X, and 4.X. Equipped with messaging, ENS offers an integrated directory for files, print, and messages, which is presently more than NetWare 4.X can offer.

Comparing ENS and Novell's NDS. ENS runs 3 tree-levels deep compared to NDS' 15 or more levels. However, ENS is not as widely distributed as NDS where a server failure may cause a partial outage.

StreetTalk is an established product, being over 10 years old. On the one hand, the bugs are out, but on the other hand, its roots go way back. For example, VINES' directory interface is not graphic whereas NDS' directory interface is graphic. However, NDS is brand new and will surely go through its own shakedown period.

ENS has updates from several servers sent to a "collector." The collectors then send the data to a central "master." The master then updates the network. NDS partitions the NDS database and replicates parts of it throughout the network as determined by the network manager. The location of the replicas should match the users as closely as possible. In this way, the partition used locally can be kept local, reducing traffic overhead.

NDS cannot presently merge directories. What this means is that if two individual departments move to NetWare 4.X, one set of directories cannot be merged into the other. Also, at present, NDS cannot search for more than one attribute at a time, whereas StreetTalk can perform multiattribute searches.

There are a few disadvantages to ENS. NetWare 4.X includes server duplexing, which ENS does not address. ENS also requires a separate server. The NDS interface is graphical, but ENS' is text-based. Lastly, Banyan has not fully disclosed its service and support plans for ENS.

Security. In an enterprise network, security is important. VINES' VAN Guard has the usual passwords and rights, but intrinsically, it authenticates a user's identification through StreetTalk before doing anything significant. This prevents the spoofing problem to which NetWare proved vulnerable. Encrypted passwords cannot be used by a spoofer to start a server session.

Like NetWare 4.X, encryption of traffic on the LAN or WAN medium is supported. This feature negates the value of data compression by routers or stand-alone compressors of VINES traffic.

Reliability and fault tolerance. VINES has good reliability, but it supports only disk mirroring and not disk duplexing. With external software, file services can be mirrored onto a separate server. If the first server dies, it uses the second server. Printer and name services cannot, however, be mirrored.

Network management. VINES network management is rather basic. VINES contains a utility called MNET for management. MNET links to SNMP manager devices through VINES SNMP Proxy Agent Option.

This makes VINES an agent that can be queried by a management system such as Cabletron's Spectrum or Hewlett-Packard's OpenView.

Banyan's market strategy.	Banyan has about 7 percent of the NOS market. Considered a high-technology company, the firm had suffered because of its "techie" image. That has changed.

NCR markets and supports VINES. Other AT&T organizations are expected to push VINES, too. ComputerLand stores, and there are over 600, offer VINES. DEC also resells VINES, at odds with its own Path-Works.

The small versions of VINES, 5-, 10-, and 20-user packs, appeal to smaller departments who still need enterprise-wide networking. Yet Novell has substantially reinforced its internetworking capability, stepping into VINES' turf. Now Banyan is doing the same thing to Novell at the low end—they hope.

It seems as though Banyan and Novell are adopting each other's strategies. Novell has strengthened its enterprise-wide networking, while Banyan has gone to resellers. Novell has made some fine alliances with other vendors, while Banyan has allied itself with DCA to gain IBM 3270 connectivity and ported VINES to Santa Cruz Operation (SCO) Unix. Other alliances are supposed to be coming.

One clear strategy of Banyan's is to link all those NetWare systems through VINES. You can see evidence of that strategy in ENS for Net-Ware.

VINES and Unix.	VINES runs on its own optimized, proprietary version of Unix. VINES is also capable of running on SCO Unix. Decoupling VINES from the operating system means that applications supported by "standard" Unix will be supported by VINES. The downside is some performance loss.

VINES on open Unix versus NetWare on Unix are different in that VINES is already Unix, so no functions are lost in porting VINES. In NetWare 4.X, not all the functions of NetWare will run successfully in a Unix environment. Running VINES on standard Unix costs more and more attention must be paid to its administration and performance, whereas running NetWare on Unix affects NetWare's functionality.

Speaking of administration, *Business Research Group* (BRG) of Newton, MA, surveyed 400 Fortune 1000-size corporations. Users said that VINES was quicker and easier to administer than other NOSs. According to BRG, VINES personnel costs were under $20,000/year network, LAN Manager was over $20,000/year network, and pre-NetWare 4.X was over $30,000/year per network. The cost difference is mainly attributed to centralized administration via StreetTalk.

In order to add to the openness of its NOS, Banyan has recently started publishing *Applications-Programming Interfaces* (APIs). Functionally similar to NLMs, APIs make it possible for third-party developers to write applications and utilities for VINES, such as management and fault tolerance. Trellis and Vortex are two such developers working on management and fault tolerance, respectively. Two mail-enabled vendors, Reach and Beyond (now owned by Banyan), offer their products for VINES. Even Lotus has gotten into the act. Banyan is again duplicating Novell's successful path.

Banyan has moved away from classical direct sales to reseller marketing. In 1992, Banyan created three reseller levels, much like Novell's Gold and Platinum reseller program.

Summary. In summary, the strengths of Banyan VINES are:

StreetTalk Distributed Directory Service

Approximately 23 VINES integrated services, e.g., token-ring bridging

Superb WAN connectivity

The Unix kernel

VINES' interoperability with other NOSs, e.g., NetWare

VINES' support for OSI and open systems

For those who need to track VINES closely, there are several periodicals and services available.[7] See Table 12.2 for advantages and disadvantages of VINES applications.

IBM's LAN Server

This LAN NOS deserves to be mentioned because it has about 6 percent of the market. It is IBM's *OS/2 LAN Server.*

LAN Server had an odd beginning. It evolved from Microsoft's LAN Manager 1.0, originally a core architecture that Microsoft licensed to others, including IBM. Microsoft later developed LAN Manager into a full-blown NOS.

IBM promised to make LAN Server compatible with applications written for LAN Manager. However, with the breakup of the collaboration between IBM and Microsoft, this never happened.

The distance that developed between Microsoft and IBM led IBM to

---

[7]Contact Wellesley Information Services at 112 Mayo Road, Wellesley, MA 02181. Their telephone number is (617) 431-7073. They publish VINES Observer, VINES Technical Bulletin, and VINES Past Bulletins Library.

TABLE 12.2 VINES Applications Profile

Advantages	Disadvantages
VINES is found in very large systems.	There are many NetWare hardware platforms and far fewer VINES platforms.
It can be used for widely dispersed networks.	More third-party software has been written for NetWare than for VINES.
It is useful where the focus is on open systems.	Support for NetWare is easier to locate and obtain than for VINES.
	Some customers are drawn by Banyan's symmetrical multiprocessing. However, the hardware must exist and the applications, presently few in number, must support VINES.

embrace NetWare in February, 1991, after having introduced LAN Server in 1989. Today, NetWare gains about 5 percent of its revenue from IBM sources.

IBM has intensified its commitment to LAN Server by introducing LAN Server 3.0, intended to run as a server on OS/2.X. LAN Server 3.0 will finally provide the Macintosh support that was promised when IBM hooked up with Apple in 1991.

Why pick LAN Server over NetWare? IBM claims that it has no internal preference. The say that customers who know what they want make the choice based on the following:

Experience with one or the other. If a customer knows NetWare, that tends to be their choice, and vice versa.

Experience with one set of applications or the other. LAN Server 2.X runs on OS/2 1.3 in the server, and LAN Server 3.0 runs on OS/2.X. Some applications require LAN Server.

Factors such as price, the balance of performance versus application, and specific functions such as Macintosh support which LAN Server 2.0 did not offer, but LAN Server 3.0 does.

Large-scale philosophical differences such as distributed processing versus shared resources, a general-purpose system versus a server-tuned system, an open NOS versus a proprietary NOS, platform service consistency versus platform-specific services, and integration versus interoperability.

LAN Manager and LAN Server look and feel the same, but there are differences in some functions. The similarities are due to their both originating from Microsoft LAN Manager 1.0.

IBM offers both advanced and entry-level versions of LAN Server. The advanced package includes a *High-Performance File System* (HPFS) and customized device drivers to speed up network file *input/output* (I/O) operations. It also has disk mirroring and duplexing. The entry-level package lacks HPFS and fault tolerance. It can, however, be run in nondedicated mode, i.e., as both a server and a workstation.

Clients can run OS/2 1.3 or 2.X, DOS, or Windows 3.X. The upgrade of LAN Server in the server to OS/2.X includes asymmetrical multiprocessing. LAN Server 2.0 and 3.0 support both token-ring and Ethernet LANs. Drivers are NDIS.

LAN Server can manage not only user accounts but also files, applications, and printers on different servers throughout the *domains,* which are subdivisions of the network. *First failure support technology* (FFST) is a way to trap and record error data. Alerts can be set and routed to LAN Network Manager or NetView.

Graphically, LAN Server claims better support for Windows applications than for LAN Manager. The presence of the OS/2 Presentation Manager *graphical user interface* (GUI) for utilities and other features enhance LAN Server's ability to manage and use big networks.

LAN Server is a NetBIOS-based LAN, as you would expect. That makes it unroutable unless it is encapsulated in TCP/IP or another similar protocol.

LAN Server is for those committed to OS/2 and for those who wish to purchase from IBM. Its performance is rarely evaluated in the trade press but is probably behind NetWare's performance.

Microsoft's LAN Manager

Microsoft's LAN Manager, also known as "LANMan," has come up in the world. It performs best with large files, and some reports show it edging out the speedy NetWare. In addition, it has good global-naming capabilities, but not as good as VINES' StreetTalk. The overall performance of LANMan is between that of NetWare and VINES (Table 12.3).

LAN Manager requires OS/2, which is LAN Manager's real problem, because Microsoft is abandoning OS/2. Microsoft has already announced that LAN Manager will be ported to Windows NT, but when is another question. In effect, OS/2-based LAN Manager is a product among the walking dead.

The current LAN Manager 2.2 handles multiservers well. The price for 10 users includes a copy of OS/2.

As mentioned above, Microsoft has announced LAN Manager for Windows NT. The main question is, "How do you upgrade?" The upgrade path is obscure, to say the least.

TABLE 12.3 NOS Performance by Application

Application	NetWare 3.1X	VINES 5.X	LAN Manager 2.2
Data entry	Best with up to 60 users (first)	Even with LAN Manager (tied for second)	Even with VINES (tied for second)
E-mail	Uniformly the best (first)	Slightly worse than LAN Manager above 20 users (third)	Slightly better than VINES (second)
Imaging	Slightly poorer than VINES (third)	Slightly better than NetWare (second)	Best (first)

Another complication is a growing industry trend: Microsoft has built networking into Windows NT and Windows for Workgroups. Why buy an NOS when it comes free in the operating system? (The answer is to obtain more functions.)

The best reason to select any Microsoft product is the Windows environment. There are three worthy Microsoft networking products to watch: Windows for Workgroups, Windows NT, and LAN Manager for Windows NT.

Networking products

Windows for Workgroups. Windows for Workgroups is DOS-based and can be used as a peer-to-peer or client-server NOS. Windows for Workgroups is also the client support element of LAN Manager and Windows NT, and includes file sharing, e-mail, and a group scheduler.

The File Manager lets users get to other local disks and LAN Manager servers. Using the Print Manager, users can print on workstation- or server-attached printers. Simple DOS workstations can access Windows for Workgroups servers but cannot act as servers.

Windows for Workgroups works with NetWare (IPX is supported), LAN Manager, and Windows NT, and has simpler installation and NIC configuration routines. However, Windows for Workgroups is clearly on a par with LANtastic, PowerLAN and Personal NetWare.

The NOS' options include remote access, tape backup, and the ability to use TCP/IP. Password encryption is standard, and security at the directory level but not the file level is supported. Once allowed into a directory, the user has access to all its files.

Windows NT. Functionally, what does Windows NT do? What can it do that LAN Manager for Windows NT cannot?

Under the basic Windows NT, clients and servers are limited to one security domain. Each NT server maintains its own rights, even if several NT servers are connected. The current NetWare operates in a similar fashion.

Windows NT servers will be limited to DOS, DOS Windows, NT Windows, and OS/2 workstations. Macintosh client support is expected. On the plus side, Windows NT will include:

Multiple redirectors to get to several networks at once

NetBEUI and TCP/IP transport protocols

TCP/IP client utilities, including Unix' *File Transfer Protocol* (FTP) and virtual terminal program Telnet (a TCP/IP terminal emulation program)

An SNMP agent for manageability

Networking services will include:

File and print server software from LAN Manager

Both client and server configurations for peer-to-peer and client-server connections.

Administration tools for Windows NT and any LAN Manager servers

LAN Manager for Windows NT. This is the large-scale solution for segmented networks. Security is centralized in servers. Thus, NT workstations ordinarily used in Windows for Workgroups as peer-to-peer devices can gain access if they logically exist in the server. But the lack of a global directory, network management, and communications software will limit acceptance of the product, at least until these features become available.

Discussion

Windows for Workgroups will most likely be used in Windows peer-to-peer applications. Because of its current lack of client support, LANtastic and other peer-to-peer NOSs will remain popular for a long time, especially since LANtastic 5.X supports Windows.

Windows NT with built-in networking has the same client problem. Clients today come in all flavors, not just DOS and Windows. Windows NT will work well as a server operating system, but it lacks many features found in standalone NOSs. The fact that networking is free will erode part of the low-end market, but Novell is not going out of business any more than is Artisoft.

LAN Manager for Windows NT presently lacks features, global naming and network management for starters, we have seen are mandatory in enterprise-wide networks. Without communications accessories and third-party software and support, LAN Manager for Windows NT will be, for a time, several steps behind NetWare 4.X, ENS for NetWare, and VINES. Table 12.4 is a comparison of basic functions of NetWare, VINES, and LAN Manager.

It is ironic that LAN Manager in its present form is a good product and that its successor will take a long time to reach the same degree of refinement. And all because of a non-Windows operating system, OS/2, that is not really relevant to a NOS. The fact, however, that LAN Manager's roots are in OS/2 means that its Microsoft days are numbered.

DEC's Pathworks

Like IBM, DEC fought the LAN rush with its DECnet and VAX. DEC, however, lost. Like IBM, DEC turned to Microsoft for help, but it was too late. The result was a set of products for LAN support collectively called Pathworks. Despite Pathworks' origins in LAN Manager, LAN Manager client software cannot run with a Pathworks server, or an IBM LAN Server, for that matter.

TABLE 12.4 Comparing NOS'

Parameter	NetWare	VINES	LAN Manager
Group size	Small to large 20–250 users	Larger groups of over 20 or so	Larger groups of 25–200
Site(s)	Single site	Multiple sites	Single site; not routable; flexible configurations
Fault tolerance	Disk mirroring; disk duplexing; hot fix; UPS	Disk mirroring; third-party disk duplexing; UPS	Disk mirroring; disk duplexing
Performance	Best in small, simple configurations; quick client-server response; small file transfers to 30 kbytes and under 50 users; more files read than written	Excels in multi-server enterprise networks; Good client-server response; larger files; excels in server-server transfers	Global naming capability (but poorer than VINES); good client-server response (NetWare is better); fastest in 20–100 users with 80 kbyte-sized files; strongest deferred disk writing ability good for applications with many writes; good for imaging or high bandwidth applications

As we said earlier, DEC sells NetWare and LAN Manager, too. NetWare is now included in the Pathworks package. However, these are "completer" products sold through DEC's system integration activity. They are not core DEC products.

DEC built a number of network application services titled *Network Application Services* (NAS). DEC licensed Windows NT from Microsoft and began building Windows clients. But the applications still run on VAX servers.

One exception is that DEC plans to port Windows NT to its new Alpha processor. Pathworks and NAS will run on that new platform. However, Windows NT contains many of the services now incorporated in NAS and Pathworks. Once again, why pay extra for the same services?

DEC has plans to metamorphose Pathworks into a true enterprisewide networking tool. Pathworks will be extended to add multivendor system support, asset management, automated backup, and support for the *Distributed Computing Environment* (DCE). DEC has committed to supporting the DCE despite the fact that most of its submissions were rejected as excessively proprietary by the Open Software Foundation.

SNMP, the management protocol, will also be supported. In fact, one of Pathworks' strengths is that it presently supports a wide variety of transport protocols, including DECnet, TCP/IP, NetBEUI for LAN Manager or LAN Server, and AppleTalk.

To help users get around in Pathworks, "navigation" tools will be added to assist users in finding resources. APIs will be added to help in the development of new applications.

Formerly, Pathworks license fees were based on the number of clients. The latest scheme is based on a maximum number of concurrent users per server. This allows occasional Pathworks users, of which there may be many, to have economical access.

When all is said and done, Pathworks is essentially a closed hardware architecture, based on DEC VAX and DECnet, although a server version exists for 386 and 486 PCs running SCO Unix. As a single-source solution, it is fine, and Pathworks has enjoyed a measure of success. But if you need interoperability and integration of clients, servers, and networks in a distributed environment, then Pathworks may not be the best choice.

The Big Picture

In selecting an NOS, first look at your needs: security, scalability, etc. Second, understand the NOS market. Read not just one NOS evaluation article, but many, and there are many. Know where the vendors are coming from and where they are going. What is their market strategy? If your direction is not the same as theirs, look elsewhere!

Third, look at the features. Do they support the clients you have? Are they an enterprise-wide NOS or a local one?

Fourth, pick *one* NOS that can grow with your evolving needs. Applications do not port well from NOS to NOS. Rewriting applications for the second to *n*th NOS is an expensive and wasteful duplication of effort.

That duplication extends to managing several NOSs. *Managing the LAN is its biggest hidden cost,* estimated at roughly *three times* the expense of an equivalent SNA network. Having to train users and support each one is yet another invisible cost. Few organizations can really afford to support several different NOSs at once, although many shops do, at great and redundant expense. See Table 12.5 for costs of various NOSs.

Peer-to-Peer LANs

Let us say this is all much too complex. You do not need all this horsepower, and you cannot afford a LAN expert. Yet you still want a LAN. What are your options?

One is to build a "zero-slot" LAN, using external adapters that plug into parallel ports, e.g., printers. Connect the adapters with 10Base2 coaxial cable or unshielded twisted pair. It is not even necessary to open the workstations' covers. Performance will be less than an ordinary LAN, but it is quick and easy.

Next, purchase a peer-to-peer NOS such as Personal NetWare or LANtastic. The cost is low: typically, it is $99 a workstation. What you get will be a good basic system for sharing files and printers, and perhaps e-mail, plus security. That is about it.

Peer-to-peer implies no dedicated server. Workstations also act as servers in the sense that they share files as do servers. Workstations can share certain files yet not others; they may also act only as workstations or only as servers. The point is that a *separate* server machine is not required. For example, Windows for Workgroups and LANtastic can work with or without a server.

Do not hire a LAN expert. The documentation and installation utilities will do if you are patient. Once running, ongoing administration tasks will be minimal.

Xircom (Calabasas, CA) sells its Ethernet-parallel port adapters and Novell's simplified peer-to-peer Personal NetWare as a package called Network Simplicity. Running on Ethernet ThinNet, Network Simplicity includes two copies of Personal NetWare, automated installation software, the cable, and e-mail software from Notework (Brookline, MA.)

TABLE 12.5 Some Comparative Prices*

NOS	5 users	10 users	20 users	50 users	100 users	250 users	Other features
NetWare 4.X	1395	3195	4695	6295	8795	15,695	500 users: 26,395 1000 users: 47,995
NetWare 3.11	1095	2495	3495	4995	6995	12,495	Router: 995 Naming service: 1995
NetWare 2.2	895	1995	—	—	—	—	SNA gateway: 2995
Personal NetWare	99	99	99	—	—	—	Maximum of 50 users
LAN Manager 2.2	1995 plus 65/ work- station	—	—	—	—	—	Unlimited license: about 18,000 Maximum number of clients per server: 256
VINES	1495	2495	3995	8495†	—	—	IP routing: 1995 Unlimited SMP: 13,995 TCP/IP: 3995 Unix support: 7495 SNA gateway: 1495
AppleShare 4.X	—	—	—	—	—	—	Supports up to 150 clients 1899 per server
LAN Server	—	—	—	—	—	—	Advanced: 2295; upgrade from 1.0, 1.2 or 1.3: 1570 Entry: 795; upgrade from 1.0, 1.2 or 1.3: 300 Per Client: 75

*Prices are in U.S. dollars and are subject to change.
†Unlimited.

Other vendors offer zero-slot Ethernet and/or token-ring adapters, but so far only Xircom and Ansel Systems package an NOS with it. On paper, Personal NetWare supports up to 50 users, although a more realistic figure is about 25. Specifics about these two vendors are listed at the end of the chapter.

The disadvantages of a zero-slot LAN include an inability to upgrade to WAN support or to customize, poorer performance relative to a standard NIC, and sometimes tying up a parallel port. The chief advantages are low cost, minimal administration, e.g., no network addresses to set, good basic file and print services, and often e-mail.

A peer-to-peer LAN

Is DOS-based and is incapable of multitasking.

Usually has no dedicated server: All the workstations can act as servers.

Is usually Ethernet-based, but it may be totally proprietary.

May or may not be NetBIOS compatible.

Has streamlined security.

Peer-to-peer NOS advantages

A peer-to-peer NOS has the following advantages:

Support for basic functions such as e-mail and file and print sharing is common.

Directory and connectivity options may be present.

Very little client RAM is required.

It lacks a single point of failure.

No expert and almost no administration is required.

It may coexist with a server-based LAN. Here the peer-to-peer NOS is used within a workgroup and a server-based LAN for internetworking. This mode of operation is becoming increasingly popular.

It is low in cost: typically, $250 per workstation, including hardware and software.

Peer-to-peer NOS disadvantages

A peer-to-peer NOS has the following disadvantages:

There is limited accessories and client support, especially for Macintoshes, OS/2, and Unix.

The number of absolute and concurrent users is typically limited.

Peer-to-peer NOS is a real "isLAN." It does not migrate well to a server-based NOS, nor does it connect very well to a host, e.g., DEC-, or IBM-based machines, or to a WAN.

Remote dial-in, bridging, or higher-layer protocols may not be supported.

Few if any fault tolerance features, such as UPS support, are found. On the other hand, no server means no central failure point.

Hard disks can be shared. Sharing can have serious security implications, especially in corporate and government environments.

Error logging, diagnostics, and remote booting exist only in high-end peer-to-peer NOSs.

Directory services are not usually found in low-end peer-to-peer systems.

Good uses for a peer-to-peer NOS

These include:

For basic file and print sharing services

Offloading a server-based LAN

For workgroups, departments, and remote offices

At the department level in a large organization

Is a peer-to-peer LAN right for you?

Here are some factors to weigh:

Do not look at where you are today. Look 2 or 3 years out. Will you need outside connectivity? Will you need access to other environments and services? How about future clients?

Do not overestimate either. You might pay for more than you need. NOSs become obsolescent quickly.

Some applications are poor peer-to-peer applications, especially databases. Most database management systems are server-based.

Consider how you would migrate to a server-based network one day.

Anticipate that you might have to start over with a server-based LAN. But if you can get 3 years' use from a peer-to-peer NOS, why not do it?

Think about security. Most peer-to-peer NOSs can restrict file and directory access, even though the client is also a server.

The price should not be the deciding factor; function should be the deciding factor.

Selection criteria

Peer-to-peer NOSs should be selected based on the following criteria:

The LAN access method: Ethernet, token ring, ArcNet, or proprietary method.

The services, e.g., e-mail or print and file sharing. For instance, Novell Personal NetWare and Sitka do not include e-mail.

The maximum number of clients. The range is from 15 users and up.

The client types that are supported and are planned on being supported.

The client RAM requirements. Less is needed if there is only one client, but more is needed if both a client and a server are present. Memory requirements may range from 2 to 120 kbytes.

The operating system: DOS (which version?), DR-DOS, or Windows.

LAN NOS features, including disk caching, error logging, on-line redirection of disks and devices, e.g., printers, dynamic node reconfiguration, remote and/or diskless booting, global resource naming, and remote diagnostics.

Security features, including password expired, audit trail, restricted logon, and access privilege control.

The sharing of modems, tape drives, etc.

Connectivity options and plans.

Hardware and cabling bundling software.

Support, warranty, and price.

Two peer-to-peer NOSs

LANtastic has about 6 percent of the NOS market share, a much greater amount than Personal NetWare's approximate 2 percent. We review LANtastic first and then NWL to give a sense of the available products, what to look for, and what to be wary of.

LANtastic. Supporting all the above features except error logging and dynamic node reconfiguration, LANtastic is a high-end peer-to-peer NOS. LANtastic is made by Artisoft of Tucson, AZ, and came on the market in 1982.[8]

LANtastic 5.0 supports up to 500 nodes per network and costs $659 for a two-node starter package that includes hardware and DOS software. The Windows version costs $100 more and uses the same NIC hardware. It is also available in four additional languages: French, German, Italian, and Spanish.

Add-on kits consisting of client software plus an adapter card and

---

[8]Artisoft may be reached at (800) 846-9726.

cost about $260 for a single-user version and up to to $2900 for a 12-user version. *Adapter-independent* (AI) NIC single-user licenses are $120. LANtastic 5.0 runs on 16-bit 80286 machines and up.

Artisoft NICs are inexpensive but are required if Ethernet NICs are not used. They can run in a NE2000 mode and are compatible with NetWare. Artisoft proprietary NICs run at 2 but not 10 Mbit/sec. AI software (LANtastic/AI) is reported to run slower than Artisoft NICs.

Internetworking. "Bridged redirectors" let LANtastic clients access another network through redirector software installed in a NetWare client. Redirectors exist for access to NetWare, Unix NFS, OS/2's HPFS, and non-LANtastic drives such as fax servers, CD-ROMs, and *write-once-read-many* (WORM) drives. The drive connections are simply defined as shared resources.

LANtastic for NetWare and LANtastic for TCP/IP are LANtastic client shells that sit above NetWare or Unix shells, respectively. They give clients peer-to-peer LANtastic connectivity plus NetWare and Unix server-based connectivity. Installed on a LANtastic server, they can bridge LANtastic users to NetWare or Unix servers.

Both connections can be maintained at once. In fact, the LANtastic side will keep running even if the NetWare server fails, making LANtastic a backup option. Using both is also a way to reduce server congestion, employing LANtastic for e-mail and file exchanges which do not require the server. LANtastic for NetWare requires Novell's NetBIOS emulation and costs about $400.

We will shortly see that Personal NetWare also uses a NetWare shell to access a NetWare LAN. This shell-on-shell approach can be a memory constraint in the client, especially if an old version of DOS only allows the client access to 512 kbytes of memory. The NetWare approach forces you to log off one in order to log into the other.

Artisoft's LANtastic for TCP/IP is most important for connectivity. This product gives LANtastic instant connectivity to Unix-based and DEC machines, to name a few, equipped with TCP/IP. The product runs on a LANtastic workstation and it communicates via terminal emulation with remote hosts using TCP/IP. This allows it to access Hewlett-Packard, Sun, DEC, and IBM systems, as well as printers, files, and applications.

Developed jointly by Artisoft and the Wollongong Group, the software supports the usual TCP/IP protocol suite: Telnet, FTP, NFS, and *packet internetwork groper* (PING). The station can emulate a variety of DEC and IBM terminals.

The other mode of operation is to load LANtastic for TCP/IP on a single dedicated machine and let it act as a TCP/IP server. As a server, it claims support of up to 255 simultaneous users. LANtastic for

TCP/IP costs about $300 per node, so the TCP/IP server approach is a way to spread around the cost.

LANtastic 5.0 encapsulates NetBIOS messages, using Novell's IPX for routing. LANtastic also supports Microsoft's *network device interface specification* (NDIS). Remote access via dial-in is optionally supported by LANtastic.

Electronic mail. LANtastic 5.0 includes built-in e-mail. However, it does not support the *Simple Mail Transfer Protocol* (SMTP), a de facto (but not very good) standard for transferring mail. The integrated mail feature cannot be used if e-mail must be meshed with other SMTP e-mail systems. Instead, a separate SMTP-compatible application must be used and run over LANtastic.

Management. Management is simple but extensive. This peer-to-peer NOS allows all network accounts to be set up from one station on a single server or workstation, and remote access allows an administrator to "take over" a user's screen remotely. Remote server management is also supported.

As in enterprise-wide NOSs, clients can gain access to global resources through a single logon. LANtastic 5.0 supports both DOS and Windows, including sound.

Bulk data jobs may be sent to designated servers after working hours. Delayed printing is also supported. Network print jobs may be spooled onto a single server, yet printed anywhere in the network at a prespecified time. LANtastic's *central station* option is a hardware docker to link resources such as printers and modems to NetWare or LANtastic LANs.

Security is very granular and extends down to the file level. Up to 12 security levels are supported. LANtastic, along with Tiara's 10Net (listed later) offer the most security options.

Client support. LANtastic supports DOS and Macintosh clients with LANtastic for Macintosh. PCs and Macintoshes can share files and printers on a LANtastic network. The product was codeveloped with Miramar Systems of Santa Barbara, CA from their own MacLAN Connect software.

LANtastic for Macintosh costs $799 for the software, LocalTalk adapter, and cabling. The software alone is $599. OS/2 and Windows NT support, LANtastic for OS/2 and LANtastic for Windows NT, respectively, is under consideration.

Market positioning. LANtastic's success pushed Novell into creating Personal NetWare. The implication is that the two are head-to-head competitors. That is not literally so.

NWL contains no e-mail and supports 25 users. LANtastic has

e-mail and supports 500 users per network. While NetWare 2.2 runs faster than LANtastic, recent releases of LANtastic have narrowed that gap. LANtastic is less expensive and has very good connectivity options, better than most peer-to-peer NOSs.

The average number of LANtastic nodes has been 6, but now some users are running as high as 100 nodes. Up to 5000 files in all the workstation and servers can be open at once.

Personal NetWare (NWL). NWL costs $99 a node, the same as LANtastic. It is also a peer-to-peer NOS, but it supports only 25 users. (Beyond 10 users, NWL begins to slow down and beyond 20 users, NetWare 2.2 is cheaper.)

Uniquely, it supports DOS, Windows, and OS/2 on both client and server platforms. For instance, NWL supports Windows by executing a simple *MS/Network compatible* command. NWL also supports both IPX and NetBIOS protocols, and, optionally, TCP/IP.

To work simultaneously with NetWare 2.2 or 3.11, you must run NETx.COM and then log into the server as noted earlier. The program comes free with NetWare 3.11 or 4.X. NWL supports adapters that work with Novell's ODI. Nine such drivers are included.

NWL, unlike higher NetWare versions, has no UPS recognition and does not support remote booting. A floppy or hard disk in each machine is required to run the software.

Rebooting a server causes users to disconnect. When asked by DOS to "Abort, Retry, Fail?", they reconnect by answering R. Some users find this disconcerting. However, network connections are automatically restored after a power surge or outright power failure.

The manual accompanying NWL is very readable, and has a choo-choo train analog to explain how LANs work. (We hope you will not need it.)[9]

NWL has a variety of flexible print options. One would expect this since printer sharing is a primary reason to buy a peer-to-peer NOS.

Security in NWL is similar to that used by higher versions of NetWare. Accounts can be created, enabled, and disabled. Supervisor privileges can be granted. Password lengths and expiration dates can be set. To simplify matters, default access rights can be set by directory. Then users can specify who will have nondefault rights. File-level security is not provided.

NWL has audit trail capability. Passwords, but not data, are encrypted.

---

[9]Technical support for NWL is via fax (900) NETWIRE or from your dealer.

NWL is copy protected through the network. The workstation client communicates with other clients to see if the same software identification number is installed. If it is, the systems freeze. NWL has no internetworking or routing capability or support, but does support up to 25 multiple servers.

As noted earlier, e-mail and a group-scheduling utility are not included. However, remote access and tape backup utilities are available.

DOS 5.0 can load all but the server into high memory; QEMM or 386Max can load it all into high memory if a 386 machine is used. Up to 635 kbytes can, thus, be used for applications.

Speedwise, NWL is fast and certainly comparable if not better than other peer-to-peer NOSs in its class. Novell suggests considering NetWare 2.2 as the number of users approaches 10 even though (on paper) NWL supports 25 concurrent users.

The NOS market outlook.   It is clear that NetWare 2.2's reason for continued existence is becoming questionable. The emphasis will shift to Personal NetWare and NetWare 3.1X and 4.0.

Novell plans to include peer-to-peer networking features in server-based NetWare. NetWare users can then share resources and files, and exchange messages without going through the server. Personal NetWare users will be able to communicate with server-based NetWare clients, as described above, and improve Windows GUI interoperability. The new client software will also permit peer-to-peer links through NetWare routers, not presently possible in Personal NetWare.

Personal NetWare and Personal NetWare will compete with Microsoft's Windows for Workgroups. However, Windows for Workgroups has e-mail whereas NWL does not.

With so many NOSs out there, there are nagging concerns about management and security, especially when clients are able to access several different NOSs simultaneously using multiple shells.

New client software is supposed to include extra management features, some of which are based on an API being developed by the Desktop Management Task Force. Novell is a member of this consortium. Under this plan, files and resources can even be delivered to mobile or transient users.

Some consultants feel that product development in NOSs is too narrow. For example, Windows for Workgroups works only with Windows. A NOS really needs to work across all the operating systems and environments. NOS vendors seem to be working toward that.

Indeed, the big picture is that the NOS, regardless of vendor, is becoming the distributor of all services throughout a network. Recognizing the need, some vendors are building network capability into their operating systems, particularly Windows NT.

On a smaller scale, Novell DOS 7.0 also contains peer-to-peer capability, as Apple machines have for some time.

Some observers prophesize that one day the entire NOS function will be absorbed into the operating system and NOSs will cease to exist as a recognizable entity. This presumes that the operating system can provide the needed functions at a reasonable cost and within reasonable memory and disk constraints, and can equal the flexibility that stand-alone NOSs have shown. Furthermore, those not needing a NOS' functionality will be paying a premium for a function they will not use.

There is a head-to-head competition brewing between the NOS-in-the-operating system makers and the peer-to-peer NOS vendors, as their functions are roughly the same. If the former does to the latter what the peer-to-peer NOS makers did to the server-based NOSs, then the peer-to-peer NOS folks will see the low end of their market erode as well.

Are LAN lightweights, whether peer-to-peer NOS or NOS-based, a small-scale answer? The answer is a qualified "Yes." They have obvious limitations that clearly restrict their applications. Yet they are easy to purchase, install, and maintain. They find themselves in law offices, consulting firms, and venture capital firms. They are in departments of large corporations and in hospital research laboratories.

Most interestingly, peer-to-peer NOSs' can underlie server-based NOSs to provide workgroup connectivity and offload servers of bulky file transfers and cycle-stealing e-mail messages. No one could have foreseen that peer-to-peer NOSs would one day complement the application they set out to replace. But that is happening.

We conclude the chapter with a listing of peer-to-peer and "starter-kit" LAN vendors. Where possible, we have included what is known about them. In the next chapter, we discuss LAN costs and the relative expense of the approaches discussed in this chapter.

Vendors

Peer-to-peer LAN vendors

Artisoft, Inc.
Tucson, AZ
(800) 846-9726
LanTastic
Considered a high-end peer-to-peer NOS.
Offers a SpecDisk on request.

CBIS, Inc.
(404) 446-1332
Network OS-Plus
Supports Ethernet, token ring, ArcNet, etc.

Hayes Microcomputer Products, Inc.
(404) 840-9200
LANstep
Requires up to 110 kbytes RAM.
Includes hardware.

Invisible Software, Inc.
(800) 982-2962
Invisible Network

Moses Computers, Inc.
(408) 358-1550
MosesAll!, PromiseLAN, and
ChosenLAN.
Low-end peer-to-peer NOS.

Net-Source Inc.
(408) 246-6679
SilverNet
Ethernet and ArcNet versions.
Includes hardware.

Novell, Inc.
(800) 638-9273
NetWare Lite v1.1
Low-end peer-to-peer NOS.
Wide client support.

Performance Technology, Inc.
(512) 349-2000
PowerLAN 2.20
Tested very fast by *Byte.*
A high-end peer-to-peer NOS.
Wide client support.
Resold by Datapoint.

Sitka Corp.
(800) 445-8677
DosTOPS, SunTOPS, and *Mac-
TOPS*
Basic security.
OpenTOPS should add wide client
support.
Based on Tiara's 10NET.
For AppleTalk-Ethernet only.

Tiara Computer Systems, Inc.
(415) 965-1700
10NET LAN OS V5.0
High-end peer-to-peer NOS
Very good security.
Includes hardware.

Webcorp
(415) 331-1449
Web NOS V3.0
A high-end peer-to-peer NOS.
Highly compatible with NetWare.
Does data compression on the cable.
Supports Ethernet, token ring,
ArcNet, etc.

LAN starter kits

Ansel Communications
(408) 452-5041
Packages NetWare Lite with 16-bit
external Ethernet interfaces, cables, and an instructional video.
Supports 2–25 PCs.
Price for two PCs: $599.
Additional PCs: $299 each (includes
hardware and software).
Portable PC connection: $399 each.
24-hour technical support.

Kodiak Technology
(408) 441-6900
External LAN Adapter.
Does not include a NOS, but does in-
clude NetWare ODI drivers.
Built-in power supply.
List price is $399.

Xircom
(800) 874-7875
Network Simplicity.
Packages NetWare Lite with its
own adapters.
Includes automated installation
and e-mail.
Expander Packs add PCs.
PPX packs add printers.
Also offers token-ring external
adapters.

Chapter

13

Determining Your
LAN Requirements

In this chapter, we bring together all the LAN components we have
discussed to help you form a cohesive purchasing and implementation
strategy. Bear in mind that this is not just for new LAN users only but
also but for those who are adding or extending their LANs.

Assessing User Needs

What you *think* your users need and what they *really* need can be two
different things. This can be a major trap. *Do not let your preconceived
notions determine your direction.*

One of the wisest things you can do is *poll your users*. Ask them what
functions they want, *not* which software or whose PC. Your task is to
uncover the functions they need. Then you can turn that into hardware
and software.

Another way to get input is to *conduct focus groups* or *brainstorming
sessions*. They can bring out some unexpected but very real needs. An
existing users' group and/or a help desk are also certainly a logical
source for input.

Getting input gives you the opportunity to control the acquisition. It
is in your organization's interest to *standardize on one or a few products* rather than to buy what everyone wants.

A limited inventory of products will get you volume discounts and
focus your support rather than spread it too thin. It also reduces training needs and helps ensure file-format and data compatibility throughout the organization.

Do not try to prevent users from acquiring another software package. The best you can do is make sure they can translate a file into and out of the format used by your standard software. However, export and import utilities are often imperfect and are always an obstacle.

If you decline to support the user's software package(s) that is often enough to discourage the user from pursuing this path. They should, of course, scan for viruses before they load their own software.

Consult your users regarding where to place equipment such as printers. What is convenient for them may not be obvious to you.

The more user input and involvement you have, the greater the likelihood of acceptance. No one likes having a fait accompli stuffed down their throat.

A matter of scale

Given the option, start your LAN small, as a pilot trial, with a small workgroup of say 10 people. Pick some individuals who are already computer literate plus a few novices and one or two power users. Their different perspectives should reflect your user community in microcosm.

Do not pick a critical operation, e.g., one that is on-line with customers. You *know* there are going to be problems, so it is wise to limit their impact. As you build your LAN, management will be watching. A highly visible disaster while you are on the learning curve will banish the LAN forever and perhaps you with it.

The same applies to internetworking. Hold off on it until your LAN is stable. Then you can add links to the outside without wondering if it was the bridge or the network that caused the network to crash.

By now you have a fairly comprehensive understanding of the options available to you. Your circumstance is one of the three below:

1. You have no LAN at all. You are in the best and worst position. The up side is that you have the chance to start with a clean slate and build it right from the ground up. You have the latest technology to work with. The down side is that you have not had the benefit of a LAN, and you have a big learning curve ahead of you.

2. You have a LAN that provides basic connections, e.g., e-mail, file transport, and basic applications. Installed on a shoestring, it may well lack the cable speed, server capability, and applications development environment needed to support mission-critical applications that are the next logical step. Your advantage is that you have some LAN experience, and you may be able to reuse parts of what you have already.

3. You are that rare company that planned their LAN for growth. You have more LAN cable speed and server capability than you pres-

ently use. You have an applications development path with trained programmers open to you. This might seem to be the best position, but the industry moves so quickly that even the most foresighted planner may be caught short.

On balance, though, this is the best position to be in. You have had the benefit of a LAN, and the steepest part of the learning curve is behind you. The industry will never be static. If you waited for that, you would never buy anything.

Those who start with a basic-connection LAN usually paint themselves into a corner. The day inevitably comes when a mission-critical application needs to be added. The result is like a twelve-car pileup. The workstations need to be upgraded. The LAN's line speed, okay for file transfers, becomes too slow for a real-time transaction-processing application. The database may be inadequate. Worst of all, there may be no real way to develop the desired applications within your current environment.

Alternatively, the preplanning folks may have overbuilt everything and selected a development environment suitable for the needs of the firm and the LAN environment. Their biggest exposure is that the high-powered, expensive technology they bought a few years ago has come way down in price. Much of it may even be obsolete.

The procrastinators may well be in the best slot. They start with the clean slate and take advantage of the latest and greatest in technology. They did not find the classic printer sharing justification for a LAN sufficiently compelling, but now a mission-critical application has come along. They can build a harmonious system, matching hardware, software, and servers into a symbiotic system. The problem, if it is one, is that they have no past experience to draw upon.

Telemarketer Company Z took the "wait-and-see" approach. They had grown their business with a combination of minicomputers and rented time on a mainframe. In the late 1980s, it became clear that the existing systems were too expensive and inflexible to keep up with their evolving needs.

Company Z studied the options. The LAN approach was appealing, but before making a full-scale commitment, they installed a prototype system. It worked. When they learned that the time to install a full system was only a few months, they decided on the LAN approach.

Today Company Z's system runs on a token-ring network with NetWare 3.1X. There are multiple servers and 60–200 386-based workstations. The database is CA-Clipper. It provides high-speed transaction processing yet contains the management tools to acquire valuable marketing data for Company Z's customers.

The system incorporates computer-integrated telephony. Originated by the network, a call goes out through the *telephone switch* (PBX). The computer record appears on the screen as the call goes through. The representative interacts with the network as the call proceeds.

Call verification is a must in telemarketing. Its purpose is to verify that the representative really did sell the item in question. Verification is best done from another call center by a different manager. To support this, a WAN links the call centers together. After verification, the result is returned to the originating center.

In the end, the full range of LAN capabilities were available to Company Z because they waited until the technology was well-developed before taking the plunge. They wound up with a well-harmonized system capable of growth and expansion.

Selection methods

Whenever you have a large variety of factors to consider, a matrix is the selection tool of choice. A sample matrix is shown in Table 13.1.

You may have already made some vital decisions. You may have to use existing cabling. Your application may require token-ring redundancy. Your environment may be multi- or single-server, or internetworked or not—or maybe in the future it will need one of these features. If these decisions are not self-evident, the matrix is the way to resolve them.

Some companies offer interoperability testing such as Interlab (Sea Girt, NJ) or the University of New Hampshire testing laboratory. The ultimate in "try before you buy," interoperability testing is a good strategy in complex or untested setups.

Specifications and Attaining Them

Estimating your traffic loads

Traffic estimation is a chicken-and-egg problem if you have no existing LAN. Most LANs running at 4 or 10 Mbit/sec will handle 10–20 users easily.

Response time is not a problem in file transfers but becomes critical in transaction-driven systems like those of Company Z above. If you must design a LAN to meet specific performance criteria, then using a design tool is appropriate.

Design tools model the behavior of a LAN under a given load. They allow you to get an accurate picture of a LAN's performance given a certain number of users, applications, and internetwork links.

Some tools include application profiles that give estimates for traffic in, for example, Microsoft Windows or in a database environment. They may also have user libraries that contain performance profiles for various pieces of equipment, such as bridges and routers. These can be

TABLE 13.1 Sample Matrix

Evaluation factor	Weight	LAN A	LAN B	LAN C
File and print services				
Workgroup e-mail				
Integrated and self-contained				
Easy to install, manage, and use				
Applications compatibility				
Reliability needed				
Ease of use by neophytes				
Risk factor(s)				
Cost-effectiveness for scale of use				
Login security				
Upward scalability				
Migration path				
Management tools				
E-mail interconnections				
LAN support skill base				
Security flexibility				
Enterprise-wide e-mail				
Applications built on e-mail				
Network management; diagnostics				
Internetwork capability				
Enterprise-level security				
Fault tolerance				
Development environment				
Total score				

plugged into the model without doing a lot of research and are a reasonable estimate of the device's throughput, delay, etc.

Design tools are not inexpensive. But if you need an engineered network, the cost of failure far outweighs that of the tool. A partial list of vendors is found at the end of the chapter.

Testing metrics

If you have an existing LAN, you can probably get reports from the *network operating system* (NOS) vendor as to the amount of traffic the NOS can carry. Many NOS run these as *value-added processes* (VAPs) or *NetWare loadable modules* (NLMs). Another traffic source measuring tool is a LAN analyzer such as a Network General Sniffer or a LANalyzer. Sniffers and LANalyzers can record traffic and through a utility, plug the information into a design tool.

If you do not care to part with $20,000 for a Sniffer, consider software emulation packages that monitor networks from a PC. Vendors can be found at the end of this chapter.

LAN traffic simulation packages generate actual LAN test traffic. By varying the size and frequency of the traffic, the effect on the LAN is measured.[1]

A simple way to make traffic is to generate a 1-Mbyte file on the server for each client. Have each station read a 10-kbyte block from the file and then randomly write a 10-kbyte block back to the file. The read to write ratio should be about three-to-one as in real life.

It is also possible to configure a single client to act as several clients. Progressive deterioration of LAN performance can be gauged as a function of client activity using just a few PCs. As a rule of thumb, one client can simulate up to 25 workstations.

Availability

Most estimates of LAN availability, in the 94 percent range, are pitiful. That is a far cry from the 99.9-plus percent availability figures that are typical of mainframe systems.

A study [2] of 100 Fortune 1000 companies showed that the average LAN is disabled about twice a month for an average of 5 h. Over a year, these outages cost them (as a group) nearly $3.5 million in lost productivity and over $600,000 in lost revenue.

Despite these losses, companies spend less than $60,000 a year for LAN maintenance, less than one-tenth of what they spend in LAN performance upgrades—over $650,000. There is also a clear positive correlation between increased size and frequency of failures.

Not surprisingly, the failure rate of LAN owners who had a protocol analyzer was only two-thirds that of nonequipped owners. Their failure periods were also shorter by about one-half hour each.

The need for availability is easily assessed. What happens if the LAN goes down? Do people just revert to "sneakernet," or does the business come to a screeching halt?

---

[1]Advertisements for traffic generating programs often appear in LAN Times, LAN Magazine, Network Computing, and Corporate Computing.

[2]"The cost of LAN Downtime," September, 1989. The study was commissioned by Network General (manufacturer of a LAN analyzer) and performed by Infonetics, Inc.

The study cited three principal costs:

1. Lost productivity caused by idle workers
2. Lost revenue caused by business going elsewhere
3. The direct expense of support needed to keep the LAN running

Your assessment of the importance of availability affects the following:

The choice of access arrangement. A token ring has the advantage.

The choice of server hardware. You may need redundant features.

The choice of mass storage, such as a *redundant array of inexpensive drives* (RAIDs).

The *uninterruptible power supply* (UPS) selection: What kind and for how long?

The NOS selection: Do you need disk and/or server mirroring and/or duplexing?

The backup selection.

The availability of support personnel, maintenance contracts, pagers. (Some servers will page you, e.g., Compaq.)

LAN Costs Assessment

Hardware and software take between 20–40 percent of the actual network's cost. The balance goes toward installation and ongoing support.

Estimate that you will spend $370–400 per workstation, including hardware and software, beside the cost of the station itself. This figure includes the cost of wiring.

If external adapters are used, i.e., a "zero-slot" LAN, opening the PC is unnecessary. All the necessary tables are set up. Installation is intuitive and mostly automatic. External adapters work both with server and peer-to-peer NOSs.

A peer-to-peer LAN will cost 25–30 percent of a full-scale LAN but is hard to expand. Peer-to-peer LANs are fine if you need nothing more such as internetworking or serious redundancy.

The cost of a peer-to-peer NOS software is about one-tenth that of a full-blown NOS. Administration is also minimal, requiring 5–20 percent of an administrator's time. While being skilled in DOS is necessary, becoming a dedicated expert is not required. Most peer-to-peer LAN owners rely on their vendor for support in the form of a maintenance or service contract. Be sure your reseller is certified by the manufacturer to service, train, and support your peer-to-peer NOS.

Administration is the biggest hidden cost of a LAN. A full-time technical support staff person will cost about $45,000 per year in salary plus $23,000 in benefits. Typically, one full-time support person is needed for every 40–100 users. (The range varies dramatically, depending in part on the environment's sophistication, user's skill levels, required availability, topological layout, and need for internetworking.)

Training always gets short shrift. Plan on recurrent training at least once a year for the administrator and for at least one person to back up the administrator.

It is becoming more common to remotely control a LAN internetwork from a central network control center, especially since the wiring hubs are often *Simple Network Management Protocol* (SNMP)-equipped. The effect is to reduce the number of highly trained administrators in the field.

Often support has devolved to the help desk as the user's first line of defense. The lack of face-to-face contact is a weakness of both strategies.

To remedy this, key LAN operators or printer administrators have been increasingly designated as first-line support people. These are already-existing employees who take on the additional task of basic LAN assistance. This diversion from their primary job is justified by the added productivity gained by the group. Table 13.2 lists recurring and nonrecurring LAN costs. Table 13.3 compares features of various cables, including *unshielded twisted pair* (UTP) and *shielded twisted pair* (STP) cables. Table 13.4 compares cable costs. Table 13.5 compares the costs of served-based LANs versus zero-slot LANs.

The Installation Process

Having decided on the media access method, is there cabling you can use? *If in doubt, ring it out.* Map each user location. The use of a wiring hub is strongly recommended.

Purchase UTP Level 5 if possible. It will adapt to any foreseeable speed or technology upgrade. This strategy does not limit your future options.

Use a cabling contractor with LAN experience. *Have another contractor check their work.* Remember than 80 percent of the problems in LANs are cable-related.

There have been many horror stories about LANs that ran intermittently because of incorrect AC wiring such as missing third-wire grounds or reversed hot and cold sides. Prevent these problems by using a licensed electrician to run the AC drops.

Document! Buy a cable management package, e.g., Microtest's CMS among many others, and use it from the start. You cannot run a LAN of any size without one.

TABLE 13.2 LAN Cost Factors

Item	Nonrecurring factors	Recurring Factors
NICs and PROMs	X	
Client software	X	
Cabling (see Table 13.4)	X	
Hubs*	X	
Server	X	
RAID	X	
UPS	X	
Backup	X	
NOS	X	
Networkable application licenses	X	X
Utility software	X	
NLMs or their equivalent	X	
Training		X
Installation of cable, client, server, and application	X	
Cable testers	X	
LAN analyzer	X	
Preventive maintenance contracts		X
Telephone support contracts		X
Off-hours support, including PC, documents, pager and compensatory time or overtime	X	X
Dial-in and dial-out toll charges, e.g., remote or fax		X
Leased-line charges for bridged or routed networks		X

*Hubs are not necessary, and they cost $100 and up per port.

Install the necessary NICs and software in server and client machines. This will require disassembly, physical installation, configuration setup, and testing. Software drivers must be installed. Memory managers may be needed to free low RAM space. If you are using a server, install the NOS on it. This will require a configuration setup, changing defaults, and setting user privileges. Today, the installation is highly automated, so this is not the problem it once was.

When all is said and done, you may have spent as much as $5000 per user!

TABLE 13.3 Cable Comparison Chart

Property	UTP	STP	Coaxial	Fiber	Wireless*
Common application	Hub network; lobe wiring	Token-ring networks	Small IEEE 802.3s (under 50 nodes)	Building or campus backbones	Temporary or often-changed networks
Cost per foot	X	2–5 X	3–5 X	4–6 X (plus hardware)	Not applicable
Bandwidth	Level-5 data grade: 100 Mbit/sec	To 500 Mbit/sec	1 GHz	1 GHz (for multimode)	S/S: <2 Mbit/sec; RF: <15 Mbit/sec; IR: <16 Mbit/sec
Maximum distance in typical application	100 m at 10 Mbit/sec	100 m at 16 Mbit/sec	600 m at 10 Mbit/sec	2 km at 100 Mbit/sec	Varies whether it is S/S, RF, or IR: generally 15–245 m
Noise immunity	Poor	Good	Better	Best	Good
Adaptability	Very good	Good	Fair	Poor	Excellent
Advantages	Low cost	Reliable	Cost per bandwidth	FDDI support†	Ability to adapt
Disadvantages	Not very noise resistant	Costs more than UTP; performance not that much better	Cable problems of all kinds	Its cost	Its cost; limited bandwidth makes it slow

*IR = infrared; RF = radio frequency.
†FDDI = fiber-distributed data interface.

TABLE 13.4   Comparing Cable Costs*

Medium	Cable size and type	New installation cost
Level-2 UTP (unshielded DIW)†	Four-pair and PVC jacket	60
Level-4 UTP (data grade)	Four-pair and PVC jacket	65
Level-4 STP (data grade)	Four-pair and PVC jacket	85
Coaxial	One cable	75
Multimode fiber‡	Single pair and PVC jacket	425

*The table estimates the average installation cost in U.S. dollars for a horizontal 100-foot run of cable types. Costs include cable, hardware, and labor. Figures vary depending on local labor expenses plus the total cable runs installed as part of a project.

†DIW = direct inside wire.

‡Fiber costs include terminations plus *optical time-domain reflectometer* (OTDR) testing of the cable. These tests produce graphs which indicate whether the cable is good and if defective, how and where. OTDR graphs should be saved for later reference as a baseline of cable performance.

Transition Issues

Early period

As a principle, it is wise to put the same applications and user software on the LAN that your customers had in their standalone PCs. It minimizes "transition anxiety." Add new packages later. Some administrators put games on the LAN at first to encourage people to use it. That is a fine idea.

Build and publish an implementation plan. Add applications gradually, one at a time, with the simplest ones first. Not only does it give people time to adapt, but you can gauge the effect on the system. Unanticipated interactions may not show up for weeks after installation.

TABLE 13.5   Costs of Server-based and zero-slot LANs*

	Server-based LAN			Zero-slot LAN		
	20†	10	5	20	10	5
Installation	1400	1500	1700	420	430	450
Yearly cost to run	2600	3300	3600	500	500	500
E-mail (optional)	650	700	750	Added	‡	‡
Total cost	4650	5500	5050	920	930	950

*Costs in U.S. dollars.

†Number of users.

‡Some peer-to-peer NOSs, such as LANtastic, include e-mail, but others, such as NetWare Lite, do not. Some NetWare Lite package vendors include e-mail at no cost.

Make haste slowly. *Document (log) every change to the system.* Otherwise, you will have no way to relate cause and effect.

Try to make as many needed changes as possible before allowing the LAN to run in production mode. Once the system enters production, changes must be made after hours, and there is no way to predict possible side effects. Simultaneous installation and production use can result in corrupted data or a crash.

Give users problem and question forms. Screen prints can be especially helpful when trouble arises.

You can speed the pace up if you are working with someone knowledgeable, perhaps your *management information systems* (MIS) department, a consultant, or a systems integrator.

It is likely that you will be using many of the same PCs as LAN workstations. Wherever possible, leave existing applications in the hard drive until the LAN is stable. Notify users when you will be coming around to remove them. (Otherwise they will never do anything new.) This is also a backup in case the LAN experiences an early-life failure.

Do some *orientation training* before the LAN is installed. Tell your customers what the LAN will be able to do and how it will benefit them by allowing easy file transfers, new applications, and quicker print service. Downplay the technical aspects. They do not care.

In and running

When the LAN is in and running, *show users how to access the network drive.* They will quickly realize that using the LAN does not feel much different from the old way of doing things. This training can be done in a group setting. It is a good idea to have a workstation and an overhead LCD panel to *illustrate the LAN's features.* You should also *prepublish an agenda* and *keep it short*—a half day at the most. Give out cheat sheets, the help desk's phone number, and any support materials you deem appropriate, especially discrepancy forms to note problems *when they occur.* Facts evaporate quickly unless recorded and are often essential to finding bugs. Screen prints can help too.

A few weeks after the LAN is in, *conduct some advanced training.* By now users will have their own questions, so let them drive part of the training session.

Thereafter, training becomes a matter of maintenance. New users, as will new applications, will come in. *Training is the key.* If a person does not know what to do, they will not use the LAN no matter how well it is designed.

You will have to be very available and very responsive in the first few weeks. The LAN will quickly become useful or come to be perceived as just another dollar drain. The perception once formed, especially if it is bad, will be hard to change later. It is important to start on the right foot. Do not plan on taking a vacation right after the LAN goes in! (Much as you may feel you need one.)

Where there is smoke, there is a fire

A month or two after the LAN is on line, *survey your users*; get some feedback. Customers rarely complain without a reason: Where there is smoke, there is usually a fire. Smoke out the problems and resolve them. Let your customers know that you have responded to their problems. Circulate more customer problem forms and question forms, and/or distribute them by e-mail.

Support Services

Preinstallation training should be provided for the administrator. In addition, back up all the software before installation.

Novell offers a NetWare System Manager class that runs for 3 days. It is recommended for all NetWare administrators. Banyan and others offer similar classes.

Novell also now offers a *Certified NetWare Administrator* (CNA) program, which is less technical than the *Certified NetWare Engineer* (CNE) program. A CNA learns how to

Add and delete users

Provide security maintenance

Perform disk management

Do system backups

Manage printers

For some students and subjects, it is not necessary to go to an instructor-led class. Novell and Banyan offer computer-based training with videos.

If possible, key operators and administrators should *participate in the installation* of the NOS and client software. *Posttraining* is a good idea after a month or two of operation to clear up any remaining questions.

LAN Expansion Strategies

Warning signals

How do you know when the LAN is becoming overloaded? Some warning signals are subtle. Almost imperceptibly, it starts taking longer for the network to paint a screen, download an application, or retrieve a file. Eventually people start to complain. *You* should notice before *they* do.

People slowly stop using the LAN's services. They resort to locally attached printers and modems. They load and keep applications on their own hard drives. No one says much, so you have to be observant. Reduced LAN traffic and a quiet phone do not necessarily mean that all is well.

Warnings come in other forms. If you have a network monitor, an unusual number of collisions in an Ethernet means unacceptable delays. The collision ratio should be very low, around 10–15 percent.

The LAN may be malfunctioning. Defective wiring, interference causing corrupted frames, or consistent beaconing in a token-ring network all mean trouble. The LAN may be mistuned. For example, the defaults that were set in the NOS may not be optimal any more compared to when you installed it or a NIC may be failing intermittently.

Many servers that reboot themselves for no apparent reason have floating electrical grounds. There should never be any voltage above ground on any exposed part of a server. If you rub your finger along the side of the machine on an unpainted surface, it should feel smooth. If you feel a vibration (there is no other way to describe it), the server chassis could be floating above ground. This could possibly be dangerous, so prompt attention is mandatory.

BNC connectors should be covered with nonconductive boots to prevent inadvertent grounding. Such grounding can cause noisy "ground loops." The symptom is usually intermittently slow network operation.

Scaled responses

What do you do? In an Ethernet, you have these options:

Do not overreact. Do some tuning to see if performance can be improved.

Be sure the LAN is not malfunctioning. Check to make sure that there are no late collisions, runt or jabber frames, or *cyclical redundancy check* (CRC)-frame rejects. Have any cabling constraints been violated? They often are, sometimes deliberately, sometimes inadvertently. Low traffic levels conceal a multitude of sins that become apparent when traffic builds.

Divide the network into smaller segments. Bridge them together. For instance, Novell supports this function internally in the server. Up to four segments can be so bridged.

Use a packet switch such as the one made by Kalpana or Artel. These devices route packets directly to the user, reducing LAN traffic.

Consider an *asynchronous transfer mode* (ATM)-based hub when it becomes available.

Consider buying a proprietary 20- or 100-Mbit/sec IEEE 802.3 version. The 20-Mbit/sec version runs on whatever cable you have; it simply makes the Ethernet a full-duplex medium.[3]

If you already have installed coaxial cable, consider using a broadband LAN to divide the logical LAN while retaining the same physical media.

In a token-ring network, you have these options:

Again, do not overreact. Check for malfunctions. Do some tuning.

Add early-token release if it is not already implemented.

Reduce the ring size; create another ring and bridge them.

Upgrade to 16-Mbit/sec equipment.

Consider the ATM hub when it becomes available.

Conclusion

As usual, the key to success lies in planning. If you understand your user community's needs, plan for them, and execute them with a little foresight, you will prevent many potential problems.

LANS are forgiving to a point. Especially in a new installation, give yourself some leeway, knowing there will be snags. Do not try to do too much, and do not commit yourself to anything without being sure you can deliver.

Applications compatibility is a question that no expert can always answer. There are many possible hidden factors that may affect the relationship between an application and a client. That is why the interoperability testing companies have come into existence and why pilot testing is so useful.

Constant sensitivity to the LAN's operation is a necessity. This applies equally to your user community. LAN performance can degrade gradually, until it is noticed by a user. Better that you should notice it first and prevent it.

In the next chapter, we discuss LAN management in more detail. Remember our guiding rule: *Never build a network you cannot manage!*

---

[3]Seeq Technology's Kodiak, Inc. subsidiary offers 8- and 16-bit ISA NICs for 20-Mbit/sec operation.

Vendors

Design tools

Some LAN design-tool vendors are

CACI
LaJolla, CA
(619) 457-9681
LANNETT II.5 LAN simulation
tool. Predicts LAN performance, including bridges, routers, and gateways.

InternetiX
Upper Marlboro, MD
(301) 420-7900
LANSIM is their large tool. Soft-
Bench is for smaller simulations
and interfaces with Spider Analyzer. SoftBench costs $995.

Comdisco Systems
Foster City, CA
(415) 574-5800
Block-Oriented Network Simulator
(BONeS). PlanNet Network Plan-
ning and Management. Sniffer
Data Interface for traffic data
transfer.

Make Systems
Mountain View, CA
(415) 941-9800
Netool is predictive and models
vendors' bridges, routers, and gateways as objects. Calculates optimum network nightly based on
that day's traffic. It is SNMP
compatible.

These systems require a 386SX or better. Some run on DOS, while others require Unix.

Monitoring software

PC-based monitor software includes Intel NetSight; NetSentry network monitoring and traffic analysis tools; the Professional protocol
analyzer; and the simpler Analyst for IPX/SPX, TCP/IP, and AppleTalk
networks. Prices range from $2000–8000.

LANPharaoh Duo is a hardware and software combination sold for
$2995 and up by Azure Technologies, Hopkinton, MA. They can be
reached at (508) 435-0448.

Digilog's (Horsham, PA; (215) 956-9570) LANVista and Progressive
Computing [Network General; (708) 574-5729] offer similar products.
Frederick Engineering [Columbia, MD; (301) 290-9000] offers a prod-
uct called Feline, which includes an optional performance analyzer.

14

LAN Management

An Overview of Network Management

Let us first define what the term "network management" means today. Please note that we are defining the activity, not a piece of equipment or software.

> Network management is the centralized function that detects and corrects impending or actual network faults, and controls the operation of the network's resources.

Like any resource, a LAN needs to be managed properly. In this sense, a LAN is no different than a WAN, a *telephone switch* (PBX), or any other asset.

Network management, then, is a generalized activity that applies across a spectrum of technologies. The *International Standards Organization* (ISO) identified and categorized the multidimensional nature of network management through the OSI management framework. These are five management functions needed in any network. Each one is called a *specific functional management area*. We itemize each of these, discuss the functions performed by each, and then show how they apply to LANs. They form the framework of this chapter and, according to a survey of network managers by the Network Management Forum, are listed in descending order of importance:

Fault management	Detecting errors and correcting them
Configuration management	Inventory, cabling, configuration issues, naming and addressing control, design and planning, and upgrades
Performance management	Traffic analysis, modeling, and tuning

| Security management | Access control, password administration, data integrity, violation detection, and disaster recovery |
| Accounting management | Billing for services, usage statistics, and software license compliance |

We begin our discussion with fault management.

Fault Management

This is what people most often think of when the term network management is mentioned, i.e., detecting faults and fixing them.

Fault management, then, is both passive and active. The passive element involves the reporting of alerts and alarms. These let the administrator know that the network has found or suspects an error. They also serve as the basis for issuing trouble tickets. Strategically, an analysis of alarm logs can identify trends and patterns, indicating a weakness in the network. Lost amid the rush of the day and a mass of detail, these patterns may not be obvious.

The active part involves invoking specific tests to isolate the malfunction. The tests may be noninterruptive, as in monitoring, or interruptive, as in generating test messages. Sometimes a series of tests invoked by a command script will be run as a group. Then all the results can be analyzed at once.

Considering the complexity of even the most rudimentary LAN, it is amazing that many shops lack even the most rudimentary testing tools. This problem usually solves itself the first time the LAN fails. These failures seem to be timed to the end-of-year closing, the busiest season, or when the CEO's PC dies. Shortly thereafter, purchase orders are quickly cut to buy whatever is needed.

If an investment is to be made in a LAN, then an equivalent, prudent investment in test equipment is only logical. The question is a matter of budgeting: What is needed and what is available.

In a nutshell, basic test equipment consists of a cable testing device and a protocol monitor if not an interactive tester. Basic tools such as screwdrivers, needle-nosed pliers, and connector crimp tools should be on hand. A simple *volt-ohm-milliammeter* (VOM) meter is very handy for checking continuity and voltages.

Monitoring: resolving common problems

Most problems occur at the physical layer—by some accounts, nearly 80 percent. Cable cuts, improper extensions, intermittent problems, poor grounding, and noisy electrical equipment all contribute their share of headaches. This is why cable testers and cable repair tools make sense.

The problems decrease as we climb up the layers. They fall to about 10 percent at Layer 2, and the remaining 10 percent is spread across Layers 3–7. It seems pretty clear where we should place our troubleshooting emphasis.

Duplicate addresses in locally administered systems cause collisions and other problems. It is important to avoid this by carefully setting each address. Protocol monitors can trap these problems easily and save a lot of downtime.

Network overload happens insidiously. More users come on board, applications are added. Sooner or later, there is no stretch left. The symptom in Ethernet is a slowly running network with many collisions. A token ring degrades more gracefully.

Changes in network configuration can precipitate problems. For instance, a token-ring card acts as a repeater. If that station is turned off, the cable between its up- and downstream stations must not exceed the allowable distance. If it does, errors or nonoperation will result.

LANs are fragile. Make changes one at a time. If you make several changes, you will not know the origin of a trouble symptom.

The following is a list of common problems (also see Chapters 6 and 7):

Missing terminators in Ethernets. These cause high apparent collision rates.

Illegal, improper, or damaged cabling. These cause corrupted frames.

Duplicate grounds. These cause noisy ground loops, corrupting frames.

Defective interface cards. These reduce efficient network accessibility.

Broadcast storms. These cause sluggish performance.

Duplicate internetwork addresses. These cause messages to be misdirected.

Duplicate network interface card (NIC) addresses. These prevent a user from logging on.

Routing inefficiencies due to misconfiguration. These cause slow performance at high transmission cost.

Overloaded segments or bridges. These cause poor response times to diskless workstations in Ethernets.

Flow control anomalies. These result in poor network performance if improper or incompatible protocols have been implemented.

Side effects from upgrades. Do one at a time!

Server configuration errors. These cause slow responses. For example, incorrect buffer size allocation will cause this problem.

Strategic management is *proactive* at the *overview* level. Strategic management is *embedded* in the network and is *centralized.*

Tactical troubleshooting is *reactive,* provides *indepth* analysis and is located at the *local* level. Tactical troubleshooting is a *single element* and is *dispatched.*

These two elements are *not* mutually exclusive. Rather, they complement one another. A management tool may indicate a specific problem to be resolved on site. Conversely, a tactical analysis may indicate a system-wide problem.

Test equipment

We discussed the available cable testers and scanners in Chapter 4. These are an essential investment. Having a simple VOM is a quick and inexpensive way of seeing if there is continuity in a cable.

Do not forget about the tools built into your *network operating system* (NOS), such as NetWare's MONITOR function. Make full use of the tools you already own!

We mentioned in Chapter 12 several software packages that let a PC act as a LAN monitor. These are not very expensive and do not need to run on a fancy PC. In fact, running them in a notebook machine makes them portable.

It is extremely valuable for you to recognize normal versus abnormal conditions. A protocol monitor is a window into your network.

Some analyzers are *passive*; they only record traffic. Others can be *active* and generate test patterns and traffic as well. Some are *dual-port* devices that look at both token-ring and Ethernet media, or on both sides of a bridge or router.

The Simple Network Management Protocol

Perhaps the single greatest management tool to come down the pike for LANs is the *Simple Network Management Protocol* (SNMP). Originally written for use on the Internet by Dr. Jeffrey Case, Dr. Marshall Rose, Keith McCloghrie, and Steven Waldbusser, it quickly became clear that SNMP was the ideal mechanism for managing LANs.

Why? For one thing, SNMP is truly simple. It takes up just 50–70 kbytes of precious RAM space in routers, bridges, and other managed devices. Secondly, SNMP imposes no polling load on the network. SNMP devices are polled on request.

SNMP accepts a variety of data transport protocols, but most often uses the User Datagram Protocol (UDP) a connectionless protocol in the *Transmission Control Protocol/Internet Protocol* (TCP/IP) suite. Like TCP, UDP works with IP.

SNMP is truly vendor-independent. Though many vendors have implemented extensions to SNMP, the core functions are universal.

SNMP has shown itself capable of managing a huge variety of devices. Today, SNMP is found in bridges, gateways, *uninterruptible power supplies* (UPSs), and even in client workstations. At the various Interop shows, SNMP has been shown managing electric toasters, robo-dogs, stereo systems, Lego-toy building sets, and soda machines. What could be next?

SNMP components. SNMP consists of three different commands that can be joined to make powerful combinations:

1. *Get messages.* These let the manager request and retrieve variable data about a device. These variables are called *objects* by SNMP. These object-variable values are passed from a device to a manager by the *agent* software as shown in Figure 14.1. You may also hear the term *proxy agent.* A proxy agent is an interface between a non-standard managed device and an SNMP-management station.

   Originally, there were about 100 such objects organized into 8 object groups. This formed what is called the *management information base* (MIB) that exists within agents. Since then, MIB-II has added 50 more objects and 2 additional groups. One is the *transmission group,* which supports transmission technologies such as Ethernet, T-1, or token ring. The other group records SNMP monitoring activity.

   Today, over 80 percent of the available agents support MIB-II. They are backward compatible with the more limited functions of MIB-I.

2. *Set messages.* These let the manager replace a value with one determined by the management system. *Set* provides the control function.

3. *Trap messages.* These set an agent to detect specific events. A status change causes a message, rather than the manager polling the device for information. SNMP specifies six conditions that can cause a trap. These conditions are called *generic traps* as contrasted to *enterprise traps,* which are vendor-specific.

Private traps and MIB objects do not make a device proprietary in the ordinary sense. They still use the basic SNMP and are compatible with the standard SNMP Structure of Management Information. Because of this, they can be run in almost any decent SNMP management

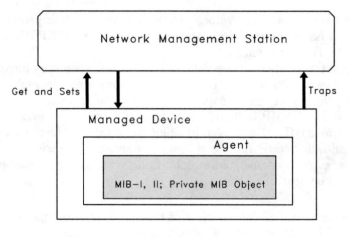

SNMP Proxy Agent

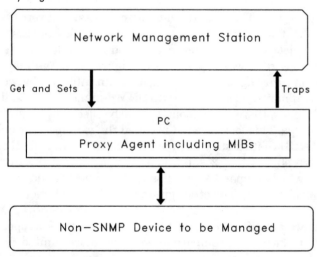

Figure 14.1 SNMP Architecture.

system. Some private MIBs are very powerful and useful. Their utility makes the public versus private argument irrelevant.

Many vendors' private MIBs are available free of charge on the Internet. Be aware, though, that they are often out of date. Since they may not be incorporated in their agents, the other half of the equation may be missing.

Management counter values tabulated by an agent will increment to $2^{32} - 1$ (4,294,967,295) and then stay there or decrement if appropriate. Counter values are not usually reset because managers look at changes, not absolute numbers.

Ordinarily, the management station and agent are linked through the network. However, devices can be dialed "out of band," so to speak, using modems, EIA-RS-232, and the *Serial-Line Interface Protocol* (SLIP).

Security has been a major concern in SNMP. SNMP's only security mechanism was a password called *Community Name.* This was woefully inadequate. For this reason, many vendors did not implement the *Set* function for fear that unauthorized parties would meddle with the agent.

SNMP Version 2.   The security and other issues have been addressed in the latest version of SNMP, called SNMP Version 2. Developed by the same team who originated SNMP, SNMP Version 2 incorporates many additions and extensions. Using a proxy agent in the management station, SNMP Version 2 and SNMP can coexist in the same network.

SNMP Version 2 adds the following features:

Bulk retrieval of data. This was not possible in SNMP.

Manager-to-manager interaction, allowing a hierarchy of managers not previously possible.

Expanded network support, including AppleTalk, NetWare, and *open systems interconnection* (OSI). Of course, UDP is still supported.

Better definition of managed objects that users want vendors to support. Vendors will also be able to better describe what their implementations can do.

Improved error handling. SNMP Version 2 produces more detailed error messages.

Configurable exception reporting. SNMP Version 2 specifies exactly where to send exception reports.

Internet users will be particularly interested in Secure SNMP for their Internet sites. Remote systems management and remote configuration become practical when adequate security mechanisms exist.

Those interested in staying in touch with SNMP Version 2 should ask their SNMP vendor for a subscription to *The Simple Times,* a free publication edited by Marshall Rose and distributed by volunteers. It is probably available by now on the Internet.

The Common Management Information Protocol

The *Common Management Information Protocol* (CMIP) is the management protocol espoused by the ISO. It is a powerful, flexible, connection-oriented protocol.

That is the problem with CMIP. All that power takes up over 700 kbytes in a bridge or router. That is too much for most vendors, and users do not want to pay for it. CMIP has suffered from political problems and is seen as slow and ungainly by many.

CMIP was on the defensive even before SNMP hit the street. Now it is even less clear that CMIP will take hold; in fact, it is doubtful. While the Network Management Forum has supported CMIP as the way to link network management systems, they have not demonstrated CMIP's viability in the LAN environment. It is simply too expensive, and SNMP does most of what users need.

Vendors are waiting for users to demand it. Users are not demanding it. A stalemate has resulted.

This is not true outside the United States; in Europe and Asia, the demand is there. In the United States, CMIP support is used as a way of qualifying vendors but is often not purchased. Current estimates are that CMIP is installed at less than 10 percent of sites, whereas over one-third have SNMP. Half of these said they had no plans to migrate to CMIP.

There is some sentiment that a trend will grow toward CMIP as distributed systems take deeper hold. IBM has also endorsed CMIP via LU 6.2, called CMOL (CMIP over Logical Link Control).

The problem with CMOL is that it cannot be routed. The *Internet Activities Board* (IAB) encapsulated CMIP in TCP/IP (called CMOT or CMIP over TCP/IP) to make it routable, but CMOT as a protocol has since been dropped by the IAB. Several Microsoft Windows-based products now support SNMP.[1]

Remote monitoring

A number of vendors are making *probe* devices, such as Hewlett-Packard's LANprobe, which sit on the network and collect data such as messages, collisions, etc. Their data can be sent across bridges and routers using the *remote monitoring* (RMON) MIB in SNMP. RMON is also commonly implemented in remote hubs.

RMON presently supports only Ethernet under the IETF, but token-ring support is coming. RMON is at heart a database. Interpreting that database is what makes it useful.

RMON gives managers a chance to be more proactive and less reac-

---

[1]WinSNMP, made by NetManage of Cupertino, CA, is Microsoft Windows-based and support SNMP. It consists of some 40 *applications programming interfaces* (APIs) grouped into five categories: agent, manager, trap, general, and utility.

Similarly, Microcom LANlord manages PCs on NetWare LANs using SNMP. LANlord also operates in the Windows environment.

tive. It gives them an actual indication of network activity from as many as nine different perspectives:

1. *Segment statistics.* Examples are collisions, runts, jabbers, and packets sent.

2. *Statistical history.* These are obtained at user-defined intervals.

3. A *host table.* This is an index that includes statistics by node.

4. *Host Top N.* This is a set of sorted user-selected host statistics.

5. *Traffic matrix.* These statistics are in grid form and indicate the traffic and number of errors between each source and destination pair of network nodes.

6. *Alarms.* These are caused by crossing high and low thresholds.

7. *Filters.* These store specified packets in a capture buffer.

8. *Packet capture.* This allows the trapping of specified packet types.

9. *Events.* These log a particular node event in a log or on an SNMP *NetWare Management System* (NMS).

RMON implementation costs vary greatly and depend heavily on the network management station platform. For example, Synoptics' platform is a very expensive Sparcstation. Others are less expensive and are based on the I960 Intel chip. Be sure to shop around!

Making sense of all the data that SNMP and RMON can generate is the biggest challenge. Many users have complained that burying the manager in a blizzard of statistics is not really "management" at all. They are right.

As a example of an RMON product, Metrix, Inc.'s *Netmetrix* uses SNMP and X-Windows to analyze remote LANs using third-party Ethernet monitors. It runs under Unix but can run on any other platform. *Netmatrix* can examine all seven protocol layers and can create simple simulations to test network configuration changes.

Analysis takes place on the remote segments to avoid polling overhead. Particular segments can be zeroed in on for detailed inspection. RMON is especially useful in multisegment networks where network analysis is required. Netmetrix is said to be highly scalable to fit in large or small networks. The product is licensed by Synoptics and is built into its Network Control Engine.

In summary, Netmetrix gives users the big picture across all the protocol layers and network segments. Then, the user can focus on a specific segment. Netmetrix is an example of RMON data put to effective use.

Many other vendors are offering RMON products, including

Hewlett-Packard and Frontier.[2] Novell's LANtern network monitor and Services Manager supports RMON. LANtern, including RMON, is supposed to appear as a *NetWare Loadable Module* (NLM).

Configuration Management

Closely related to fault management, configuration management is viewed by network managers as second only to fault management in importance. Configuration management establishes the inventory of resources to be managed or the domain of resources that will be subject to fault management.

The network configuration is always evolving: Lobes are being added, and bridges link networks. Change management and cable management are required to avoid chaos.

Similarly, the inventory of equipment and software are in a constant state of flux as are the users who come and go. They all need NIC addresses, passwords, and user names. Someone must assign and replace them when they get stale or if someone forgets. As new applications appear, directory services keep users up to date on them.

The following is a summary of LAN management tasks associated with configuration management.

Printer management

Of all the configuration tasks, printer management is the one most often exercised. The administrator is responsible for making sure that essential jobs are printed first and on the most appropriate machine. The print management function is so common that some administrators have broken out this task and delegated it to a "key printer operator."

As mentioned earlier, a LAN administrator can support up to about 40 users. By delegating the print management function, up to about 60 users can be supported by one administrator.

Print queue management

As mentioned before, it is becoming common to designate a person as the print-control operator. This person is responsible for making sure that print jobs are properly prioritized and printed on the right machine. A few hours' training by the administrator can relieve him or her of a major, recurring burden best handled departmentally.

---

[2]From Software Concepts Design, New York, NY.

Configuration management

The LAN configuration exists in physical and logical senses. Both must be fully documented. This responsibility is divided between the support team that installed the LAN on the physical side and by the administrator who assigns users their logical addresses, rights, and group membership.

It is important that the administrator keep online records of his or her activity, especially unusual actions taken for nonetheless logical reasons. This establishes continuity as administrators come and go, and gives the technical support people an ongoing reference if maintenance is needed or if trouble occurs.

Support teams need to keep accurate cabling records of lengths, routes, cable type, and postinstallation qualification test results. Only in this way can the LAN be extended or reconfigured without violating cabling rules. The test results allow technicians to see if the cable has deteriorated or changed, causing a possible malfunction.

Scanning software in client machines can tell managers which hardware and software is loaded in their clients. One such system is Tally Systems *PC Census* (NH); there are many others. In addition, SNMP can poll for configuration data.

Upgrade management

At one time, it was standard procedure to upgrade software or firmware with each new release. Today, we must be more discriminating.

A warning bell should go off in your mind when considering any upgrade or new product whose version number ends in ".0." If you elect to proceed, bear in mind that in effect you are debugging the vendor's product for them, using your staff time and resources. If the product is used for essential production purposes, the warning bell should go off louder.

An upgrade to a previous upgrade may be desirable. Presumably it will work better than the last version, but not always! It may well be *worse* than what you had. Backup *everything* before going to an upgrade. An upgrade from a .0-product may be effectively mandatory to make it work as it is supposed to.

Weigh the pros and cons. Some new features may mean little or nothing to you. If so, there is small benefit and a lot of risk. If that is the case, *do not do it*. As a reality check, ask yourself, "*Why* should I do this?"

One reason to perform an upgrade might be for continuity of support. Vendor support for older versions may be weak or even nonexistent. Some software support contracts call for having the current release online, by a version that has not been superseded by more than two releases, or some contractual variation thereof.

What effect will your current environment have on the upgrade, and vice versa? Systems can interact in funny and unpredictable ways. Try to anticipate any possible interactions, and to the extent you can, prepare for them.

Be prepared to go back if you decide to go forward. That is your safety net.

Adding and deleting users

As users come and go, they must be added and deleted from the database. Their rights and privileges must be set. Group assignments may be made. Login identifications and passwords need to be set and changed periodically. A directory structure needs to be in place. Drive-usage identifiers that specify the network drive letter (e.g., F:) must be determined.

Address administration

It is essential that NIC addresses be managed, especially if local administration is used. Recall from Chapter 9 that one decision you must make is whether to use locally or universally assigned addresses, or both. The former are set by you; the latter is burned into each NIC's ROM and is guaranteed to be the only card so addressed.

Recall that the address field is six bytes, i.e., XX XX XX XX XX XX; 12 hex digits in all.

Local administration. Local administration gives you the opportunity to organize the addresses by department, LAN segment, ring number, application, building and floor, etc. One method for source-routing bridges is to assign the first digit of a ring source address to a building, the second to a floor, and the third to a ring on the floor.

Sometimes workstations that access a mainframe will be given a separate block of addresses followed by a number assigned to the user. You may wish to assign addresses in sequence to NICs of the same or similar type. Creativity is encouraged. Build enough information into the addressing to be useful, but try not to be too rigid. Leave enough address space to accommodate a lot of growth. You only get to do this once.

Some addresses are not valid for workstations. For example, FF FF FF FF FF FF and C0 FF FF FF FF FF are the all-call broadcast addresses. You will have others that must be dedicated. You may have group addresses you wish to assign as well. An assigned Internet class address or use of TCP/IP will further restrict your options.

Local administration allows for NIC replacement while retaining the original address. This may also be desirable for some software programs that use the NIC address themselves. Note that the address must be installed by hand in the replacement NIC.

By the same token (no pun intended), local administration allows a convenient block of addresses to be filtered or forwarded through a bridge or router.

Universal administration. With universal administration, the buyer has no idea what the address will be except for the first three bytes assigned to the vendor. (Did you ask?) This makes advance address planning impossible. Similarly, replacement NICs will have a different and unknown address, with rippling effects throughout the network, unless local administration is used to match the defective card's address with the new NIC's address. In any case, the NIC-adapter test routine is needed to discover the NIC's universal address.

While this discussion may seem canted toward favoring local administration, it is fairly standard policy to use universal administration for the orthodox workstations, servers, and bridges. Stations with different configurations—those needing to access the mainframe or those that can boot as OS/2 as well as DOS machines—are locally administered. There is every reason to mix and match as long as care is used.

Documentation. Documenting addresses is essential for troubleshooting and adding new stations. Keeping orderly and up- to-date records is essential. Manual systems are cumbersome, but they are always there even if the system is down. However, they are in one place, making remote access difficult. They are only as current as the latest printout, which is inevitably outdated. You *must* develop procedures and policies for updating this information periodically and systematically.

Should you need motivation, be advised that duplicate addresses are one of *the* most common LAN problems. They can cause bizarre symptoms that will tie you up for days. Furthermore, the sheer preponderance of users will bury you unless you have a system to maintain order and avert chaos. Like many things in life, if you do not manage it, it will manage you.

Some shops keep their address information in an online database with a printout for backup. This way, the database can be updated from anywhere. It is still, however, essentially a manual process.

Intelligent wiring hubs contain network management, one of whose capabilities is address management. These hubs, however, are not inexpensive and may call for expensive and disruptive rewiring.

Protocol analyzers can build a database of addresses, but disconnected clients will not register. Also, some NICs can use the local address at one time and the universal address at another. If TCP/IP is used, each node will have an IP address, too. Correlating these from a protocol analyzer is inconvenient and time-consuming, but is at least a real-world problem. If the data can be imported into a database application and then manipulated into proper order, this may be a viable option.

Along with addresses, you should maintain a database containing the user's room location, phone number, configuration, patch panel port, *medium attachment unit* (MAU) port, and other useful information. Ideally this information would be kept in a groupware application, perhaps Lotus Notes. Then the information would be available everywhere—as long as the network and server are up.

Performance Management

A survey of network managers placed performance management third in relative order of importance. Put simply, does the network run the way it is supposed to? Does it meet the business purpose for which it was intended? If a 2-sec response time is needed, does the network deliver it? If network components are found to be highly reliable, is redundancy unnecessary?

With answers to these questions, managers are comparing performance to cost and learning how to more effectively manage the resources available to them. With time, network managers see their task increasingly as resource allocators, making sure that their firm acquires only the resources needed and then gets the most out of them.

A metric of network quality

Correct network operation is not just a matter of being functional. It must pass traffic in a timely manner and contribute to productivity by delivering prompt responses to inquiries and requests. Performance management is a metric to evaluate the operation of the objects being managed.

At a minimum, performance management monitors data being passed in the network and records volumes, response time elements, errors and delays, buffering, and queuing. This information can be analyzed informally or may become the platform for sophisticated analytical tools to assess trends and evaluate alternate configurations.

Poor performance is considered a "soft" failure. Yet performance analysis has taken a quantum leap in complexity with the advent of intelligent devices such as communications servers and routers. Accordingly, it becomes more important to have accurate data from each of the elements involved.

Performance data answers questions such as whether a new application can be accommodated. It affects expenses as managers seek to purchase the optimum bandwidth for their needs. Traffic dynamics may permit managers to route their traffic over a less costly path, resulting in a savings. Network managers who see themselves in this role, as resource managers, truly understand their real value to their firms.

Tuning the NOS

Within the NOS itself, performance can be enhanced by tuning a wide variety of parameters such as buffer sizes, packet lengths, and the like. Some NOSs will suggest changes based on accumulated data. Tuning and testing for possible malfunctions should be the first response to degrading LAN performance.

It is extremely useful to have a traffic profile for all the clients on the LAN as well as a general idea of usage throughout the day. These profiles allow the manager to spot trends before users begin to notice a decrease in performance.

Network modeling

In recent years, network modeling has become less of a black art as vendors have flooded the market with WAN and LAN design and modeling tools. Some of these vendors were listed in Chapter 12.

Much of the mathematics has been embedded in the software, so that only some very basic knowledge of statistics is needed. The ability to ask, "What if we speed the network up to 16 Mbit/sec?" may save a lot of time and money by keeping a manager from going off in the wrong direction. Working scientifically is preferable to relying on fallible intuition, especially where large sums of money are involved.

Disk management

Rapid file access means that the disk must be well-organized and not fragmented. The administrator must recognize when the disk approaches capacity and transfer outdated files to an archive system.

Files can be lost if there is corruption of the *file allocation table* (FAT). The administrator must know how to recover these and other kinds of unintentionally lost files.

Security Management

Viewed from several perspectives, security management encompasses user authentication and authorization, encryption techniques, antivirus measures, and physical security. Security management will take on increasing importance as the enterprise-wide user community expands. Internetworking and use of the network by external users as in *electronic data interchange* (EDI) will increase security needs in ways as yet undefined. ———

Access control

Of increasing concern as networks become larger, control of access to the network, authentication of users and encryption to prevent reading, writing or tampering with information belonging to the enterprise have become major aspects of security management. Some operators make a distinction between protecting the network itself and the applications, user data, and databases accessed by the system.

In larger systems, user accounts are established, and connections are counted and timed for backbilling purposes. Using the NetWare bindery makes this task much easier. In fact, products such as Bind-View Plus (LAN Management Group, Dallas, TX) allow documentation, security audits, and management reports to be created. BindView Plus is also very customizable, as each user will have their own reporting requirements.

System security, including password control and rights management, take up a lot of time. Security really has two levels: system security and file and resource confidentiality. You will be working at both levels.

Security maintenance. It is important that users change their passwords periodically. Sometimes a user will forget or will let a password expire. In this case, the administrator must help the user to create a new one.

System backup. The administrator is specifically responsible for establishing a backup strategy, ensuring that it is carried out, and restoring the file(s) or disk data that may be lost due to media failure. This responsibility extends to keeping essential backups off-site in case of a major disaster.

Backup management is important. Automate it if possible, but do it manually if you must. Some LAN owners think that server duplexing as in *System Fault Tolerance III* (SFT III) will reduce the need for *redundant array of inexpensive drives* (RAID)-like devices. We will not really know until SFT III has been out for awhile.

Fault tolerance. This is a mixed blessing. It adds reliability and availability, but adds complexity, too. Failures have occurred that were masked by the fault tolerance of the machine. Keep an eye on your machine so that fault messages are not missed. Some servers will broadcast an alarm or call a pager to indicate a fault or security breach. If the alarm goes only to the server console in a locked room or, more probably, if the console is turned off, the stage is set for a total failure sooner or later.

General security notes

Managers recognize the increasing value of the information contained in servers and traveling across LANs. Often the value of the data in the server far outweighs whatever the machine itself cost.

Novell plans to introduce a system of numbers and letters, keys really, that a user must match in order to use particular services. Novell may resell Intel's LANprotect, mentioned earlier, as virus protection software for NetWare.

Microsoft will certify Windows NT at the federal C2 level and at the B level later.

Decentralized organizations have trouble maintaining security. For example, at a major hospital, research scientists often set up their own LANs, neglecting traditional safeguards. *Management information systems* (MIS) finds out about these only by accident.

Decentralized LANs create security problems for banks, too. For one bank, the lack of security is limiting its implementation of LANs at the branch level.

Some companies have given their staff indepth training concerning security. Closed user groups prevent casual browsing through servers that contain confidential memoranda or e-mail.

Kerberos

Kerberos, for you who are not up on Greek mythology this week, was the three-headed dog that guarded the entrance to Hades. Kerberos software guards access to systems and applications in today's computing world, which sometimes might feel like Hades.

Kerberos was a result of Project Athena, a joint effort by IBM and DEC to develop computing at the undergraduate level. The "guinea pig" platform was the Massachusetts Institute of Technology.

Kerberos is transparent to the user. Kerberos was incorporated by the Open Systems Foundation as the security mechanism for the *Distributed Computing Environment* (DCE). Hewlett-Packard, IBM, and Sun all support DCE. Solaris 2.0 will contain Kerberos security.

In Kerberos, a user logs on with a personal identification code. Sent to an authentication server, the user requests a "ticket" for the session.

An authentication exchange between user and server checks to see if the user has real authorization. The user's computer then asks the ticket-granting server for a ticket.

A correctly encrypted ticket grants the various permissions needed during the session. User-server messages are encrypted using *data encryption standard* (DES). DES has been in use since 1986 at MIT, and the school now authenticates all users of its computer systems this way.

The following are the steps taken when using Kerberos:

The user requests a ticket-granting service (TGS) from Kerberos.

A ticket is given by Kerberos for TGS.

A request is made for a server ticket from the TGS server.

A server ticket is granted by the TGS server.

The user requests service from the desired server.

Thus, the user must pass through two levels to get to the server: through Kerberos first and the TGS server second. Only then does the user access the server. (That makes three heads.) Expect to see Kerberos in the future as we migrate to true client-server networks.

Securing Ethernet

Ethernet is hard to secure because it is one big party line. Furthermore, the presence of a hub is a clear target for those trying to tap into the system.

An unauthorized PC or analyzer on a vacant port, or a protocol analyzer on a live node is all it takes to crack Ethernet security. Step one, then, is to lock up the hub and any protocol analyzers you have. This is "physical layer" security.

Unused ports should be shut off. Most hubs can do this easily.

Tapping into a live port with an analyzer is a real problem. To combat this, some hub vendors, such as 3Com, SynOptics, and Ungermann-Bass, are using *application-specific integrated circuits* (ASICs) to forward data-carrying packets *only to the intended destination*. Every other station gets gibberish. The strategy is illustrated in Figure 14.2.

Working at the *media access control* (MAC) sublayer, the first MAC packet's address from a node is noted. The node number and address are stored in an ASIC-created table. Then packets intended for that node will be turned into gibberish on every other node. Note that a tap on the lobe will capture data to or from that node.

Similarly, the system can be set to accept nodal access only on a specific port. This prevents pretending to be a node (spoofing) from some-

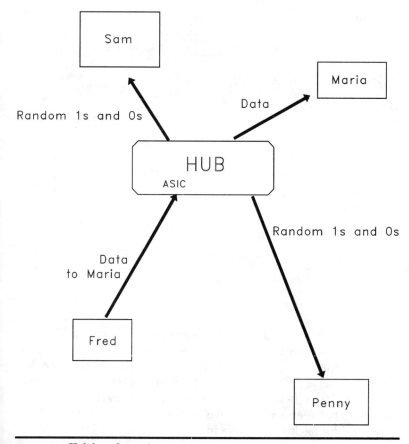

Figure 14.2 Hub-based security.

where else. Alarms occur when a mismatch is noted. The incremental cost of all this is about $60 per port.

Not all vendors are on this bandwagon. Chipcom claims its customers want physical security and that tapping in with an analyzer is too James-Bond-like, even though analyzer software is available for your PC for a few hundred dollars. Chipcom feels that the best security comes from segmenting networks using bridges and routers into secure and nonsecure nets. This can be done in the same hub.

The IEEE 802.10B LAN Security Working Group

The IEEE security panel is working to produce a secure data-exchange protocol for all LAN devices, not just hubs. Working at the *logical link control* (LLC) sublayer (see Figure 14.3), the protocol will specify the

Handling security

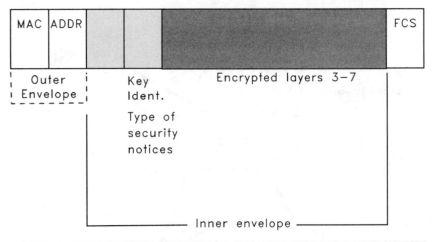

| MAC | ADDR | | | | FCS |

```
 ┌ Outer ┐        Key          Encrypted  layers  3-7
 └ Envelope ┘     Ident.

                  Type of
                  security
                  notices


                          ──── Inner  envelope ────
```

Figure 14.3   Proposed IEEE 802.10B secure data packet.

frame format and processing needed to encrypt and decrypt at the LLC sublayer. It will identify the encryption keys that are used but not the encryption scheme. That, they say, will be left to the marketplace, but most likely it will be DES. The protocol will also identify the types of security notices that take place in an association between two machines, such as between a client and a server.

The secure data packet will have inner and outer headers, or "envelopes." The outer envelope will contain address and handling information. The inner envelope will contain security information. Then comes the encrypted upper-layer information.

Intruders, as well as routers and bridges, can read the outer envelope. But the inner header and the data are unreadable.

SNMP security

As mentioned earlier, SNMP needed beefing up in its security. These have been boiled down to four basic features:

1. *Origin authentication.* This stops an unauthorized user from masquerading as a management station.

2. *Replay protection.* This prevents delaying an SNMP packet and reissuing it later.

3. *Message integrity.* This prevents tampering with a packet's contents.

4. *Data encryption.* This allows SNMP to be encrypted.

The plumbers

Watergate was not the only house with leaks. Networks leak, too. Here are some sources and what you can do about them.

Resolving the conflicting goals of security versus open and interoperable networks is not easy. The right balance is based in part on the time-value (how quickly the information loses its worth) of the data and how much effort an adversary would go to to get it. Contributing factors are the potential damage it could do and possible legal requirements to safeguard the data.

Server security. Server security is affected by three systems:

1. The operating system and the NOS

2. The server's file-sharing controls

3. The application's own file access controls

You need to look at all three levels for possible leaks.

Operating system security holes. Unix, DOS, and OS/2 have known security holes. In some Unix versions, entering an input message far exceeding the operating systems's input buffer capacity can return a superuser prompt. This can reportedly happen in OS/2 as well.

There can be leaks in the file server software. Is it possible to access directories, change permissions, or read and write privileges? Are there any limits on copying files? Sometimes the server's documentation may give a clue.

NOSs have their own holes. In NetWare, login scripts contain security commands, like an AUTOEXEC. So do audit packages.

Just before login, if you type IPX, NET, and ATTACH, the scripts will not run but server access will occur. Unless server security is in effect before the "attach point," this sequence will work and security will fail.

Holes like this are prevented by software such as Centel's Net/Assure. Net/Assure checks the logon attempt for a valid NIC address and for Net/Assure software in the PC. Invalid users' machines are frozen.

The application itself has access controls. Access should be limited to give users the least amount of privileges consistent with their work needs. Archive servers should have the same security as on other database or file servers. In some systems, a request for an archived file must come from an automated system, not a user directly. This adds a layer of security.

Removable media are a prime leak. If you copy data onto a diskette and put it in your drawer, you have just bypassed all the system security.

Security software encrypts files before storing them. If copied onto disk, they are still encrypted.

Backup disks and tapes are a source of leaks. Backups should be encrypted or at least be password protected.

Many people know that deleted files are not really deleted. Only their names are. These files can be readily recovered until the space is overwritten. Some PC security utilities write random 1s and 0s to an erased file. Such utilities are National Security Agency (NSA) classified A1.

Access controls on a hard disk are common but are easily breached. Just put a bootable disk into the A: drive and reboot. Once security is bypassed, Norton Disk Doctor and other utilities can grab data, change privileges, or alter security provisions.

Data network leaks. Users that connect via *modems* are the major problem. Data and viruses can be transported in and out. Communications or terminal servers should be interposed between modems and file or application servers as blocks to unauthorized callers.

It is fairly easy to record modem data (if its not too fast, say not over 2400 bits/sec), then play it back into the system. This way, even encrypted passwords can be breached since they are played back after having been encrypted.

Time-sensitive passwords prevent this spoofing attack. SecureID from Security Dynamics (Boston, MA) creates a new password several times a minute. A user must have a smart card that displays the current password. This way a password is valid for only a few seconds.

Many LAN owners have dial-back modems. They can be beaten by call-forwarding the return call to a "hacker partner."

Newer systems use caller-identification to check the caller's number, then call back quickly. In principle, a dishonest caller cannot enter a call-forward code fast enough to beat the return call.

T-1 channel service units (CSUs) are another breach source. A T-1 analyzer connected to a T-1 CSU can read data easily, as the formats are very fixed and quite public. CSUs and analyzers should be locked up. Encryption should be considered, too.

Fiber is considered untappable, but it is not. The right tools let a little bit of light pass through a breach in the cladding. Hard to do but not impossible. *Fiber repeaters* convert light to electrical signals then back to light again. Electrical signals are easy to tap.

Conventional thinking says that hiding cables in walls presents a barrier to tapping. In fact, it can hide a tap. Instead, buy brightly colored cable and put it in public view. Then taps will be noticed immediately.

Spread-spectrum LANs are fairly secure, as they frequency-jump often. Internal snooping is still possible. Check the cone of visibility and use encryption.

Similarly Very Small Aperture Terminals (*VSATs*) and satellite *microwave* links are readily intercepted. Encrypt!

Switches, bridges, and routers can leak, too, and they should be physically secure. If a person learns the network identification numbers and device addresses, they can go anywhere by tricking the router into thinking they are an approved user.

Hackers have learned how to assault routers. They can observe packet addresses and data, reroute packets, or introduce errored packets. Ask your router vendor where the machines are vulnerable, and button them up. Some new routers have encryption, but even those that do not can still handle encrypted packets as long as the headers are in plain text.

Internet routers are a particular problem, because the Internet goes so many places and is a huge hacking medium. If the Internet is not in use, turn the IP-routing protocols off. When open, allow only specific source, destinations, and functions through.

Remove potentially problematic protocols that could help hackers. These include FINGER, TELNET, TFTP, RLOGIN, and *File Transfer Protocol* (FTP). Filter *packet internetwork grouper* (PING) out at the router. The object is to stop someone from browsing your network and finding host names using inquiry protocols. Certainly, you do not want them stealing files using your FTP!

Gateways are a risk because a hacker can work anywhere in the protocol stack. For instance, if a hacker gains control of the session layer, the hacker could wait until a user logs out, then nullify the user's command to close the session.

The network system should be configured to terminate any session that does not close properly. The network should never leave a session dangling. If a session has been quiet for say, 50 sec, then it should be closed, regardless of who the user is.

Network analyzers are a major source of leaks for data and passwords. Keep them locked up. Some newer ones require passwords.

"Eyeball" leaks

Unauthorized users can read terminal screens, printer output, faxes, and the like. Send printer output to secure areas. Screen savers or utilities will wipe display screens. Similarly, unused applications should be automatically logged off. Faxes should fall into a locked container or even better, go to a fax mailbox or a workstation acting as a secure fax receiver. Destroy Mylar printer ribbons that retain an impression.

Employee awareness

Security is best maintained by employees sensitized to the risks. Outside attacks by high-tech spies happen, but they are rare. More commonly, leaks are caused by insiders, often carelessly. Those with identifications and passwords bear watching, not so much for deliberate leaks, but for the innocent and unintentional exposure of information by carelessness or slipshod procedures.

A television news magazine showed how easy it was for a young hacker to gain access to a major corporate network. He simply called a user at random, identified himself as being from the computer center, and asked the user to log on. In the course of conversation, he casually asked, "What's your password so I can see it on the system"? The user promptly gave it to him.

The company had given him 2 weeks to crack their system. He did it in 2 hours.

Virus and worm protection

A lot has been said about viruses and worms in the LAN environment. LANs seem to be the ideal way to rampantly propagate viruses. The scare factor has been multiplied by the Morris Internet worm and Michelangelo. There has been a lot of self-serving hype. Most of the concern has turned out to be hypochondria.

A study by IBM's Thomas J. Watson Research Center found that for every 1000 PCs in a business, a virus infects less than 4 a year. The primary path of infection has been via contaminated disks, not networks. According to the Virus Research Center of ICSA, 63 percent of organizations have had a viral infection. Of those, 69 percent said it did little or no damage.

That does not mean that damage cannot happen. How about the other 31 percent? According to the Burton Group, a consulting firm in Salt Lake City, an infection on a networked PC costs about $15,000 in lost data, manpower, and replacement software.

A virus in a server could be triggered by the innocent action of a manager. Then the virus could delete all the files on the server, scramble user passwords, and even shut the server down. Being at the heart of the LAN, the server could infect any client connected to it through file transfers or e-mail. The virus could pass anywhere in a network. While it has not happened so far, can it be far off?

Antivirus programs.   There are three types:

1. *Scanners.* These search a PC's memory, boot area, and executable files for the bit pattern that indicates a known virus. Examples are McAfee's Netscan and Microcom's Virex/PC.

Scanners can be fooled by newer viruses and "stealth" viruses with no particular signature. Stealth viruses change their signature and hide anywhere in programs to avoid detection. Scanners must also be run periodically to work.

2. *Active monitors.* Programs like Virex/PC and Flu Shot+ both intercept DOS and ROM BIOS calls, looking for virus-like actions. Flu Shot+ is made by Software Concepts Design (see Footnote 2).

Since it is a *terminate-and-stay resident* (TSR) program, the use of an active monitor brings up applications compatibility issues. Some applications require the memory taken up by an antivirus TSR.

3. *Integrity checkers.* These tack a *cyclical redundancy check* (CRC) onto a program. When the program is pulled up, it is checked against a database. If it does not match, the program may be infected.

Of course it may not be. It may have been modified quite legitimately. But cyclical redundancy checkers merely look for changes. They do not need updating and do not chase signatures.

The problem is that none of these techniques are very suitable for servers. Intel offers a real-time scanner for servers, LANprotect, but it works only with NetWare 3.X servers. It needs an integrity-checker, too. LANprotect finds over 400 viruses.

Macintoshes are just as vulnerable. Virex from Microcom is also available for Macintoshes. There are certainly other products, as well.

Central Point's Antivirus for NetWare protects the client, server, and enterprise-wide levels with three sets of software. CentralTalk speaks to CentralAlert, which can call a pager, send a *message-handling system* (MHS)-based message, or use NetWare's broadcast facility. Central Point even has a rapid-notification virus protection service and a quick-response virus eradication team that can reach a site within 24 h to deal with viral problems.

This program recognizes that most infections start at a client, then propagate to a server. Central Point recognizes that a virus can be propagated through a WAN, too.

Symantec's Norton Antivirus detects over 1400 viruses. It, too, is a scanner, looking for patterns that identify viruses. The advantage of Antivirus is that it can be loaded and administered from a central server.

This product works with AT&T's StarLAN, VINES, NetWare, LAN Manager, and 3Com's 3+ Open. It can be configured to scan various domains, e.g., all the executable files or all or some disks. In addition, you can tell it when to scan. The configuration can be the same for everyone, different for different workgroups, or even individually specified.

Newer viruses mutate by themselves each time they are executed, making them hard to detect. They are called *polymorphic viruses*. Many polymorphic viruses use a *mutation engine* to change their signature. These engines can create 900,000 new virus versions in just a few days, each of which a scanner would consider a different virus. Norton Antivirus detects such viruses, in part by looking for signs of a mutation engine, and also looking for virus-like signatures.

Stealth viruses can mask changes in file sizes. They record the file size before an infection and alter the directory and FAT so the original value appears there. This can defeat some scanners. Norton Antivirus uses the CRC method to detect altered files.

Scanners need periodic updates. For instance, Norton Antivirus is updated quarterly.

Virus detection is being built into other products, such as AppMeter, menuing and inventory systems, and asynchronous communications software such as Hyperaccess.[3] Hyperaccess can even stop a file transfer if a virus is detected.

Active-monitor virus protection is memory-resident. Either a device driver loaded through CONFIG.SYS or a TSR loaded through AUTO-EXEC.BAT can be used. Some products offer both variants, which can be used on a client-by-client basis.

The TSR can be booted when the PC starts. It can also be on a server, so that all users can share its use. The downside is that the user must log onto the server to get to the TSR. This lag creates a window through which a virus can crawl. For instance, it could be loaded after an infected COMMAND.COM.

TSRs can be installed from a login script to the network. They can also be removed from memory without a reboot to handle a large application. Some users find out sooner or later that they can bypass the scan by hitting ESCAPE.

Device-driver programs live on the PC and are loaded at powerup by CONFIG.SYS. This leaves no window for a virus. Device drivers cannot be loaded by login script. Nor can they be removed without altering CONFIG.SYS and rebooting.

TSRs should scan programs during loading, while executing, during copies, and while writing. Virus-infected files should be caught before they run. The TSR should allow only the manager to reconfigure the program.

Server protection works in two ways. The TSR should screen files coming from the server as well as those going to it. Not all antivirus

---

[3]Hyperaccess/5 is by Hilgraeve.

TSR products do this. Server protection is important because about one-half of all office PCs use a LAN server for storage, making the server an ideal place to hide a virus, especially since most virus protection software is intended for clients and not servers.

In evaluating antivirus software, see how much time the TSR adds to the boot process. Excess time will cause users to seek ways around the scan.

Similarly, the memory occupied by the TSR can affect other applications. Memory requirements range from about 5 kbytes to 40 kbytes (Symantec Antivirus) or even 50 kbytes (Microcom's Virex).

The products should be easy to install and offer advice when choices are given. Excessive reliance on documentation is a negative. The documentation itself should be adequate. This includes details on specific viruses, virus protection, and policies, as well as procedures related to preventing and dealing with viral attacks.

Reporting and messaging should be customizable. A detected virus should be reported and logged. The log should include the date, file infected, and nature of the infection.

Alert messages may be customizable. Some have an audible warning and advise an action along with an alert. Often, the alert can be sent to a number of workstations.

Antivirus software itself can be infected. Accordingly, antivirus software should have a self-test feature that prevents it from being used until it checks properly. TSRs may be loaded after a virus is on board and may not catch the virus or operate as expected. That is the plus for the device-driver approach.

Resident programs may not catch all viruses. *Vienna* executes quickly in memory and looks for another file to infect, which it does over and over. Some programs do not screen out an infected file that a user wishes to copy. In one test, no popular TSR or device driver program caught a Cascade-infected floppy inserted into the A: drive when a DIR was done. These programs seem to treat floppy boot sectors differently from the way they treat infected files.

Caveat emptor! Read the industry trade journal evaluations and the detailed reports from the *International Computer Security Association* (ICSA) Virus Research Center in Washington, DC.[4]

Pricing for antivirus packages varies significantly, but LAN versions for 10 users run around $600–700. Pernode pricing falls quickly for 100- and 1000-user licenses. NCSA found that there is no direct correlation between price and performance, so buying the most expensive

---

[4]ICSA may be reached at (202) 364-8252.

product does not mean that you are necessarily getting the best. As always, your needs first and then your budget should dictate what you buy.

Antivirus protection strategies. The following are antivirus protection strategies:

Use antivirus software.

Use diskless workstations that cannot be contaminated.

Forbid the use of unscanned disks. Scan on a stand-alone PC.

Use stand-alone PCs for outside communication.

Outlaw the use of shareware. (Easier said than done!)

Prohibit downloading programs from bulletin boards. (Ditto!)

Write-protect floppy disks.

Use file encryption.

Automate scanning. Scan from the server each time a user logs on. Add scanning to the AUTOEXEC.BAT file or as a device driver.

Periodically check PC-based bridges and routers since they can propagate viruses everywhere. Perform no bridge or router upgrades without scanning the disks first.

What can you do if you are infected? Many experts do not trust virus scrubbers. Scrubbers may not remove the entire virus or may damage the file so that it cannot return to its original state.

If you elect to try to clean a file, copy it and run the virus scrubber on it. If the program runs fine and the file size is no smaller than its original size, then use the product to disinfect any other files. Antivirus scrubbers can leave extra bytes in a file after the virus has been removed. This is not usually a problem.

Some experts prefer restoring the files from backups far enough in the past to be surely uninfected. There will be data loss, but at least you know the virus is gone. Since most viruses come from disks brought from home, that often becomes the "gate date."

Accounting Management

Accounting management includes not only traffic-based cost allocation but other overhead costs generally regarded as invisible, such as disaster-recovery protection and network management. With time, network managers will be required to total these costs and allocate them to different enterprise elements.

Chargeback systems have their advantages and disadvantages. Some advantages include:

They are fair.

They provide a way of showing value.

They recover costs.

Some disadvantages are:

Chargeback systems add complexity to the administration of the systems.

Department managers do not like them because they are a variable cost.

Users get "taxi meter syndrome," knowing they are being charged each time they use the network. Some managers may restrict network usage.

One option is to charge each password holder a flat fee per year. Some network managers will reduce their own budgets so that departmental managers can have money to pay them for the LAN.

The Importance of Usage Statistics

It is important to be able to show management that the LAN is useful. The best way to do this is with a one-page summary report illustrating the usage of the LAN and perhaps the cost per character processed. Charts showing progressively more usage by application are especially impressive.

Relevance to the organization's mission should be stressed. For example, if LAN resources were utilized to assemble a particularly comprehensive sales proposal, that fact should be made evident to management.

Continued LAN support in all its facets, including staffing and expansion, is contingent upon the ability to justify the LAN, year in and out. It is a serious mistake to assume that its value (and by inference, your value) is self-evident. Failure to maintain management support will mean reduced funding, lack of policy support (e.g., for antiviral measures), and, in the extreme case, the LAN's demise.

Licensing and Software Issues

The LAN administrator is responsible for making sure that software licenses are not violated. In practice, it is almost impossible to avoid violating a license agreement sooner or later. In large measure this is because the licensing terms vary so much from vendor to vendor. The best you can do is often a matter of meeting the spirit rather than the letter of the law.

The Software Publishers Association has made a number of well-publicized surprise inspections of users sites. They do not need a warrant: They simply threaten lawsuits. Sometimes this works through intimidation. So—do not be intimidated!

Most managers prefer a software site or server license, covering as many users as there are at a given location or on a given server. This seems rather excessive, so some vendors allow a certain number of concurrent users instead.

Concurrence is more realistic and fair, but software is required to limit the number of concurrent users and queue those that are waiting. Sometimes, it will log out users who have been inactive for a time, e.g., iconized.[5]

Menu systems often have addons for metering, such as *Saber Menu* (Saber Software, Dallas, TX) and *Sitelock* (Brightwork Development, Tinton Falls, NJ). These let an administrator build a database of the applications and number of copies of each that should be installable. Tracking can be by the number of copies in use at one time or by the maximum number allowed.

If you cannot afford one of these, then you must build an inventory of where each application is installed, how many copies have been bought, and how many copies are being used at once. Some copies may have been made illegally and stored locally or on the server. Inventory programs sniff out all of these.

These programs, however, are imperfect. They key on common applications and file names, which are often outdated or incomplete. Sometimes file names are duplicated between applications: Did you know that at least three different programs have the file name WP.EXE? Further filtering, as by size, date, or a signature byte are needed.

Like every policing mechanism, metering can be beat. If the menu is bypassed or an application is loaded from a local hard disk, metering can be avoided.

Some networked applications have their own metering. They track all active users, often on several file servers. Ultimately, NOSs will have an API in which all applications will be available on all servers.

---

[5]Examples of metering software are *LAN Automatic Inventory* from Brightwork Development (Tinton Falls, NJ); *Network HQ* from McGee Enterprises (Norcross, GA); *Parsec Auditor* from Parsec Information Corp (New York, NY); and, *AppMeter* from Funk Software (Cambridge, MA; (800) 828-4146 X421).

Using the global-naming feature, licenses will be held in a central repository. They will be doled out and recovered as users come and go. This utopia will require that NOS and application vendors cooperate. If the application vendors really want users to manage the use of their software (even though it's not necessarily in their interest), then it is to their benefit to work with the NOS vendors, who are already discussing the API.

The LAN Administrator

The concept of a LAN administrator is that of an individual who may design, install, and maintain a LAN. In small organizations, one person may receive this assignment as a secondary responsibility to their primary job. This person will focus on day-to-day operations rather than on design or installation issues. This specialized work often falls to consultants or systems integrators. In larger shops, another internal organization, often MIS, will carry out this responsibility.

In the most basic form, a LAN administrator will handle routine questions and problems, and escalate them to the help desk or MIS if the problem goes beyond that. Users strongly appreciate having someone right there, especially a coworker who understands their problems. At the same time, the help desk and MIS are relieved of the simpler difficulties that do not make full use of their expertise.

Even the simplest LAN requires some degree of administration. If the task is not delegated, administration will be haphazard. It is important to give someone the responsibility and the authority to see that the LAN is properly maintained.

The benefit is three-fold. First, the administrator quickly comes up to speed. Second, it establishes specific accountability. Third, designating an individual establishes consistency and prevents several people from working at cross-purposes.

Administrator training

LAN administrators need not be very technically oriented. They should be comfortable in the operating system used by your NOS and client workstations, and should have attended a 3-day class on administering their specific NOS. This class typically teaches software basics and how to set up users, directories, and security. NOS utilities are also discussed, as well as when and how to invoke them. Monitoring and backup procedures for the NOS are practiced. To ease user access, login scripts and menus are created in group exercises.

Some NOS vendors, including Novell, offer advanced system manager classes. This level, of course, covers management strategies, performance management, advanced print functions, and remote management. A first look at protocols and the NetWare Name Service is included along with trouble-prevention and maintenance strategies.

Engineer-level support

Certified NetWare Engineers (CNEs) and *Certified Banyan Engineers* (CBEs) take a series of courses. Students in a CNE course need a foundation in DOS and microcomputer concepts, followed by both administrator courses discussed above. From there, they take a class in service and support and a class on networking technologies. This bring them to the CNE level. They can optionally take TCP/IP and NetWare Network File System to become enterprise-wide CNEs.

Clearly, this level of skill is well beyond that needed for an office administrator. CNEs and CBEs are second-level support for problems that administrators cannot handle, especially where internetworked LANs are involved.

In our concluding chapter, we touch on selected current and emerging LAN topics. LAN technology moves quickly, so much of the discussion will be based on recent industry developments. Our emphasis is on near-term developments that may affect your network or networking plans.

Chapter

15

Coming Attractions

Advances in LAN technology are occurring rapidly and cover a broad range of LAN functionality. We have discussed many of these advances. In this chapter, we summarize the latest trends.

New applications drive LAN development and strongly influence future strategic planning. So the particular focus of this chapter is to expand our scope and try to spot emerging applications before they overtake us.

Advances in LAN Technology

LAN technology is advancing on every front, but the key areas are:

Advances in *network operating systems* (NOSs)	Examples of these advances are Microsoft Windows NT and the incorporation of NOS functions in operating systems such as IBM-DOS 6.1, which includes three NOS shells, collectively called DOS LAN Services. New operating systems such as Windows NT support true symmetrical multiprocessing and, more importantly, *structured query language* (SQL) applications that will replace even more mainframes. Novell's NetWare running atop the multitasking Unix operating system will give Windows NT stiff competition, especially since each element is proven and Windows NT lacks NetWare's and Unix' well-established track record.
Asynchronous transfer mode (ATM)	For both LANs and WANs, ATM will make seamless networks practical. ATM provides

the right mix of speed, delay, and cost to make new applications feasible.

| High speeds over cable media | Specifically, we are referring to 100Base-VG or an equivalent technology, e.g., *copper digital data interface* (CDDI), supporting 100 Mbit/sec over Level-5 copper cable. This technology can be combined with ATM. |
| Increased interconnection with mobile users | Cellular systems designed for data make it possible for the roving "road warrior" to gain access to all the resources that this individual would have in the office. Now in its infancy, this technology will increase dramatically in use and decrease just as dramatically in cost. |

Microsoft Windows NT Advanced Server

Windows NT Advanced Server (as opposed to the desktop version) seems to be the product that will help LAN-based computing evolve from workgroup computing to strategic, mission-critical applications. Some key influential factors are:

The product's scalability. It works effectively in small and large applications, allowing easy growth.

Its multiprocessor support. Windows NT supports true symmetric multiprocessing, and was designed from the start to do so.

Its price and performance. It is well suited to client-server applications, and it runs on PCs instead of the more expensive Unix workstations.

Its compatibility with existing LANs, including TCP/IP and IPX/SPX.

The multidomain administration features.

The remote server support.

The well-known Windows interface, which minimizes retraining.

Its range of common *applications programming interfaces* (APIs), allowing integration of off-the-shelf and custom applications.

Its ability to perform transaction processing via SQL Server for NT, which is closely integrated with the Windows NT operating system itself.

Expert Systems

Expert systems are finding their way into the LAN environment. They are surfacing in network management systems and test instruments.

They are being instituted for competitive business applications as well as technical ones, and their applicability should not be viewed in only a narrow technical context.

Employees will accept an expert system if they are so overworked that they do not care who (or what) brings relief. Expert systems solve recurring problems; people like new ones. The two are complementary.

Expert systems almost never replace employees. Instead, they keep the head count down by letting employees devote their time to new projects and problems.

When does an expert system make sense? Here are some common-sense guidelines:

The problem to be solved is important.

The problem has a solution.

An expert system is cost effective. (Some run on a PC.)

The competition has one.

Live experts are scarce and/or expensive.

Turnover is high.

The problem occurs over and over.

It is possible to define a set of rules and a set of facts to solve the problem.

Agreement on a set of correct diagnoses and prescriptions can be reached by live experts ("liveware").

The environment is stable. Little reprogramming if any will be needed.

The problem takes more than 15 min but less than 8 h to solve by hand.

There are a defined number of outcomes.

If you decide to implement an expert system, select *one* expert to work on the project. This way the knowledge engineer who is programming the rules will not be confused.

There have been some tremendous successes (New York Telephone's MAXX) and some major-league flops (do not ask). The common theme in the flop scenarios seems to be that the expert systems were too rigid and did not account for the fact that users learn as they use the systems. The systems forced them to go through a series of screens when the operator was ready to jump ahead and speed up the process. Other failed systems often ran afoul of one or more of the guidelines listed above.

For those interested in developing an expert system, the *Interna-*

tional Association of Knowledge Engineers (IAKE) has set up an online job bank matching *artificial intelligence* (AI) experts with potential employers and clients around the world. The job bank holds the resumes of engineers who design and build expert systems as well as job openings at corporations, universities, and government agencies.

IAKE is a Maryland-based nonprofit organization that sets and standardizes qualifications for knowledge engineers. IAKE has members in 42 countries.[1]

Multimedia

Is it really coming? You can see it at the trade shows, in the press, but in a few offices. Is it a toy or will it be genuinely productive?

As yet, multimedia is too cumbersome and too expensive to implement on a broad scale. More fundamentally, the user community is not convinced that the added complexity and cost will yield the dramatic payback that LANs have, for instance.

Is multimedia too bulky and complex to use when many people still fear the most basic computer? An absolute sine qua non for multimedia is that it be dirt-simple to use. Second only to finding "killer" applications, the user interface will make or break this technology.

Clearly, high-speed LANs are an "enabling technology" for multimedia. This is a fancy way of saying that without a suitable LAN, multimedia is not possible.

"Suitable" boils down to the following characteristics: high speed, microscopic delay, and reasonable cost. The last, the cost, includes being able to reuse existing cable.

Document Imaging

So far, efforts to create the paperless office have fallen flat, but vendors keep trying. It makes so much sense to eliminate reams and reams of paper. Most critically, the ability to find all that you need, and when you need it, is strategically vital in the fast-paced, competitive business climate. Saving a tree or two is not a bad idea, either.

Storing and retrieving documents calls for high resolution, rapid access, ubiquity of availability, and integration with other systems such as file and facsimile services. All of these are things that LANs do well.

It seems likely that 100-mbits/sec LANs will be needed as the docu-

---

[1]The IAKE job bank may be used by both members and nonmembers and may be reached by dialing the IAKE bulletin board at (301) 816-2473. To talk to a representative, call (301) 231-7826.

ments in bit form will be large, even when compressed. Imaging "juke-boxes" will appear as document servers on the LAN.

A major problem is not technical but legal and perhaps ethical. Will scanned paper documents or electronically created documents be accepted in a court as originals? How do we ensure that a contract agreed to and stored electronically has not been altered? How about a will?

These questions are not radically different from the ones that arose upon the introduction of the fax machine. Is a signed, faxed contract binding? In the banking industry, it generally is not, but a telex is.

Look for document imaging to overcome these problems and become another LAN service. Some limited applications are already running.

Object-Oriented Systems

Object-oriented systems treat information as blocks of related data. The effect on a LAN will depend on where processing occurs. If the processing is at the local level, the effect will be minimal. If the processing is at the object's level, then each time a block is transferred, the LAN's utilization will jump momentarily. The difference between that and today's "bursty" traffic pattern is that these objects are much larger, much more like a file transfer than an interactive transmission in size.

A large number of objects will clutter up an Ethernet, creating delays. If the object must be parsed for transmission through an internetwork, the receiver must reassemble it, creating a delay again.

Clearly, object-oriented systems favor speed and more speed in an effort to increase data density so as to permit more users to access the LAN. Perhaps data compression can be used effectively before a speed jump is required. This is an area where modeling may yield some clues as to direction.

Distributed Computing and Cooperative Processing

Is there a *distributed computing environment* (DCE) and a *distributed management environment* (DME) in your future? The DCE is intended to be the generic, distributed, object-oriented architecture of the future. Technically ambitious, the DCE is beginning to appear on the market. All the major computing vendors have contributed to and endorsed the DCE effort. The DCE's management element, the DME, will make it possible to manage individual client workstations that are presently beyond our management reach, except for *Simple Network Management Protocol* (SNMP) or SNMP Version 2 agents that can reside in workstations.

Cooperative processing, a part of the DCE, will process, invisibly to the user, portions of applications on different processors.

All of this will place burdens on the network, which increasingly obeys the oft-heard dictum that "the network *is* the computer." Indeed, the DCE and DME are further obscuring that distinction.

Increased User Expectations from (Management) Information Systems

At each higher step of technology, the user's contentment period seems to shorten. As each advance is presented, it is quickly absorbed and then the users—our customers—want more. They become even more demanding once they see what apparent miracles can be wrought, how they can be used competitively, and save head count.

There is no end to this spiral, and that is good. However, it imposes upon us an ever-increasing burden to exceed our past accomplishments. As in the entertainment industry, each new plateau makes the next increment smaller and harder to attain.

How do we keep users—our "customers," really—happy with our efforts?

Be responsive to present needs.

Anticipate short-term future scenarios.

Look for new technology that will help your organization meet its mission. *Organizational relevance supersedes all other criteria.*

Be your customers' advocate in the technology marketplace.

Communicate with your customer base and your management.

Information: The Lifeblood of the Organization

In the face of globally intense competition, tactical and strategic use of information will help separate the winners from the losers. In all organizations, information is critical to allocating resources in the most effective way and leveraging them as fully as possible. The fact that LANs have evolved into enterprise-wide networks and now into global area networks is proof of the need for timely, complete, and accurate information in order to spend the world's precious resources wisely.

To that end, the *management information systems* (MIS) departments and its attendant information technology is penetrating to the core of the organization. This evolution is a stark contrast to the "Chinese wall" that once separated MIS from whatever else the organization did.

The former failure to adopt our organization's mission and to be responsive to our user community sparked a roll-your-own, let-us-do-it-ourselves rebellion among users.

Until we adapted, we were for a time less relevant, even irrelevant. Some were not paying attention to the advance of technology, caught up in the daily routine, walking around with blinders on. Some were unwilling to change.

Collectively, we have learned a hard lesson. In the words of Norman Mailer, "One must grow or else pay more for remaining the same."

Today, we bring the discipline and the experience of the past to the technology of today and tomorrow. We have recaptured our relevance and integrated ourselves into the heart of our organizations. The spotlight has been turned on us as management realizes that information is truly the lifeblood of the organization.

This book then, is not just at an end but also the mark of another beginning. If technology is always a moving target, and it is, then we can never be completely content with our knowledge, for we are not dealing with a finite topic. This book is a success if it leads you to new topics of interest or stimulates you to dig deeper into a subject that interests you. We wish you well in that quest.

Glossary

You will find the following terms useful in working with LAN data communications.

Access The method by which data enters a common network. ITU-TSS X.25 is an access method for a public network. A local operating company provides an access line for linking a premises with an interexchange carrier's point of presence.

ACK An acknowledgement of receipt of correct data to the sender.

Address A unique identifier associated with a station, line, path, or unit. In LANs, addresses are assigned by *local* or *universal* administration.

Algorithm A set of well-defined rules or processes to solve a problem in a finite number of steps.

Alternate A secondary communications path used to reach the destination.

Amplifier A device that reproduces and enlarges an electrical signal. It is not the same as a *repeater* that completely regenerates a digital signal.

Analog A continuously varying electrical signal with an infinite number of amplitudes.

Application The use to which a system is applied.

ARQ The acronym for *automatic repeat request*. Incorrectly received data is rejected and a request for a repeat is initiated. See the unit on data link layers.

Asynchronous Occurring at any point in time; no specific time relationship.

Baud A unit of signaling speed, not necessarily the bit rate.

Bit The smallest possible unit of information in a digital system.

Bit order The order of transmission in a serial system. Typically, the *least significant bit* (LSB) is sent first.

Bridge A *media access control* (MAC) networking device that works at Layer-2 of the *open systems interconnection* (OSI) model.

Brouter Brouters perform both bridging and routing at Layers 2 and 3, respectively. (See Chapter 11.)

Byte A sequence of 8 bits in a row. Also called an *octet*.

Carrier A base analog signal that is modulated to carry information.

Clock   A signal used to synchronize the transmitter and receiver in a *synchronous* system.

CRC   The acronym for *cyclical redundancy check*. It ensures the validity of received data.

Demodulation   The process of recovering information impressed on a carrier signal by *modulation*.

Emulator   A computer program that makes a programmable device imitate another device, producing the same results.

Frame   In bit-oriented protocols (e.g., SDLC, HDLC, or ADCCP), a frame consists of a flag (Hex 7F), address, control, data, frame check sequence, and an ending flag. The frame check sequence is a 16-bit CRC. Using the term *frame* implies Layer-2 functions of the OSI model.

Front-end processor   A specialized computer that relieves the main CPU of line control, message handling, code conversion, and error control.

Gateway   A networking device that works at Layers 3–7 of the *International Standards Organization* (ISO) model.

Handshake   A predetermined exchange between two entities in order to establish communication.

Idle character   A character sent when there is no information to send. Idle characters keep the line alive and ensure that both ends stay synchronized.

Intelligent workstation   A terminal containing processing capability, e.g., an intelligent workstation or PC.

Interface   A shared boundary between two systems such as data communications (terminating) equipment (DCE) and data terminal equipment (DTE). Also a boundary between adjacent layers of the ISO model.

Kernel   The core functions of an operating system.

Kilo (k)   The Greek word that means 1000. For memory sizes, it means 1024.

LAN   The acronym for *local area network*. Typically, it denotes a short-distance and high-speed network.

Leased line   A full-time link between two or more locations leased from a local or interexchange carrier.

LSB   The acronym for *least significant bit*. It stands for the bit with the least binary weight in a character.

Mark   A binary 1.

Mega (M)   The term for 1 million, as in megabits or millions of bits per second.

Modeling   An analytical process based on mathematical network behavior formulas called *models* to predict the performance of a data network.

Modem   Contraction of the term *modulator-demodulator*. It converts digital signals to analog signals for transmission over the analog network and back again.

Modulation   The process of impressing information on a carrier signal.

Monitor   A passive activity for observing, evaluating, and verifying correct operation of a link or process.

MSB   The acronym for the *most significant bit*. It stands for the bit with the greatest weight in the binary system and is usually the last bit sent in a character.

Multiplexer   An electronic device that combines several signals into one to save transmission costs. *Time division multiplexing* (TDM) and *frequency division multiplexing* (FDM) are used in various aspects of LAN data communications.

NAK   The acronym for a *negative acknowledgement*. It indicates that the data was not received correctly, the device was not ready, or an error condition.

Network   A series of points connected by communications channels. Public networks can be used by anyone; private networks are closed to outsiders.

NLM   In NetWare 3.1X, it is the acronym for *NetWare Loadable Module*. An NLM provides a specific function or utility and can even be an application.

Network management   A systematic approach to planning, organizing, and controlling networks.

Node   A point in the network where lines from many sources meet.

Packet   Data grouped for transmission through a public network such as ITU-TSS X.25.

Packet switching   A transmission system in which a circuit shares the transmission of packets to different destinations. In contrast to circuit switching, routing of the packet is determined during rather than before packet transmission.

Physical   The actual wire connection between devices. Compare with *virtual*.

Polymorphic   A virus that mutates to avoid detection.

Protocol   A formal set of rules setting the format and control of data exchange between two devices or processes.

RAID   The acronym for *redundant array of inexpensive disks*.

Redirector   A redirector in a workstation sends data to the network or keeps it in the workstation for local use, as appropriate.

Router   A networking device that works at Layer 3 of the ISO model.

Routing   The process of reaching a destination. If the primary path is not available, several alternate paths may be tried.

SDLC   The acronym for *synchronous data link control*. A Layer-2 protocol that was created by IBM and based on ADCCP. It is a bit-oriented protocol and is very similar to HDLC.

Simulate   A technique for evaluating the performance of a network before building it. Simulation employs timers and sequences as opposed to mathematical models to produce expected network behavior.

SLED   The acronym for *single large expensive disk*. Compare with *RAID*.

SNMP   The acronym for *Simple Network Management Protocol*, an Internet creation used widely to manage LANs.

SONET   The acronym for *synchronous optical network*. It is a fiber optic network that operates in up to 48 segments of 51.84 Mbit/sec/segment or 2.48832 Gbits/sec.

Space   A binary 0.

SNA   *Systems Network Architecture*, a communication architecture developed by IBM to facilitate mainframe-to-terminal and mainframe-to-mainframe communication. With LU 6.2, terminals can communicate with other terminals directly.

Statistical multiplexer   A multiplexer that allocates time on the channel to active inputs but not to inactive ones. It greatly increases line capacity.

Store and forward   Typical of ITU-TSS X.25, a transmission system in which messages are sent, stored, and then forwarded on to their destinations.

STP   The acronym for *shielded twisted pair* wiring. It is used mainly in IBM 16-Mbit/sec LANs.

Synchronous transmission   A data link in which the components of the network are all controlled by a single timing source.

T-1 and T-3   A digital communications path operating at 1.544 or 44.736 Mbit/sec, respectively.

Universal addressing   Uses the built-in address in a *network interface card* (NIC). It is used in large networks to ensure that addresses are not duplicated.

Unreliable   A message sent without expectation of an acknowledgement.

UTP   The acronym for *unshielded twisted pair* wiring. It is used in token ring and as Ethernet 10BaseT wiring.

VAP   The acronym for a *value added process*, such as a utility, in NetWare 2.2. It is similar in function to a NetWare 3.1X NLM.

Virtual   The way a network is logically organized, regardless of the physical connections involved.

WAN   The acronym for a *wide area network* and is a network extending more than a few miles.

Workstation   A highly intelligent terminal often found on a LAN.

Index

Index note: The *f.* after a page number refers to a figure; the *n.* to a note; and the *t.* to a table.

ABOUT THE AUTHOR

Fred Simonds has more than 19 years of experience in the field of data communications, and is presently an independent consultant who specializes in streamlining data networks and teaching data communications for corporations and universities. He previously worked in hardware design and systems engineering at Motorola Codex, and in applications engineering at Racal-Datacom. Mr. Simonds was a pioneer in the application of Token Ring technology.

ABOUT THE SERIES

McGraw-Hill Series on Computer Communications is McGraw-Hill's primary vehicle for providing communications professionals with timely concepts, solutions, and applications. Jay Ranade, series advisor and editor in chief of the J. Ranade IBM, DEC, and Workstations Series, has more than 125 published titles in various series.